Sports on Film

Recent Titles in Hollywood History

The Vietnam War on Film
David Luhrssen

The American West on Film
Johnny D. Boggs

The Civil War on Film
Peg A. Lamphier and Rosanne Welch

World War II on Film
David Luhrssen

The Cold War on Film
Paul Frazier

Sports on Film

Johnny D. Boggs

Hollywood History

 ABC-CLIO®

An Imprint of ABC-CLIO, LLC

Santa Barbara, California • Denver, Colorado

Library of Congress Cataloging-in-Publication Data

Names: Boggs, Johnny D., author.
Title: Sports on film / Johnny D. Boggs.
Description: Santa Barbara, California : ABC-CLIO, [2021] | Series:
  Hollywood History | Includes bibliographical references and index.
Identifiers: LCCN 2021008700 (print) | LCCN 2021008701 (ebook) | ISBN
  9781440875557 (Print : acid-free paper) | ISBN 9781440875564 (eBook)
Subjects: LCSH: Sports films—History and criticism. | Sports in motion
  pictures. | Motion pictures—United States—History—20th century. |
  Motion pictures—United States—History—21st century. | LCGFT: Motion
  pictures.
Classification: LCC PN1995.9.S67 B64 2021 (print) | LCC PN1995.9.S67
  (ebook) | DDC 791.43/657—dc23
LC record available at https://lccn.loc.gov/2021008700
LC ebook record available at https://lccn.loc.gov/2021008701

ISBN: 978-1-4408-7555-7 (print)
       978-1-4408-7556-4 (ebook)

25 24 23 22 21   1 2 3 4 5

This book is also available as an eBook.

ABC-CLIO
An Imprint of ABC-CLIO, LLC

ABC-CLIO, LLC
147 Castilian Drive
Santa Barbara, California 93117
www.abc-clio.com

This book is printed on acid-free paper ∞

Manufactured in the United States of America

Contents

Series Foreword

Just exactly how accurate are Hollywood's film and television portrayals of American history? What do these portrayals of history tell us, not only about the events they depict but also the time in which they were made? Each volume in this unique reference series is devoted to a single topic or key theme in American history, examining 10–12 major motion pictures or television productions. Substantial essays summarize each film, provide historical background of the event or period it depicts, and explain how accurate the film's depiction is, while also analyzing the cultural context in which the film was made. A final resources section provides a comprehensive annotated bibliography of print and electronic sources to aid students and teachers in further research.

The subjects of these Hollywood History volumes were chosen based on both curriculum relevance and inherent interest. Readers will find a wide array of subject choices, including American Slavery on Film, the Civil War on Film, the American West on Film, Vietnam on Film, and the 1960s on Film. Ideal for school assignments and student research, the length, format, and subject areas are designed to meet educators' needs and students' interests.

Preface

The first motion picture, some argue, was a sports movie.

On June 19, 1878—years before the movie camera was invented—Eadweard Muybridge (1830–1904) set up still cameras to photograph a horse being ridden at a racetrack in Palo Alto, California.

An English-born bookseller-turned-photographer, Muybridge teamed with Leland Stanford (1824–93), the founder of Stanford University and a horseracing enthusiast, to prove that all four of a horse's feet came off the ground simultaneously during a gallop.

Muybridge used white paint and a white sheet on the walls and layered the track with white dust and lime so that Sallie Gardner, Stanford's dark-colored mare, would stand out in the photographs. Trip wires connected to multiple cameras, positioned at intervals of 27 inches, triggered the shutters to snap photographs as the horse sped along. After developing the film on site, Muybridge put together a series of chronophotographic images that proved all four feet of Stanford's racehorse went completely aloft during a gallop.

Within a couple of years, Muybridge had created the zoöpraxiscope, which rapidly projected images to give the illusion of motion. Though Muybridge's invention would more likely be associated with today's graphics-interchange-format (GIF) technology, it paved the way for Thomas Edison (1847–1931) and William K.L. Dickson (1860–1935) to invent the Kinetoscope—the first motion-picture camera—in the early 1890s, and the movie industry was born.

In nickelodeon theaters in the early 1900s and in larger theaters later, filmmakers often documented sporting events. Baseball (1909's *His Last Game*), boxing (1910's *Dooley Referees the Big Fight*), golf (1910's *The Golf Fiend*), motorsports (1915's *The Little Mademoiselle*), horse racing (1915's

Winning the Futurity), football (1921's *Two Minutes to Go*), rodeo (1925's *Let 'er Buck*), sprinting (1925's *Nine and Three-Fifths Seconds*), basketball (1927's *The Fair Co-ed*), and tennis (1928's *The Cardboard Lover*) had been well-chronicled on celluloid long before talking pictures hit theaters.

Sports on Film examines ten movies about sports history. *Field of Dreams* (1989) is a great baseball film, and golf fanatics adore *Caddyshack* (1980), but those are fictional stories. The movies chosen for this book are based on actual people and/or events. Each film is arranged chronologically by year of first release. Chapters compare Hollywood's version of the truth to what most historians believe happened.

Picking these movies was difficult.

Although I despise the New York Yankees, I love *Pride of the Yankees* (1942), but to me, there's no more important moment in American sports than when Jackie Robinson broke Major League Baseball's color barrier in 1947. *42* (2013) might be a better film than *The Jackie Robinson Story* (1950), but my editors and I wanted to start this book with a bang.

The Basketball Fix (1951), arguably the least known movie featured in this volume, edged out *Glory Road* (2006) because the former was released during the height of a nationwide scandal that threatened the integrity of college basketball.

With a domestic gross of more than $255 million, the football film *The Blind Side* (2009) is the highest-grossing sports movie of all time, but *Paper Lion* (1968) was made in the 1960s about the 1960s and offered an inside look at how an ordinary Joe could compete in a professional football training camp.

8 Seconds (1994) fairly accurately depicts a professional rodeo cowboy, but *Junior Bonner* (1972) was filmed during one of America's oldest rodeos and, although a box-office failure, remains one of director Sam Peckinpah's most endearing movies.

A League of Their Own (1992) could have been pulled for another baseball movie based on a historic event, *Eight Men Out* (1988), but the former offers a women's perspective and that great line: "There's no crying in baseball."

Ali (2001) might not be the best boxing biopic—I'm a sucker for *Somebody Up There Likes Me* (1956)—but you can't write about sports without including "The Greatest," Muhammad Ali.

Seabiscuit (2003) could have been scratched for *The Story of Seabiscuit* (1949), but the editors and I wanted to open with Robinson.

Miracle (2004) was never questioned. *Sports Illustrated* named the U.S. hockey victory over the Soviet Union in the 1980 Olympics the No. 1 moment in sports history.

Battle of the Sexes (2017) made the cut for its look at tennis and women's lib in the 1970s. *I, Tonya* (2017) was considered, but we already had an Olympic story in *Miracle*, while *The Game of Their Lives* (2005), which chronicled U.S. men's soccer team's World Cup upset of England in 1950, was reluctantly canceled.

Motorsports biopics *Greased Lightning* (1977) and *Heart Like a Wheel* (1983) were in the running, but *Ford v Ferrari* (2019)—the *Moneyball* (2011) of auto-racing films—won out because of its glimpse at the business of sports.

Rocky (boxing, 1976) and *Chariots of Fire* (running, 1981) might be the only two sports movies to win Academy Awards for Best Picture, but sports films have often been hits.

I write mostly about the American West, and have always been a sucker for film *noirs*, but I spent decades in newspaper sports departments. As an assistant sports editor in Dallas-Fort Worth, I would not have challenged Ray Didinger and Glen Macnow's statement: "When done well, sports movies do more than entertain—they reflect our culture and, in some cases, become woven into its fabric. We see these films, we discuss them, we benefit from them, and we even quote them in our daily lives" (Didinger and Macnow 2009, 11).

Ready? On your mark . . . let 'er buck . . . start your engines . . . let's play ball.

FURTHER READING

Didinger, Ray, and Glen Macnow. 2009. *The Ultimate Book of Sports Movies: Featuring the 100 Greatest Sports Films of All Time*. Philadelphia: Running Press.

Gartland, Dan. 2017. "These Are the Top 10 Highest-Grossing Sports Movies." *Sports Illustrated*, December 4, 2017. https://www.si.com/extra-mustard/2017/12/04/best-sports-movies-ever-box-office-money

"100 Greatest Moments in Sports History." 2016. *Sports Illustrated*, March 8, 2016. https://www.si.com/100-greatest/

Patrick, Neil. 2016. "Filmed in 1878, 'The Galloping Horse' Is the First Motion Picture Ever Made." *The Vintage News*, July 27, 2016. https://www.thevintagenews.com/2016/06/27/46591-2/

Shah, Haleema. 2018. "How a 19th-Century Photographer Made the First 'GIF' of a Galloping Horse." *Smithsonian Magazine*, December 13, 2018. https://www.smithsonianmag.com/smithsonian-institution/how-19th-century-photographer-first-gif-galloping-horse-180970990/

Introduction

When the first European settlers landed on the Atlantic seaboard in the 1600s, they brought their sports, such as skating and foot races, with them. Native Americans, however, were already playing their own games, including various forms of stickball or lacrosse, and other contests. Influenced by culture, geography, and economics, sporting events varied regionally.

Historian Murry R. Nelson wrote: "Native Americans inhabited what became the United States long before the British appeared. Africans arrived by 1618, and thousands upon thousands of them were forcibly shipped from their homelands late into the eighteenth century. Other European ethnic groups also migrated to the New World, and all of these peoples and their traditions affected the form and forums of early American sports" (Nelson 2009a, 2).

Cricket and lawn bowling were introduced in the 1600s. By the 1650s, tennis and an early version of miniature golf were being played in what is now New York state, where horse racing in New York City was forbidden by Governor Peter Stuyvesant (c. 1610–72), and other sporting events were prohibited during religious services. Considered the first organized sport in the United States, horse racing gained ground in the mid-1660s with the establishment of the Newmarket Course at Hempstead Plains in present-day Garden City, New York. Colonial Governor Richard Nicholls (1624–72) said he was opening the racecourse "not so much for the divertissement of youth as for encouraging the bettering of the breed of horse which, through great neglect, has been impaired" (Jeansonne 2008). The track remained open for a century.

South Carolina established the South Carolina Jockey Club—America's first—in 1758. Horse racing continued to spread in popularity in the colonies, usually for the wealthy. On February 15, 1792, Washington Race Course in Charleston, South Carolina, held its first race, and Race Week became an annual event each February where "the great Lowcountry planters gathered to show their horses, make bets, attend a few balls, seal a few business deals, drink fine Madeira wine, and introduce their daughters to the right sort of people in the reserved seating section" (Handal 2019, 30). Harness racing—in which a trotting horse pulls a driver in a two-wheeled sulky—emerged in the early 1800s. By the 1840s, horse racing had reached the masses, not just the elite.

The early 1800s saw the opening of America's first archery club (in Philadelphia); swimming school (in Boston); curling club (in Orchard Lake, Michigan); and college gymnastics program (Harvard). Yachting clubs were formed in Detroit in 1839 and New York in 1844. By the 1850s, croquet had come to America, and the United States scored an international victory when the New York Yacht Club's schooner *America* won the inaugural America's Cup in 1851 against British yachts in a 53-mile race around the Isle of Wight.

Town ball, an Americanized version of England's rounders, rose in popularity in Boston in the 1830s and likely led to the creation of baseball, which grew in the following decade and by 1850 was considered America's pastime. In 1869, more than a thousand clubs were playing baseball across the nation, the *New York Times* reported. The games were played by amateurs, yet 1869 also saw the formation of the first all-professional baseball team: The Cincinnati Red Stockings went undefeated in sixty-three games, including exhibition contests, and changed the sport forever. In 1876, the professional National League formed. In 1901, the American League became a second major league, and when the champions of both leagues played in a best-of-nine series, the World Series was born as the Boston Americans defeated the Pittsburgh Pirates in eight games. In the following decades, standouts like George Herman "Babe" Ruth (1895–1948), Ted Williams (1918–2002), and Hank Aaron (1934–2021) became worldwide celebrities.

Americans' interest in sports led to the founding of the monthly magazine *American Turf Register and Sporting Magazine* in 1829 and *Spirit of the Times*, a New York City–based weekly newspaper that began covering sports, theater, and agriculture in 1831. The entertainment weekly *New York Clipper*, established in 1853, became known for its coverage of baseball. In 1886, *The Sporting News*, a weekly newspaper, was founded in St. Louis, Missouri.

After the Civil War (1861–65), spectator sports saw massive growth. "Before that conflict," George Gipe wrote, "going to an athletic event was simply not a regular part of the average person's life; after, it gradually became commonplace" (Gipe 1978, 2). America's sports evolution between 1870 and 1900 was:

an era of experimentation as well as rapid change in technology and social attitudes. People did strange things then, such as jumping off the Brooklyn Bridge or pushing a wheelbarrow from coast to coast; women engaged men in athletic competitions, formed baseball teams, and proved they could do stunts hanging from a balloon as well as their male counterparts. Young people even rebelled then. When informed by their elders that bicycle riding was not lady-like, the ladies kept right on doing it. True, there were more timid folks than iconoclasts, but the adventurous spirit was applauded, either aloud or secretly. (Gipe 1978, 2–3)

Bowling alleys thrived in the 1870s—but the racket led a newspaper to call a Fort Scott, Kansas, alley's "continual rolling, clattering and smashing a considerable nuisance to the neighborhood" and request that since "the 'pursuit of happiness' in the ten-pin way usually reaches to a late hour in the night, we think some slight regard should be had to the comfort of the people who are compelled to woo slumber in the vicinity where these places of muscular recreation are located" (Untitled article 1870, 3).

While some sports boomed, boxing, known then as prizefighting, fought controversy. After a fighter's death in a match, London Prize Ring rules were established in 1838. These rules made butting, gouging, scratching, kicking, and biting illegal, and also outlawed using hard objects such as stones concealed in a boxer's bare fists. Those rules did not help Thomas McCoy, a twenty-year-old, who was killed in a $200 match against Christopher Lilly in New York in 1842. During the 120 rounds that lasted 2 hours, 43 minutes, McCoy was knocked down eighty-one times. The *New-York Daily Tribune* reported: "And in that moment of freezing horror—when it would seem that the blood of the hardiest ruffian must have curdled with conscious guilt and remorse, and a shadow darkened the most indurated brow—even then, in reference to the fact that *another* fight had been arranged to come off on this occasion, one voice was raised in the crowd, exclaiming, 'Come, *carry off your dead, and produce your next man!*'" ("The Horrible Death of McCoy" 1842, 2).

Little wonder that many states and territories outlawed prizefighting. Adopted in 1867, "Marquess of Queensberry" rules made boxing more palatable by requiring padded gloves and weight classifications, but not until 1884, when Jack "Nonpareil" Dempsey (1862–95) knocked out George Fulljames (1852–88) for the middleweight championship, did a professional fight in the United States follow the Queensberry rules. Only in the late 1890s and early 1900s did boxing become a sport that did not have to be held surreptitiously.

College sports, on the other hand, surged in popularity. In 1873, four years after Rutgers beat what is now Princeton University, 6–4, Columbia, Princeton, Rutgers, and Yale officials agreed on a code of rules for American football. The rules, resembling soccer more than today's football, were later abandoned in favor of rugby-inspired rules. In December 1875, the Intercollegiate Association of Amateur Athletes of America was formed for track and field, with the first national championships contested the following year. By the 1890s, the Canadian-created sport of ice hockey had reached college campuses in the United States.

Other sports began organizing. In 1881, the United States National Lawn Tennis Association was formed, rules were standardized, and the first national championships were held in Newport, Rhode Island. Before long, the National American Croquet Association (1882), U.S. Intercollegiate Lacrosse Association (1883), American Football (soccer) Association (1884), American Trotting Association (1887), United States Golf Association (1894), and the American Bowling Congress (1895) had been organized. Also in 1887, the Amateur Athletic Union was formed to protect amateur athletes from "unscrupulous promoters" and "to preserve 'sport for sport's sake'" (Carruth and Ehrlich 1988, 43).

Although Santa Fe, New Mexico (1847), and Deer Trail, Colorado (1869), cite earlier competitions, cowboys in the American West began competing for prizes in tournaments that became known as rodeos in Pecos, Texas, in 1883; Prescott, Arizona, in 1888; Cheyenne, Wyoming, in 1897. By the late 1920s, the Rodeo Association of America had been organized, leading to the founding of the Rodeo Cowboys Association in 1945 and the Professional Rodeo Cowboys Association in 1975.

New sports also came into vogue. Softball is believed to have been developed in Chicago in 1887—as an indoor game to be played in winter—and the Mid Winter Indoor Baseball League of Chicago adopted rules in 1889. In 1891, James Naismith (1861–1939) used a soccer ball and two peach baskets to introduce basketball at the YMCA Training School in Springfield, Massachusetts. In 1895, one of Naismith's students, William G. Morgan (1870–1942), blended basketball, baseball, handball, and tennis to invent volleyball.

On Thanksgiving Day 1895, Frank Duryea (1869–1967) drove the gas-powered Duryea Motor Wagon, which he and his brother Charles (1861–1938) had designed, to victory in a six-vehicle motorized race sponsored by the *Chicago Times-Herald*—America's first motorsports event. After the winning auto covered the 54 miles in 10 hours, 23 minutes, *Scientific American* acknowledged that "for looks [the Duryea] could hold its own with the average horse carriage of today. Undoubtedly the motocycle has come to stay" (The Chicago Times-Herald Motor Race 1895).

Motorsports in America was also here to stay. In 1911, Ray Harroun (1879–1968) won the first Indianapolis 500 at Indianapolis Motor Speedway. Drag racing, typically pitting two "hot rods" racing side by side for a quarter mile, began as illegal competitions in the 1930s. Wallace "Wally" Parks (1913–2018) brought legitimacy to the sport by helping create the Southern California Timing Association in 1938, and then founded the

National Hot Rod Association in 1951. "Wally Parks's passion for hot rodding led to formation of NHRA as an avenue for safe, sanctioned drag racing open to men and women Sportsman and Professional [classification] racers," said John Sturbin, a reporter for RacinToday.com (John Sturbin, interview with author, March 22, 2020).

Road races, sanctioned by the American Automobile Association after its founding in 1902, were being staged as early as 1908. According to legend, stock-car racing, another American-born sport with illegal roots, got its start in the Southern Appalachians when moonshiners began illegally transporting liquor during and after Prohibition (1920–33). Whiskey runners began racing their souped-up cars against one another, and in 1947, Bill France Sr. (1909–92) helped establish the National Association for Stock Car Auto Racing in Daytona Beach, Florida, where beach races had been held as early as 1903. NASCAR's first race was held at Daytona in 1948. In 2020, the total purse for the Daytona 500, NASCAR's biggest race, was $23.6 million, the highest in American motorsports history.

American sports joined the international stage in 1896 when the Olympic Games were revived in Athens, Greece. After traveling by steamship from New Jersey to Greece, the Americans dominated. James B. Connolly (1868–1957) became the first modern Olympic champion when he won the triple jump, and U.S. athletes won ten other titles while placing second in seven events and third in two. The gold, silver, and bronze medals weren't introduced until 1904, when the games were held in St. Louis, Missouri. The Americans' Olympiad success paved the way for gold medalists such as pentathlon and decathlon standout Jim Thorpe (1887–1953) in 1912; track and field competitors Babe Didrikson Zaharias (1911–56) in 1932, and Jesse Owens (1913–80) in 1936; sprinter Wilma Rudolph (1940–94) in 1960; swimmer Mark Spitz (1950–) in 1968 and 1972; the U.S. men's hockey team in 1980; gymnast Mary Lou Retton (1968–) in 1984; and swimmer Michael Phelps (1985–) in 2004, 2008, 2012, and 2016.

The biggest growth in American sports came in the twentieth century. The Professional Golfers Association organized in 1916, followed in 1920 by the American Professional Football Association, which became the National Football League two years later. The National Basketball Association was established in 1949 when the Basketball Association of America and the National Basketball League merged. Both organizations faced challenges from new leagues, the American Football League in 1959 and the American Basketball Association in 1967, before mergers—NFL–AFL completed in 1969; the NBA–ABA in 1976—established the leagues still in existence today.

In 1947, African American baseball players Jackie Robinson (1919–72) of the National League's Brooklyn Dodgers and Larry Doby (1923–2003) of the American League's Cleveland Indians broke big-league baseball's color barrier. By the 1960s, Hispanic golfers Lee Trevino (1939–) and Juan Antonio "Chi-Chi" Rodriguez (1935–) were winning regularly on the PGA

Tour. Women also made inroads. The Ladies Professional Golfers Association was founded in 1950; Althea Gibson (1927–2003) in 1950 became the first African American, man or woman, to compete in tennis's U.S. Nationals, then in 1963 became the first Black woman to join the LPGA tour; and Janet Guthrie earned starting spots in the Indianapolis 500 and Daytona 500—a first for women—in 1977.

Title IX of the Educational Amendments Act of 1972, which prohibited sexual discrimination by schools and colleges receiving federal aid, gave women's sports its biggest boost. Only 64,390 women competed in intercollegiate sports in 1981–82, the first year the National Collegiate Athletic Association began compiling men's and women's sports participation figures. In 2018–19, 218,496 women played intercollegiate sports.

New forms of media brought sports to the masses. A Pittsburgh radio station broadcast a live boxing match on April 11, 1921, followed by a Philadelphia Phillies-Pittsburgh Pirates game that August. On May 17, 1939, NBC televised a live college baseball game between Princeton and Columbia. Short newsreels features in movie theaters often included sports news, and live radio and TV sports broadcasts soon became commonplace. *Sports Illustrated*, a weekly magazine, was launched in 1954. On September 21, 1970, the Cleveland Browns defeated the New York Jets, 31–21, as ABC introduced *Monday Night Football*, "the NFL's first permanent excursion into prime time" (Fox 1970, 97). ESPN, an entertainment and sports cable network, was founded in 1979. In 2016, *The Athletic,* a subscription-based sports-journalism website and app, launched and had more than 100,000 subscribers two years later.

The media reported scandals that rocked sports.

In 1921, eight Chicago White Sox players, accused of colluding with gamblers to throw the 1919 World Series against the Cincinnati Reds (who won the best-of-nine series in eight games), were acquitted in a trial. "As cheers filled the courtroom and hats and confetti were tossed into the air, it became obvious that it was baseball, itself, that had been on trial. Something had to be done to restore the public's faith in the game" (Ross 2019, 97). Kenesaw Mountain Landis (1866–1944), a retired federal judge hired as baseball's first commissioner, responded by banning the eight players from professional baseball for life. In 1989, Reds manager Pete Rose (1941–) accepted a lifetime ban from baseball for betting on games, including Reds games, although he said he always bet on his team to win. Late in 2019, reports of the Houston Astros' intricate sign-stealing practices tainted the Astros' 2017 World Series, cost several their jobs, and led a baseball executive to ask, "Where's the moral compass of our game?" (Lacques 2020).

The scandals weren't limited to professionals. Seven colleges and thirty-two players were implicated in a widespread point-shaving scandal that rocked college basketball in the 1950s. Point-shaving incidents continued, at Boston College in 1978–79, Tulane in 1985, Arizona State in 1994, and

Northwestern in 1994–95. Pay-for-play and other recruiting and academic violations decimated several college football programs, most significantly in 1987 when the NCAA gave Southern Methodist University the "death penalty," eliminating the program for the 1987 and 1988 seasons. In 2011, Penn State coach Joe Paterno (1926–2012) retired after defensive coordinator Jerry Sandusky (1944–) was charged with—and later convicted on—forty-five counts of sexually abusing young boys in the 1990s and 2000s. "Once regarded as one of the greatest coaches in college football history, Paterno died as a vilified man . . . because of the possibility that he knew what was going on and looked the other way" (Miller 2017).

The use of performance-enhancing drugs (PEDs) tarnished the reputations of several major-league baseball players including Mark McGwire (1963–), who hit 70 home runs in 1998, and Barry Bonds (1964–), who hit 762 career home runs. Performance-enhancing drugs also resulted in track star Marion Jones (1975–) being stripped of five medals—including three golds—won at the 2000 Olympics and cost seven-time Tour de France cycling champion Lance Armstrong (1971–) $75 million in endorsements.

"The growth of the mass media transformed sportswriters from idol-creating cheerleaders to myth-shattering critics," said Frank Wooten, a retired newspaper editor and columnist who worked in Baltimore, Dallas, and Charleston, South Carolina. "Home-run king Babe Ruth, a womanizing alcoholic, was generously cast as a larger-than-life, happy-go-lucky hero who loved kids, dogs, hot dogs and mink coats. Home-run king Barry Bonds was rightly condemned as a sullen, steroid-swollen cheater. These days, the Houston Astros play—again, fairly enough—the villains as high-tech sign stealers. Something has been gained in this journalistic evolution from glorious-legend builders to hard-truth tellers. But has something also been lost?" (Frank Wooten, interview with author, March 22, 2020).

"The days of bland acceptance of sports are past," James Michener wrote. "The entire program in this country will have to be subjected to most careful scrutiny and the most biting criticism. Those who defend sports and their enormous budgets will have to justify them as never before and many hallowed preconceptions will be challenged" (Michener 2015, 18).

Sports earn big money in the United States—the North American sports market was expected to reach $73 billion in 2019.

As Christine Emba wrote for the *Washington Post*: "Studies have shown that for fans, being identified with a favorite team is more important than being identified with their work and social groups, and is as or more important to them as being identified with their religion. Sociologists have hypothesized that sports subcultures work as 'totems,' serving as points of connection for communities and an outlet for ritual and religion in a time when actual religiosity continues to decline. Support for a certain team or club can serve as a point of identity and belonging, either crossing lines of age, race, and background or reinforcing them" (Emba 2016).

But Americans love their sports.

"Sports may often be considered nothing more than a silly game, but they've played a major role in our society," Drake Oz wrote. "Sports have excited. They've disappointed. They've turned immature boys and girls into exceptional men and women. Sometimes sports truly transcend anything they were ever supposed to accomplish" (Oz 2010).

FURTHER READING

Carruth, Gorton, and Eugene Ehrlich. 1988. *Facts & Dates of American Sports: From Colonial Days to the Present.* New York: Perennial Library.

"Chicago Times-Herald Motor Race, The." 1895. *Scientific American,* December 1895. https://www.scientificamerican.com/article/the-chicago-times-herald-motor -race/

Cottom, Ric. 2017. *Your Maryland: Little-Known Histories from the Shores of the Chesapeake to the Foothills of the Allegheny Mountains.* Baltimore, MD: John Hopkins University Press.

Crabtree-Hannigan, James. 2020. "Daytona 500 Purse, Payout Breakdown: How Much Prize Money Will the Winner Make in 2020?" *Sporting News,* February 18, 2020. https://www.sportingnews.com/ca/nascar/news/daytona-500-purse -payout-2020-prize-money-breakdown/1k8vnlp3t4m5s1tm2k93r62zhk

Ellison, Betty Boles. 2014. *The Early Laps of Stock Car Racing: A History of the Sport and Business through 1974.* Jefferson, NC: McFarland & Company, Publishers, Inc.

Emba, Christine. 2016. "Why Do We Care about Sports So Much?" *The Washington Post,* March 14, 2016. https://www.washingtonpost.com/news/in-theory/wp /2016/03/14/why-do-we-care-about-sports-so-much/

Eschner, Kat. 2016. "The Forgotten Car That Won America's First Auto Race: The Zippy Roadster Won America's First Automobile Race in 1895 with an Average Speed of 5 mph." *Smithsonian Magazine,* November 28, 2016. https://www.smith sonianmag.com/smart-news/model-t-came-duryea-wagon-180961218/

Fox, Larry. 1970. "Browns Hold Off Super-Penalized Jets, 31-21." *New York Daily News,* p. 97.

Gems, Gerald R. 2014. *Boxing: A Concise History of the Sweet Science.* Lanham, MD: Rowman & Littlefield.

Gipe, George. 1978. *The Great American Sports Book: A Casual but Voluminous Look at American Spectator Sports from the Civil War to the Present Time.* Garden City, NY: Doubleday & Company, Inc.

Goldstein, Richard. 2007. "Wally Parks, Drag Racing Pioneer, Dies at 94." *The New York Times,* October 4, 2007. https://www.nytimes.com/2007/10/04/sports/other sports/04parks.html

Halberstam, David J. 2019. "Eighty Years Ago Today, NBC Experimented with the First Ever Telecast of a Sporting Event: A Baseball Game between Columbia and Princeton Was Produced Using Only One Camera. Perhaps a Few Hundred Saw The Flickering Picture." *Sports Broadcast Journal,* May 17, 2019. https://www

.sportsbroadcastjournal.com/eighty-years-ago-today-nbc-experimented-with
-the-first-ever-telecast-of-a-sporting-event/

Handal, Leigh Jones. 2019. *Lost Charleston*. London: Pavilion Books.

Hickok, Ralph. 2002. *The Encyclopedia of North American Sports History, Second
Edition*. New York: Facts On File, Inc.

"Horrible Death of McCoy, The." 1842. *New-York Daily Tribune*, September 19,
1842, p. 2.

Irick, Erin, preparer. 2019. *Student-Athlete Participation 1981–82 – 2018–19:
NCAA® Sports Sponsorship and Participation Rates Report*. Indianapolis, IN:
National Collegiate Athletic Association.

Jeansonne, John. 2008. "Horse Racing History. Nothing New for Li." *Newsday*,
May 27, 2008. https://www.newsday.com/sports/horse-racing-history-nothing
-new-for-li-1.499605

Jussim, Matthew. n.d. "The 15 Biggest Steroid, P.E.D., and Doping Scandals in
Sports History." *Men's Journal*. https://www.mensjournal.com/sports/15-biggest
-steroid-ped-and-doping-scandals-sports-history/

Lacques, Gabe. 2020. "'Where's the Moral Compass of Our Game?': Houston Astros
Cheating Scandal Exposes MLB's Problems." *USA Today*, February 27, 2020. https://
www.usatoday.com/story/sports/mlb/columnist/gabe-lacques/2020/02/27
/astros-cheating-scandal-mlb-front-office-baseball/4880978002/

Michener, James. 2015. *Sports in America*. New York: Dial Press Trade Paperback.

Miller, Kerry. 2017. "College Football's Biggest Scandals Since 2000." *Bleacher Report*,
July 12, 2017. https://bleacherreport.com/articles/2720980-college-footballs-big
gest-scandals-since-2000#slide1

Nelson, Murry R., ed. 2009. *Encyclopedia of Sports in America: A History from
Foot Races to Extreme Sports. Volume 1: Colonial Years to 1939*. Westport, CT:
Greenwood Press.

"100 Greatest Moments in Sports History." 2016. *Sports Illustrated,* March 8, 2016.
https://www.si.com/100-greatest/

Oz, Drake. 2010. "The Top 10 Greatest Sports Speeches Ever." *Bleacher Report*,
December 2, 2010. https://bleacherreport.com/articles/532457-the-top-10-great
est-sports-speeches-ever#slide0

Peckham, Eric. 2018. "The Tactics Behind The Athletic's Breakout Success in Sports Sub-
scriptions." *Tech Crunch*, October 31, 2018. https://techcrunch.com/2018/10/31
/theathletic-interview/

Romano, Frederick B. 2017. *Boxing on Radio and Television: A Blow by Blow History from 1924 to 1964*. New York: Carrel Books.

Ross, Thom. 2019. *The Black Sox: A Century Later*. Santa Fe, NM: Art Guild Press
LLC.

Seymour, Harold. 1989. *Baseball: The Early Years*. New York: Oxford University
Press.

Singer, Mike. 2013. "Ranking the 10 Most Shocking Scandals in College Basketball History." *Bleacher Report*, May 1, 2013. https://bleacherreport.com/arti
cles/1625497-ranking-the-10-most-shocking-scandals-in-college-basketball
-history#slide2

Sloan, Wm. David, ed. 2002. *The Media in America: A History, 5th edition*. San
Ramon, CA: Vision Press.

Sperber, Murray. 1998. *Onward to Victory: The Crises That Shaped College Sports*. New York: Henry Holt and Company.

Streible, Dan. 2008. *Fight Pictures: A History of Boxing and Early Cinema*. Berkeley, CA: University of California Press.

Sullivan, Dean A., ed. and compiler. 1997. *Early Innings: A Documentary History of Baseball, 1825–1908*. Lincoln, NE: Bison Books.

Svrluga, Barry, and Dave Sheinin. 2020. "The World Just Learned of the Astros' Cheating. Inside Baseball, It Was an Open Secret." *The Washington Post*, February 11, 2020. https://www.washingtonpost.com/sports/mlb/astros-cheating-open -secret/2020/02/11/1830154c-4c41-11ea-9b5c-eac5b16dafaa_story.html

Untitled article. 1870. *Fort Scott Daily Monitor*, June 24, 1870.

Wagman, John. 1990. *On This Day in America: An Illustrated Almanac of History, Sports, Science, and Culture*. New York: Gallery Books.

Williams, Randy. 2006. *Sports Cinema: 100 Movies: The Best of Hollywood's Athletic Heroes, Losers, Myths, and Misfits*. Pompton Plains, NJ: Limelight Editions.

"Women Pioneers in Sports History." 2019. *Newsday*, March 8, 2019. https://www .newsday.com/sports/women-s-sports/women-pioneers-in-sports-history-1.47 11159

Chronology

August 22, 1851 — The schooner *America* of the New York Yacht Club beats fourteen British ships in a 53-mile regatta around the Isle of Wight, winning the first of what becomes known as the America's Cup—the oldest continually contested sports trophy in the world.

November 6, 1869 — Before about a hundred spectators in New Brunswick, New Jersey, Rutgers defeats the College of New Jersey (renamed Princeton in 1896), 6–4, in what is considered the first American football game.

November 8, 1869 — The Cincinnati Red Stockings, the first all-professional baseball team, routs the Cincinnati Picked Nine, 34–5, to finish the season with a 64–0 record, including exhibition games.

July 4, 1870 — The *Rob't E. Lee* arrives in St. Louis, Missouri, at roughly 11:30 a.m., beating the *Natchez* by six and a half hours in a 1,154-mile Mississippi River steamboat race from Natchez, Mississippi, that Mark Twain will record in *Life on the Mississippi*.

May 17, 1875 — Nineteen-year-old Oliver Lewis rides Astrides to victory in the first running of the Kentucky Derby before a crowd estimated at ten thousand at Churchill Downs in Louisville, Kentucky.

July 4, 1883	What has started out as two area cowboys trying to determine who is the better roper expands to competition for other cowboys in Pecos, Texas, and the West of the Pecos Rodeo—arguably the first rodeo in America—is born.
May 1, 1884	Moses "Fleetwood" Walker plays for Toledo in an American Association game in Louisville, Kentucky, becoming the first African American player in the major leagues. In September, Walker is released because of an injury. Racial prejudice and pressure from the Chicago White Sox's Cap Anson leads to an informal ban of Black players that lasts more than sixty years.
July 4, 1888	Cowboy Juan Leivas is declared the winner of a "cowboy tournament" in Prescott, Arizona Territory, beginning an uninterrupted rodeo tradition.
December 21, 1891	Physical education instructor James Naismith develops a game for bored male students at the YMCA in Springfield, Massachusetts, in what becomes the first basketball game in history.
January 1, 1902	In the first postseason college football game, the University of Michigan routs Stanford, 49–0, at Tournament Park in Los Angeles in the Tournament of Roses football game, now known as the Rose Bowl.
October 13, 1903	The American League's Boston Americans shuts out the National League's Pittsburgh Pirates, 3–0, in the eighth game to win the best-of-nine series in baseball's first "World Championship" that becomes known as the World Series.
May 30, 1911	Ray Harroun drives a Marmon Wasp to victory, averaging 74.59 miles per hour at Indianapolis Motor Speedway to win the International 500-Mile Sweepstakes Race—motorsports' first Indianapolis 500.
January 27, 1913	The Amateur Athletic Union rules that Jim Thorpe, a member of the Sac and Fox Nation, is a professional athlete because he played two summers in a *semipro* baseball league in 1900 and 1910, allowing the International Olympic Committee to strip the athlete of the gold medals he won in the all-around pentathlon and decathlon during the 1912 Stockholm Olympics. In 1982, the medals are posthumously restored.

June 11, 1919   Kentucky Derby and Preakness winner Sir Barton easily wins the Belmont Stakes, becoming the first "Triple Crown" winner of American horse racing—although that term won't come into vogue until the 1920s.

September 19, 1920   *Headin' Home*, a movie staring George Herman "Babe" Ruth (in his first year with the New York Yankees) as himself, premieres in New York City.

August 3, 1921   One day after eight Chicago White Sox players are acquitted of conspiracy charges in a high-profile trial, Judge Kenesaw Mountain Landis, Major League Baseball's first commissioner, bans the eight "Black Sox" for taking bribes and throwing the 1919 World Series against the Cincinnati Reds.

March 25, 1934   Horton Smith's 20-foot putt for birdie on the 17th hole gives him a one-stroke victory over Craig Wood in the first Augusta National Invitation Tournament—also known as the Masters—in Augusta, Georgia.

August 9, 1936   African American track and field standout Jesse Owens wins four of the United States' eleven gold medals, embarrassing Germany Führer Adolph Hitler at the Berlin Olympics.

November 1, 1938   Seabiscuit defeats Triple Crown winner War Admiral before a crowd of forty thousand in a match race at Baltimore's Pimlico Race Course in a horse race promoted as "The Race of the Century."

July 4, 1939   Calling himself "the luckiest man on the face of the earth," New York Yankees first baseman Lou Gehrig announces his retirement from major-league baseball, weeks after being diagnosed with the fatal disease amyotrophic lateral sclerosis (ALS), more commonly called today "Lou Gehrig's Disease."

May 30, 1943   The first season of the All-American Girls Baseball League begins with games in Rockford, Illinois, and Racine, Wisconsin. The four-team league will bring 176,612 customers during its inaugural season.

April 15, 1947   Brooklyn Dodgers first baseman Jackie Robinson breaks the color barrier by becoming the first African American player in major-league baseball since 1884.

August 3, 1949   The professional National Basketball Association is formed after the Basketball Association of America and the National Basketball League merge.

June 29, 1950   The United States soccer team of part-time players upsets powerful England, 1–0, in a FIFA World Cup first-round game in Brazil.

February 18, 1951   Three City College of New York men's basketball players are arrested at Penn Station and charged with bribery that is just the start of an investigation that rocks college basketball nationwide.

August 12, 1952   The Southeastern Conference suspends the University of Kentucky's men's basketball team from competing in the 1952–53 season for the program's involvement in the national "basketball fix" scandal.

July 3, 1954   Two years before her death from colon cancer, Babe Didrikson Zaharias, who earned three medals during the 1932 Olympic Games, wins the U.S. Women's Open golf tournament by twelve strokes.

September 8, 1960   Wilma Rudolph sets world records in the 100- and 200-meter sprints and the 4 × 100-meter relay in Rome, becoming America's first female track and field athlete to win three gold medals during one Olympic Games.

October 1, 1961   The New York Yankees' Roger Maris hits his 61st home run of the season in his last game of the season, breaking the record held by Yankees legend Babe Ruth since 1927.

February 25, 1964   Cassius Clay pummels Sonny Liston in Miami Beach, Florida, in seven rounds, winning his first heavyweight boxing title and declaring, "I am the greatest." The next day he announces his conversion to Islam, and on March 6 becomes Muhammad Ali.

March 19, 1966   Coached by Don Haskins, Texas Western University defeats the University of Kentucky, 72–65, in College Park, Maryland, to become the first National Collegiate Athletic Association team to win the men's national basketball championship after starting five African American players.

January 15, 1967   The National Football League's Green Bay Packers defeat the American Football League's Kansas City Chiefs, 35–10, at Los Angeles Memorial Coliseum in the first AFL-NFL World Championship Game—later to become known as the first Super Bowl.

September 8, 1968   Arthur Ashe defeats the Netherlands' Tom Okker in five sets at West Side Tennis Club in Queens, New York, to become the first African American male to win the U.S. Open men's singles championship.

November 14, 1970   An airplane crash in West Virginia kills all seventy-five passengers and crew, including thirty-six Marshall University football players in what is considered the worst air disaster in American sports history.

June 23, 1972   President Richard Nixon signs into law Title IX, which requires that all schools—at any level—receiving federal funding provide fair and equal treatment of the sexes in all areas. That leads into an increase in women's participation in high school and college athletics.

September 2, 1973   Billy Jean King defeats Bobby Riggs, 6–4, 6–3, 6–3, at Houston's Astrodome in a nationally televised tennis match billed as the "Battle of the Sexes."

April 2, 1974   Producer Kieth Merrill's *The Great American Cowboy*, which documents professional rodeo cowboy Larry Mahan's 1973 season that earned him a record sixth All-Around Cowboy title, wins the Academy Award for best documentary feature.

March 29, 1975   UCLA men's basketball coach John Wooden announces his retirement after the Bruins defeat Louisville, 75–74, in overtime in the NCAA semifinals—and calls it quits two days later after a 92–85 victory against Kentucky for UCLA's tenth title in twelve years. He finishes with a 664–162 overall record at UCLA at Indiana State.

October 22, 1978   Cale Yarborough's victory in the American 500 at North Carolina Speedway in Rockingham gives him a record third consecutive Grand National Winston Cup Series championship in the National Association for Stock Car Auto Racing, a record held until Jimmie Johnson wins five in a row from 2006 to 2010.

February 22, 1980   Scoring two third-period goals, Team USA upsets the Soviet Union's men's hockey team, 4–3, in Lake Placid, New York, during the Winter Olympics in what becomes known as the "Miracle on Ice." The Soviets, four-time defending gold medalists, have to settle for the silver medal, while the Americans beat Finland, 4–2, in their final game to secure the gold.

July 24, 1983   George Brett's two-run, two-out home run in the ninth inning at Yankee Stadium is disallowed after the umpires rule that his bat has too much pine tar on it. Brett is declared out, giving the New York Yankees a 5–4 victory over the Kansas City Royals, and an irate Brett is ejected. But the Royals protest, the American League rules the umpires were wrong, and the game resumes August 18, ending with a 6–5 Royals victory in what becomes known as "the Pine Tar Incident."

February 25, 1987   The National Collegiate Athletic Association shuts down Southern Methodist University's football program for the 1987 season for paying several players during the early 1980s. The ruling—known as the "death penalty" for repeated rule violations—forces the Dallas school to cancel its 1988 season, too.

August 9, 1988   National Hockey League fans are shocked when the Los Angeles Kings acquire Edmonton Oilers great Wayne Gretzky in a trade.

August 24, 1989   Major League Baseball Commissioner A. Bartlett Giamatti bans Pete Rose, the former Cincinnati baseball star now managing the Reds, from baseball for life for betting on baseball games.

February 11, 1990   Buster Douglas, a 42-to-1 underdog, knocks out undefeated heavyweight champion Mike Tyson in the tenth round in Tokyo in one of boxing's biggest upsets.

January 6, 1994   While practicing for the Olympic figure-skating trials in Detroit, Nancy Kerrigan is attacked by man hired by rival skater Tonya Harding's ex-husband. Despite an injured knee, Kerrigan goes on to win the silver medal at the 1994 Olympics in Lillehammer, Norway.

September 6, 1995   The Baltimore Orioles' Cal Ripken Jr. plays in his 2,131st consecutive major-league baseball game, breaking Lou Gehrig's record. Ripken goes on to play in 2,632 consecutive games, ending his streak on September 20, 1998.

April 13, 1997   Playing in his first major golf championship since turning professional, twenty-one-year-old Tiger Woods wins the Masters tournament by shooting an 18-under-par 270, 12 strokes ahead of runner-up Tom Kite.

February 18, 2001   Forty-nine-year-old Dale Earnhardt is killed in a crash on the last lap of the Daytona 500 at Daytona (Florida) International Speedway, three years after the seven-time NASCAR Winston Cup champion won the prestigious race for the first time in his career.

April 16, 2008   As a member of the winning 4 × 100-meter medley relay, Michael Phelps earns his eighth gold medal in the Beijing Olympics. That gives him the most gold medals by an athlete at one Olympic Games since swimmer Mark Spitz won seven in Munich, Germany, in 1972.

June 28, 2011   By defeating Florida in Omaha, Nebraska, the defending national champion University of South Carolina's baseball team becomes the last school to win the College World Series at Omaha's historic Rosenblatt Stadium and the first to win the CWS at the new TD Ameritrade Park.

June 6, 2015   American Pharoah's Belmont Stakes victory makes the horse the first Triple Crown winner since Affirmed in 1978, and—with its 2015 Breeders' Cup Classic victory—the first to win thoroughbred racing's Grand Slam.

Chapter 1

The Jackie Robinson Story (1950)

Jackie Robinson (1919–72), who in 1947 became the first African American to play major-league baseball since the 1880s, was at the top of his game in 1950. Coming off the 1949 season in which he was voted the National League's Most Valuable Player and led the Brooklyn Dodgers to their second World Series in three years (losing again, as in 1947, to the New York Yankees), Robinson became the highest-paid player in Dodgers' history when he signed for $35,000 in January. Baseball, however, would just be a small part Robinson's income. After leading the National League with a .342 batting average in 1949, Robinson had endorsement deals with Chesterfield cigarettes (despite not smoking), Wheaties breakfast cereal, and clothing lines. His total income avenues were expected to drive his earnings up to $100,000. One of those revenue streams came from Hollywood.

Robinson plays himself in *The Jackie Robinson Story,* which follows the athlete from childhood—Howard Louis MacNeely (1940–) plays Robinson as a child—through Robinson's historic 1947 season with the Dodgers. Living with his mother (Louise Beavers, 1902–62) and brother Mack (Joel Fluellen, 1908–90), Robinson exceeds his brother's accomplishments as a star athlete at Pasadena Junior College. At UCLA, he excels in football, basketball, track and field, and baseball. Despite his mother and girlfriend Rae's (Ruby Dee, 1922–2014) reservations, Robinson drops out of college with hopes of landing a job as a high school coach. No schools are interested in hiring him, but Robinson is drafted into the army during World War II (1941–45).

After serving stateside as a lieutenant, Robinson resumes his search for a coaching career after the war. Instead, he is hired to play for the Black Panthers, a professional African American baseball team. Robinson is a great player, but the life is hard. "We sleep and we eat and we play ball," a team-mate tells him. "Then we get on a bus and do it all over again." After one game, Clyde Sukeforth (Billy Wayne, 1897–1970), who identifies himself as a Brooklyn Dodgers' scout, says Dodgers' general manager Branch Rickey wants to see Robinson. Thinking that a joke is being played on him, Robinson blows off Sukeforth, but the scout is legitimate, and Robinson meets Rickey (Minor Watson, 1889–1965) in New York.

Robinson thinks he can play organized baseball, but Rickey warns him that his success will depend on more than what shows up in a box score. "You know," Rickey says, "a box score is really democratic, Jackie. It doesn't say how big you are or how your father voted in the last election, or what church you attend. It just tells you what kind of ballplayer you were that day."

"Well, isn't that what counts?" Robinson asks.

"It's all that ought to count," Rickey replies. "And maybe someday it's all that will count."

Integrating baseball will be difficult, Rickey says, warning Robinson that he will have to take insults and vicious plays. "But if we fail, no one will try again for twenty years."

After talking to his mother, brother, and a minister (Laurence Criner, 1898–1965), Robinson signs a contract and is assigned to Montreal, the Dodgers' top minor-league team. Robinson marries Rae, and they report to spring-training camp in Florida. Robinson's ability wins over many doubt-ers, including Montreal Royals' manager Clay Hopper (Richard Lane, 1889–1982). An exhibition game against the Dodgers is canceled because of an ordinance prohibiting interracial games, and the International League president fears that Robinson's appearance will destroy the minor leagues. But Robinson leads the Royals to the minor-league championship. The next year, Rickey squashes a petition that a handful of Dodgers players have started to keep Robinson off the team, and Robinson is promoted to the Dodgers for the 1947 season.

He endures racial taunts from fans and opposing players, battles out of a hitting slump, and powers the Dodgers to the World Series, clinching the National League pennant with his hitting and base-stealing prowess. He is invited to speak at Congress, and Rickey assures him that he should. "Now," Rickey says, "you can fight back." The narrator concludes that Robinson's victory is one that can only happen "in a country that is truly free, a country where every child has the opportunity to become president or play baseball for the Brooklyn Dodgers."

Robinson's financial adviser brokered a deal to obtain movie rights from Greenberg, a small company that published Robinson's 1948 as-told-to memoir, *Jackie Robinson: My Own Story*, written by African American sportswriter Wendell Smith (1914–72). The movie deal arranged for Robinson to be paid $50,000 in two installments, and receive 15 percent of net profits. Robinson had to pay the screenwriters, Lawrence Edmund Taylor and collaborator Louis Pollock (1904–64). Taylor had approached studios about a movie after Robinson's rookie year, but was rejected. "Every major studio in town was offered the picture," producer Mort Briskin (1913–2000) said, "and was scared to take it" (Clary 1950, 4).

Hollywood had often avoided racial issues, but after World War II some filmmakers began tackling anti-Semitism (1947's *Gentleman's Agreement*), prejudice against African Americans (1949's *Home of the Brave*), and the mistreatment of Hispanics (1949's *Border Incident*) and Native Americans (1949's *The Cowboy and the Indians*).

"We don't preach," Robinson said of *The Jackie Robinson Story*. "We show it on the screen. We don't talk it" (United Press 1950b, 10).

Eagle-Lion Films, a low-budget production company best known for film *noirs* like *T-Men* (1947) and *Raw Deal* (1948), handled distribution.

Rickey reportedly insisted that Robinson play himself, and having a baseball player star as himself wasn't unheard of in Hollywood. New York Yankees star George Herman "Babe" Ruth (1895–1948) played himself in several shorts and features, including *Headin' Home* (1920) and *The Pride of the Yankees* (1942). The subject of the latter film, Ruth's teammate Lou Gehrig (1903–41), starred as himself in the comic western programmer *Rawhide* (1938). Rickey also wanted a hand in the script, so he sent his assistant, Arthur Mann, to California when production began in February 1950. Given credit as technical adviser, Mann began writing his own biography of Robinson, *The Jackie Robinson Story*, which he said would provide legal arguments to dismiss claims by Greenberg or others about copyright infringement. However, the film credits only Taylor and Mann and cites no original source material.

With spring training set to begin in March in Florida, the cast and crew faced a tight deadline to finish the film.

"For 16 days I worked day and night, going on the lot at 9 o'clock in the morning," Robinson said. "We had to work fast. I played a doubleheader every day" (Burr 1950, 15). Yet when Robinson completed shooting and arrived at the training camp, he was 15 pounds overweight.

Robinson arrived in Hollywood on February 4, bringing his three-year-old son, Jackie Robinson Jr. (1946–71) with him. Rachel "Rae" Robinson (1922–) had just given birth to a daughter, Sharon (1950–) and stayed in New York but soon brought their baby to California. Said Dee, who played Rachel: "The moment I talked with her, I had the feeling I wasn't doing her justice. She was a much more outgoing person than I was portraying. . . . I remember feeling, Gee, I wish I had known her before I took this part. She was a stronger woman than I portrayed. I had listened to too many directors about not undercutting the star. I hadn't imagined Rachel as she really was" (Rampersad 1997, 225).

Despite being nervous and seldom relaxed, Robinson impressed director Alfred E. Green (1889–1960). "I simply explained what we wanted, and he did it with all the feeling we asked," Green said (Rampersad 1997, 225). Yet just before the film wrapped, Pollock, who was not credited as a screenwriter, sued Robinson, production company Jewel Pictures Corp. and Eagle-Lion for 5 percent of the profits. Robinson said: "Before I left the lot in California one of our script writers came up to me with his hand behind his back and said, 'Jackie, I hate to do this. You're my favorite ball player,' his hand whipped into sight and he liked to have slapped me in the face with that old legal paper. And then he asked me for my autographed picture" (Burr 1950, 15). Screenwriting, then and now, is often a collaborative effort. Writers come and go, and an arbitration hearing sometimes determines final credit. Robinson said the suit was settled out of court, but no details have surfaced.

The Dodgers trailed the Philadelphia Phillies in the National League standings by one game when *The Jackie Robinson Story* premiered on May 16 at Manhattan's Astor Theater. The proceeds were donated, per Robinson's request, to Youth United, a Brooklyn-based youth organization.

The *Brooklyn Eagle's* Jane Corby singled out Robinson's performance. "He doesn't act in 'The Jackie Robinson Story,' he's just natural. Added to this remarkable poise, Jackie has the looks to make his performance as a screen player effective. His splendid physique and his expressive face give him an assist in putting over his story, and the personality which won him success over tremendous handicaps comes across in telling style" (Corby 1950, 12). Kate Cameron of the *New York Daily News* gave the movie a three-and-a-half-star rating on a four-star scale, writing that Robinson's "innate courage shines through the picture and it is that quality that gives the film biography its special appeal to the heart of the beholder" (Cameron 1950, 78).

"Told simply and with a minimum of heroics," Henry Ward wrote in *The Pittsburgh Press,* "'The Jackie Robinson Story' . . . is a frank, and sincere film. It is as American as the game of baseball" (Ward 1950, 32). Wood Soanes of the *Oakland Tribune* called the movie "excellent entertainment, inspirational, in a way, in that it brings into the open the matter of American prejudices and how they may be met and conquered" (Soanes 1950, 39).

The film's commercial success was uneven, falling below expectations in major markets but dominating in smaller towns, such as Salt Lake City, Utah, where the movie opened simultaneously in six theaters, "a move unprecedented in Utah movie history" ("Jackie Robinson Story Set in Six S.L. Theaters" 1950, 2F). Overall, *The Jackie Robinson Story* grossed $2.7 million, but although it "proved to be one of the more successful sports movies of the era . . . [because of] the often mysterious way of Hollywood accounting, Jack made little additional money from the movie" (Rampersad 1997, 226). The fact that Eagle-Lion ceased production and was taken over by United Artists in 1951 didn't help, either.

Years later, Robinson said, "I realized that it had been made too quickly, that it was budgeted too low, and that, if it had been made later in my career, it could have been done much better" (Robinson 1972, 101).

HISTORICAL BACKGROUND

Although how Americans came to create baseball, which descended from the English game of rounders, is difficult to trace, the modern game began in 1845 when Alexander Cartwright (1820–92) drafted rules and bylaws for the New York City–based Knickerbocker Base Ball Club. In 1866, the *New York Clipper* noted that "nearly every trade and occupation has its votaries in the game of base ball" (Seymour 1989, 41–2), and a game that year between the Brooklyn Atlantics and Philadelphia Athletics reportedly attracted 40,000 spectators. "Business houses closed," historian Harold Seymour wrote, "bosses and clerks bet on the game; men, women, and children rushed to the scene, crowding windows, housetops, and trees. Unfortunately, they swarmed over the playing field as well, forcing the clubs to call the game" (Seymour 1989, 42). Baseball had become "the American National Game" (Hickok 2002, 57).

When the sport's governing body, the National Association of Base Ball Players, was founded in 1857, amateurs and mostly amateurs (or presumably amateurs) played baseball. Paying men to play games was frowned upon. At the December 1868 convention, however, the association divided players into amateur and professional status, with professionals being those who "play baseball for money, or who shall, at any time, receive compensation for their services as players" (Ryczek 1998, 166). In 1869, center fielder Harry Wright (1835–95), who came to Cincinnati in 1866 to play professionally for the city's Union Cricket Club, captained the first all-pro baseball team, the Cincinnati Red Stockings, to a 63–0 record including exhibition games.

American baseball would never be the same. The distinction between professional and amateur players was removed at the 1869 convention. In 1871, the National Association of Professional Base Ball Players was established. The professional National League was formed in 1876, but the league's stance against playing Sunday games and selling of alcohol at all games led to the formation of the American Association—dubbed "the beer and whiskey league"—after the 1881 season. Although that league would fold after the 1891 season, the Western League took its place in 1892, changing its name to the American League after the 1899 season. On January 9, 1903, the American and National leagues and minor-leagues association signed an agreement, creating modern professional baseball and baseball's first World Series.

New Yorkers had long been passionate about baseball, and Brooklyn had teams in the professional National Association from 1871 to 1875. From 1884 through 1889, Brooklyn fielded an American Association team before moving to the National League in 1890. Eventually the National League club became known as the Trolley Dodgers because pedestrians had to avoid trolleys on crowded thoroughfares. The name was shortened to the Dodgers. Locals more affectionately called them "Bums." These "Bums," who had not won the National League pennant since 1920, made it to the World Series in 1941 only to lose to the New York Yankees in five games. Despite winning 104 games in 1942, the Dodgers finished second to the St. Louis Browns. In late October 1942, the Dodgers signed Branch Rickey (1881–1965) to a five-year contract as president and general manager.

Born in Ohio, Rickey earned degrees from Ohio Wesleyan College and Allegheny College before earning a law degree from the University of Michigan, where he coached the baseball team. He had played major-league baseball for parts of four seasons and managed the St. Louis Browns and St. Louis Cardinals, eventually becoming the Cardinals' general manager—and that's where Rickey found his biggest success. Unable to outbid wealthier teams for minor-league prospects, Rickey decided to buy stock in minor-league teams. "Experience had taught us that a partial share of a minor-league team was unsatisfactory; the solution was to own the minor-league team outright," Rickey said (Frommer 1982, 53). Baseball commissioner Kenesaw Mountain Landis (1866–1944) ruled in 1938 that a major-league team could control only one team in each minor league, but Rickey's farm system worked. Between 1926 and 1943, the Cardinals won four World Series, won three other National League pennants, and finished second in the league five times. "The only thing he couldn't do in St. Louis," Jimmy Breslin wrote, "was move Black fans out of the broiling one-hundred-degree sun of the bleachers and into the shaded grandstand" (Breslin 2011, 6). When Rickey tried to get Cardinals' owner Sam Breadon (1876–1949) to abandon integrated seating, Breadon refused, saying, "Business is business" (Breslin 2011, 7).

Rickey recalled coaching an African American player at Ohio Wesleyan named Charlie Thomas (1881–1971). The details varied during the multiple times Rickey told the story, but, in essence, a hotel refused to allow Thomas to stay until Rickey said the player would stay in Rickey's room. There, Rickey discovered "this fine young man, sitting on the edge of a chair, crying. He was crying. He was pulling at his hands as though he could tear the very skin off. 'It's my skin, Mr. Rickey . . . . If I could just pull it off'" (Eig 2007, 116).

In 1945, Rickey announced the formation of the United States Negro League, which would include teams of African American players in Detroit, Pittsburgh, Chicago, Toledo, Brooklyn, and Philadelphia. But that was a ruse. Rickey's actual plan was to integrate major-league baseball, and he found a needed ally in A.B. "Happy" Chandler (1898–1991), who in 1945 became Major League Baseball's commissioner. "If a Black boy can make it in Okinawa and Guadalcanal, hell, he can make it in baseball," Chandler said (Frommer 1982, 104).

Rickey sent his scouts to look at African American players in the Negro Leagues. African Americans had been playing baseball almost as long as baseball had been played, and some had made it to the major leagues before

RICKEY AND THE COMMISSIONER

Baseball commissioner A.B. "Happy" Chandler was often the man behind the scenes in 1947. The former Kentucky governor warned Philadelphia Phillies owner R.R.M. Carpenter (1877–1949) to control his team—especially manager Ben Chapman (1908–93), known for his racial taunts of Robinson—or face punishment. Before that, though, Chandler had an even bigger part in Robinson's success.

In the early 1980s, Chandler told Stan "Tex" Banash, author, historian, and speechwriter, that Rickey met Chandler at a cabin behind Chandler's home in Versailles, Kentucky.

"He then explained I was sitting in the chair where Rickey sat when they decided to bring Jackie Robinson to the major leagues," Banash recalled. "He told how they discussed Robinson's talent. Chandler said he couldn't face his Maker if he didn't give a ballplayer with the talent and skills that Robinson demonstrated a chance in the major leagues" (Stan "Tex" Banash, interview with author, March 31, 2020).

In January 1947, major-league owners voted 15–1 against allowing Rickey, the lone dissenting voter, to promote Robinson to the Dodgers. Chandler overruled the vote, which was not announced publicly.

"While Robinson deserves credit for tolerating verbal abuse and unacceptable behavior from white fans, players and managers, credit Rickey for standing by him and Chandler for making it all happen," Banash said. "Had Chandler not made that decision, it might have taken decades before an African American broke baseball's color barrier" (Stan "Tex" Banash, interview with author, March 31, 2020).

Source
Griffin, Richard. 2010. "January 1947: Baseball Owners Vote 15-1 against Allowing Jackie Robinson to play with the Dodgers." *The Star*, January 20, 2010. https://www.thestar.com/sports/baseball/2010/06/20/january_1947_baseball_owners_vote_151_against_allowing_jackie_robinson_to_play_with_the_dodgers.html

the pros segregated baseball. Early attempts to form professional African American baseball leagues failed until the Negro National League was formed in 1920 in Kansas City, Missouri. That came after eight members of Chicago White Sox conspired with gamblers to throw the 1919 World Series. Raymond Doswell, vice president of curatorial services at the Negro Leagues Baseball Museum in Kansas City, explained:

Keep in mind that at this time, after African Americans had successfully proved themselves as American citizens through their efforts in World War I, many Black soldiers and others returned from the war expecting full rights of citizenship, but were rebuffed. The country explodes in race riots, Chicago, East St. Louis, Texas, other places. The Black community responds strongly to that, but out of that comes the Harlem Renaissance, that sense of race pride and affirmation of culture and a level of independence, too. This is also a period that coincides with the Black migration with African Americans moving out of rural areas into mostly urban areas in the North. The Negro Leagues kind of come out of this, as well. The creation of the Negro National League is meant to show stability by comparison to the major leagues, which are reeling from that [White Sox] scandal. And to show that they belong because they knew that they belonged ability-wise. (Raymond Doswell, interview with author, February 19, 2020)

Hurt by the Great Depression (1929–39), the Negro National League folded after the 1931 season, but in 1937, the Negro American League was formed.

Rickey's scouts narrowed their choices to catcher Roy Campanella (1921–93), pitcher Don Newcombe (1926–2019), outfielders Larry Doby (1923–2003) and Monte Irvin (1919–2015) and Robinson, then playing shortstop for the Kansas City Monarchs. Catcher Josh Gibson (1911–47) and pitcher LeRoy "Satchel" Paige (1906–82) were considered but believed to be too old. On August 28, 1945, Robinson met Rickey in Rickey's Brooklyn office. On October 23, the Dodgers announced that Robinson had signed a contract and would likely be playing for the Montreal Royals, Brooklyn's top minor-league (Class AAA) team in the International League, in 1946.

Robinson was what Rickey wanted. Having lettered in four sports at UCLA, Robinson served as an officer in the U.S. Army during World War II. At Camp Hood, Texas, a driver ordered Robinson to move to the back of the bus. Robinson refused, citing the Army policy prohibiting segregation on military posts. The exchange grew heated, military police were called, and Robinson faced a general court-martial but was acquitted. Jonathan Eig wrote:

Had Rickey wanted a pacifist, he might have selected any one of a half a dozen men with milder constitutions than Jack Roosevelt Robinson's. It is a testament to Rickey's sophistication and foresight that he chose a ballplayer who would become a symbol of strength rather than assimilation. It is a testament to Robinson's intelligence and ambition that he recognized the importance of turning the other cheek and yet found a way to do it without appearing the least bit weak. So long as he showed restraint when fans and players baited him, he could fight like hell on the ball field. No one could fault him for playing hard. (Eig 2007, 28)

On February 10, 1946, Robinson married Rachel Isum. She came with him—the only player's wife allowed by Rickey—to the Dodgers' spring training in Florida, where Robinson began "probably the most crucial [year] in my life" (Robinson 1948, 65). Robinson also had to endure the South's segregation policies of the time, riding in the back of a bus with Rachel to Daytona Beach. A game in Jacksonville, Florida, was canceled because of a law prohibiting interracial games on city-owned property. In Deland, Florida, another game was canceled because the lights were allegedly being repaired. "Asked just what the lights had to do with a daytime game, authorities replied that the electricians were available only on that day, and that the teams couldn't use the field" (Mann 1951, 144). Games were also canceled in Savannah, Georgia, and Richmond, Virginia.

Robinson played that season for Montreal, where he led the league with a .349 batting average and helped the Royals to 100–54 record. The Royals then won the "Little World Series" in five games against the Syracuse Chiefs. In 1947, Rickey moved the Dodgers' spring training to Cuba and Panama, where Robinson had to deal with racism but also learn a new position. The Dodgers had popular Harold Henry "Pee Wee" Reese (1918–99) at shortstop, while Eddie Stanky (1915–99) played a solid second base. Rickey and manager Leo Durocher (1905–91) agreed to move Robinson to first base, a position he had played briefly for Montreal because of a sore throwing arm. "I had hated the position then; and now, of all times, I didn't want to be shifted from a position I could play to one that I knew literally nothing about," Robinson recalled (Robinson 1948, 119).

On April 10, 1947, in his last spring-training game, Robinson hit into a double play to end an exhibition against the Dodgers while Mann was passing out a release in the press box that read "The Brooklyn Dodgers today purchased the contract of Jackie Roosevelt Robinson from the Montreal Royals" (Robinson 1948, 122). The color barrier in the majors had been broken, and Robinson opened the season for the Dodgers at first base on April 15. His jersey number was 42. Exactly fifty years later, Major League Baseball retired the number for all teams. Thirteen players were told they could continue wearing 42 for the rest of their careers, although six changed numbers after the 1997 season. The last major-leaguer to wear 42 was New York Yankees pitcher Mariano Rivera (1969–), who retired after the 2013 season.

Rumors of a potential boycott of Dodgers games by several St. Louis Cardinals players persisted, but nothing ever happened (a petition circulating among some Dodgers players to keep Robinson from making the major-league roster was squashed during spring training). Yet Robinson heard racial slurs from spectators and players. The Philadelphia Phillies "used rotten language," Robinson said. "Philadelphia . . . was the worst of all, the fans, the players, everything" (United Press 1950b, 10). Minor-league fans had flocked to games in the International League in 1946, and major-league fans filled stadiums across the country in 1947 when the Dodgers played. Even St. Louis had to ignore its segregated seating policy when African American spectators overflowed into sections typically reserved for whites. Robinson finished the season with a .297 batting average and led the National League with twenty-nine stolen bases. He was chosen as baseball's first Rookie of the Year. Major League Baseball awarded only one rookie award in 1947 and 1948 before presenting awards to American and National League rookies in 1949. Before the regular season ended, fans arranged for a "Jackie

Robinson Day" at Brooklyn's Ebbets Field. The Dodgers won the National League Pennant, and despite losing to the New York Yankees in seven games in the World Series, Robinson said, "All in all, I had had a very lucky year" (Robinson 1948, 164).

The following year Robinson moved to second base after the Dodgers traded Stanky to the Boston Braves. Robinson followed his MVP season in 1949 by hitting better than .300 in the next five seasons, losing to the Yankees again in the 1952 and 1953 World Series before finally beating the Yankees in seven games in the 1955 World Series. Rickey, however, left after the 1950 season and became executive vice president and general manager of the Pittsburgh Pirates in 1951 before retiring in 1955. Rickey died in 1965 at age eighty-three. Two years later, he was inducted into the Baseball Hall of Fame.

Robinson still faced racism. Jack L. Smith (1929–2016), a University of Oregon standout signed by Rickey in 1952 and later invited to try out for other major-league teams in the mid-to-late 1950s, recalled a spring-training game when "Robinson was walking by our dugout when one of my team-mates jumped up on the fence and began acting like a monkey. That guy was a real b—, but Robinson, he just kept walking" (Jack L. Smith, interview with author, December 22, 2014). Other opponents played cleanly. After knocking Robinson down while stretching to catch an errant throw, Pirates first baseman Hank Greenberg (1911–86) asked Robinson if he was okay, then offered to share "a few things I've learned through the years that might help you and make it easier" (Robinson 1948, 147). After a collision at second base, St. Louis Cardinals shortstop Marty Marion (1916–2011) asked if he had spiked Robinson. After Robinson said he wasn't hurt, Marion said, "I got new spikes on and they'd cut pretty deep. I'm glad I didn't" (Eig 2007, 163).

Robinson retired after the 1956 season in which the Dodgers lost again to the Yankees in the World Series. He finished his ten-year career with a .311 batting average and was inducted into the Hall of Fame in 1962. The Dodgers, who moved to Los Angeles after the 1957 season, retired Robinson's number in 1972. Plagued by diabetes and having suffered a heart attack in 1968, Robinson died on October 24, 1972, ten days after throwing out the ceremonial first pitch before Game 2 of the World Series in Cincinnati.

"The word for Jackie Robinson is 'unconquerable,'" *New York Times* columnist Red Smith wrote after Robinson's death. "The point is, he would not be defeated. Not by the other team and not by life" (Smith 1972, 53).

DEPICTION AND CULTURAL CONTEXT

In a newspaper interview days before *The Jackie Robinson Story*'s premiere, Robinson said, "We don't name cities where things happened, or ball clubs, either. Otherwise, they'd lose a lot of fans" (Lewis 1950, 15). But for a period when Hollywood wasn't known for staying close to history, *The Jackie Robinson Story* kept things fairly accurate.

"When you get into the minutiae, obviously there were licenses taken," Doswell said, "but I think the intensity of what [Robinson] went through and some of the things that he had to deal with were handled as appropriately as they could be" (Raymond Doswell, interview with author, February 19, 2020).

Robinson and his brother Mack are depicted as living with their mother, Mallie Robinson (1889–1968), but other siblings—Edgar (1910–94), Frank (1911–39), and Willa Mae (1916–97)—are left out. Robinson's parents had separated and in 1920, his mother took the children from their sharecropping farm near Cairo, Georgia, to Pasadena, California.

Most likely, Mack's prowess in athletics inspired Robinson to take up sports.

Robinson's college career in the movie closely follows his actual path. In 1938, Robinson's jump of 25 feet, 6 1/2 inches at the Southern California Junior College track meet broke the national junior college record for the broad jump of 25 feet, 5 1/2 inches, which Mack had set at the Drake Relays in Des Moines, Iowa, in 1937. Having missed the 1932 Olympic Games in Los Angeles because of a heart ailment, Mack won a spot on the U.S. Olympic team that competed in Berlin, where he won a silver medal in the 200-meter dash behind teammate Jesse Owens (1913–80), who won four golds in Germany. Despite Mack's sports success, the only job Mack found was as a street sweeper in Pasadena. "May not be a great job," Mack says in the film, "but it's steady."

"In a really important way," Jonathan Eig said, that scene "showed how a lot of black athletes, even black heroes, were treated at the time and that a good steady job was a street cleaner" (Jonathan Eig, interview with author, February 24, 2020). Several people wondered how an Olympic medalist could do such menial labor, Mack said later. "I never did understand those people," Mack said. "I had to take whatever I could get" (Rampersad 1997, 56).

Robinson's army career gets little screen time—it was the subject of a Turner Network Television movie, *The Court-Martial of Jackie Robinson*, in 1990—but Robinson's brief career in the Negro Leagues is well covered—only instead of playing for the Kansas City Monarchs, the team is called the Black Panthers. Today, that rings with a touch of irony. Founded in 1966 in Oakland, California, the Black Panther Party, or the Black Panthers, was formed to protect African American neighborhoods from police brutality during the turbulent 1960s but grew into a "revolutionary" organization. Although Robinson was a strong supporter of African American rights, Doswell said, "he wasn't a big fan of the Black Panther movement" (Raymond Doswell, interview with author, February 19, 2020). Many African American teams were given names like Black Sox, Brown Dodgers, Black Barons, and Black Yankees, however, so Black Panthers fit.

The bus travel is accurately depicted. The Monarchs paid Robinson $400 a month, but he said, "it turned out to be a pretty miserable way to make a buck" (Robinson 1972, 35). In one scene, the team bus stops at a roadside diner and Robinson is sent in to "See if we can eat inside. Two, see if we can wash up. Three, if we can't eat inside, see if they'll fix up sandwiches." The chef agrees to make sandwiches to go, but the manager says the restroom is "out of order."

The incident didn't happen at a restaurant but at a gas station, Robinson said, but the film's depiction of road life for African American baseball players was certainly realistic. Robinson later recalled:

> This fatiguing travel wouldn't have been so bad if we could have had decent meals. Finding satisfactory or even passable eating places was almost a daily problem. There was no hotel in many of the places we played. Sometimes there was a hotel for blacks which had no eating facilities. No one even thought of trying to get accommodations in white hotels. Some of the crummy eating joints would not serve us at all. . . . You were really living when you were able to get a plate of cold cuts. You ate on board the team bus or on the road. (Robinson 1972, 36)

In August 1945, Brooklyn Dodgers scout Clyde Sukeforth (1901–2000) introduced himself to Robinson before a game in Chicago. Although the film places the introduction after a ballgame, the reaction of Robinson and his teammates is a faithful recreation of what really happened. "We all got a great kick out of it," Robinson said. "The possibility of a Big League scout spending his time looking at Negro players was nothing but a joke" (Robinson 1948, 16). Sukeforth had to convince Robinson that he was legitimate and that Rickey really wanted to meet Robinson. Certainly, Robinson had reason to be skeptical. *The Pittsburgh Courier,* an African American newspaper, had arranged for Robinson, Cleveland Buckeyes outfielder Sam Jethroe (1917–2001), and Philadelphia Stars second baseman Marvin Williams (1923–2000) to try out at Boston's Fenway Park on April 16 before Red Sox manager Joe Cronin (1906–84) and general manager Eddie Collins (1887–1951). "After the workout they shook hands with us and told us we might hear from them," Robinson recalled. "We never did" (Robinson 1948, 15). In 1959, the Boston Red Sox became the last major-league team to integrate.

"It still takes 12 years between Robinson's debut in '47 to 1959 before every team has at least one black or Latino player on its roster," Doswell said. "Robinson played in 10 of those 12 years in his career. It was a slow process" (Raymond Doswell, interview with author, February 19, 2020). The Negro American League disbanded in 1960, although a few teams continued to barnstorm across the country. The last of those teams, the Indianapolis Clowns, folded in 1973.

On August 28, 1945, Robinson met with Rickey. The movie's depiction is fairly accurate to what historians believe happened, and closely follows the account of the meeting that appeared in the May 13, 1950 issue of the *Saturday Evening Post*. But that article appeared right before *The Jackie Robinson Story* began playing at theaters, and it was written by Mann, Rickey's publicist and Robinson's biographer who got a screenwriting credit for the movie. As one sportswriter wrote: "Naturally, Mr. Rickey doesn't lose any saintliness through Mr. Mann's worshipful pen" (Lewis 1950, 15).

"The movie was being made a couple of years after the events had occurred so they're all on the same page, they're all telling the story the same way," Eig said. "Either that means it really happened that way or they all came up with a fable they liked and they decided to share it. You never really know since we didn't have a recorder or a secretary or a tape recorder" (Jonathan Eig, interview with author, February 24, 2020).

Rickey asked Robinson if he had a girl. "Rickey loved to ask ballplayers the girl question, because he learned something about their character, and he liked employees who had families relying on them to work hard and behave responsibly" (Eig 2007, 27). He interrogated Robinson to find out how he would react to racial slurs, taunts, and physical confrontations, and Robinson asked if Rickey wanted a ballplayer who was afraid to fight back.

"I never will forget the way he exploded," Robinson recalled years later. "'Robinson,' he said, 'I'm looking for a ballplayer with guts enough not to fight back'" (Robinson 1972, 46).

The movie has Robinson telling Rickey that he signed no contract or had any agreement with the Black Panthers. The film goes no further with that story, but in 1945 the Monarchs were not happy. "I had taken it for granted that Negro Baseball would universally hail the event as the long-sought opening wedge into the Big Leagues," Robinson recalled. "But [Monarchs owners J.L. Wilkinson (1878–1964) and Tom Baird (1885–1962)]—who, by the way, are white men—were anything but pleased by the news" (Robinson 1948, 51).

"If players are going to be taken from the Negro League, I believe some sort of an arrangement should be worked out between the major leagues and the Negro League," Baird said. "We are not trying to keep any Negro ball player from the major leagues" (United Press 1945, 17). Rickey countered that the Negro Leagues "were not leagues at all. I failed to find a constitution, by-laws or a uniform player's contract, and I learned that players of all teams became free agents at the end of each season, with no written guarantee or consideration" (Rickey Counters Piracy Charge 1945, 59).

The Negro American League lacked a reserve clause, which bound a player to a specific team for a long period (the clause in professional baseball was abolished in 1975), and, like the major leagues, did not allow players to become free agents and, providing they were not under contract, sign with any team.

Did Robinson have a contract with the Monarchs?

"He probably had a contract," Eig said. "Even if he didn't, the Negro Leagues probably had a legitimate claim that they should have been compensated for him . . . . [The Dodgers organization] treated Negro Leaguers as if they were fair game" (Jonathan Eig, interview with author, February 24, 2020).

"It depended on the team, but there were contracts," Doswell said. "In fact, by the mid-1930s some teams were using basically major-league baseball players contracts" (Raymond Doswell, interview with author, February 19, 2020). After Robinson signed with the Dodgers, player contracts became the norm for Negro American League teams. "In essence, they became a farm system for Major League Baseball," Doswell said. "They protected themselves in that way" (Raymond Doswell, interview with author, February 19, 2020).

What *The Jackie Robinson Story* leaves out, however, is the fact that Robinson wasn't the only African American at the Dodgers' spring-training camp in 1946. On January 29, John R. "Johnny" Wright (ca. 1916–90), a pitcher for the Homestead Grays, signed with the Montreal Royals. Wright and Robinson, both "tense," arrived in Sanford, Florida. "Johnny and I both realized that this was hostile territory—that anything could happen any time to a Negro who thought he could play ball with white men on an equal basis," Robinson recalled. "It was going to be difficult to relax and behave naturally" (Robinson 1948, 67).

In April, the Dodgers signed Campanella and Newcombe to play for Brooklyn's Class B affiliate in Nashua, New Hampshire. Campanella was promoted to the Dodgers in 1948, but a car accident prematurely ended his big-league career before the 1958 season. He was inducted into the Hall of Fame in 1969. Newcombe joined the Dodgers in 1949, spent ten years in the major leagues despite missing the 1952 and 1953 seasons because of military service, and won the Cy Young and Most Valuable Player awards in 1956. Wright's career, however, was brief. He made two relief appearances for the Royals before being optioned to the Dodgers' Class C team in Three Rivers, Quebec, where he finished the season. Released by the Dodgers that winter, Wright returned to the Homestead Grays. "John had all the ability in the world, as far as physical abilities were concerned," Robinson said. "But John couldn't stand the pressure of going up into this new league and being one of the first" (Peterson 1970, 196).

Regarding the petition by some Dodgers players to keep Robinson off the 1947 team, Robinson said, "Branch Rickey wanted that scene in the picture" (United Press 1950b, 10). The movie, however, leaves out Durocher's part in ending the petition.

"The petition is very much in dispute," Eig said. "I think it's almost certain that there was some kind of petition. Of course, years later nobody would admit to having signed it. But the big difference was it was really Leo Durocher who confronted the players. It wasn't Branch Rickey. Branch Rickey was aware of it and told Leo Durocher to handle it and Durocher called a meeting and summoned everybody to the kitchen of the hotel and read them all the riot act" (Jonathan Eig, interview with author, February 24, 2020). Rumors at the time alleged that St. Louis players also signed a petition saying they didn't want to play against Robinson, either, but most historians dismiss the Cardinals' reaction as a bluff. Still, resentment among white players certainly didn't surprise Rickey—even on his own team. "Some players with us now may even quit," Rickey said after signing Robinson. "But they'll be back in baseball after working a year or two in a cotton mill" (Turkin 1945, 59).

The hostility Robinson faced in the minor and major leagues is also toned down, yet the depictions remain effective. The incident in which fans give Robinson a black cat as his companion actually happened at an International League game in 1946, and the cat was brought by the team, not fans. "At the time I thought it was funny," Robinson said. "I laughed inwardly but of course I couldn't let them know" (United Press 1950b, 10). Yet the movie shows racial taunts; even the word n— is used, and this came when Hollywood's Production Code Administration, formed in 1934, had strict rules against vulgarities, obscenities, and profanity.

The Jackie Robinson Story leaves out an iconic scene that has become part of the Robinson mythology—a scene that is included in *42*, a 2013 movie directed and written by Brian Helgeland (1961–) about Robinson's first year in the major leagues.

According to legend, in a 1947 game in Cincinnati, while fans mercilessly hurled insults at Robinson, Dodgers shortstop "Pee Wee" Reese, a native of Kentucky, walked over to Robinson and put his arm over his teammate's shoulder in a show of support. The moment became the subject of a popular 1990 children's book, *Teammates*, written by Peter Golenbock and illustrated by Paul Bacon. A statue depicting the moment was unveiled in Brooklyn in 2005. Another account puts the event in Boston. But did it actually happen?

The first mention of anything resembling the incident was published in the *Brooklyn Daily Eagle* on August 24, 1949, in Robinson's "as-told-to" article written by Ed Reid, but in this version players, not fans, on an opposing team were screaming insults at Reese, and Reese did not put an arm around his teammate:

> They were joshing him very viciously because he was playing on the team *with me* and was on the field nearby. Mind you, they were not yelling at me; I supposed they did not have the nerve to do that, but they were calling him some very vile names and every one bounced off Peewee and hit me like a machine-gun bullet.
>
> Peewee kind of sensed the sort of hopeless, dead feeling in me and came over and stood beside me for a while. He didn't say a word but he looked over at the chaps who were yelling at me through him and just stared. He was standing by me, I could tell you that.
>
> Slowly the jibes died down like when you kill a snake an inch at a time, and then there was nothing but quiet from them. It was wonderful the way this little guy did it. I will never forget it. (Robinson 1949, 11)

"There's a reason Robinson left that scene out in the movie," Eig said. "That whole incident with Pee Wee really didn't become part of the mythology for several decades after it occurs. Clearly to me it didn't happen in 1947 and when it did happen later it was no big deal because Robinson was already on the team. . . . His wife said to me it's the wrong story because it makes the white man the hero and it suggests that Jackie couldn't have done it without Pee Wee's embrace. And that's not only incorrect factually, it's the wrong message" (Jonathan Eig, interview with author, February 24, 2020).

The movie ends with Robinson speaking to Congress after his rookie season, but that appearance took place in 1949. In a speech given in April in Paris, Paul Robeson (1898–1976), an actor, singer, and civil rights advocate, was quoted as saying, "It is unthinkable that American Negroes would go to war on behalf of those who have oppressed us for generations against a country which in one generation has raised our people to the full dignity of mankind" (Rampersad 1997, 211). That led Georgia Congressman John Stephens Wood (1885–1968) to request Robinson, who said he didn't even know Robeson, to appear before the House Un-American Activities Committee (HUAC). The HUAC had been established in the 1930s but grew in stature during the early years of the Cold War (1947–91) when unfounded fears arose over subversive communist activities in America. The movie aims to end on a patriotic note with Robinson testifying that: "I do know that democracy works for those who are willing to fight for it, and I'm sure it's worth defending. I can't speak for any 15 million people. No one person can. But I'm certain that I, and other Americans of many races and faiths, have too much invested in our country's welfare to throw it away, or let it be taken from us."

In reality, HUAC and fears of communism led to the blacklisting of roughly five hundred people in the entertainment industry for more than a decade. Some actors, writers, and directors couldn't find work. That list included Pollock, the screenwriter denied a credit for *The Jackie Robinson Story*.

By 1954, Pollock's screenwriting career dried up, and no one would tell him why. He had to sell his house. Five years later, he learned that he had been blacklisted because HUAC labeled him an "unfriendly witness." Pollock, however, had never been subpoenaed by the committee, and had no communist sympathies, but a California clothier named Louis Pollack had refused to testify before the committee. "[N]obody ever asked me once: 'Are you this man?'" Pollock said. "Nobody ever asked me" (Hollywood Script 1964, 12). The case of mistaken identity ended Pollock's screenwriting career until he began getting some television work in 1963. Pollock died of a heart attack in 1964.

CONCLUSION

The Jackie Robinson Story isn't as well known as *42* (2013) or as well regarded as baseball biopics like *The Pride of the Yankees* (1942), *The*

Stratton Story (1949), or *Fear Strikes Out* (1957). Yet many viewers are often amazed at how well it plays today, how faithful it is to history, how it still gets its message across, and how it can still pack a punch.

"It's pretty sweet, harmless movie," Eig said. "It doesn't exaggerate tremendously. It seemed like Jackie was very earnest in trying to tell the story" (Jonathan Eig, interview with author, February 24, 2020). "It's a good movie," Doswell said. "It's a movie of its time. It's an important part of understanding his story and baseball history in general. We're fortunate to have that as an artifact" (Raymond Doswell, interview with author, February 19, 2020).

FURTHER READING

Associated Press. 1945. "New League Formed: For Negro Ballplayers—Branch Rickey Announces Formation." *The Cincinnati Enquirer*, May 8, 1945, p. 10.

Associated Press. 1950a. "To Portray Life Story: Jackie Robinson Slated to Step Before Movie Cameras." *The Galveston Daily News*, January 30, 1950, p. 5.

Associated Press. 1950b. "Dodger Star Arrives for Filming of Life." *The Sioux City Sunday Journal*, February 5, 1950, p. 1.

Associated Press. 1950c. "Robinson Sued in Row Over Movie." *Oakland Tribune*, February 28, 1950, p. 31.

Belson, Ken. 2013. "Rivera Is Taking Robinson's 42 to Its Last Stop." *The New York Times*, March 13, 2013. https://www.nytimes.com/2013/03/14/sports/baseball/mariano-rivera-carries-banner-for-final-42s-and-for-jackie-robinson.html

"Boro Invades Times Sq., Flies Pennant for 'Jackie' Film Bow." 1950. *Brooklyn Eagle*, May 17, 1950, p. 3.

Breslin, Jimmy. 2011. *Branch Rickey*. New York: Viking.

Brimner, Larry Dane. 2018. *Blacklisted!: Hollywood, the Cold War, and the First Amendment*. Honesdale, PA: Calkins Creek.

Brody, Richard. 2013. "When Jackie Robinson Played 'Jackie Robinson'." *The New Yorker*, April 19, 2013. https://www.newyorker.com/culture/richard-brody/when-jackie-robinson-played-jackie-robinson

Broeg, Bob. 1950. "It Must Be Spring—Browns and Cardinals Open: Taylor Is Forced with Four Holdouts." *St. Louis Post-Dispatch*, March 1, 1950, p. 4B.

Burr, Harold C. 1950. "Hollywood Proves No Great Help to Robinson's Plunging Waistline: Jackie Reports to Vero Beach 15 Pounds Over." *Brooklyn Eagle*, March 7, 1950.

Cameron, Kate. 1950. "Jackie Robinson Story Touches the Heart: Life of Star Tells a Vivid Tale of Courage, Humility." *New York Daily News*, May 17, 1950, p. 78.

Clary, Patricia. 1950. "Hollywood Film Shop: Production Manager's Job Is Arduous One." *The Latrobe Bulletin*, March 13, 1950, p. 4.

Coates, Paul. 1964. "Louis Pollock's Death Recalls Tragedy of Wrong Identification." *Los Angeles Times*, August 28, 1964, Part II, p. 6.

Corby, Jane. 1950. "'The Jackie Robinson Story,' 'Johnny Holiday' New Arrivals." *Brooklyn Eagle*, May 17, 1950, p. 12.

Dixon, Phil S. 2002. *The Monarchs 1920–1938: Featuring Wilber "Bullet" Rogan, the Greatest Ballplayer in Cooperstown*. Sioux Falls, SD: Mariah Press.

Duncan, Garrett Albert. 2020. "Black Panther Party." *Encyclopedia Britannica*, March 16, 2020. https://www.britannica.com/topic/Black-Panther-Party.

Eig, Jonathan. 2007. *Opening Day: The Story of Jackie Robinson's First Season*. New York: Simon & Schuster.

Frommer, Harvey. 1982. *Rickey & Robinson: The Men Who Broke Baseball's Color Barrier*. New York: Macmillan Publishing Co., Inc.

Golenbock, Peter. 1986. *Bums: An Oral History of the Brooklyn Dodgers*. New York: Pocket Books.

Gould, Ben. 1946. "Dodgers Sign 2 Negro Aces for Nashua Farm." *Brooklyn Daily Eagle*, April 5, 1946, p. 15.

"Grays' Hurler Is Signed by Dodger Farm: John Wright Leaves Posey to Enter Organized Baseball." 1946. *Pittsburgh Post-Gazette*, January 30, 1946, p. 13.

Hickok, Ralph. 2002. *The Encyclopedia of North American Sports History, Second Edition*. New York: Facts On File, Inc.

"Hollywood Script." 1964. *The Boston Globe*, August 26, 1964, p. 12.

International News Service. 1950. "Jackie to Leave for Dodger Camp." *The Arizona Republic*, March 4, 1950, p. 18.

"'Jackie Robinson Story' Set in Six S.L. Theaters: Gem, Crest, Arcade, Apollo, Ute and Park Vu to Open Film Aug. 31." *Deseret News*, August 23, 1950, p. 2F.

Kahn, Roger. 1973. *The Boys of Summer*. New York: Signet.

"Late Sport." 1942. *The Ithaca Journal*, October 29, 1942, p. 1.

Lewis, Dave. 1950. "Once Over Lightly." *Long Beach Independent*, May 13, 1950, p. 15.

Mann, Arthur. 1951. *The Jackie Robinson Story*. New York: Grosset & Dunlap.

Margolies, Jacob. 1993. *The Negro Leagues: The Story of Black Baseball*. New York: Franklin Watts.

Misler, Buster. 1946. "Buster Misler's Time Out." *The New York Age*, November 23, 1946, p. 11.

Nemec, David. 2004. *The Beer & Whiskey League: The Illustrated History of the American Association—Baseball's Renegade Major League*. Guilford, CT: The Lyons Press.

Nilsson, Jeff. 2011. "Grace Under Pressure: Jackie Robinson: First Told in the Post, Robinson's Story Is Still Breaking Barriers with the Release of 42." *The Saturday Evening Post*, January 29, 2011. https://www.saturdayeveningpost.com /2011/01/grace-pressure-jackie-robinson/

Paige, Leroy (Satchel) as told to David Lipman. 1962. *Maybe I'll Pitch Forever*. Garden City, NY: Doubleday & Company, Inc.

Peterson, Robert. 1970. *Only the Ball Was White: A History of Legendary Black Players and All-Black Professional Teams*. Englewood Cliffs, NJ: Prentice-Hall, Inc.

Quinlan, David. 1991. *Quinlan's Illustrated Guide to Film Directors*. London: B.T. Batsford, Ltd.

Rampersad, Arnold. 1997. *Jackie Robinson: A Biography*. New York: Alfred A. Knopf, Inc.

"Rickey Counters Piracy Charge." 1945. *New York Daily News*, October 24, 1945, p. 59.

Robinson, Jackie as told to Alfred Duckett. 1972. *I Never Had It Made: An Autobiography*. New York: G.P. Putnam's Sons.

Robinson, Jackie as told to Ed Reid. 1949. "Jackie Robinson Tells His Story." *Brooklyn Daily Eagle*, August 24, 1949, pp. 1, 11.

Robinson, Jackie as told to Wendell Smith. 1948. *Jackie Robinson: My Own Story.* New York: Greenberg.

Robinson, Ray. 2006. *Iron Horse: Lou Gehrig in His Time.* 2006. New York: W.W. Norton & Company.

Ryczek, William J. 1998. *When Johnny Came Sliding Home: The Post-Civil War Baseball Boom, 1865–1870.* Jefferson, NC: McFarland & Company, Inc., Publishers.

Sandomir, Richard. 2017. *The Pride of the Yankees: Lou Gehrig, Gary Cooper, and the Making of a Classic.* New York: Hachette Books.

Seymour, Harold. 1989. *Baseball: The Early Years.* New York: Oxford University Press.

Slide, Anthony. 2013. *The New Historical Dictionary of the American Film Industry.* New York: Routledge.

Smith, Red. 1972. "Death of an Unconquerable Man." *The New York Times*, October 25, 1972, p. 53.

Smith, Wendell. 1946a. "The Sports Beat." *The Pittsburgh Courier,* April 13, 1946, p. 14.

Smith, Wendell. 1946b. "'Robinson Plays or No Game,' Rickey's Answer to Dixie Bias." *The Pittsburgh Courier*, April 13, 1946, p. 14.

Smith, Wendell. 1946c. "Jackie in Lineup against Jersey City." *The Pittsburgh Courier*, April 20, 1946, p. 15.

Smith, Wendell. 1946d. "Jackie Robinson Sensational in Opening Game: Jackie Hits Homer, Scores 4 Runs as Royals Win First." *The Pittsburgh Courier*, April 27, 1946, p. 16.

Soanes, Wood. 1950. "Jackie Stars in Role at T&D." *Oakland Tribune*, June 22, 1950, p. 39.

Studio Briefs. 1950. *Los Angeles Times*, February 16, 1950, Part III, p. 10.

Turkin, Hi. 1945. "Dodgers Sign Negro Star, 1st in 70 Baseball Years." *New York Daily News*, October 24, 1945, p. 49.

United Press. 1945. "Robinson Worth 50 G's, K.C. Owner Says." *Brooklyn Daily Eagle*, October 24, 1945, p. 17.

United Press. 1950a. "Over-Weight Robby Tries to Calm Rickey." *Brooklyn Eagle*, February 23, 1950, p. 23.

United Press. 1950b. "Real Life Different, Robinson Says of Film." *The Asheville Citizen*, March 2, 1950, p. 10.

Ward, Henry. 1950. "Pride of Brooklyn: 'The Jackie Robinson Story' Stars Robinson at Barry: Baseball Star Plays Himself in Drama of a Sportsman." *The Pittsburgh Press*, June 8, 1950, p. 32.

Whitaker, Matthew C., ed. 2011. *Icons of Black America: Breaking Barriers and Crossing Boundaries: Volume 1.* Santa Barbara, CA: Greenwood.

Wright, Marshall D. 2000. *The National Association of Base Ball Players, 1857–1870.* Jefferson, NC: McFarland & Company, Inc., Publishers.

Young, Dick. 1950. "DiMag Signs for 100Gs; Robby Gets Top 35." *New York Daily News*, January 25, 1950, pp. 1, 4.

Zang, David W. 1995. *Fleet Walker's Divided Heart: The Life of Baseball's First Black Major Leaguer.* Lincoln: University of Nebraska Press.

Chapter 2

The Basketball Fix (1951)

"Ripped from the Headlines" is not a recent advertising phrase for the motion picture and television industries. As early as the 1930s, studios, trying to cash in on topical news, frequently used "Ripped from Headlines" or similar phrases in their advertisements. In the fall of 1951, with college basketball still reeling from a point-shaving scandal involving players earlier that year, "Torn from Sports Headlines" advertisements gave *The Basketball Fix* immediacy.

The movie opens with big-city sports columnist Pete Ferreday (John Ireland) recalling the rise and fall of Johnny Long (Marshall Thompson), a star high school basketball player who signs a scholarship with State College (what state is never revealed). With his father in a sanatorium, Long needs part-time jobs to take care of his kid brother, Mickey (Bobby Hyatt), and struggles financially (the mother's whereabouts are never revealed). So State College basketball coach Nat Becker (Walter Sande) gets Long a job at an exclusive country club where another State player, Jed Black (Johnny Sands), is employed. There, Long meets gambler Mike Taft (William Bishop).

As a freshman, Long powers State to national prominence, but grows tired of not having money. He can't afford to buy Christmas presents for Mickey or his girlfriend, Pat Judd (Vanessa Brown). Taft says Long's scoring ability helped the gambler win bets, so he offers Long $100 as walking-around money. After Long turns down the cash, Taft shrugs off the rejection as "usual first reaction: scruples, indignity."

During the Christmas break, however, Long asks Taft for a job during the Christmas break. Taft instead offers him $500. He's not asking Long to lose a game deliberately, Taft explains, just miss a basket or lose the ball once in a while. Gamblers like Taft can clean up by betting that a heavily favored team doesn't cover the point spread (the margin by which a team is favored to win a game). Again, Long refuses.

But with money pressure building and wanting to buy Judd a $1,000 engagement ring, Long relents after learning that Black has been paid to miss shots and commit turnovers so that Taft can win his bets. Reluctantly, Long begins "fixing" games for the gambler. But when he pays cash for Judd's ring, the suspicious salesman calls the police.

Guilt-ridden by his brother's idolatry of him, Long soon reverses course and begins playing up to his ability to lead State to the national championship game. But Taft threatens him, even has Long beaten up, and so when Judd doesn't show up for the title game, Long mistakenly fears that Taft has kidnapped his fiancée. Once Long starts to fix the game, Taft, Black, and Long are arrested. Judd arrives—vice-squad investigators, not Taft's thugs, had detained her—and seeing Long escorted away in handcuffs, Ferreday sadly comments, "It looks like it is going to cost him more than he figured."

Jack Broder (1904–79) became interested in movies as a kid selling candy at a theater counter in Detroit. Later, he ran a theater chain. After World War II, Broder moved to Beverly Hills, California, and bought Realart Pictures, which had great success rereleasing classic Universal horror films of the 1930s and 1940s to theaters. That segued into Broder's founding of Jack Broder Productions, Inc., which produced low-budget features that Realart distributed. By the time *The Basketball Fix*, Broder's first film, was released, he still owned three Detroit theaters and two others in Los Angeles.

"Broder hasn't had any trouble lining up talent," *Detroit Free Press* columnist Helen Bower noted before *The Basketball Fix*'s September 21 release in Detroit.

That talent included tall, lanky Marshall Thompson (1925–92), who started his career in the early 1940s typecast as naive boys but was moving to rawer parts—including a psychopathic killer in *Dial 1119* (1950) and a conspirator to assassinate presidential-elect Abraham Lincoln in *The Tall Target* (1951). "If the exposé in this picture goes just one step toward cleaning out the racketeers from college athletics, I'll consider myself a very capable heel—and much more valuable than the run-of-the-mill hero," Thompson said (Majestic 1952, 12).

Born in Vienna as Smylla Brind, Vanessa Brown (1928–99) had appeared on Broadway in *Watch on the Rhine* when she was thirteen, made her first movie appearance in 1944, and acted on the stage, on radio, and in film and television. During *The Basketball Fix*, after director Felix Feist (1910–55) declared a scene perfect after only one take, Brown quipped, "You mean we don't have to do it again? Gosh, movies are getting just like television" (Johnson 1951b, 4).

Johnny Sands (1928–2003), born Elbert Hart Jr., hitchhiked to Hollywood when he was thirteen and appeared in his first movie in 1946. "I don't look like a juvenile anymore," he said while filming *The Basketball Fix*. "I'm a leading man at last, not a jerk" (Johnson 1951a, 4). Around 1953, Sands left acting altogether. Disillusioned with Hollywood, he moved to Honolulu and became a realtor.

Top-billed John Ireland (1914–92) had earned praise for his film debut as an infantry soldier in *A Walk in the Sun* (1945) and received an Academy Award nomination for best supporting actor in *All the King's Men* (1949), adapted from the Pulitzer Prize-winning novel by Robert Penn Warren (1905–89). Although Ireland continued to work steadily until his death, instead of rocketing after *All the King's Men*, Ireland's career floundered in B movies with occasional supporting roles in big-budget features. Scandals that were splashed across movie magazines and gossip columns, often involving alcohol and women, helped stagnate Ireland's career. So did Ireland's politics. Partially fueled during the Cold War (1947–91) by rhetoric from U.S. Senator Joseph R. McCarthy (1908–57), "Red Scare" hysteria led to the blacklisting of several actors, writers, and directors in the 1950s for suspected communist leanings. Film historian C. Courtney Joyner elaborates: "As far as I know [Ireland] was never fingered 'officially' as a communist, but he was certainly considered 'pink,' and was denied work during the fall-out from the McCarthy hearings. He did sue some TV producers for backing out on a series deal, which he claimed was due to his politics. That's another thing—lawsuits. Ireland was quick with the lawyers against producers and studios for all kinds of reasons, and I'm sure that didn't make him very popular, even when he was right" (C. Courtney Joyner, interview with author, May 19, 2020).

One of those suits was against Broder. In 1953, Ireland and his wife, actress Joanne Dru (1922–96), sued Broder and his production companies, claiming that Broder had promised to deliver a Western movie, *Hannah Lee*, which starred Ireland and Dru, to a major studio but instead released the film himself. Broder countersued, claiming that Ireland's "erratic ideas" delayed production and skyrocketed costs. The outcome of the suits was not reported, but *Hannah Lee* was the last movie released by Jack Broder Productions.

While Broder is remembered mostly for campy movies like *Bride of the Gorilla* (1951) and *Bela Lugosi Meets a Brooklyn Gorilla* (1952), he tackled serious subjects such as gambling in *Two Dollar Bettor* (1951) and *The Basketball Fix*.

The Basketball Fix earned mostly lukewarm reviews.

"It isn't an entertaining film," Edith Rosenblatt wrote for the *Pittsburgh Post-Gazette*, "but it is informative and might well be seen by youths tempted to try for a fast buck. . . . The picture is adequate. It serves its purpose. But still it's a shame somebody didn't polish up the dialogue" (Rosenblatt 1951, 12). But *New York Daily News*'s Wanda Hale said, "For a speedy job, 'The Basketball Fix' is pretty good, especially in production, direction and acting" (Hale 1951, 75).

Jay Carmody of *The Evening Star* in Washington, D.C., praised the film for its "documentary fidelity," adding that, "A good news editor could very well regard 'The Basketball Fix' as a sound pictorial treatment of one of the year's hottest news stories" (Carmody 1951, A-24). The *New York Times*'s Oscar Godbout, however, called the film a "curiously uneven story" that "merely dribbles adroitly past some interesting questions." Godbout concluded that despite being "on the timid side, it is worth the effort put into it, and points the way to better and more constructive social comments" (Godbolt 1951, 21).

Variety gave *The Basketball Fix* "only mild chances" at the box office and said the film's "overall outlook is for lowercase, programmer release" (The Basketball Fix 1951, 6). Filmed fast and released quickly to cash in on the collegiate scandal, *The Basketball Fix* was also soon forgotten. As one historian noted, the movie's "narrow focus frustrated reviewers and audiences more than it pleased or enlightened them" (Sperber 1998, 417).

HISTORICAL BACKGROUND

Working at the International YMCA Training School in Springfield, Massachusetts, in 1891, James Naismith (1861–1939) was given an assignment: Combine factors of known sports and create a new game—one that would be interesting to play and watch, not difficult to learn, and could be played during the winter with artificial light.

Athletics had become such a part of the culture, men sought out baseball, bicycling, or other athletic clubs, or the YMCA during warmer months—but the only opportunities young men had in the winter were gymnastics. Most men had no interest in gymnastics, and the younger generation played sports "for pleasure and thrill rather than physical benefits" (Naismith 1996, 33).

Naismith, who had been working at the YMCA school for roughly a year, had always been something of an inventor. As a child in Canada, he made his own ice skates by setting old files into strips of hickory. As captain of the rugby team at Montreal's McGill University, he invented a warm-up exercise in which players tossed balls into a box.

So when he started trying to come up with a new sport, he remembered his rugby exercise and a game he played as a young boy, "Duck on a Rock." In that game, players tried to knock a small stone, called a "duck," off a larger stone—guarded by another player—by throwing their own "ducks." The best way to knock the duck off the rock, players learned, was to toss stones in the air, over the reach of the defending player, and hit the target.

After a janitor brought two peach baskets—Naismith had asked for a couple of boxes—Naismith nailed those to the bottom rails on the gym's balcony. He got a soccer ball and determined rules, including fouls and two 15-minute halves (with sudden-death overtime to break a tie if team captains agreed). Players could not run with the ball; it had to be thrown or batted. The goal was to put the ball into the basket.

In late December, Naismith introduced the sport to his class of eighteen, which was divided into two teams of nine players. Only one goal was scored, but the game became popular. "Word soon got around that they were having fun in Naismith's gym class," Naismith recalled, "and only a few days after the first game we began to have a gallery" (Naismith 1996, 57). Naismith's new sport, which he called "basket ball," was off and running. The association with the YMCA propelled the sport across North America rapidly. Women were playing basketball by the spring of 1892, and Native Americans played it on a South Dakota reservation that summer.

Rules were adjusted. Because someone had to climb a ladder to get the ball out of the basket—slowing the game's pace—a wire basket with the bottom cut out replaced the peach basket in 1892, but that still required someone to push the ball out of the basket with a pole. Other adjustments were made until open-bottom nets were officially approved in 1912–13. The first official basketball, produced by Overman Wheel Company, a bicycle manufacturer, replaced the soccer ball in 1894. Passes—by bouncing or throwing—were allowed; so was dribbling, although juggling and double-dribbling were prohibited in 1898.

While early teams ranged from three to forty players, the standard became five or nine in 1893, which was standardized to five at the beginning of the 1897–98 season. Points started as one, then increased to three in 1894–95 with a foul resulting in an extra point. In 1896–97, the free throw was introduced for foul shots (one point)—the free-throw distance changed over the years—with field goals reduced to two points. One player per team was designated to shoot all free throws until 1923.

Basketball also found its way onto college campuses, played as an intramural sport by men's and women's teams, and soon intercollegiately. By 1901, Columbia, Cornell, Harvard, Princeton, and Yale formed the Eastern Intercollegiate league. Historians seem uncertain if the first professional game was played in 1893 in Herkimer, New York, or in 1896 in Trenton, New Jersey, but in 1898, the first National Basketball League began play with six teams—two in New Jersey; six in Pennsylvania—but professional basketball would not see its popularity rise nationally until after 1950. By 1936, men's basketball became an Olympic sport (women's basketball came forty years later).

In 1931, with the nation mired in the Great Depression (1929–39), New York Mayor Jimmy Walker (1881–1946) asked Ned Irish (1905–82), a sportswriter for the *New York World-Telegram*, to put together college-basketball event with proceeds going to help the poor and unemployed. Irish's event—a tripleheader of New York teams on New Year's Eve, attracted fifteen thousand. Irish arranged similar events over the next two years, left newspapers and became a full-time sports promoter. In 1934, he began bringing in out-of-state teams to play New York colleges at the Madison Square Garden, helping men's intercollegiate basketball reach the national level.

After Naismith created a men's basketball championship in 1937 for small colleges in the National Association of Intercollegiate Athletics, the postseason National Invitation Tournament (NIT) began play in 1938 at Madison Square Garden. The National Collegiate Athletic Association (NCAA), collegiate sports' governing body, started its national tournament the next year. In 1943, the Garden was the site of the NCAA's title game.

Originally an old railroad station rebuilt as a hippodrome in 1874 by showman P.T. Barnum (1810–91) and renamed Madison Square Garden five years later, the facility had gone through several owners by 1925, when new owner George Lewis "Tex" Rickard (1870–1929) decided in 1925 to build a new Madison Square Garden at a new location. The $6 million, eighteen thousand-seat arena on Eighth Avenue held bicycle races, basketball games, boxing matches, hockey games, tennis matches, and track and field competitions.

Early in 1940, syndicated sports columnist Joe Williams wrote that in New York City, "college basketball is the biggest gambling sport in town" (Williams 1940, 15), and by the early 1950s, Madison Square Garden became "the clearinghouse for New York City's gambling establishment," historian Charley Rosen wrote. "Even the popcorn vendors regularly know the point spread" (Rosen 1999, 4).

In 1950, City College of New York defeated Bradley in the final games of the NIT and the NCAA tournament, both held at Madison Square Garden. That marked the only time a school won both tournaments in the same year. Soon after City College of New York's double championship, NCAA rules mandated that a team could play in just one national tournament; in 1971, the year after Marquette spurned an NCAA bid to play in the NIT, the rule was amended to say that no team could turn down an NCAA bid to play in another postseason tournament.

The Beavers were hailed as triumphant underdogs after finishing the 1949–50 regular season with a 17–5 record; they had been one of twelve unseeded teams (the top four seeded teams did not have to play in the first round) invited to the NIT. City College won four consecutive games, including a 65–46 victory over defending champion San Francisco and an 89–50 rout of perennial powerhouse Kentucky. After defeating Bradley, 69–61, in the final, City College entered the NCAA tournament, defeating Ohio State, North Carolina State, and Bradley.

Across New York City's boroughs, City College's 1950 championships were celebrated. The school did not give athletes scholarships because tuition was free for all students. Recalled author Stanley Cohen, a native of the Bronx:

To us, this was our guys playing against middle America. We didn't recruit people. They weren't brought in from all over the country. You had to live in the city and you had to make the grade. We beat [Bradley] twice. This justified us, and we were on top of the world. It was a heroic place to us, because we were really on the low end of the economic scale. The guys in my neighborhood, almost all of us were sons of immigrants. City College, to us, was like Mecca. This was what was all about. You could go here. You could get a degree. You could become somebody. (Stanley Cohen, interview with author, February 3, 2020)

The basketball players who helped City College win those national titles "were our heroes," Cohen said (Stanley Cohen, interview with author, February 3, 2020).

A year later, a national scandal crushed not only City College of New York, it led the *New York Herald Tribune*'s Irving Marsh, a City College graduate, to declare that intercollegiate basketball "is through as a big-time sport" (Rosen 1999, 6).

The first news broke in January 1951. Former Manhattan College player Henry Poppe (1924–2000), the team's cocaptain the previous season, approached Manhattan College standout Junius Kellogg (1927–98) and promised to pay Kellogg $1,000 if he helped Manhattan lose to DePaul, a 10-point favorite, by more than 10 points. "He also said it was worth my life to keep my mouth shut about it," Kellogg recalled (Wilner and Rappoport 2014, 56).

Kellogg told coach Ken Norton (1914–96), who alerted the authorities. Police investigators asked Kellogg to meet with Poppe and agree to the fix. "Everybody was betting on De Paul with the points," a bookie recalled. "Guys who never bet more than ten bucks in their life suddenly wanted to get down for three hundred dollars. They were breaking their necks running up the stairs to make their bets" (Rosen 1999, 40).

Poppe; Manhattan co-captain, John A. Byrnes (1928–); and three other men were charged with conspiracy and bribery charges. Manhattan upset DePaul, 62–59.

On February 19, 1951, while City College of New York was struggling with an 11–7 record but still considered likely to receive an NIT bid, district attorney Frank S. Hogan (1902–74) announced that three Beavers players had been charged with bribery. City College's twenty-year-old center Edward Roman (1930–98) of the Bronx; twenty-one-year-old forward Edward L. Warner (1929–2002) of upper Manhattan; and twenty-one-year-old guard Alvin Roth (ca. 1929–) of Brooklyn were arrested early the previous morning at Penn Station after a road game at Temple University. Roman and Warner were team cocaptains.

New York University player Harvey "Connie" Schaff and Long Island University's Eddie Gard, a senior whose college basketball eligibility had expired, also faced bribery charges. Jewelry manufacturer and gambler Salvatore Sollazzo, forty-five, also arrested, had approached Gard at a Catskills resort where the player was working the previous summer and persuaded him act as a go-between and line up other players willing to fix the games, Hogan said.

Hogan said Warner, Roman, and Roth accepted $500 to $1,500 per game for fixing games against Missouri, Arizona, and Boston colleges during the 1950–51 season. Although City College lost all three games, the players had only agreed to make sure the Beavers won by no more than the three-point spread. "But of course," Hogan said, Sollazzo "was very happy when they lost the games" (Associated Press 1951c, 14).

Schaff, who was not a starter, was charged with trying to persuade a New York University starter to throw games. Two days later, Long Island University players Sherman White, Adolf Bigos, and Leroy Smith were arrested for fixing games.

"This," Irish said, "could be a blow for all sports" (Turkin 1951, 46).

Upon learning that City College players had conspired with gamblers in Arizona's 41–38 victory December 28, 1950, at Madison Square Garden, Wildcats coach Fred Enke (1897–1985) said, "Our boys played very good that night, but unfortunately this takes the luster away from our victory" (Turkin 1951, 46).

"Basketball is the biggest sport in the nation," University of Kentucky coach Adolph Rupp (1901–77) said in August. "It's the biggest in attendance and is by far our greatest active participation sport. We can't expect it to remain completely untainted." But saying his players were always supervised, Rupp added: "The gamblers couldn't get at our boys with a 10-foot pole" (Associated Press 1951d, 6). In 1949, City College coach Nat Holman (1896–1995) made similar remarks before a game in San Francisco: "My boys would tell me about it if any one tried to put them in the bag. We haven't had the slightest bit of trouble and perhaps we can take that as a compliment. The gamblers know better than to monkey with us, so they lay off" (Sullivan 1951, 35).

The scandal, though, was far from over. City College, banned from post-season tournaments, canceled its remaining games, and declared that it would eliminate its athletic program "as an athletic power in the future" (Devlin 1951, 11). Tennessee Senator Estes Kefauver (1903–63), chairman of the Senate Crime Committee, announced: "We have been investigating this particular basketball scandal for some time" (Turkin 1951, 45). Before the year was over, thirty-two players from seven schools were charged with intentionally losing games or shaving points since 1948. That included three players from the University of Kentucky's national-championship teams of 1948 and 1949. The Southeastern Conference suspended Kentucky's basketball program and Rupp for the 1952–53 season.

A newspaper editor said: "One fact we refuse to face is that there are no amateurs in big-time college sports; there are only underpaid professionals" (Goodman 2019a).

The NCAA withdrew its 1952 championship tournament from Madison Square Garden and recommended that NCAA athletic programs boycott the facility. Long Island University immediately suspended its basketball program, reviving it six years later. Two players were handed jail sentences and banned from the National Basketball Association (NBA). The other players were banned from NBA play, expelled from school, given suspended sentences, and put on probation. Eventually, the NCAA tournament overtook the NIT in prestige.

City College fans were stunned.

"When it all came out we were like, 'Can't be . . . they got it all wrong . . . they're trying to smear them'," Cohen recalled. "We were absolutely dismayed and shocked to find out they were dumping games" (Stanley Cohen, February 3, 2020, interview with author).

DEPICTION AND CULTURAL CONTEXT

In 1934, the Production Code Administration was established to maintain morality and ethics in all American-made movies, which had to be approved by before release. The Code required criminals to be punished and prohibited vulgarity, nudity, and explicit violence. Although the Code remained in force, its power lessened after World War II (1941–45) and the beginning of the nuclear age. Filmmakers understood that audiences could accept grimmer movies, questionable morality, and not-so-happy endings. Many of these postwar movies were filmed in gritty black and white with plenty of shadows (often to hide the low budgets). These postwar movies became known as *film noir*, a term coined by French critic Nino Frank (1904–88) in 1946. *The Basketball Fix* has been called a *film noir*.

In his first meeting with gambler Mike Taft in *The Basketball Fix*, sportswriter Pete Ferreday says college players probably deserve some sort of stipend. "It stands to reason that some of the big money made by college sports should rub off on those responsible for it," he says.

Historian Michael Goodman wrote:

> On a college basketball night, other than the fans who had paid to get in, nearly every individual inside the Garden was in some way deriving income from the games. The coaches, the athletic directors, the referees, the ushers, the ticket takers, the food vendors, and countless others—not to mention to the bookmakers who handled as much as $300,000 in bets for each Garden game—all owed their income, at least in part, to the enormous profits that were generated by New Yorkers' desire to watch high-quality college basketball. The only ones not reaping those profits were the players themselves: the very ones whose talent made all the rest of it possible. (Goodman 2019a)

Ferreday's point wasn't new in 1951, and it grew more pronounced after the "fix" broke.

"Let's pay college athletes a reasonable amount of money and clear up this mess," Washington & Lee coach George Barclay (1910–97) said. "There is no way of enforcing recruiting and subsidy rules now. Maybe an open, above-board payment to athletes would give the conferences a chance to keep control on things" (Grady 1951, 5-B). Southern Conference commissioner Wallace Wade (1892–1986) of Duke University, however, argued that "Such an allowance would rise to objectionable proportions. . . . I am in favor of a boy receiving his room and board, as is approved by conference rules. An allowance would be something else" (Grady 1951, 5-B).

"Show me a strictly amateur sport and I'll show you a sport which doesn't have gate receipts that amount to anything," United Press sportswriter Oscar Fraley opined. "So why not pay the lads who draw the money—pay 'em right out in the open—and eliminated the dishonest dollar?" (Fraley 1951, 10).

The debate continues today.

"Paying student-athletes might sound like a fairer way to treat students who generate so much money and attention for their colleges (not to mention the television networks that broadcast their games). But paying athletes would distort the economics of college sports in a way that would hurt the broader community of student-athletes, universities, fans and alumni," Cody J. McDavis, a former collegiate basketball player, wrote in an opinion column for *The New York Times* in 2019. "A handful of big sports programs would pay top dollar for a select few athletes, while almost every other college would get caught up in a bidding war it couldn't afford" (McDavis 2019).

Sports Illustrated's Pat Forbes, however, countered: "When the college sports landscape was torn up and put back together a decade ago for the sole purpose of maximizing broadcast revenues, it was time to quit regarding this enterprise as amateur athletics. The Big Ten, SEC, ACC, Big 12 and Pac-12 realigned in ways that were damaging to rivalries and geographic sensibilities—but they made a bucket load of money, so why not? If that was the acknowledge[d] guiding principle of college sports, then it became increasingly untenable to prevent revenue-creating athletes from being part of the profit-making machinery. Now it's time to correct that fundamental wrong" (Forbes 2020).

College basketball was big in the 1950s, but it is big business today. In 2016, the NCAA signed an eight-year, $8.8 billion contract extension with CBS and TBS to televise the NCAA basketball tournaments through 2034. The California Legislature passed a bill in 2019 that allowed college athletes to earn money for endorsement deals. As other states began passing similar bills, and politicians started questioning the merits of the NCAA's antitrust exemption, the NCAA had to act. In 2020, the NCAA approved, reluctantly, a rule change that would allow athletes to be paid by third parties for the use of their images and likenesses for marketing/advertising purposes. The

NCAA hoped to have a plan in place by 2021. "There is big money in college sports," the *Pittsburgh Post-Gazette* editorialized, "and the time has come for the athletes who play those sports to get their share of it" (Editorial Board 2020).

In *The Basketball Fix*, screenwriters Peter R. Brooke (1921–99) and Charles K. Peck Jr. (1921–96) accurately captured how gamblers and their go-betweens persuaded athletes to fix games.

Taft's argument—"Can you put glory in the bank?"—eventually resonates with Long, and gamblers and fixers used similar evidence when approaching college athletes.

"I would look up and the stadium was always full, eighteen thousand," a former City College of New York player recalled. "And I would think to myself, 'Every one of those people paid to get in tonight.' And where did that money go? Not to me" (Goodman 2019a).

In the movie, Jed Black tells Long that, because of Black's income for fixing games, he'll be able to open a sporting-goods store when he's out of college. Poppe used a similar tactic when he tried to lure Kellogg into the conspiracy. "He told me that rah rah stuff doesn't get you any good," Kellogg said. "He said he and Jack Byrnes worked together last year. Now he had a new car, some money in the bank and bonds" (Associated Press 1951b, 38).

State College coach Nat Becker can't pay Long to play basketball in *The Basketball Fix*, but Belker does get Long a job at a tony resort—where Long first meets Taft. The setting for that meeting is also accurate. In post–World War II New York, pricey hotels and resorts in the Catskill Mountains became a popular place for college basketball players to land cushy jobs. Though usually employed as bellhops or waiters, their main job was to play summer basketball. Grossinger's Catskill Resort Hotel in Liberty, Klein's Hillside Hotel in Parksville, Kutscher's Hotel in Thompson, and the Tamarack Lodge in Greenfield Park fielded basketball teams and often recruited top players; an estimated five hundred college players might be employed in the Catskills' fifty hotels and resorts during the summer. "If truth could be told, they were paid to play basketball," Cohen wrote, "but that would have made them professionals and would have cost them their college eligibility" (Cohen 2001, 99). It wasn't just basketball players; the Catskills employed an estimated twenty thousand collegians during the summer of 1950. The Catskills also attracted college basketball coaches who were recruiting players.

Eddie Gard landed summer jobs at the Catskills while playing at Long Island University. In 1950, Gard, who had previously fixed games, was looking for someone to bankroll him. "Eddie was lovable," historian Charley Rosen wrote, "but he was larcenous" (Rosen 1999, 37). While working at Grossinger's that summer, Gard met Salvatore Sollazzo, "the kind of a guy who would bet on two cockroaches running across the floor" (Goodman

2019b, 201). Sollazzo found his go-between. For a percentage of the profits, Gard would line up college players willing to fix games. The players would be paid a flat rate.

"Nobody's asking you to throw a game," Wade tells Long in *The Basketball Fix*. "It's merely a matter of points. Keep the scores close together. That way you're not letting anyone down. Becker still wins his ballgame."

This was an argument that gamblers used to lure college players into the conspiracy.

Gard's pitch to Long Island player Sherman White (1928–2011) went like this, according to White: "'We control the game. We're good enough to beat these guys anyway and we can make some money. They ain't giving you no money here at L.I.U.' The same old story. We can control the game and nobody will get hurt except the gamblers. Now I'm one of the guys. Peer pressure" (Anderson 1998, 9).

Before the point spread, or line, was introduced, bets were made on teams or individuals to win or lose, although odds could be offered (5-to-1 odds meant if someone bet $5 on the favored team, a winning bet would earn $1; a winning $1 bet on the underdog would earn $5). The point spread, on the other hand, meant the favored team had to win by a certain number of points or runs. A football team favored by 2.5 points had to win by three points to cover the spread. A three-point favorite that won by three points meant the bet was a tie, or push.

Charles McNeil (1903–81), a genius in mathematics, is commonly credited for creating the point spread in the 1930s, although other bookies have also been cited as the inventors. After losing his job as a securities analyst during the Great Depression, McNeil, who also loved gambling, created what he called "wholesaling odds" (Millman 2020). Instead placing bets on money-line odds, he used point spreads, and by the early 1940s, had opened his own bookmaking shop in Chicago, giving his "wholesale odds" on National Football League games first before moving to college football and finally college basketball. Because baseball games on average are decided by small margins, bettors rarely wager on point spreads.

Other bookmaking operations picked up on the point spread, which soon became "the gambler's delight and balm for the bookmaker; it made every game a toss-up" (Lang with Cohen 2009, 110).

Bookies could be found easily, especially in major cities. "I was fully aware of our local bookie when I was in my teens," Cohen recalled. "He sat at a table in a Bronx cafeteria, often alongside the beat cop, plying his trade" (Stanley Cohen, interview with author, June 12, 2020). That bookie, known as Joe Jalop, was arrested with Jack Molinas (1931–75) for fixing basketball games in 1961. Newspapers, naturally, printed Jalop's real name, Joe Hacken. "When I saw his name in the newspaper, I said, 'I don't know who this guy is'," Cohen said, "but when I saw his picture, I said, 'Oh, Joe Jalop'" (Stanley Cohen, interview with author, February 3, 2020).

Even before the scandal broke in 1951, sports columnist Jimmy Cannon called college basketball "the slot machine of college sports" (Gustkey 2001, D-11). Basketball had become "the most heavily bet sport in America" (Cohen 2001, 59).

"The team still wins," Ferreday says in *The Basketball Fix*, "the bookie wins, and the betting public loses." State College wins the games Long and Black fix, but in reality, the team with the player or players fixing the game did not always win.

"When you were a 12-point favorite, it's not too hard to take the money, win by eight, and win your game," Cohen said. "You didn't disgrace your college, and you got the money as well. City [College], they'd be a two-point favorite, and though they won the tournaments, they weren't a dominant force during the year. These guys weren't looking to lose the games, but if you're a three-point favorite, it's kind of tough [to fix the game but not lose]" (Stanley Cohen, interview with author, February 3, 2020).

Long Island player Sherman White (1928–2011), who served eight months, twenty-four days of a one-year prison sentence for his role in the 1951 point-shaving scandal, recalled Long Island's 80–52 loss to Syracuse in a fixed game during the 1950 NIT. "We were hoping to play City College," he told the *New York Times* years later. "But we lost that Syracuse game outright. In trying to keep the game a certain way, it got out of control. It takes something away when you go into a game knowing it's not on the up and up" (Anderson 1998, 9).

As the scandal broke, newspaper sports sections took criticism for publishing point spreads. Newspapers in the eastern United States, Rupp said, "quote odds and play directly into the hands of the gamblers" (Cohen 2001, 105).

"In the days before the scandal, the point spread was treated as any other bit of info, often included in the headline of the story on game day," Cohen recalled. "I have always assumed it got to the papers, much like the other news about the game, via wire-service teletype. Of course, it is not unlikely that someone in the sports department at every paper just phoned a local bookmaker to get the spread" (Stanley Cohen, interview with author, June 12, 2020).

In the wake of the point-shaving arrests, campaigns were launched to make newspapers quit running point spreads, and the *New York Post* quickly announced that it would no longer publish betting odds. Not all newspapers printed gambling information. Even as early as 1944, *The Hartford Courant* "ignored efforts to have us buy a weekly service that offered to provide the proper odds on college basketball games" and had been "refusing for years to publish the same sort of form figures on college football, another sport on which millions are bet" (Lee 1945, 13).

Today, many newspapers publish betting lines, supplied by wire services from Las Vegas, Nevada, oddsmakers, in sports sections, but the debate over the ethics of running gambling information is still debated. Former Texas newspaper executive Gary Hardee recalled a staff meeting at the *Dallas*

Times Herald in the early 1990s. The sports editor questioned if the newspaper should continue publishing the daily point spread, arguing that it promoted illegal gambling. Hardee, then the assistant managing editor overseeing the sports department, remembered: "I would have argued then, as I would today, that the point spread gives many readers and sports fans who would never even consider placing a bet, legally or illegally, a sense of which team is favored and by how much. I feel that the spread can be a point of sports debate between non-betting fans, not unlike college football rankings or pro sports power ratings. Sports conversations are dominated by statistics and data of all kinds. A point spread is just another data set, albeit today perhaps a less-used one because there are so many others to use" (Gary Hardee, interview with author, December 19, 2019).

Historian Murray Sperber criticizes *The Basketball Fix* for ignoring "the culture of corruption that surrounded college basketball at this time; instead of entire teams and legions of gamblers, we watch one player [technically two, Long and Black] and one fixer" (Sperber 1998, 417).

When the scandal broke early in 1951, many people limited the corruption to New York City and Madison Square Garden. Attempts to fix games at the Garden did not start with the 1950–51 season. In 1944, University of Utah coach Vadal Peterson (1892–1976) reported to the police that a gambler had attempted to bribe him to throw the NCAA tournament championship game against Dartmouth at the Garden. Peterson said he slammed the door in the man's face; witnesses said he knocked the man to the floor with a punch to the jaw. Utah defeated Dartmouth, 42–40, in overtime. In 1945, Brooklyn College expelled six players for accepting bribes. Four men were charged in 1949 for attempting to bribe a George Washington University player to fix a game. After that news broke, *Hartford Courant* sports editor Bill Lee wrote that college basketball became "big business" once Madison Square Garden started holding games and "It wasn't long before form sheets on college basketball teams were being printed and distributed to the gambling spots. Teams and players were rated just like horses" (Lee 1945, 13).

But the 1951 scandal reached far beyond New York City. According to a grand jury's findings, eighty-six games had been fixed in twenty-three cities in seventeen states, making the fix the biggest American sports disgrace since the "Black Sox" incident of 1921, in which eight Chicago White Sox players were permanently banned from major-league baseball for conspiring with gamblers to throw the 1919 World Series to the Cincinnati Reds.

College athletics dominated sports headlines for the rest of the year, and basketball wasn't the only sport criticized. Proposals to ban football bowl games were introduced. Eventually, the NCAA began to wield more power in cracking down on recruiting violations.

But the aftermath did not eliminate scandals. It didn't even come close. In 1954, Holman warned sportswriters that "some gambler somewhere is going to approach a kid one of these days, and we'll have another dirty mess on our hands" (Cohen 2001, 226).

THE ARMY FOOTBALL SCANDAL

The 1951 college sports scandal was not limited to basketball. In August, news broke that the United States Military Academy had expelled ninety cadets, including thirty-seven football players, for violating the code of honor. The cadets, who had been cheating academically, were later allowed to resign.

Under coach Earl "Red" Blaik (1897–1989), Army's football team had compiled a 57–3–1 record over the previous seven seasons and won three national championships. One of the expelled football players was Blaik's son, Bob (1930–). But the scandal was not limited to football: twenty-three of the expelled cadets played other intercollegiate sports, and most of the nonathletes expelled were tutors.

"Out of historical context, the crimes of the Army athletes seem minor compared to those of the basketball fixers," historian Murray Sperber wrote. But in 1951, with the American soldiers dying in the Korean War (1950–53), the news rocked the country. "Intercollegiate sport is rotten to the core and the Army episode proves it," *New York Times* sports columnist Arthur Daley wrote, adding: "The West Point scandal might not seem to be even vaguely related to the basketball scandals. But they are blood brothers, spawned by overemphasis, commercialism and bigness" (Daley 1951, 3).

Army went 2–7 in 1951, its first losing record since 1940. Like the New York colleges that de-emphasized their basketball programs in wake of the point-shaving scandal, Army began de-emphasizing its football program. Although the Cadets finished the 1958 season 8–0–1 and ranked third in the nation, Army has never again finished in the top ten Associated Press rankings.

Sources

Ambrose, Stephen E. 1999. *Duty, Honor, Country: A History of West Point*. Baltimore, MD: The Johns Hopkins University Press.

Daley, Arthur. 1951. "Sports of *The Times*: Dark Disillusionment." *The New York Times*, August 12, 1951, Section 5, p. 3.

DeFord, Frank. 2000. "Code Breakers: Fifty Years Ago Red Blaik's Football Powerhouse at Army Was Decimated by the Loss of Players Who Violated the Military Academy's Honor Code. But Who Really Acted Dishonorably?" *Sports Illustrated*, November 13, 2000. https://vault .si.com/vault/2000/11/13/code-breakers-fifty-years-ago-red-blaiks-football-powerhouse -at-army-was-decimated-by-the-loss-of-players-who-violated-the-military-academys -honor-code-but-who-really-acted-dishonorably

Heller, Dick. 2009. "Heller: Shame, Blame at West Point." *The Washington Times*, August 3, 2009. https://www.washingtontimes.com/news/2009/aug/03/heller-shame-blame-at-west -point/

Sperber, Murray. 1998. *Onward to Victory: The Crises That Shaped College Sports*. New York: Henry Holt and Company.

Jack Molinas, a former Columbia University basketball star, was suspended from the NBA's Fort Wayne Pistons in 1954 for betting on games. Out of professional basketball, he turned to fixing college games. He led a ring that involved thirty-seven players from twenty-two colleges in 1961. Convicted on five charges and sentenced to ten to fifteen years, Molinas was paroled after serving five years. "In my opinion, you are a completely immoral person," the judge told Molinas after the conviction. "You are the prime mover of the conspiracy and you were the person most responsible. You callously used your prestige as a former all-American basketball player to corrupt college basketball players and defraud the public" (Rosen 2001, 284). In 1975, Molinas was murdered at his Los Angeles home.

Boston College players were linked to a point-shaving conspiracy involving nine games during the 1978–79 season. One player wasn't charged, another was acquitted, but a third was sentenced to ten years in prison, later reduced to twenty-eight months. Other point-shaving incidents implicated players at Tulane (1985), Arizona State (1994), and Northwestern (1994–95).

"It's not something that's easy to control, and part of it is because it's baked into the original recipe," Cohen said. "The more you try to keep something clean, sometimes, the more corrupt it becomes" (Stanley Cohen, interview with author, February 3, 2020).

CONCLUSION

By the 1950s, sports movies started depicting less rah-rah and more reality. Besides *The Basketball Fix,* Columbia's *Saturday's Hero* (1951), starring John Derek (1926–98) and Donna Reed (1921–86), painted a grim picture of college football. Also in 1951, Warner Bros. released *Jim Thorpe—All-American*, a biopic about Native American Jim Thorpe (1887–1953). Thorpe rose to fame at Carlisle (Pennsylvania) Indian School before his amateur career was ruined after he was stripped of his two gold medals won at the 1912 Olympics; the medals, revoked because Thorpe had been paid as a minor-league baseball player in 1909 and 1910, were posthumously restored in 1983. In Universal-International's *The All-American* (1953), a star football player's parents are killed in an auto accident but the college coach doesn't tell the player until after the game has been won. *Trouble Along the Way,* a 1953 Warner Bros. release, cast John Wayne (1907–79) as a football coach who uses shady methods to rebuild a college program.

The Basketball Fix might have oversimplified the point-shaving scandal, but it offered a fairly accurate account of how gamblers and collegians came to rock the U.S. sports world earlier that year—and would dismay the public again in years to come. Basketball had changed a lot since Naismith invented it in 1891.

"Dr. Naismith cared about his players as people first, as students second, and as athletes third," University of North Carolina men's basketball coach Roy Williams (1950–), a 2007 Basketball Hall of Fame inductee, wrote in the introduction to a 2009 biography of Naismith. "He put their well-being ahead of all other issues. He valued those young men who had high morals and values, and he viewed success in terms of the impact he had on the lives of those young people—not whether his team won or lost" (Rains with Carpenter 2009, viii–ix).

FURTHER READING

Advertisement. 1952. *The Bismarck Tribune*, January 2, 1952, p. 3.

Anderson, Dave. 1998. "When Sherman White Threw It All Away." *The New York Times*, March 22, 1998, Section 8, pp. 1, 9.

Associated Press. 1951a. "Bribe Probe Hints Scandal in College Basketball 'Fix' May Increase in Scope." *Democrat and Chronicle*, January 18, 1951, p. 30.

Associated Press. 1951b. "Manhattan Star, Who Foiled 'Dump,' Gives Details of Bribery Proposal." *Democrat and Chronicle*, January 19, 1951, p. 38.

Associated Press. 1951c. "Three Members of City College Team Arrested." *The Times Record*, February 19, 1951, p. 14.

Associated Press. 1951d. "Cat Cagers Caged: Fixers Can't Get to U.K. With 10-Foot Pole, Says Rupp, Because of Constant Supervision." *The Courier-Journal*, August 16, 1951, p. 2-6.

"The Basketball Fix." 1951. *Variety*, September 19, 1951, p. 6.

Bower, Helen. 1951. "Star Gazing: Payton Hassle Ties in with Detroiter's Film." *Detroit Free-Press*, September 20, 1951, p. 23.

Brody, Richard. 2014. "'Film Noir': The Elusive Genre." *The New Yorker*, July 23, 2014. https://www.newyorker.com/culture/richard-brody/film-noir-elusive-genre-2

Broomfield, Fred. 1950. "Hometown to Roll Out Red Carpet For Mature." *Valley Times,* July 11, 1950, p. 13.

Carmody, Jan. 1951. "'The Fix' Is On: Trans-Lux Film Tale of Fallen Sports Idol." *The Evening Star*, September 26, 1951, p. A-24.

Cohen, Stanley. 2001. *The Game They Played*. New York: Carroll & Graff Publishers, Inc.

Davies, Richard O., and Richard G. Abram. 2001. *Betting the Line: Sports Wagering in American Life*. Columbus: The Ohio State University Press.

Devlin, James. 1951. "Up to Colleges to Keep Athletics Clean: Streit: Governor Asks for Probe Into Program at Maryland." *The Sioux City Journal*, November 21, 1951, p. 11.

Editorial Board. 2020. "Paying College Athletes: NCAA Takes First Step in Allowing Players to Cash in: The Governing Body of American College Athletics Has Been Under Increasing Pressure in Recent Years to Drop the Pretense That College Athletes Are Amateurs." *Pittsburgh Post-Gazette*, May 6, 2020. https://www.post-gazette.com/opinion/editorials/2020/05/06/Paying-college-athletes-NCAA-takes-first-step-in-allowing-players-to-cash-in/stories/202005050014

Forbes, Pat. 2020. "The NCAA Supporting Athlete Compensation Is the Right Thing—and It's Time to Embrace It: There Are Many Logistical Challenges Ahead, but Change Is (Finally!) Coming to the NCAA Over Student-Athletes' Name, Image and Likeness Rights." *Sports Illustrated*, April 29, 2020. https://www.si.com/college/2020/04/29/ncaa-name-image-likeness-rules-college-sports

Fraley, Scar. 1951. "Let's Pay College Athletes and Eliminate the Dishonest Dollar." *Binghamton Press*, March 3, 1951, p. 10.

Godbolt, Oscar. 1951. "Behind College Basketball Scenes." *The New York Times*, September 14, 1941, p. 21.

Gold, Ben. 1951. "On the Rebound." *Brooklyn Eagle*, February 24, 1950, p. 17.

Goodman, Matthew. 2019a. "What a 70-Year-Old Basketball Scandal Has to Do with College Players Earning Money Today: Under the Surface of This Point Shaving Scandal Lies Systemic Inequality Still Intact between Players and Leadership." *USA Today*, November 8, 2019. https://www.usatoday.com/story/opin ion/2019/11/08/ncaa-basketball-earn-money-point-shaving-scandal-city-college -column/2519349001/

Goodman, Matthew. 2019b. *The City Game: Triumph, Scandal, and a Legendary Basketball Team*. New York: Ballantine Books.

Grady, Sandy. 1951. "'Pay College Athletes above Table and Clear Up This Mess'— W&L's Barclay: Wade Says It Won't Work." *The Charlotte News*, February 9, 1951, p. 5-B.

Griffin, John. 1951. "'Cinderella Kids' Find Glory Road Slippery Place." *The Times Record*, February 19, 1951, p. 14.

Gustkey, Earl. 2001. "This Problem Still Hasn't Been Fixed: Gambling: Point-shaving Scandal Rocked College Basketball in 1951, and Others Have Followed." *Los Angeles Times*, March 30, 2001, pp. D-1, D-11.

Hale, Wanda. 1951. "'The Basketball Fix' A Pertinent Picture." *New York Daily News*, September 14, 1951, p. 75.

Hickok, Ralph. 2002. *The Encyclopedia of North American Sports History, Second Edition*. New York: Facts on File, Inc.

Holmes, Tommy. 1951. "Cage Game Again Gets on the Spot." *Brooklyn Eagle*, January 19, 1951, p. 19.

"Ireland, Wife Ask Receiver for Picture." 1953. *Los Angeles Times*, September 29, 1953, p. 15.

Isabella, Sean. 2018. "Notable Point-Shaving Scandals in NCAA History." *CNHI Sports*, June 30, 2018. https://www.cnhinews.com/cnhi/news/article_b6131e40 -7334-11e8-ba2e-efb580f8e189.html

Johnson, Erskine. 1951a. "Arlene Dahl Gets Contract Release to Be with Mate." *The San Bernardino Daily Sun*, August 3, 1951, p. 4.

Johnson, Erskine. 1951b. "Hollywood: Filmdom Already at Work on Film Dealing with the Basketball Fix." *Denton Record-Chronicle*, August 15, 1951, p. 4.

Katz, Ephraim. 2001. *The Film Encyclopedia, Fourth Edition*. New York: HarperResource.

Kubala, Christopher. 2015. *Collegiate Basketball: A History of Madness!* Thorold, Ontario: Ruckus Books.

Lang, Brandon with Stanley Cohen. 2009. *Beating the Odds: The Rise, Fall, and Resurrection of a Sports Handicapper*. New York: Skyhorse Publishing, Inc.

Lee, Bill. 1945. "With Malice toward None." *The Hartford Courant*, February 1, 1945, p. 13.

Maes, Jack. 1952. "Let's Go to the Movies!" *The Atchison Daily Globe*, February 10, 1952, p. 7.

"Majestic: 'The Basketball Fix' and Rex Allen Western Film Coming to Local Screen." 1952. *Schamokin News-Dispatch*, March 6, 1952, p. 12.

McDavis, Cody J. 2019. "Paying Students to Play Would Ruin College Sports: A Handful of Programs Would Pay Top Dollar for a Select Few Athletes, While Other Schools Would Get Caught Up in a Bidding War They Couldn't Afford."

The New York Times, February 25, 2019. https://www.nytimes.com/2019/02/25/opinion/pay-college-athletes.html

Millman, Chad. 2020. "The Mavericks Who Remade Sports, Part I: Charles McNeil, Father of The Point Spread." *Chicago Tribune*, June 1, 2020. https://www.chicagotribune.com/gambling/sns-actnet-mavericks-who-remade-sports-part-i-point-spread-20200601-rzikvzhnzjefbdrinxij3fwrzu-story.html

Murtha, William and James Desmond. 1951. "Cage Stars, Big Bettor Seized." *New York Daily News*, February 19, 1951, pp. 1, 28.

Naismith, James. 1996. *Basketball: Its Origin and Development*. Lincoln: University of Nebraska Press.

Nelson, Murry R. 2009a. *Encyclopedia of Sports in America: A History from Foot Races to Extreme Sports: Volume 1*. Westport, CT: Greenwood Press.

Nelson, Murry R. 2009b. *Encyclopedia of Sports in America: A History from Foot Races to Extreme Sports: Volume 2*. Westport, CT: Greenwood Press.

Piereson, James. 2017. "The Big Fix: Looking Back at College Basketball's First Great Scandal, with Dethroned the Game from Its Place Atop New York Sports." *City-Journal*, October 1, 2017. https://www.city-journal.org/html/big-fix-15466.html

Rains, Rob with Hellen Carpenter. 2009. *James Naismith: The Man Who Invented Basketball*. Philadelphia: Temple University Press.

Rosen, Charley. 1999. *Scandals of '51: How the Gamblers Almost Killed College Basketball*. New York: Seven Stories Press.

Rosen, Charley. 2001. *The Wizard of Odds: How Jack Molinas Almost Destroyed the Game of Basketball*. New York: Seven Stories Press.

Rosenblatt, Edith. 1951. "'Basketball Fix' 'Man with My Face'—Palace." *Pittsburgh Post-Gazette*, November 30, 1951, p. 12.

Special to *The New York Times*. 1975. "Molinas's Past Sifted for Clues." *The New York Times*, August 6, 1976, p. 57.

Sperber, Murray. 1998. *Onward to Victory: The Crises That Shaped College Sports*. New York: Henry Holt and Company.

"Suit Cites Slump in 3-D Popularity." 1953. *Valley Times*, November 27, 1953, p. 3.

Sullivan, Prescott. 1951. "The Low Down." *San Francisco Examiner*, February 19, 1951, p. 35.

Thompson, William N. 2001. *Gambling in America: An Encyclopedia of History, Issues, and Society*. Santa Barbara, CA: ABC-CLIO.

Turkin, Hi. 1951. "Cage Scandal Bars City from March Tourneys." *New York Daily News*, February 19, 1951, pp. 46, 50.

Vorsino, Mary. 2004. "Johnny Sands Jr. / 1928–2003: Actor Left Big Screen to Focus on Family and Ocean." *Honolulu Star-Bulletin*, January 6, 2004, p. C-10.

Williams, Joe. 1940. "Stanford University Decides not to Play any More in Rose Bowl." *Tampa Morning Tribune*, January 10, 1940, p. 15.

Wilner, Barry and Ken Rappoport. 2014. *Crazyball: Sports Scandals, Superstitions, and Slick Plays*. Lanham, MD: Taylor Trade Publishing.

Chapter 3

Paper Lion (1968)

Between the time George Plimpton's *Paper Lion* was published in 1966 and the movie version premiered in 1968, America had undergone radical change. In 1968 alone, the Vietnam War (1965–75) had escalated, leading to protests across the country; civil rights leader Martin Luther King Jr. (1929–68) and Democratic presidential candidate Robert Kennedy (1925–68) were assassinated; and riots had broken out in more than ten cities. In a year of antiestablishment and cynical movies like *Bullitt, Petulia, Rosemary's Baby,* and *Planet of the Apes,* would moviegoers want to see lighthearted fare about a fake National Football League quarterback?

George Plimpton (Alan Alda), a part-time writer for *Sports Illustrated* magazine, wants to join a National Football League (NFL) team's training camp to see what it's like to play professional football. Most teams laugh off his request, but Detroit Lions coach Joe Schmidt (himself) and the owner (Plimpton) agree to let Plimpton try out. Pretending to be a semipro football player from Newfoundland, Plimpton arrives at camp that summer. Schmidt asks defensive tackle Alex Karras (himself) to look after Plimpton, but it doesn't take long before most of the players realize Plimpton is a phony. When Plimpton's girlfriend/secretary (Lauren Hutton) visits as the magazine's photographer, she chides him because he thinks he really can play with the pros.

Eventually, Plimpton earns the respect of most players, who still enjoy tormenting him, and even get him drunk. In a preseason game against the St. Louis Cardinals and the Lions leading with time running out, Schmidt sends Plimpton into the game.

It's a disaster. A nervous Plimpton loses forty-one yards in three plays before the game ends, but his teammates present him with a game ball. Plimpton returns to his real life and real job in New York City.

In 1963, Plimpton posed as a quarterback trying out for the Detroit Lions. His articles about that experience appeared in *Sports Illustrated*, a weekly national sports magazine, in 1964 and 1965, and in 1966, Harper & Row published *Paper Lion*, which quickly became a national bestseller.

Syndicated sports columnist Red Smith wrote, "If there is anybody who has not read about George Plimpton's 'Paper Lion' . . . he must have been living in a cave lately, for the Sunday book sections have featured it, the mid-week reviewers have saluted it, Newsweek leads its current 'Press' department with it, and excerpts have been appearing in assorted magazines for a year or two" (Smith 1966, 2D).

Plimpton "makes the reader feel the speed, force, and the pain of it, shows how the plays are put together," the *San Francisco Examiner's* Brian Fuller wrote, "and gets technique from the best sources—the men make this book the odd gem it is" (Fuller 1966, 40).

In March 1967, New York–based Stuart Millar Productions, Inc. bought the movie rights to Plimpton's book for $50,000. Millar (1929–2006) had helped produce acclaimed films such as *Birdman of Alcatraz* (1962) and *The Best Man* (1964). *Paper Lion* was budgeted at $2 million. United Artists handled distribution.

By April, Millar announced that NFL players and coaches would play themselves in the movie. Plimpton, who had hoped to play himself, got the small part of the Lions owner. That summer, Millar, screenwriter Lawrence Roman (1921–2008), and a camera crew filmed footage of the Lions' training camp in Detroit and at Detroit's exhibition game in St. Louis.

Alex March (1921–89), who had worked mostly on television series, was hired to direct.

At a December party in New York City celebrating the first anniversary of the book's publication, Plimpton announced that Alda would play Plimpton in the movie version. The son of actor Robert Alda (1914–86) had starred in *The Owl and the Pussycat* and *The Apple Tree* on Broadway, earning a Tony Award nomination for the latter; *Paper Lion* was his first major film role. Hutton, a model, also made her first screen appearance.

Alda had never been a sports fan. "It was just a pain in the neck to me," he said. "Very boring. And all that yelling by the crowd made no sense" (Lardine 1968, 4). He almost didn't get the part. When told that Millar wanted Alda to meet him at Central Park for a game of touch football, Alda asked for a delay because he didn't know how to play touch football. After the Central Park audition, Millar said: "I don't think this is going to work out. We need someone that can handle himself a little better" (Lardine 1968, 4).

Alda kept his job by saying he could be coached, and Millar had several professional quarterbacks instruct Alda, but the players had different approaches, confusing the actor even more. Still Alda kept his job, and principal filming started in February 1968 in Boca Raton, Florida, where the St. Andrews School for Boys was familiar with pro football players (the Miami

Dolphins trained there) and resembled the Lions' camp at Cranbrook, a private prep boarding school in Bloomfield Hills, Michigan.

The slow pace of shooting a movie frustrated Joe Schmidt (1932–), a reluctant actor. "That was my big objection," he recalled. "You're going to sit on your a— for a long time. Then they'll take a shot. Then you're sitting. You're not accustomed to that and you know you have work to do. I wanted to coach. But we'd go to the set in the morning, be there into the night" (Joe Schmidt, interview with author, February 20, 2020).

But if filming a movie was foreign to pro football players, working with pro football players often frustrated filmmakers. Linebacker Mike Lucci (1939–) described the shooting in Florida as "kind of anarchy. They really had not a lot of control over anybody" (Mike Lucci, interview with author, March 8, 2020).

"Marsh simply could not fathom the inner world of pro football," recalled Alex Karras (1935–2012). "Sometimes it would take him hours to round up the Lion players to do a scene[.] 'What's wrong with you people!' he'd shout. 'Can't you take directions?' If one of us laughed, or farted, or—God forbid—cursed, Marsh would throw up his hands and scream, 'I'm dealing with animals! Animals!'" (Karras 1978, 229).

Roman, however, enjoyed working with the players. "The number of lines a player had became a bit of a thing," he recalled. "Off to the side, a group would gather with a full script and count, much like a neophyte actor (and some veteran actors too). Then if turned loose in a scene with one line to say, somehow it would come out three and it seemed as though you'd need a hook to get him off. . . . Coach Schmidt, in particular. Turn him loose on a scene and you wanted everything he had to say. Anything superfluous could be handled in the cutting room" (Roman 1968, 16). Much of the dialogue involving players and coaches was adlibbed.

The players also had fun at Alda's expense. Karras told Lucci that Alda was becoming delusional. "He said, 'This a— really thinks he can play. Hit him'." So during a scene highlighting contact drills, Lucci knocked Alda to the ground. "The director ended up screaming at me" (Mike Lucci, interview with author, March 8, 2020). Said Alda: "I took a worse beating than George Plimpton had" (Bonderoff 1982, 83).

The barroom scene in which Lions players get Plimpton drunk took twenty-seven takes, Karras recalled. With real beer served, "Alda joined in to prove he could lift his glass with anyone in the joint" (Karras 1978, 230). "We kept egging [Alda] on about having another beer, and it kind of backfired on us because he ended up getting about half drunk and we had to stop shooting," Lucci said. "We ended up working till about 5 o'clock in the morning when we were supposed to be done about 1 o'clock in the morning" (Mike Lucci, interview with author, March 8, 2020).

On September 30, 1968, World Series reporters previewed the film in St. Louis before *Paper Lion* opened October 2 in Detroit. Reviews were mixed.

The Boston Globe's Bud Collins praised Alda for capturing Plimpton's "gawkishness and boyishness," and singled out the Lions players: "But if Alda does well as the skinny writer amidst the brutes, it is the brutes themselves—the Lions—who are the stars of this flick. In fact the[y] are extremely Plimptonian in reverse: professional athletes making it as actors. Unselfconsciously Coach Joe Schmidt, linemen Alex Karras (a gigantic Buddy Hackett), Mike Lucci, Roger Brown, John Gordy, quarterback Karl Sweetan and the other players handle their roles as themselves terrifically. Gratifyingly—and amazingly—here is a sports picture that is quality by any standard" (Collins 1968, 15).

"Many football players and coaches appear to play themselves," wrote William Mootz, film critic for *The Courier-Journal* of Louisville, Kentucky. "Each of them is surprisingly adept before the cameras. No Sir Laurence Oliviers, mind you, but each of them contributes an authentic air to the film's peek-a-boo atmosphere of catching some of pro football's greats both at work and at play" (Mootz 1968, 35).

The *Detroit Free Press*'s Susan Stark wrote that the movie would appeal to "Football nuts," but added, "For the rest of us, me included, 'Paper Lion' amounts to a pretty dull and pointless movie" (Stark 1968, 6-C). *New York Times* critic Renata Adler praised the real football people in the movie, but said Alda "is charming as a Harvard boy" but "at no point is it convincing that this man is a reporter" (Adler 1968, 54).

The movie failed to find an audience, earning an estimated $1.7 million. "In a year exceptionally notable for sensitive male screen performances—evidenced by Peter O'Toole's [*The*] *Lion in Winter*, Alan Arkin's *The Heart Is a Lonely Hunter*, Alan Bates' *The Fixer* and Cliff Robertson's [*Charly*]—[Alda's] portrayal of a daredevil journalist turned football player seemed lightweight by comparison" (Bonderoff 1982, 84–5). Alda would not find stardom until he played "Hawkeye" Pierce in the hit CBS-TV sitcom *M*A*S*H* (1972–83). "There simply wasn't anything that outstanding about the film" (Strait 1983, 95).

HISTORICAL BACKGROUND

"As played in the United States," Gary Bellsky and Neil Fine wrote, "football is foremost a game of territorial acquisition, fitting for a sport born in the century that saw Manifest Destiny emerge as the national credo" (Belsky and Fine 2016, 75).

Early colonists from Europe brought an early version of the sport, a mixture of rugby and soccer, to America only to find Native Americans playing games similar to European football, better known in the United States as soccer. Near Jamestown, Virginia, Captain Henry Spelman (1595–1623) saw Powhatans playing two versions of football games. One game featured women and boys trying to kick a ball to a goal, but the players "never fight nor pull one another [down]" or "strike up one another's [heels], as we do" (Eisen and Wiggins 1995, 3–4) while in the men's game, players dropped a ball from their hands and kicked it—similar to the modern football's punt—with the winner being the man who kicked the ball the farthest. Massachusetts colonists also noticed similar games played by Native Americans.

In the sport's early development, teams from two Massachusetts towns reportedly competed in a football game in 1685, and students at various colleges were playing the sport in the late 1700s, but American versions of football were soon banned on some college campuses, and the sport did not take root across the country until the nineteenth century.

In 1869, college students at Rutgers challenged the College of New Jersey (renamed Princeton University in 1896) to a series of three football games. Princeton's William S. Gummere (1852–1933), later the New Jersey Supreme Court's chief justice, and his Rutgers counterpart agreed on the rules: a field 360 feet long and 225 feet wide on which players would try to score by kicking or batting the ball in the air between two goal posts eight paces apart; there was no crossbar. Throwing the ball and running with the ball were prohibited; tripping and holding were fouls. Each team would field twenty-five-men players. The first team to score six goals would be the winner. Four judges and two referees would serve as officials.

On November 6—a Saturday, because there were no classes on that day, and playing on a Sunday was prohibited—a crowd estimated at a hundred or more watched the first game of the proposed series. There was no admission fee. The first intercollegiate football game in the United States began a little after 3 p.m. "Princeton had something to learn about tactics, for it chose to kick off into the wind and shanked the ball to one side. This enabled Rutgers to take over in excellent field position, from where it began dribbling toward Princeton's goal. Both teams appear to have played a crude zone defense, posting a few men to guard the goal and assigning everyone else to cover certain parts of the field rather than a specific man on the other team. By carefully shielding the man with the ball, Rutgers was able to score first, about five minutes into the game" (Bernstein 2001, 7).

The ball kept going flat, and had to be inflated, but after a little more than three hours, Rutgers had earned a 6–4 victory. The second game was played a week later, with Princeton winning, 8–0. The deciding third game, however, was never played because "faculty at both schools had become alarmed at the passionate attention the new game generated among students, and ordered the match canceled" (Bernstein 2001, 7).

More colleges took up the sport, but rules varied from school to school, so in 1873 Yale, Princeton, and Rutgers sent representatives to New York City for a meeting to codify football rules. Although Columbia chose delegates, it did not send any to the meeting. Harvard, however, refused to attend because it favored "Boston game," a variation of rugby, and sent a letter, explaining: "We even went so far as to practice and try the Yale game. We gave it up at once as hopeless" (Bernstein 2001, 9).

Harvard thought differently after a two-game set played in Cambridge, Massachusetts, against McGill University of Montreal. The teams agreed to play the first game under Harvard rules, and the second under McGill's Canadian style. "The ball used by the McGills is simply a bladder covered with leather, and is much harder to kick with than the ordinary rubber ball," *The Boston Globe* noted (Notes 1874, 2). Harvard won the first game, 3–0, playing under its rules, then played McGill to a draw the following day under McGill's rules. Harvard players, however, decided they liked the other game better and met Yale the following year to be played under "'concessionary rules,' actually pretty much Harvard's" (Hickok 2002, 178). In an 1876 meeting in Springfield, Massachusetts, Columbia, Harvard, Princeton, and Yale formed the Intercollegiate Football Association with games to be played under a modified version of the game McGill had taught Harvard. By the 1890s, football had replaced baseball on most college campuses as the favorite sport.

"At first the play was crude in the extreme," Walter Camp (1859–1925) recalled, "but even in its earliest stages it proved distinctly more satisfactory to both player and spectator than the kicking and shoving which marked the English method" (Camp 2018, 8). A graduate of Yale, Camp, known as the father of American football, became Yale's football coach in 1888. More importantly, he served on the college rules committee and was instrumental in decreasing the number of players on the field to eleven for each team; instituting concepts such as the quarterback calling signals; the line of scrimmage (instead of a rugby scrum); the system of yards and downs; and a new method of scoring.

Rules were tweaked over the years. A touchdown went from four points to five in 1898 and up to six points in 1912. Field goals decreased from five points to four in 1904 and to three in 1909.

With interest in amateur football growing in the United States, professional football had to follow.

On November 12, 1892, William W. "Pudge" Heffelfinger (1867–1954), an 1889 All-American selection from Yale now playing for the Chicago Athletic Association team, was paid $500, plus expenses, to play for the Allegheny Athletic Association in a game against the Pacific Athletic Club. The 6-foot-3, 195-pound guard picked up the ball fumbled by his teammate and ran it in for a touchdown, the only score of the game to give the Allegheny team a 4–0 victory at Pittsburgh's Recreation Park, making him the first known professional football player. In 1893, a Pittsburgh Athletic Club player—believed to have been halfback Grant Dibert—was signed to a season-long contract that paid him $50 a game but stipulated that Dilbert, or whoever the player was, could not compete for another team. Dilbert was out of the starting lineup after the fourth game and quickly faded from history.

With players being paid to play, a professional football league could not be far behind. In 1895, a professional team from Jeannette, Pennsylvania, lost, 12–0, to a YMCA-sponsored team from Latrobe, Pennsylvania. More professional and semiprofessional teams began forming.

In 1902, major-league baseball's Philadelphia Athletics and Philadelphia Phillies formed professional football teams and created, along with the Pittsburgh Stars, the short-lived National Football League. In 1920, the American Professional Football Association was formed in Canton, Ohio, eventually fielding fourteen teams from five states with the Akron Pros, finishing with a league-best 8–0–3 record. By 1922, the league had eighteen teams and a new name, the National Football League (NFL).

The new NFL spent more than twenty years without competition until 1946, when the All-America Football Conference (AAFC) was formed with teams in Brooklyn, Buffalo, Chicago, Cleveland, Los Angeles, Miami, and San Francisco. The AAFC and NFL merged as the National Football League in 1949, and the following year the NFL divided into two conferences: the American (Chicago Cardinals, Cleveland Browns, New York Giants, Philadelphia Eagles, Pittsburgh Steelers, Washington Redskins) and National (Baltimore Colts, Chicago Bears, Detroit Lions, Green Bay Packers, Los Angeles Rams, New York Yanks, San Francisco 49ers).

Again, the NFL monopolized professional football in the United States until the American Football League (AFL) launched in 1960, signing a five-year contract with ABC-TV. The NFL signed a broadcasting contract with CBS in 1964; the following year, the AFL jumped to NBC. The real winners were the players; competing leagues led to bidding wars for players. In 1965, quarterback Joe Namath (1943–) signed a four-year contract for $25,000 a year with a $250,000 signing bonus to play for the AFL's New York Jets. In 1966, the two leagues agreed to merge, although the merger was not completed until 1970. At the end of the 1966 season, the AFL and NFL champions met in the NFL World Championship game, now known as the Super Bowl.

When *Paper Lion* was filming, the oldest continuing professional football operation was the St. Louis Cardinals, whose roots dated to Chicago in 1899, when plumber and painter Chris O'Brien (1881–1951) organized the amateur Morgan Athletic Club, a sandlot football team on Chicago's south side. After moving the team to Normal Park on Racine Avenue, the team was first renamed the Racine Normals and then the Racine Street Cardinals (after the team's red jerseys). O'Brien had to suspend operations in 1906, reformed it briefly before America entered World War I (1914–18) in 1917, but in 1920 O'Brien traveled to Canton, Ohio, and his Chicago Cardinals became a charter member of the American Professional Football Association. O'Brien sold the team in 1929. The Cardinals moved to St. Louis in 1960 and Phoenix in 1988. The team, renamed the Arizona Cardinals in 1994, remains the oldest continuing professional football operation.

The NFL had attempted to field teams in Detroit three times without success in the 1920s, but in 1934 local radio-station owner George A. Richards (1889–1951) bought the Portsmouth (Ohio) Spartans for $8,000 and moved the franchise, renamed the Lions, to Detroit. The following year, the Lions won the NFL championship, beating the New York Giants in the title game. Chicago department-store executive Frederick L. Mandel Jr. (1908–73) bought the team in 1940 before selling it to a group of stockholders in 1948. The Lions saw their biggest success in the 1950s, winning NFL championships in 1952, 1953, and 1957. Quarterback Bobby Layne (1926–86) led the team before breaking his leg late in the 1957 season. The Lions traded Layne to the Pittsburgh Steelers early in the 1958 season. Detroit has never won an NFL title since. The *Detroit Free-Press* opined in 1995:

> Perhaps it's the Curse of . . . Bobby Layne.
>
> Just as the Red Sox haven't won a World Series since trading Babe Ruth, and the Indians haven't since trading Rocky Colavito, and the Cubs haven't even reached the Series since refusing to admit a goat to Wrigley Field, the Lions haven't won an NFL title since trading Layne . . . in October 1958.
>
> Layne, a Hall of Fame quarterback, led the Lions to championships in 1952, '53 and '57. But after two games in '58, he was sent to Pittsburgh. The Lions never explained why. And they still can't explain why they have been one of the most fruitless franchises in professional sports ever since. (Foiled Again 1995, 1D)

The Boston Red Sox won World Series championships in 2007, 2013, and 2018; the Cubs won the World Series in 2016; and while the Cleveland Indians still haven't won a World Series since 1948, they advanced to the championship series in 1954, 1995, 1997, and 2016. But the Detroit Lions have made the playoffs only twelve times since 1957 and are 1–13 record in those appearances.

During "the 1960s the Lions weren't big winners," recalled Loren D. Estleman, a Michigan native best known for his Detroit-set mystery novels, "but their defensive line was feared throughout the NFL" (Loren D. Estleman, letter to author, January 12, 2020).

That's the world George Plimpton (1927–2003) entered in 1963. Educated at Harvard and Cambridge, Plimpton (1927–2003) became the unpaid editor of *The Paris Review*, a literary journal, in 1953, but was best known as a "participatory journalist" in which he gave readers a taste of what it actually felt like to try to compete in professional sports. Having pitched to major-league players and boxed against a professional, he thought playing in a professional football game would be an interesting experience.

DEPICTION AND CULTURAL CONTEXT

During the opening credits, *Paper Lion* notes: "This film is an amiable fiction based on the book 'Paper Lion' by George Plimpton and is not intended to be a literal depiction of its author."

The first obvious change filmmakers made was moving the story from 1963, when Plimpton attended the Detroit Lions' training camp, to the present—shooting some footage from the 1967 season before principal filming began in early 1968.

In flashbacks, Plimpton is seen pitching to American and National League All-Stars at Yankee Stadium and trying to box three rounds with "Sugar" Ray Robinson (1921–89). The All-Stars hammer him in the baseball appearance and Robinson decks him in the boxing exhibition.

On October 13, 1958, Plimpton pitched before an exhibition game that pitted National League All-Stars led by San Francisco Giants outfielder Willie Mays (1931–) against American League All-Stars led by New York Yankees outfielder Mickey Mantle (1931–95) at New York's Yankee Stadium (a different event than baseball's annual All-Star Game). *Sports Illustrated* agreed to put up $1,000 that would be divided among the players for the team that hit Plimpton the hardest. The terms were that Plimpton would face eight National and American League All-Stars; scoring would be one point for a single, two for a double, three for a triple, and four for a home run. The first two players Plimpton faced, Philadelphia Phillies outfielder Richie Ashburn (1927–97) and Mays, popped out. "That is all of that day I really care to remember," Plimpton wrote (Plimpton 1961, 95). Cincinnati Reds outfielder Frank Robinson (1935–2019) doubled; Chicago Cubs shortstop Ernie Banks (1931–2015) saw twenty-three pitches before flying out; Pittsburgh Pirates third baseman Frank Thomas (1929–) hit a 400-plus-foot home run into the upper deck; Los Angeles Dodgers first baseman Gil Hodges (1924–72) singled; Philadelphia Phillies catcher Stan Lapota (1925–2013) grounded to Detroit Tigers shortstop Billy Martin (1928–89), who "first gave a little startled jump as if in surprise to hear the whack of the ball being hit, then moved for it on legs that seemed 'stiff from disuse' . . . and promptly fumbled" the ball (Plimpton 1961, 133). When the Pirates second baseman Bill Mazeroski (1936–) came to bat, Yankees manager Ralph Houk (1919–2010) relieved Plimpton, who, looking shellshocked, returned to the American League dugout, where Yankees pitcher Whitey Ford (1928–) told him: "We've been making book here in the dugout as to when you'd keel over" (Plimpton 1961, 140). The film shows Plimpton pitching to several New York Yankees, but in reality he never pitched to any American League player.

Robinson, welterweight and five-time middleweight champion, had retired as a professional boxer in 1965. Plimpton never boxed against Robinson, but in 1959 he went three rounds with Archie Moore (1916–98), a light-heavyweight champion, at a New York gym before roughly two hundred "Literary people, television and stage people, society people" (Hand 1959, 13). *Sports Illustrated* arranged that fight for Plimpton; a *Sports Illustrated* writer served as referee and announcer. "At the end of the second [round], George's nose was red. At the end of the third and last round Plimpton's bloody nose had stained Archie's shirt" (Hand 1959, 13). Plimpton's bloody nose depicted in the film is accurate enough, but Moore, taking it easy, never sent Plimpton to the canvas.

Plimpton's inspiration for becoming a participatory journalist was Paul Gallico (1897–1976), a *New York Daily News* sportswriter who boxed with Jack Dempsey (1895–1983) in 1923 and later caught pitches thrown by major-leaguer curveball specialist Herb Pennock (1894–1948), golfed with Bobby Jones (1902–71), and rode with speedboat racer Gar Wood (1880–1971) and race-car driver Cliff Bergere (1896–1980) "just for the sensation" (Holtzman 1974, 66). "If I weren't a writer, there'd be no reason to do it," Plimpton said. "If I just did it for the hell of it, I'd really be a lunatic" (Davidson 1967, 46).

"There's a lot of interest in pro ball. It's damn near the national sport," the *Sports Illustrated* editor (David Doyle, 1929–97) says in the film while proposing that Plimpton pose as a rookie quarterback trying to make an NFL team, which could fulfill his contract with six articles for the magazine. *Sports Illustrated* managing editor Andre Laguerre (1915–79) arranged the

---

PAUL GALLICO ON SPORTS

Paul Gallico became a participatory journalist so that he could be a better sports-writer. "If I knew what playing a game felt like," he explained, "particularly against or in company of experts, I was better equipped to write about the playing of it and the problems of the men and women who took part in it" (Gallico 1945, 284). Therefore he knew that being knocked down by Jack Dempsey was "a good deal like having a building fall down on you" (Gallico 1923, 22).

In the late 1930s, Gallico left newspapers to write fiction and for film. By that time, he had already witnessed in sports "the coming of the million-dollar gate, the seventy-thousand-dollar horse-race, the hundred-thousand-dollar ballplayers, the three-hundred-thousand-dollar football game, the millionaire prizefighter, and the fifty-thousand-dollar golfer" (Gallico 1945, 8). "I'm a rotten novelist," he said. "I'm not even literary" (Holtzman 1974, 80). One of his novels, *The Poseidon Adventure* (1969), was turned into a 1972 movie, grossing more than $84 million and launching a disaster-film craze. He also wrote the original story and contributed to the treatment of *The Pride of the Yankees* (1943), writing a movie-tie hardcover published by Grosset & Dunlap. That movie, a biopic of New York Yankees star Lou Gehrig (1903–41), is consistently rated among the best sports movies of all time.

Sources

Gallico, Paul. 1923. "How Jack Dempsey Hits, by One Who Knows: News Sports Writer Tests His Punch: Curious, Gallico Offers Chin in Interests of Science; One Round—He's Satisfied." *New York Daily News*, September 10, 1923, p. 22.

Gallico, Paul. 1945. *Farewell to Sport*. New York: Pocket Books.

Holtzman, Jerome, recorder and ed. 1974. *No Cheering in the Press Box: Recollections—Personal & Professional—By Eighteen Veteran American Sportswriters*. New York: Holt, Rinehart and Winston.

trip, and Plimpton did contribute articles to the magazine, but Plimpton also wrote pieces for *New York* and *Harper's Magazine*. Yet the "national sport" quote rings true. During the three years CBS televised the NFL season from 1961 to 1963, ratings for NFL games rose 50 percent; in 1964, CBS paid the NFL $14.1 million per year for a two-year TV deal. In 2015, NFL's total revenues were reported at $13 billion, compared to Major League Baseball's $9.5 billion. The idea to play for an NFL team was Plimpton's, but how he came to the Detroit Lions' training camp was roundabout.

At first, Plimpton wanted to play in the annual Pro Bowl game, the NFL's version of baseball's All-Star Game, an idea he called "grandiose" (Plimpton 1966, 10). Western Conference coach Red Hickey (1917–2006) called Plimpton crazy and said he had no chance of playing in the game, but Hicks gave Plimpton a ticket to watch the game from the bench.

In the movie, Plimpton meets with Green Bay Packers coach Vincent Lombardi (1913–70). Lombardi, who plays himself, good-naturedly rejects Plimpton's proposal and suggests that he try the American Football League. After finding no support from the Los Angeles Rams and other teams, Plimpton asks Frank Gifford (1930–2015), who retired in 1964 after twelve seasons with the New York Giants, to put in a word for him with the Giants. "I've got a good word for you George," Gifford, who also plays himself, tells him. "Forget about being quarterback." "It has to be quarterback," Plimpton says. "That's the nerve center of the team."

Although Plimpton had considered playing every position, he came to think that quarterback was the position he needed to play. "It's the position everyone would want to read about it," he told the Lions coaching staff (Plimpton 1966, 69), but he never reached out to Lombardi, whom Plimpton called "tough and dictatorial" (Plimpton 1966, 20). "A guy like Vince Lombardi would have thrown his a— straight out the door," Schmidt said (Joe Schmidt, interview with author, February 20, 2020). After Plimpton was rejected by the Giants and the American Football League's New York Titans (renamed the New York Jets in 1963), he tried the Baltimore Colts before a director with the Detroit Lions agreed to mention his idea to Lions coach George Wilson (1914–78), who surprised Plimpton by writing back and inviting the writer to the Lions training camp. "Only a coach as easygoing as George Wilson would have tolerated such an encroachment," Jerry Wynn, a sportswriter for the *Long Beach Independent*, wrote (Wynn 1964, C-1).

"The front office asked [Wilson] if it was OK for [Plimpton] to come out and hang out and do certain things," Schmidt recalled. "It was unusual, but it's not like today. When I was playing, training camp was four to six weeks and difficult. We played six preseason games and never got any money for it. The Lions were the only team that paid players for training camps. We got 25 bucks a week" (Joe Schmidt, interview with author, February 20, 2020).

The casting of 1967–68 Detroit Lions players as themselves also led to several differences between the film and the book. The principal Lions in the movie are Schmidt, Karras, Lucci, John Gordy (1935-2009), Pat Studstill (1938–), Roger Brown (1937–), and offensive coordinator Bill McPeak (1926–91).

A linebacker out of the University of Pittsburgh, Schmidt played thirteen seasons, 1953–65, with the Lions. He was one of the team's leaders when Plimpton arrived at training camp in 1963. After his retirement as a player, the Lions hired him as an assistant coach for the 1966 season under head coach Harry Gilmer (1926–2016), who had replaced Wilson after the 1964 season. When Gilmer was fired after the 1966 season, Schmidt became the Lions head coach. Schmidt resigned as coach in 1973, saying, "I promised my family and myself when I started coaching that I would get out when it stopped being fun. Unfortunately, it's reached that point" (Vincent 1973, 1D). Schmidt compiled a 43–34–7 record, making the playoffs once and finishing second in the division four consecutive times. In 1973, Schmidt was inducted into the Pro Football Hall of Fame.

In the film, Schmidt reveals Plimpton's true identity to Karras and asks the star defensive lineman to look after the writer. Karras was an intimidating player. "If I told you I don't enjoy ripping [Packers quarterback] Bart Starr's head off, I'd be lying to you," he said. "Knocking down an offensive lineman and breaking his head open is something I enjoy" (Cope 1968, 89). Karras, a first-round draft pick out of the University of Iowa in 1958, played his entire twelve-year career with the Lions, but he did not take part in Detroit's training camp with Plimpton. In April 1963, NFL commissioner Pete Rozelle (1926–96) fined Gordy, Schmidt, and three other Lions players $2,000 each for betting on NFL games, and Karras was suspended indefinitely. All players had bet on the Packers to win. Green Bay running back Paul Hornung (1935–2020) was also suspended for one year. "There is no evidence that any player has given less than his best," Rozelle's report said. "There is no evidence that any player ever bet against his own team. There is no evidence that any player has sold information to gamblers" (Puscas 1963, 4-A). Karras missed the entire 1963 season before being reinstated in 1964.

Linebacker Lucci spent his first three years in the NFL with the Cleveland Browns, and didn't join the Lions until he was traded in 1965. He wasn't familiar with Plimpton's training-camp adventures until talks about the movie began in earnest. "We talked about [Plimpton] here and there, but it really wasn't a big discussion," Lucci said. "When they started talking about the movie, then of course I read the book and we had more discussions with the guys who were there in '63" (Mike Lucci, interview with author, March 8, 2020).

Studstill and Brown were at Cranbrook with Plimpton in 1963, but by the time the movie was released, both players had become Los Angeles Rams. The Lions traded Brown in September 1967, which caused a script update in which Schmidt announces the trade to his players in the movie. Studstill was traded in May 1968 while *Paper Lion* was still being filmed. He flew to California after the trade, but rejoined the production.

Offensive lineman Gordy, the Lions' offensive captain, was one of the principal characters in Plimpton's book, and gives one of the most effective monologues in the movie when he tells Plimpton: "George, this is a team effort. Everybody has to know what everybody else is doing, or somebody can get hurt. I've had a good life in pro football. I'd like to keep it that way. I don't want to be messing around with somebody like you and get hurt. Like a ligament. Ligaments don't heal, George. Now what I'm trying to say to you is this: Why should I play for you? So you can get some kicks? I've got to lay it on the line."

That speech proved prophetic.

In July, Gordy and tackle Roger Shoals (1938–), dissatisfied with the Lions' salary offers for their 1968 contracts, briefly walked out of training camp. A day after returning to practice, Gordy tore a ligament in his left knee that required surgery. After missing the entire season, the thirty-three-year-old announced his retirement from the NFL on January 15, 1969, and accepted the position of executive director of the NFL Players Association.

"Injury is the most nightmarish aspect of football because its threat is impossible to handle—its nature unpredictable, even quixotic," Plimpton wrote. ". . . So much—even a championship—depends on the health of a team, and often on the condition of one star player" (Plimpton 1966, 194). That was on Lucci's mind during filming. "We did [takes] over and over again," he said. "We screwed around a lot but it was also like, 'OK, that was our livelihood and if someone got hurt, I don't really know legally if we'd have any recourse if someone had gotten hurt '" (Mike Lucci, interview with author, March 8, 2020).

In the film, Plimpton finds a bloody knife pinning a note to his pillow with the message: "WRiTER BEWARE! YOU'RE going TO GET YOUR BUTT KICKED IN." Karras explains the prank as, "Guess the guys didn't want to waste a good nosebleed." That scene was invented. "Some [scenes], of course, don't go right along with the book," Karras said (Alex Karras on 'Paper Lion' 1968, 13).

But where the film excelled was in its training-camp scenes. Karras's comic rookie-show performance was unscripted but typical antics for Karras during his career. Rookies and veterans were segregated in the dining room, as depicted, and veterans often hazed first-year players to sing their school songs. "No one seemed much put out," Plimpton wrote. "Everybody went on eating. . . . Nobody put down their forks to listen. It was apparent that the singing was secondary to the indignity to which the rookie was put; he was being embarrassed so that he would keep the rigorous caste system firmly in mind" (Plimpton 1966, 26).

The film's depiction of training camp "was pretty accurate" for the 1960s, Lucci said. "I was looking at the negotiations today with the [Collective Bargaining Agreement] and you look at how much they're allowed to hit and what they're allowed to do. At training camp [in 1968], we scrimmaged and had two-a-days, four out of five days some days. Linemen did it all the time. We were hitting a lot more than they ever think about hitting today. The contracts are so much bigger [today], they're worried about public opinion and things like that. So training camp [in the 1960s] in many ways was tougher than the games" (Mike Lucci, interview with author, March 8, 2020).

The scene in which Lucci dons a fright mask to scare Plimpton is not far-fetched, either. "Sometimes, late at night, the 'natives would get restless,'—as John Gordy would say, and in the dormitory the hi-jinks would begin," Plimpton wrote. "It was a way of letting off energy not consumed by the day's practice. The mode changes from year to year. It was water pistols one year. My year it was fright masks" (Plimpton 1966, 122).

"We were bored," Lucci said, "and needed to pass the time. So we'd go in there and screw around with their clothes or lock them out or who knows? When you think back now, you laugh about it. It many ways, it was break-ing the monotony" (Mike Lucci, interview with author, March 8, 2020).

The finale, set during a preseason game in St. Louis against the Cardinals, looks authentic, too, with dirty, sweaty players on the sidelines—because second-unit photography was shot at the 1967 Lions-Cardinals exhibition game in which the Lions won, 21–7. But Plimpton's performances in the scrimmage and the exhibition game are fabrications.

In the movie, Plimpton guides his team to a touchdown in the scrimmage, only to learn that the Lions defense and coaches arranged for the journalist to look good. In reality, Wilson let Plimpton run five plays in the scrimmage. On the first play, Plimpton took too long trying to control the ball after taking the snap and was knocked down by his own teammate, Gordy, who was pulling on the play. Plimpton fumbled, but recovered the ball. He lost his balance after taking the snap on the second play and fell down for another loss. On the third play, he was too slow to hand off the ball to fullback Danny Lewis (1936–2015) and was stopped by Brown. "I had lost twenty yards in three attempts," Plimpton wrote, "and I had yet, in fact, to run off a complete play" (Plimpton 1966, 238). His fourth attempt was an incomplete pass. On Plimp-ton's last play, he lateraled the ball to Nick Pietrosante (1937–88), who was tackled at the one-yard line for another loss. When Plimpton walked back to the bench, he was greeted with applause, some of it coming from spectators "who had enjoyed the comic aspects of my stint" (Plimpton 1966, 241).

The film depicts Schmidt sending Plimpton into the game with just more than a minute left in the game and the Lions leading the Cardinals by 14 points. On the first play, Plimpton lines up behind Gordy, the guard, instead of the center, resulting in a five-yard penalty for delay of game. He stumbles after taking the snap and falls to the ground for a nine-yard loss on the next play. Then he gets tackled for an eight-yard loss. Defying Schmidt's instructions to call only handoffs, Plimpton calls a pass play and runs into the goalpost, knocking himself out as time expires. After being revived in the locker room, Schmidt tells him he did all right. "I must have set some kind of record," Plimpton says. "Three plays and I lost 41 yards." The players, however, give him the game ball.

None of that happened. Before the Lions played the Cleveland Browns in an exhibition game, Wilson told Plimpton he might play if Detroit had at least a 20-point lead, but at halftime Lions general manager Edwin Anderson (1902–1987) informed Plimpton that the deal was off. Anderson had called Rozelle, and the commissioner refused to allow Plimpton in the game. "There's no way they'd let him play in a game," Lucci said (Mike Lucci, interview with author, March 8, 2020). When the team returned to Michigan, Plimpton decided to leave camp, and Wilson and the players promised to send Plimpton a gold football on a pedestal that proclaimed Plimpton "THE BEST ROOKIE IN DETROIT LION HISTORY" (Plimpton 1966, 342).

Plimpton wasn't finished with the Lions, however. "He occasionally suits up with the Lions in practice and has made the Western trip with them," the *Independent* of Long Beach, California, reported before a September 19, 1964, game against the Los Angeles Rams. "If he gets into the game, the Rams really will be in trouble" (Wynn 1964, C-1). He "has occasionally been on the Lion bench during games and once represented them at a player draft meeting," the *San Francisco Examiner's* Brian Fuller noted two years later (Fuller 1966, 40). In 1971, Plimpton ran four plays at quarterback for the Baltimore Colts during halftime of an exhibition game against the Lions for part of a TV special. "You know," Plimpton said, "I was the last player Alex Karras tackled" (Green 2003, 8C). The Lions released Karras shortly after that game.

Plimpton continued practicing participatory journalism, playing goaltender for the National Hockey League's Boston Bruins, playing with the New York Philharmonic, and playing a villain that gets decked by John Wayne (1907–79) and shot and killed by Jorge Rivero (1938–) in a saloon gunfight in the 1971 Western movie *Rio Lobo*. The year *Paper Lion* hit theaters, Harper and Row published his book about competing in professional golf, *The Bogey Man*. Plimpton even inspired another participatory journalist, *Wall Street Journal* reporter Stefan Fatsis (1963–), to try out as a placekicker for the NFL's Denver Broncos in 2006.

In 2003, Plimpton attended a forty-year reunion of *Paper Lion* participants in Detroit. Four days later, on September 25, Plimpton died of a heart attack in his New York City apartment. He was seventy-six. "It was shocking," Brown said. "We had a good time last weekend. I told him how he was a light in my life" (Bock 2003, A10). In one of his last interviews, Plimpton said: "I go every Sunday to watch the Lions at a place called The Blue Moon, where they have several TV sets, here in New York. I'm the only one watching. I've been doing it for years" (Green 2003, 8C).

CONCLUSION

Many of Plimpton's books remain in print, but the movie *Paper Lion* is mostly forgotten. Wood Knapp released the movie on videocassette in 1988, but at this writing, the movie has never been released on DVD or Blu-ray and rarely shows up on television, although it has appeared on some streaming services. Interest in the movie has "died," Schmidt said. "People every once in a while people will say something about it," Schmidt said, "but it's been so long ago . . ." (Joe Schmidt, interview with author, February 20, 2020).

Despite some realistic football scenes, the movie might be best known for helping launch an acting career for Karras. In 1969, Karras landed a small part in an episode of the TV series *Daniel Boone* and went on to appear in other TV series and TV movies, but might he be best remembered for playing Mongo, a brainless brute in *Blazing Saddles*, a 1974 spoof of the Western movie genre by director Mel Brooks (1926–). Karras continued acting for film and television, including 150 episodes of the TV series *Webster*, which ran four seasons on ABC (1983–87) and two in first-run syndication (1987–89).

Paper Lion "turned out to be quite a nice excursion through life," Schmidt said. "Alex Karras became a movie star and George Plimpton became a household name, so to speak, so I guess it took its place in history" (Joe Schmidt, interview with author, February 20, 2020).

FURTHER READING

Adler, Renata. 1968. "The Screen: 'Paper Lion': Real Football Players Provide Authenticity." *The New York Times*, October 24, 1968, p. 54.

"Alex Karras on 'Paper Lion.'" 1968. *Detroit: The Magazine of Michigan's Metropolis*, October 13, 1968, p. 13.

"Alex March Directs 'Paper Lion' Movie." 1968. *The Pittsburgh Press*, February 16, 1968, p. 17.

Arber, Edward. 1895. *Capt. John Smith. Works. 1608–1631*. Westminster, England: Archibald Constable and Co.

Associated Press. 1967. "Grier's Replacement: Rams Trade for 300-lb. Lineman." *San Pedro News-Pilot*, September 8, 1967, p. 7.

Associated Press. 1968a. "Rams Trade QB Munson." *Daily Capital News*, May 2, 1968, p. 16.

Associated Press. 1968b. "Rozelle Lets 49ers Have Hardy, Saint Draft Choice." *The News-Palladium*, July 27, 1968, p. 14.

Associated Press. 1968c. "Paper Lion Becomes Tissue Soft." *Wisconsin State Journal*, August 11, 1968, Section 3, p. 4.

Beal, Borden. 1967. "A Week in Which We Let 'Serendipity' Reign." *The Herald-Tribune*, February 5, 1967, p. 6-B.

Belsky, Gary and Neil Fine. 2016. *On the Origins of Sports*. New York: Artisan.

Bernstein, Mark F. 2001. *Football: The Ivy League Origins of an American Obsession*. Philadelphia: University of Pennsylvania Press.

Bock, Hal. 2003. "Detroit Team Recalls Their 'Paper Lion.'" *Daily Record*, September 27, 2003, p. A10.

Bonderoff, Jason. 1982. *Alan Alda: An Unauthorized Biography*. New York: Signet.

"Broadway Star Picked for 'Lion.'" *The Austin Statesman*, December 13, 1967, p. A58.

Broeg, Bob. 1968. "'Paper Lion': Pros Add Realism to Movie." *St. Louis Post-Dispatch*, October 1, 1968, p. 2B.

"CAMBRIDGE." 1874. *The Boston Globe*, May 16, 1874, p. 8.

Camp, Walter. 2018. *American Football*. Frankfurt, Germany: Outlook Verlag.

"Chris O'Brien, Pro Football Pioneer, Dies." 1951. *Chicago Daily Tribune*, June 4, 1951, p. 1.

Collins, Bud. 1968. "'Paper Lion' a Well-Handled Sports Movie." *The Boston Globe*, October 14, 1968, p. 15.

Cope, Myron. 1968. *Broken Cigars*. Englewood Cliffs, NJ: Prentice-Hall, Inc.

Davidson, Sara. 1967. "The Unsecret Life of George Plimpton." *The Boston Globe*, September 10, 1967, pp. 44–48.

"Detroit Lions Team History." https://www.profootballhof.com/teams/detroit-lions/team-history/

Dow, Bill. 2003. "Karras Eager for 'Paper Lion' Reunion: Ex-Lion to Be in Detroit for 1st Time in 20 Years." *Detroit Free Press,* September 9, 2003, pp. 1D, 3D.

Eisen, George, and David K. Wiggins. 1995. *Ethnicity and Sport in North American History and Culture*. Westport, CT: Praeger Publishers.

Fatsis, Stefan. 2008. *A Few Seconds of Panic: A 5-Foot-8, 170-Pound, 43-Year-Old Sportswriter Plays in the NFL*. New York: The Penguin Press.

Fernandez, Bernard. 1989. "Boxing Loses Its Greatest Ever." *Philadelphia Daily News*, April 13, 1989, p. 82.

"Foiled Again." 1995. *Detroit Free-Press*, October 24, 1995, p. 1D.

"Football History." https://www.profootballhof.com/football-history/history-of-football/

Fuller, Brian. 1966. "The Rookie with a Notebook." *San Francisco Examiner*, November 13, 1966, p. 40.

Green, Jerry. 2003. "Plimpton Was Real Paper Lion as a Great Writer and Storyteller." *The Detroit News and Free Press*, September 28, 2003, p. 8C.

Hand, Jack. 1959. "Writer Wants to Fight Champ—So Archie Moore Obliges." *Reno Evening Gazette*, January 16, 1959, p. 13.

Hickok, Ralph. 2002. *The Encyclopedia of North American Sports History, Second Edition*. New York: Facts On File, Inc.

Holtzman, Jerome, recorder and ed. 1974. *No Cheering in the Press Box: Recollections—Personal & Professional—By Eighteen Veteran American Sportswriters*. New York: Holt, Rinehart and Winston.

Horrigan, Joe. 2019. *NFL Century: The One-Hundred-Year Rise of America's Greatest Sports League*. New York: Crown.

Karras, Alex with Herb Gluck. 1978. *Even Big Guys Cry*. New York: Signet.

Katzowitz, Josh. 2013. "Remember When: Grant Dibert Signs First Pro Football Contract: On Oct. 4, 1893, Grant Dibert Apparently Was the First Football Player to Sign a Pro Contract." October 4, 2013. https://www.cbssports.com/nfl/news/remember-when-grant-dibert-signs-first-pro-football-contract/

Kutz, Steven. 2016. "NFL Took in $13 Billion in Revenue Last Season—See How It Stacks Up against Other Pro Sports Leagues." *MarketWatch*, July 2, 2016. https://www.marketwatch.com/story/the-nfl-made-13-billion-last-season-see-how-it-stacks-up-against-other-leagues-2016-07-01

Lardine, Bob. 1968. "Thrown for a Gain: Alan Alda Took Beating in Football Movie, 'Paper Lion,' But It Could Make Him a Star." *Sunday New York News: Coloroto Magazine*, October 27, 1968, pp. 4, 7.

Larson, Al. 1968. "'Senseless to Remain with Rams Now'—Pope." *Independent*, May 6, 1968, p. C-4.

Lewis, Dan. 1968. "The Paper Lion Flicks His Tale." *The Record Magazine,* March 23, 1968, pp. 12–13.

Lyons, Leonard. 1967a. "The Lyons Den: Thant Finds His Job Has Conflicts." *The Morning Call*, March 21, 1967, p. 15.

Lyons, Leonard. 1967b. "The Lyons Den: Exile Isn't Killing the Living Theater." *The Morning Call*, April 20, 1967, p. 22.

Lyons, Leonard. 1967c. "On Broadway." *The Cedar Rapids Gazette*, December 24, 1967, p. 24.

Martin, Betty. 1967. "Movie Call Sheet: Director Jerry Paris Signed." *Los Angeles Times*, October 14, 1967, p. 17.

Monarrez, Carlos. 2012. "'There Was No One Like Him': Lions Great Karras a Rough-and-Tough Star with a Hollywood Persona." *Detroit Free Press*, October 11, 2012, p. C4.

Mootz, William. 1968. "'Paper Lion' Roars on the Screen." *The Courier-Journal*, October 24, 1968, p. 34.

Morrison, Robert. 1968. "Actor Alda Loves Big Red." *St. Louis Post-Dispatch*, May 14, 1968, p. 4-C.

Nelson, Murry R., ed. 2009a. *Encyclopedia of Sports in America: A History from Foot Races to Extreme Sports: Volume One: Colonial Years to 1939*. Westport, CT: Greenwood Press.

Nelson, Murry R., ed. 2009b. *Encyclopedia of Sports in America: A History from Foot Races to Extreme Sports: Volume Two: 1940 to Present*. Westport, CT: Greenwood Press.

NFL's Official Encyclopedic History of Professional Football. 1973. New York: MacMillan Publishing Co. Inc.

"Notes." 1874. *The Boston Globe,* May 11, 1874, p. 2.

Peterson, Robert W. 1997. *Pigskin: The Early Years of Pro Football*. New York: Oxford University Press.

Plimpton, George. 1961. *Out of My League*. New York: Harper & Row, Publishers.

Plimpton, George. 1966. *Paper Lion*. New York: Harper & Row, Publishers.

Plimpton, George. 2016. *Shadow Box: An Amateur in the Ring*. New York: Little, Brown and Company.

Puscas, George. 1963. "Lions Cry 'Double-Cross,' Seek Appeal of Penalties." *Detroit Free Press*, April 18, 1963, pp. 1-A, 4-A.

Puscas, George. 1987. "'Paper Lion' Gang Still Telling Stories." *Detroit Free Press*, June 30, 1987, pp. 1D, 2D.

Roman, Lawrence. 1968. "Football Pros in 'Paper Lion' Den." *Los Angeles Times*, November 10, 1968, Calendar Section, pp. 16–17.

Rosenfeld, Arnold. 1968. "The Three Little Worlds of Alex Karras." *Detroit: The Magazine of Michigan's Metropolis*, October 13, 1968, pp. 12, 15–18.

Rowley, Christopher. 2015. *The Shared Origins of Football, Rugby, and Soccer*. Lanham, MD: Rowman & Littlefield.

Severo, Richard. 2003. "George Plimpton, Urbane and Witty Writer, Dies at 76." *The New York Times*, September 26, 2003. https://www.nytimes.com/2003/09/26/obituaries/george-plimpton-urbane-and-witty-writer-dies-at-76.html

Smith, Red. 1966. "The Sweaty Literati." *Democrat Chronicle,* November 3, 1966, pp. 1D–2D.

Snyder, Cameron C. 1971. "Five Colt Rookies Impress." *The Sun*, August 24, 1971, pp. C1, C5.

Special to the Constitution. 1967. "Alda to Play the 'Paper Lion.'" *The Atlanta Constitution*, December 30, 1967, p. 4-A.

Sports Illustrated Staff. 2016. "Write Stuff: As Baseball Has Changed So Have the Dreams of Those Who Try to Get Inside It, from Finding Glory on the Field to Calling the Shots from on High." *Sports Illustrated*, May 9, 2016. https://vault.si.com/vault/2016/05/09/write-stuff

Stark, Susan. 1968. "Football Fans Loved It … but." *Detroit Free-Press*, October 4, 1968, p. 6-C.

Strait, Raymond. 1983. *Alan Alda: A Biography*. New York: St. Martin's Press.

Tamte, Roger R. 2018. *Walter Camp and the Creation of American Football*. Urbana: University of Illinois Press.

Tatham, Dave. 1967. "Movie Based on Detroit Lions Book to Be Filmed at Boca's St. Andrews." *The Palm Beach Post-Times*, December 23, 1967, p. 10.

Tatham, Dave. 1968. "No. 0: A Squad of Pro Football Heavies Turn Pro Actors for the Florida Filming of 'The Paper Lion'." *Pensacola News-Journal all Florida*, May 12, 1968, pp. 6–10.

Ulin, David L. 2014. "For April Fools' and Baseball Season: George Plimpton." *Los Angeles Times*, April 1, 2014. https://www.latimes.com/books/jacketcopy/la-et-jc-for-april-fools-baseball-season-george-plimpton-20140401-story.html

United Press International. 1958. "Mantle and Mays Choose Up Sides: Expect All-Star Game to Draw 40,000 Fans." *The Terre Haute Star*, September 9, 1958, p. 8.

United Press International. 1968. "Gordy Suffers Torn Ligament." *The Holland Evening Sentinel*, August 2, 1968, p. 4.

United Press International. 1969. "Gordy Retires from Gridiron War." *The State Journal*, January 16, 1969, p. D-6.

Vincent, Charles. 1973. "'Fun' Gone … Schmidt Quits: Lions Have 6 or 7 Candidates for Coach." *Detroit Free Press*, January 13, 1973, pp. 1-D, 4-D.

Wynn, Jerry. 1964. "Plum Is Ripe! Detroit QB Now Team Player, Hot Passer." *Independent*, September 18, 1964, p. C-1.

Chapter 4

Junior Bonner (1972)

By the early 1970s, Westerns were falling out of favor among studios and moviegoers, and films depicting the contemporary West, while not unheard of (1936's *The Last Outlaw*, 1962's *Lonely are the Brave*, 1963's *Hud*), had never been a Hollywood mainstay. So it came as a surprise when five contemporary rodeo movies—Plateau International's *Squares*, Columbia's *J.W. Coop*, United Artists' *The Honkers*, 20th Century Fox's *When the Legends Die*, and Cinerama Releasing Corporation's *Junior Bonner*—were released in 1972. The last starred Steve McQueen (1930–80) and was directed by Sam Peckinpah (1925–84). McQueen was the highest paid movie star in 1971 with plenty of box-office success—*Bullitt* (1968) grossed more than $42 million—while Peckinpah was riding a wave of success after the extremely violent, controversial, and critically acclaimed *The Wild Bunch* (1969). The producers hoped McQueen and Peckinpah would help drive *Junior Bonner* to critical acclaim and box-office success.

Rodeo cowboy JR "Junior" Bonner (McQueen) returns to his hometown of Prescott, Arizona, to compete in the city's historic annual rodeo over Independence Day weekend, but JR's homecoming is disappointing. Nursing minor injuries sustained in the bull-riding competition from the previous weekend's rodeo, JR is also broke. His parents, Ellie (Ida Lupino) and Ace (Robert Preston), remain separated. His brother, Curly (Joe Don Baker), a wealthy real-estate developer, has sold Ace's ranch, put Ellie's home up for sale, and plans to have Ellie live in the mobile-home park that Curly owns. Ace, a womanizing drifter, has been hospitalized after wrecking his truck.

JR enters several contests in the rodeo, including the wild-cow-milking competition with his dad, and bribes stock contractor Buck Roan (Ben Johnson) to let him ride the bull that injured him in the previous rodeo.

Ace leaves the hospital, borrows (without permission) JR's horse for the rodeo's inaugural parade, and asks his son for money so he can prospect for gold in Australia, only to learn that JR is busted. The family supper at his mother's doesn't go well, either, when JR knocks Curly through a window during an argument about their father.

JR has a rough start at the rodeo. He's bucked off a saddle bronc a second short of a qualifying ride, then scores a quality time in steer wrestling only to lose to a rival's faster time. Ace and JR almost win the wild-cow-milking contest, but Ace trips over his dog—which somehow got into the arena— and spills the milk out of the bottle.

In The Palace Saloon, Curly gets even by knocking JR to the floor. Ace and Ellie are briefly reunited, and JR has a dalliance with Charmagne (Barbara Leigh), another cowboy's date, which leads to a barroom brawl. When the rodeo resumes, however, JR scores 92 points (out of 100) on his rematch with Sunshine—becoming the first cowboy to ride the bull in thirty attempts.

Most of JR's $950 prize money goes to a first-class airline ticket to Australia for his father before JR drives to his next rodeo.

In 1970, Jeb Rosebrook (1935–2018) was vacationing with his family in Phoenix when a friend invited him to attend the Frontier Days and Rodeo in Prescott, roughly a hundred miles northwest. That was something of a homecoming for the struggling screenwriter and novelist. Born in New York City, Rosebrook suffered asthma as a child, so his parents sent him to school at a working cattle ranch in central Arizona when he was nine. The 1970 visit to Prescott revived Rosebrook's career. "It was a return to a world I had known: cowboys, rodeo competition . . . cowboy bars, and Country-Western music," Rosebrook recalled (Rosebrook 2018, 10).

As Rosebrook started developing ideas for a screenplay, his agent called him over Labor Day weekend with news: Actor Robert Redford (1936–) wanted a rodeo story. Rosebrook sent an outline. Redford never responded, but Joe Wizan (1935–2011), a producer at Warner Bros., wanted a screenplay for McQueen. After a meeting, Rosebrook was paid $1,800 to write the script, which, if produced, would earn the writer $50,000. "My dad was writing about himself," said Rosebrook's son, Stuart Rosebrook. "The life of a screenwriter is reflected in Junior's coming back home" (Stuart Rosebrook, interview with author, July 17, 2020).

McQueen liked the script. So did Peckinpah, who was sold on the concept after reading only six pages. Peckinpah's mother was selling his father's ranch to developers, and Rosebrook's premise touched Peckinpah, whose *Ride the High Country* (1962), *The Wild Bunch,* and *The Ballad of Cable Hogue* (1970) also used End-of-the-West themes.

"Prescott was the location in the script, and it all had to be timed perfectly to be in Prescott by the end of June to film the parade live, and then film as much as they could over the Fourth of July rodeo week," Stuart Rosebrook said, adding that putting a major film together that quickly was "highly unusual," but once Wizan had signed Peckinpah and Bonner "it was a matter of script revisions, casting and locations" (Stuart Rosebrook, interview with author, July 3, 2020).

Robert Preston (1918–87), a Tony Award–winning actor for *The Music Man* and *I Do, I Do* and whose last film role had been in 1963, *All the Way Home*, said he "took the role of Ace Bonner because I felt it had overtones of Harold Hill, 'The Music Man'" (Strassberg 1972, N-5). Although Academy Award–winner Susan Hayward (1917–75) was sought, Ida Lupino (1918–95), an actress (1941's *High Sierra*) who moved into directing (1953's *The Hitch-Hiker*), was cast as Ellie. "I hadn't read the script for this picture but my agent said it was a colorful role and that Sam Peckinpah was directing," Lupino said. "That sold me" (Strassberg 1972, N-5).

Joe Don Baker (1936–) and Bill McKinney (1931–2011), graduates of the Actors Studio in New York, were cast as Curly and JR's rodeo rival, Red Terwiliger. Fashion model Barbara Leigh (1946–) was hired to play Charmagne, while Ben Johnson (1918–96) was Peckinpah's only choice for Roan. Johnson, whose performance in *The Last Picture Show* (1971) would win the Oscar for supporting actor, was a former world champion team roper. Two other rodeo champions, bronc rider Casey Tibbs (1929–90) and steer wrestler Ross Dollarhide (1921–77), were hired as rodeo consultants and stuntmen. Lucien Ballard (1908–88), a frequent collaborator with Peckinpah, came in as cinematographer.

Three black bulls were used for Sunshine. The bull in the opening credits in which Junior gets hung up was a Mexican fighting bull. "This bull was special," said Bill Pierce, a rodeo official who plays himself in the movie. "He was a mean S.O.B." (Bill Pierce, interview with author, July 20, 2020). The bull that McQueen sits on in the chute for the Prescott competition was "a tame bull," Pierce recalled. "My 9-year-old daughter actually rode that bull every day" (Bill Pierce, interview with author, July 20, 2020). A stuntman rode a bull from the Prescott rodeo string during the scene depicting Junior's successful rematch with Sunshine.

The eighty-fourth rodeo celebration, held Friday, July 2, through Monday, July 5, drew roughly four hundred competitors. In the parade, Wizan served as one float's announcer, and McQueen surprised spectators when he moved through the crowd and headed for the fictional mobile-home park's float. "The town," Preston said, "was our audience" (Strassberg 1972, N-5).

Sets on a Peckinpah film were seldom congenial. Before filming the parade scene, Peckinpah issued a warning: "An airplane flew most of you over here. F— up and you're on the bus [to home]" (Rosebrook 2018, 93). Lupino threatened to quit after Peckinpah made a caustic remark about her lipstick. Peckinpah didn't think Leigh was a good actress, but she and McQueen became involved romantically, and McQueen, making $850,000 for *Junior Bonner*, wasn't about to let his new girlfriend be replaced. Peckinpah fired several second-unit directors. He also tried to get Rosebrook to quit so

Peckinpah could hire Max Evans (1924–2020), Peckinpah's frequent drinking pal and under-the-table script doctor. Evans, who declined Peckinpah's offer, recalled: "Imagine how Jeb was feeling: here's his chance to get a big film with the biggest movie star in the world, and here's this madman Peckinpah putting people on the bus" (Evans 2014, 177).

Action scenes were filmed during the rounds of competition, known in rodeo as go-rounds. "They then used the arena for all the pickups and close-ups after the crowds were gone," Stuart Rosebrook said (Stuart Rosebrook, interview with author, July 3, 2020).

Despite what Evans called "the usual madness that erupted on all of Sam's pictures" (Evans 2014, 175), production wrapped after eight weeks of filming. McQueen wanted *Junior Bonner* to open slowly in art houses, but *Junior Bonner* premiered in June at Grauman's Chinese Theater in Hollywood as a major release.

Critical reaction was mixed.

In Tucson, Arizona, David Nix of *The Arizona Daily Star* called *Junior Bonner* "Peckinpah's best film to date," noting that the "man-eating violence" depicted in *Straw Dogs* (1971) and *The Wild Bunch* "is supplanted by the bone-rattling roughness of the rodeo—violence, perhaps, but the violence of work, not of destruction" (Nix 1972, 10). But the *Tucson Daily Citizen's* Micheline Keating panned the acting, writing, directing, and pacing. "Maybe people in other parts of the country will relish the riding, roping and roughhouse. But it is not for Arizonans" (Keating 1972, 6).

William Mootz, film critic of *The Courier-Journal* in Louisville, Kentucky, called *Junior Bonner* "a nostalgic, warm-hearted and quite lovely movie about the way we Americans are gradually giving away our sacred right to stand tall and live independently" (Mootz 1972, B26). But the *San Antonio Express's* Tom Nickell declared *Junior Bonner* the "saddest event of the film year," calling it "an odd technical success" in its rodeo scenes but overall "absolutely awful" (Nickell 1972, 12-A).

The movie tanked at the box office. With a budget of $3.2 million, it earned an estimated $2.8 million, for a total loss (including postproduction expenses) of $4 million. *Junior Bonner* died, Jeb Rosebrook said, "with an obituary of losing money" (Rosebrook 2018, 168).

HISTORICAL BACKGROUND

Few eras are wrapped in mythology more than the heyday of the American West's working cowboy. Cattle and horses reached the New World in 1493, Mexico by 1521, and Texas probably by 1541. By the mid-1840s, ranchers were being established in Texas, where cowboys copied the methods and outfits of their Mexican counterparts, *vaqueros*, who herded cattle on the vast haciendas and rancheros. After the Civil War (1861–65), the beef market in the

United States rocketed. Texans began driving cattle to the railheads, mostly in Kansas, and cowboys worked on ranches across the West. The cowboy soon became recognized throughout America and, eventually, the world. Cowboys were "Fearless and intrepid riders," an *Austin State Gazette* correspondent noted, ". . . riding half-broke horses, fiery and vicious" to "naturally become what is commonly called a dare-devil . . ." ("Middle Texas," 1869, 1). Dime novels, pulp magazines, and the 1902 novel *The Virginian* by Owen Wister (1860–1938) helped popularize the image of a dashing, heroic cowboy, while *The Great Train Robbery* (1903) proved so successful, Western-theme motion pictures dominated the industry for decades.

Mythology, likewise, shrouds rodeo's origins. The sport's roots trace to early sixteenth-century New Spain, where ranchers staged *charrería*, an event that included roping, riding, horse breaking, and working with bulls—contests created by Spanish conquistadors. In the West, rodeos began as bragging-rights competition between cowboys, but the first rodeo is difficult to document. Some suggest Santa Fe, New Mexico, in June 1847, but the source—a letter allegedly written by a novelist to a friend, first cited in Clifford P. Westermeier's rodeo history *Man, Beast, Dust: The Story of Rodeo* (1947)—has been debunked. Deer Trail, Colorado, cites a July 4, 1869, gathering in which cowboys competed in various ranching chores. A cowboy competition was held in Pecos, Texas, on July 4, 1883. In August 1884, cowboys gathered near Payson, Arizona, to compete in ranch-related contests. Prescott, Arizona, charged admission for a cowboy tournament in July 1888. All claim "firsts."

But Austin, Texas, reportedly held a steer-roping contest, then known as "steer busting," in 1882, with the winner receiving a $300 saddle. Plus a cowboy tournament was held on June 9, 1888, in Williamson Valley near Prescott, roughly a month before Prescott's first rodeo. And cowboys were showing off their skills in the popular exhibitions of William F. "Buffalo Bill" Cody (1846–1917) and other Wild West shows in the late 1800s. "An exact date of the first exhibition of the daily work and, later, of the sport of the cowboy cannot be given," Westermeir wrote. "If such an attempt were made, it would bring forth vehement and justified protests from the various parts of the West" (Westermeier 1948, 30).

Even the first use of *rodeo* for these competitions is disputed. In the 1800s Southwest, *rodeo* meant the roundup in which cowboys gathered calves for branding. Since these roundups usually included dances, festivals, and competitions, cowboy tournaments eventually adapted the name *rodeo*. Many historians say Prescott first used *rodeo* for its cowboy tournament in 1924, but newspaper accounts show some journalists were calling Prescott's event a rodeo at least three years earlier. Likewise, historians often cite the earliest use of *rodeo* in any cowboy competition as 1916, but Los Angeles staged an event called simply "The Rodeo" in 1913, while the year before, the "Great Southwestern Interstate Cowboy Contests" (Advertisement 1912,

2) at nearby Santa Anita was commonly called a rodeo. On February 9, 1913, The Rodeo—advertising four hundred contestants and five hundred head of stock—opened (a day late because of rain) at Los Angeles Stadium. That first day's competition drew a standing-room-only crowd of twenty-five thousand. General admission tickets cost 50 cents. Events included a quarter-mile horse race, cattle-cutting competition, an 18-mile cowgirl relay race, and a fancy/trick-roping performance. A $10 prize was offered to any rider who could stay on a bull named Black Sharkey for 10 seconds. "One cowboy stayed on for two seconds and there were no other entries" (Waddell 1913a, 2). Men's bucking and a men's relay race were also held. The Rodeo "was surely a success financially if not otherwise" ("Big Financial Success" 1913, 7).

Cheyenne, Wyoming, held its first Frontier Days rodeo in 1897. Pendleton, Oregon, put on its inaugural Round-Up in 1910. The Stampede in Calgary, Alberta, debuted in 1912. The Southwestern Exposition and Livestock Show, held in Fort Worth, Texas, since 1886, introduced a rodeo at North Side Coliseum in 1918, believed to be the world's first indoor rodeo.

At the beginning, rodeos were organized loosely, if at all, but in 1929, rodeo committees, stock contractors, and sponsors formed the Rodeo Association of America (RAA), dividing North America into fifteen districts with national headquarters in Salinas, California. Although promoter Van "Tex" Austin (1885–1938) began a string of "World's Championship" rodeos at New York City's Madison Square Garden in 1922 and in Chicago in 1925, the RAA eventually developed a points system to determine world champions in sanctioned events: saddle-bronc riding, bull/steer riding, calf roping, steer roping, steer decorating, steer wrestling, team roping, and wild-cow milking.

In 1921, rodeo competitors discussed organizing to lobby for better compensation, rules, and government, but not until 1936 did several competitors, demanding more prize money and better judges, walk out of the Madison Square Garden rodeo and boycott the next rodeo in Boston. Colonel W.T. Johnson (1875–1943), a top rodeo promoter, gave in to the strikers, who, because they took so long before they stuck their necks out, called themselves the Cowboys' Turtle Association. That led to the formation of the Rodeo Cowboys Association in 1945 and the Professional Rodeo Cowboys Association (PRCA) thirty years later.

The National Finals Rodeo, the championship tournament for PRCA cowboys, began in Dallas in 1959, moved to Los Angeles in 1962, to Oklahoma City in 1965, and has been held in Las Vegas, Nevada, since 1985.

Sanctioned events changed over the years, but their roots came from Western ranching.

Saddle-bronc riding, "the cornerstone of rodeo" (Groves 2006, 71), dates to when ranch hands had to train—often called "break" or "gentle"—a wild horse until it accepted saddle, bridle, and rider. Bareback riding, considered rodeo's toughest event, was first introduced at the Calgary Stampede in 1912 and didn't become a regular feature in rodeo until the 1930s. The PRCA recognizes Smoky Snyder (1908–65) in 1932 as the first bareback world champion; other event champions date to 1929.

Bull or steer riding, which started in rodeos as exhibition events, finds its roots on Mexico haciendas as on offshoot of bullfighting called *jaripeo* in which a contestant rode the bull to death. Cowboys, legend has it, rode bulls or steers on dares or bets. Bull riding started as an official event in Prescott in 1925. Brahma bulls, "Hump-backed, floppy-eared, pointy-horned, and exceptionally strong" (Nance 2020, 145), became the prominent breed used. In 1935, brothers Earl Bascom (1906–96) and Weldon Bascom (1912–93), called the "Fathers of Brahma Bull Riding," first used the breed in a rodeo in Columbia, Mississippi.

Bull riding, considered rodeo's most dangerous event, grew so popular that in 1992, twenty PRCA bull riders formed Professional Bull Riders, Inc., as a separate sanctioned competition. The PRCA still sanctions bull riding.

Saddle-bronc, bareback, and bull riding are roughstock events. Contestants must ride for eight seconds, holding on with just one hand; two judges can award up to 25 points for each rider and animal for a total of 100 points. Only one rider, Wade Leslie, has ever scored perfection in PRCA competition, recording a 100-point ride on a bull named Wolfman in Central Point, Oregon, in 1991. Two saddle-bronc riders have scored 95 points; four bareback riders have reached 94 points.

In early competitions, cowboys used spurs and quirts to encourage bucking. Today, spurs are blunt—sharp spurs are grounds for disqualification—and, contrary to myth, fleece- or neoprene-lined flank straps are not tied to a bull's or horse's testicles to make the animal mad.

> Instead of painful spur-and-quirt bucking, or cowboys spurring and waving their hats to frighten and disorient a horse, the flank rope encouraged horses to kick back and up since it triggered the sensation of being attacked by a predator on the haunches. Certainly less bloody or visually violent to spectators, the flank rope was perhaps just masking or sanitizing a horse's experience for audiences since the use of it did not require a rider to whip a horse harshly to draw blood on his hide to extract the necessary behavior. For several decades, flank ropes were just that: ropes or bare leather straps. It would be some years before people began applying a wide, leather flank strap with a wool [fleece] sheath that eliminated the skin abrasions that bare flank ropes caused as horses bucked and kicked. (Nance 2020, 91)

Other events are timed. In steer wrestling, a cowboy leaps off a horse—running almost 30 miles per hour—and wrestles a steer to the ground. The event, originally known as bulldogging, was invented by African American cowboy Bill Pickett (1870–1932) in the 1800s. Having seen dogs bring down cattle by biting the animals' lower lips, Pickett did the same and began giving bulldogging exhibitions in 1888. Today's rodeo cowboys just grab steers by the horns and usually keep their mouths closed.

In team roping, two mounted cowboys rope a running steer. The header ropes the steer around the horns; the heeler lassos the hind legs. Once the header turns his horse around to face the heeler, the clock stops. "Cowboys learned that treating or branding these large, strong steers was too difficult—impossible most of the time—for one man alone. Therefore, they developed the system of team roping" (Groves 2006, 103).

In tie-down roping, formerly called calf roping, a galloping contestant ropes a running calf, and, as the horse slides to stop, secures the end of the lariat to the saddle horn, dismounts, races to the calf, throws it to the ground, and ties any three of the calf's legs with a short roped called a "piggin' string." Once the cowboy signals, the clock stops, but the contestant has to remount the horse and ride forward, causing the rope to slacken. The calf must remain tied for six seconds before the recorded time becomes official.

Rodeos became targets of animal-rights activists. Steer busting was banned in many states in the early 1900s. A court-ordered injunction prevented twelve officers of the Society for Prevention of Cruelty to Animals from interfering with the calf-roping competition at the 1922 Madison Square Garden rodeo. "Although the calves sometimes went down with a bump," the *New York Times* noted, "they did not seem to mind any more than a football player when tackled successfully" ("Cowboys Do Tricks in Rodeo at Garden" 1922, 20).

Rodeos remain targets of groups including the American Society for the Prevention of Cruelty to Animals (ASPCA), Animal Legal Defense Fund (ALDF), and People for the Ethical Treatment of Animals (PETA). The PRCA, which sanctions roughly six hundred rodeos in the United States and Canada (of an estimated ten thousand annual rodeos), implemented rules to protect rodeo animals in 1947. A PRCA study in 2015 reported that a survey of more than sixty thousand animal exposures in 218 rodeo performances and slack (overflow competitions done before and after the main rodeo) resulted in twenty-eight injuries, an injury rate of 0.00046 percent, compared with injury rates of 1–3 percent for animals hurt on farms and ranches. Animal-rights groups dispute those findings, but cowboys are far more likely to be injured than animals. One study said 11 percent of all contesting cowboys were likely to be injured.

Rodeo has always been dangerous. Saddle-bronc rider Pete Knight (1903–37), bronc-riding champion of 1932, 1933, 1935, and 1936, died after being thrown and trampled at a rodeo in Hayward, California. Lane Frost (1963–89) was gored by a bull and killed during the Cheyenne Frontier Days rodeo; Frost became the subject of a 1994 movie, *8 Seconds*. Bull rider Brent Thurman (1969–94) died after a head injury sustained at the National Finals Rodeo. Said bull rider Sean Willingham (1981–): "Football players are tough too, but their sport is nowhere close to what we have to

---

NOT JUST CLOWNING AROUND

When the rodeo announcer in *Junior Bonner* says, "The safety of our cowboys may very well depend on the daring of our rodeo clowns," he's not joking. "These guys are something else," Bill Pierce said (Bill Pierce, interview with author, July 7, 2020).

A typical rodeo employs a barrel man and two bullfighters. The barrel man often doubles as comic relief between events, but the main job for all three is to distract bulls and protect the cowboys.

"If it comes time when you have to offer your body to keep a bull rider from getting hit," bullfighter Loyd Ketchum (1961–) said, "you've got to do it" (Boggs 1996, 6). That's what Ketchum did in September 2009 at a rodeo in Ellensburg, Washington. Protecting a bull rider in trouble, Ketchum was tossed by the bull. "I flew about 15, 20 feet in the air," he said. "I thought I was going to make the landing, but my momentum carried me over. I knew my back was broken. I thought I'd never walk again" (Kusek 2010). Ketchum, whose bullfighting career began in 1987, recovered and continued in rodeo until retiring in 2014.

"It's a contact sport," bullfighter Ronny Sparks (1964–) said (Boggs 1996, 6).

Sources

Boggs, Johnny D. 1996. "Clowning Around At the Rodeo." *Boys' Life*, April 1996, p. 6.
Kusec, Joe. 2010. "Joe Kusec: Broken Back Can't Slow Ketchum." *Billings Gazette*, December 22, 2010. https://billingsgazette.com/sports/rodeo/joe-kusek-broken-back-cant-slow-ket chum/article_ac60acff-b515-5262-bd6b-30285cb50007.html
Westermeier, Clifford P. 1948. *Man, Beast, Dust: The Story of Rodeo*. Denver, CO: World Press.

---

deal with every day. Of course, they get hit by 300-pound men. We're getting hit by a 1,500-pound bull" (McKinney 2018).

Not until the early 1990s did protective vests and helmets become common safety equipment for rodeo competitors. Professional Bull Riders requires protective vests be worn by all competitors and helmets for athletes born on or after October 15, 1994. The PRCA has no requirements for adult contestants. "It's just a cowboy thing," said Ty Murray (1969–), a seven-time PRCA all-around cowboy champion (Branch 2009).

Today's rodeos usually include barrel racing, a timed event for women that started in 1948, in which riders race around three barrels in a cloverleaf pattern. But many women competed in roughstock events into the early twentieth century. In a bucking contest during The Rodeo in 1913 in Los Angeles, "Prairie Rose" Henderson "rode the wild animal clear across the arena, over the fence and half way around the track, where he was roped and she dismounted amid the cheers of the thousands" (Waddell 1913a, 2). Historian Melody Groves said: "Although managed by men, rodeo allowed more and more women to compete. At the 1903 Cheyenne Frontier Days rodeo, women rode professionally for the first time, but instead of labeled as 'competitors,' they were called 'sweethearts' or 'queens' of rodeo. They gained momentum in this sport until 1929, when a female bronc rider was killed in the arena. The world gasped and traditional gender roles were reapplied. Men decided a woman's place in rodeo was to be as a smiling, waving rodeo queen, not on the back of an untamed animal" (Melody Groves, interview with author, June 27, 2020).

The Girls Rodeo Association, formed in 1948 and renamed the Women's Professional Rodeo Association in 1981, has more than three thousand members today competing in barrel racing, team roping, tie-down roping, and breakaway roping (a calf-roping variation).

Cleo Hearn (1939–), the first African American to attend college (Langston University) on a rodeo scholarship, turned professional in 1959 and in 1970 became the first African American cowboy to win a calf-roping event at a major rodeo. Hearn started producing rodeos for African Americans in 1971, and his Cowboys of Color showcases more than two hundred cowboys and cowgirls of diverse racial backgrounds in rodeos today. The Bill Pickett Invitational Rodeo started in Denver in 1984 and has grown into a multicity series of rodeos that celebrates the legacy of African American cowboys and cowgirls.

Rodeos became team sports for many high schools and colleges. Inmates began competing in prison rodeos open to the public, including maximum-security facilities in Huntsville, Texas (1931–86); McAlester, Oklahoma (1940–2010); and Angola, Louisiana (1965–).

Rodeo cowboys became celebrities. Casey Tibbs made the cover of *Life* magazine in 1951. Larry Mahan (1943–) made the cover of *Sports Illustrated* in 1973. Rodeo also became a big business. Total payoff for contestants competing in the 2019 National Finals Rodeo was $10 million. Jess Lockwood (1997–) won $1,391,500 for winning the Professional Bull Riders world championship in 2019.

"When I was a kid, folks told you if you wanted to make some money, you needed to become a professional person, a doctor or lawyer or somethin'," said Jim Shoulders (1928–2007), pro rodeo's all-around champion in 1949, 1956, 1957, 1958, and 1959. "Now, they say get into sports. I never heard of a doctor gettin' out of medical school and signin' a multimillion-dollar contract. I thought I was rich if I won a $40 go-round" (Boggs 2005, 36).

DEPICTION AND CULTURAL CONTEXT

There's a common flaw in most rodeo movies, according to Mahan, pro rodeo's all-around cowboy from 1966–1970 and 1973. "Hollywood had to put a twist on the storyline," he said (Boggs 2002, 95). A lot of films had good rodeo footage, Mahan said, but few captured the essence of the sport. *Junior Bonner* came close. As film critic Tom Nickell pointed out:

"Peckinpah's rodeo footage is watchable work for what it is—and honest rodeo film for a change!" (Nickell 1972, 12-A).

That's evident in the opening in which Junior gets hung up on Sunshine, a scene filmed at night after Prescott's rodeo had ended. Local bull rider Chucky Olson, who was paid $500 to ride the Mexican fighting bull, used a "suicide wrap" in which the rope the cowboy grips is wrapped around the rider's pinky finger. Olson was dating Bill Pierce's oldest daughter at the time. Pierce, who played one of the rodeo clowns in the scene, recalled:

> They told Chucky to ride maybe six-seven seconds and then just buck off. Well, when the bull actually bucked him off you can see him swinging out there. If you look close you can see two clowns and a third clown with a straw hat on—and that's me—going in there trying to get him unhooked because I would have a crying daughter the rest of my life if he got hurt real bad or whatever. So we got him off. But during the time we were getting him off, Sam was yelling, "Keep rolling, keep rolling, keep rolling" to Lucien Ballard. I don't know what I could have done. The real guys got over there. I was yelling at him, "Let go, let go, let go." Then he fell off, and we both ran. That is how that scene came about, and they did it with one take because it was some kind of ride. (Bill Pierce, interview with author, July 7, 2020)

It might not have been scripted, Jeb Rosebrook wrote, "But it made for damned good film" (Rosebrook 2018, 90).

A hung-up bull rider is frightening for competitors and spectators. Usually, a cowboy is freed in a few seconds. Being tossed about like a rag doll for 10 seconds is rare, but in the 1990 National Finals Rodeo, Richard "Tuff" Hedeman (1963–), a three-time PRCA bull-riding champion and the 1995 Professional Bull Riders world champion, got hung up on a Mexican fighting bull named Stinger for 58 seconds. The *New York Times* described the scene:

> Suddenly Tuff was skimming parallel to the ground, stemmed to the beast by his left arm, orbiting like a carny airplane ride. The nonpareil rodeo bull fighter, Rob Smets, whose task is to divert bulls from fallen riders, took Stinger on horns-first, and ricocheted like a duckpin. A dozen off-duty bullfighters streamed out of their seats, led by Tuff's older brother, Roach, who flung himself across the bull's back to reach the snagged handhold.
>
> "I was settin' with my folks in the stands," recalled Tuff's wife, Tracy, "and I've never had that feeling before. Everybody was going wild, and I was just watchin' it, in a zone."
>
> After 30 seconds of chaos, Tuff managed to gain his footing without getting tromped on. "It was like runnin' through a war zone," he'd say later, in his thick Texas twang. (Coplon 1992, 36)

Hedeman made qualifying rides on his next three bulls in the finals.

In the Prescott rodeo scene where the bronc rears in the chute after Junior mounts him, McQueen wasn't acting. "The look on Steve's face says it all," Rosebrook remembered. "It certainly wasn't in the script" (Rose-brook 2018, 113). C.E. "Chuck" Sheppard (1916–2005), manager of the nearby K4 Ranch and a world-champion team roper inducted into the Pro Rodeo Hall of Fame in 2000, owned that horse. Sheppard had turned the former bucking horse into a working horse that he used as one of the pickup horses during the Prescott rodeo. "He was as gentle as he could be," Pierce said, "but he remembered spurs" (Bill Pierce, interview with author, July 7, 2020). McQueen accidentally spurred the horse, which reared. "Steve said, 'He scared me to death'," Pierce recalled (Bill Pierce, interview with author, July 7, 2020).

Those unscripted scenes fit perfectly in a rodeo movie because, as Mahan said, "the main thing I like about rodeo is that it's so unpredictable" (Van Steenwyck 1977, 45).

Junior treats his own injuries in the movie, often the case for rodeo cowboys. "In my day," Shoulders said, "you was on your own. There were a few major rodeos that would have a first-aid thing, but as far as a crisis fund or anything like that to kinda help you out . . . well, it was like if you asked me what the retirement fund was when I quit rodeoin'. I'd say it was whatever you had in your a— pocket" (Boggs 2005, 36).

"I really consider myself fortunate because of the amount of riding I did," Mahan said. "I probably went to 1,200 rodeos and got on 6,000 head of stock between the bucking horses and bulls, and I might have had a half-dozen injuries that kept me out of the game a while. Broke my jaw the year before I turned pro, and all that did was shut me up for a while. Broke my leg pretty good one time, then pulled a bicep loose, which kept me out for a while. And then just a few aches and pains. Broke a few ribs on different occasions. And broke my foot. But hey—don't know how many times I've had my heart broken" (Boggs 2002, 95).

Today's rodeo competitors often hire professional trainers, and medical services are provided at all rodeos. In 1989, the PRCA, Justin Boot Company, and the Women's Professional Rodeo Association formed the Justin Cowboy Crisis Fund to offer financial assistance for competitors who sustained catastrophic injuries. Good Samaritans have also helped injured rodeo cowboys. In 1998, after stock-car driver Bobby Labonte (1964–) won NASCAR's Busch Grand National race in Darlington, South Carolina, he donated his $26,875 purse to twenty-five-year-old Jerome Davis (1972–), a bull rider who was paralyzed from the chest down after a bull threw him headfirst into the ground, breaking his neck, in a Professional Bull Riders event in Fort Worth, Texas.

The movie also highlights a main difference between rodeo competitors and many other professional athletes. Junior is so broke, he is forced to sleep in a bedroll instead of a hotel on the way to Prescott.

"You only get paid if you win," said Pete Hawkins (1974–), who qualified for six National Finals Rodeos during his career. "You don't have a

$17 million contract and a Benz and a Bentley parked in the garage" (Boggs 2005, 36).

Traveling from rodeo to rodeo is one of the biggest expenses for professional cowboys, then and now. Logging as many as 100,000 miles a year is not atypical, and in a sport in which paychecks aren't guaranteed, many cowboys travel together to cut down on expenses—especially for competitors who travel with their own horses—by sharing motel rooms and splitting travel expenses.

"We have to travel up and down the road, put fuel in the truck, pay for feed for horses, food for ourselves," steer wrestler Luke Branquinho (1980–) said. "There's a lot of expense behind the curtain that nobody sees. I think one year I had a $230,000 year, but I spent at least half that getting up and down the road. If we could go to less rodeos and win more money, it cuts your expenses down and have more money in the bank" (Harkins 2010).

On the other hand, Mahan decided early in his career that he needed to travel faster to make the best-paying rodeos. He took flying lessons and eventually bought a two-seat Cessna 120 so he could fly from city to city.

Most cowboys drive pickup trucks, but Junior pulls his horse trailer in a Cadillac convertible. That wasn't usual, Pierce said, but: "I did with my kids. I had a 1966 Cadillac Limited convertible. I put a hitch on it, painted the horse trailer the same color, and we went to rodeos that way even though I had a pickup in the garage" (Bill Pierce, interview with author, July 7, 2020).

The key element in the film's plot is when Junior asks Roan, the stock contractor, to rig the bull-riding draw to set up the rematch on the unridden bull. A fix? In rodeo? Say it ain't so! As syndicated sports columnist Red Smith wrote in 1963: "A realist viewing the sports field would conclude that if there is any branch of athletic competition where there are no short cuts, it has to be rodeo. You can't bribe a bucking horse or bull, and if you could dope him, what would it get you? Slip him a fast pill and he'd pitch you into the mezzanine; slow him down and you'd get no score riding him. The only possible place to cheat is in the draw for livestock" (Smith 1963, 12).

That's what happened at a Memphis, Tennessee, rodeo in September 1963. Rodeo secretary R.C. "Judge" Tolbirt (1913–84) held out a top bucking horse at a rodeo for bareback rider Paul Mayo (1942–) in the draw. At the time, Mayo led the world standings in bareback riding with $16,829 in winnings. The plan might have worked, but two rodeo judges remembered that neither horse's nor rider's name had been called during the draw and reported the incident to the Rodeo Cowboys Association. Mayo denied knowledge of the fix, but Tolbirt admitted to his part and said Mayo instigated the plot, which RCA president Dale Smith (1928–2017) called "a low blow to all of us" (RCA Suspends Bronc Rider For Cheating 1963, 2). The Rodeo Cowboys Association suspended and fined both men $500, who were reinstated eight months later. The RCA board of directors, Smith said, did not want "to hand out life suspensions for a first mistake" (UPI 1964, 19).

Tolbirt resigned in 1965, but Mayo continued competing and was inducted into the Pro Rodeo Hall of Fame in 2010.

In the movie, Junior tells Roan that most cowboys would pay the stock contractor not to draw Sunshine. But Red Smith, one of the best-known newspaper columnists of the time, offered another perspective: "You see, a rodeo cowboy who cheats isn't just clipping a bookmaker or stealing from some faceless monolith like an insurance company. He's jobbing his own guys, and there's no other sport or business where friendship is deeper than in rodeo. Cowboys compete against one another for prize money, their only income. When a good horse is held out for one cowboy, it can cost his roommate a chance for a pay day on that horse" (Smith 1963, 12).

Pierce said the chance of such a fix was "none" because stock contractors have "too much at stake, if they're a successful stock contractor" (Bill Pierce, interview with author, July 7, 2020). On the other hand, Pierce said, a cowboy might honestly get a reride. "It could happen sometimes," Pierce said. "A guy comes to the next rodeo and he draws the same bull. What are the percentages? Who knows?" (Bill Pierce, interview with author, July 7, 2020).

Jeb Rosebrook, however, opted to include the fix for dramatic effect. Rodeo historian Kristine Fredriksson said the 1963 incident was "One of the very few scandals, if not the only one, that have ever shaken the sport" (Fredriksson 1993, 113). Mayo won Prescott's 1970 bareback riding event with a 69-point ride, but whether Rosebrook knew about the 1963 incident is unknown. History, however, was on Rosebrook's side. No one can say such cheating never happened in pro rodeo.

On the other hand, Junior offered Roan half the prize money if Junior rides Sunshine. Had Roan collected, Junior wouldn't have enough money to buy his dad an airline ticket to Australia. Roan tells Junior that he is traveling back to Wyoming after the Prescott rodeo to rest his stock rather than provide animals for the Salinas rodeo. Roan obviously knows the value of his animals. Harry Vold (1924–2017), a noted stock contractor from Avondale, Colorado, said: "Rodeo is an investment" (ProRodeo Livestock, 12). Rodeo bulls can sell for $60,000, and bucking horses for more than $80,000, making a rigged draw for one cowboy far less likely to happen today.

Sunshine, in fact, is one of the stars at the Prescott rodeo, and it wasn't—and still isn't—uncommon for bucking stock to become rodeo stars in their own right. In the Los Angeles rodeo of 1913, a bucking horse named Cyclone got much attention during the rodeo's ten-day run, and was finally ridden by Art Acord to a standstill on the last day. As the crowd cheered, "The conquerer [sic] sat quietly on the trembling conquered and waved his broad-brimmed hat" (Waddell 1913b, 2)—much like the ovation Junior gets after riding Sunshine before his hometown crowd.

The legend of Steamboat, a famous bucking horse from 1900–14, endures today. A 1903 photo of the horse, with that year's world champion cowboy (Guy Holt) riding him in Laramie, Wyoming, was used to design the

University of Wyoming Cowboy bucking horse logo in 1921, and Steamboat is believed to have been used as the model for the image used on Wyoming's state license plate. Added Wyoming historian Candy Moulton, author of *Steamboat, Legendary Bucking Horse: His Life and Times, and the Cowboys Who Tried to Tame Him:*

> For over a dozen years, the great bucking horse Steamboat thrilled crowds at early rodeos including Cheyenne Frontier Days and the Denver Festival of Mountain and Plain. This horse, born and bred on the Two Bar Ranch in eastern Wyoming, also became the star animal in the Irwin Brothers Wild West Show and appeared all across the continent from Cheyenne to the Pendleton Roundup in Oregon, Madison Square Garden in New York City, and the Calgary Stampede. A lot of cowboys tried to ride him; only a very few succeeded. In those days a cowboy had to stay on until the horse came to a standstill. . . . Steamboat was well known and widely respected as an equine athlete, so famous that upon his death an obituary for the horse was written and published in the *Cheyenne Daily Leader*, October 14, 1915. (Candy Moulton, interview with author, July 19, 2020)

Junior Bonner's wild-cow-milking scene is accurate, too. From 1936 to 1981, Prescott offered wild-cow milking, not a sanctioned event but generally a favorite among spectators. Other rodeos still include the event, which is sanctioned by the Working Ranch Cowboy Association, founded in 1995 to showcase ranch cowboys at work in ranch-related activities such as team branding, team penning, and team doctoring.

Junior Bonner also accurately depicts another common event in rodeo: the parade. Prescott held its first Independence Day parade in 1864, and rodeo contestants were reportedly required to ride in the parade, or be disqualified, from 1888 to around 1950. Prescott's rodeo parade, though canceled in 2020 because of the COVID-19 pandemic, is one of the oldest in Arizona, and the July 4 holiday has always been popular for rodeos—so much that the PRCA calls the Independence Day run "Cowboy Christmas." Twenty-seven PRCA rodeos were held on June 30–July 9, 2019, while the following year, despite forced cancellations because of the coronavirus pandemic, fourteen rodeos were staged between June 29 and July 6, including Prescott's "World's Oldest Rodeo."

The parade attracts thousands, and in 1971—when *Junior Bonner* was filmed—the 70-minute parade attracted a record crowd estimated at thirty thousand. Tibbs served as grand marshal, riding horseback despite being injured during the previous night's rodeo.

Yet *Junior Bonner* accurately depicted more than just rodeo events and the rodeo parade. The Palace Saloon "was depicted exactly as it was," Pierce said (Bill Pierce, interview with author, July 7, 2020).

The original saloon opened in 1877 on what became known as "Whiskey Row." Founded in 1864, Prescott was Arizona's first territorial capital

(1864–66) and again from late 1877 until 1887, when the capital moved to Phoenix. By the late 1800s, reportedly forty saloons could be found on "Whiskey Row." In 1898, a traveler recalled these observations from a trip down Whiskey Row two years earlier:

> Of the ten saloons, several had a sort of continuous show bulletined to fit. For instance, in one resort, at 8:45, Miss Lizzie would sing the latest songs; at the next place at 9:00 Professor Rubberneck was booked for a contortion act; 9:15 was set in the next saloon for the appearance of the Stein sisters in their novelties and at the fourth Madamoiselle Sangalle was down on the bill for an operatic selection. The programmes were evidently arranged so that the crowds might rotate from one saloon to the other in their desire to get the worth of their money. Beyond was a neat looking place where, with a friend, I called and found only the barkeeper in attendance. Drinks were called for and passed out. I passed in a dollar and the barkeeper dropped it out of sight, totally oblivious of the fact that change was forthcoming. Prescott is a great town, ain't it? ("Passing Thoughts" 1898, 2)

On July 14, 1900, a fire started in a Prescott hotel and burned much of downtown. Several men pulled the 24-foot-long bar of carved oak out of The Palace, which was destroyed. By 1901, much of Whiskey Row—including The Palace—was back in business, with stone and brick buildings going up for better fire protection.

The Palace and Whiskey Row remain popular during rodeo week, as they were during the 1971 rodeo.

"It's a state highway, so you can't shut it down," Pierce said. "But the mayor was a friend of mine and he put two backhoes, one on each end of the row, and said we're having water problems. We set up two bandstands across the street, brought beer out and had street dances" (Bill Pierce, interview with author, July 7, 2020). Herbert "Shell" Dunbar (1898–1977), who owned The Palace, is one of the men playing poker with Roan in the saloon's back room in *Junior Bonner*.

Junior Bonner ends with Junior driving to another rodeo. He might be old, but viewers know he'll keep on rodeoing as long as he can. "When I can't reach down and pull up a bunch of want-to out of myself," Mahan said, "I'll know it's time to quit" (Fredriksson 1993, 118).

Or as Shoulders put it: "That's why I quit rodeoin'. I couldn't beat nobody and the ground got too hard" (Boggs 2005, 38).

CONCLUSION

Junior Bonner was doomed by timing. It was released after three other 1972 rodeo movies: *J. W. Coop* and *Squares* (January) and *The Honkers*

(March); *When the Legends Die* hit theaters in August. More importantly, moviegoers expected action and violence in films starring McQueen, whose previous, nonviolent movies in which he starred, *The Reivers* (1969) and *Le Mans* (1971), also performed poorly. After *The Wild Bunch* and *Straw Dogs* (1971), audiences especially expected bloodshed in a Peckinpah film. "I made a film where nobody got shot," Peckinpah said of *Junior Bonner,* "and nobody went to see it" (Eliot 2011, 265).

Hollywood wasn't done with rodeo. In 1974, *The Great American Cowboy*, which focused on the 1973 rodeo competition between Phil Lyne (1947–) and Mahan for the all-around cowboy title, hit theaters and won the Academy Award for best documentary. Meanwhile, *Junior Bonner* wasn't forgotten. McQueen called it his favorite movie, and others agree. Its quiet look at family dynamics and a changing West strikes a chord, while its depiction of a rodeo rings true. *Junior Bonner* might have been underappreciated in 1972, but today it is usually ranked among Peckinpah's best films, often just behind *The Wild Bunch* and *Ride the High Country.*

"*Junior Bonner* is the best rodeo film that's ever been made," Max Evans said. "It was the best script Sam ever got his hands on" (Rosebrook 2018, 104).

FURTHER READING

Advertisement. 1912. *Los Angeles Times*, March 5, 1912, Section III, p. 2.

Applebome, Peter. 1989. "Wrangling Over Where Rodeo Began." *The New York Times*, June 18, 1989, Section 5, p. 45.

Bernstein, Joel H. 2007. *Wild Ride: The History and Lore of Rodeo*. Salt Lake City, UT: Gibbs Smith, Publisher.

"Big Financial Success." 1913. *The Redondo Reflex*, February 21, 1913, p. 7.

Boggs, Johnny D. 1998. "Busch Driver Dedicates Purse to Hurt Bull Rider." *Fort Worth Star-Telegram*, March 22, 1998, Section C, p. 10.

Boggs, Johnny D. 2002. "Telling It Like It Is … Larry Mahan." *Santa Fean*, January–February 2002, pp. 94–96.

Boggs, Johnny D. 2005. "More Bucks and Other Changes: Comparing Pro Rodeo Today with the 1950s Version." *True West*, July 2005, pp. 36–38.

Boggs, Johnny D. 2016. "Bulls, Buckles and Prison Bars at 'the Wildest Show in the South.'" *Roundup Magazine*, August 2016, pp. 9–10.

Branch, John. 2009. "Bull Riders Start Trading Hats for Helmets." *The New York Times*, January 9, 2009. https://www.nytimes.com/2009/01/10/sports/othersports/10helmets.html

Camp, Ray. 1944. "Cowboy Turtle Association Is an Odd Name, but There's a Reason, Riders Say. 'Fort Worth Star-Telegram'." March 14, 1944, p. 7.

Coplon, Jeff. 1992. "Riding Ugly: World Bull-Riding Champion Richard (Tuff) Hedeman Is Philosophical about the Manic Pas De Deu He Must Perform Night Andfter Night with a Partner from Hell. Sometimes You Get the Bull, and Sometimes the Pull Gets You." *New York Times Magazine*, April 12, 1992, pp. 34–36, 53, 56–58, 61.

"Cowboys Do Tricks in Rodeo at Garden: Fancy Riding, Calf Roping and Wrestling with Steers Thrill Spectators. Wild Horse Race a Draw: Courts Enjoin S.P.C.A. from Interfering with Part of the Program." *The New York Times*, November 5, 1922, p. 20.

Craven, Scott. 2018. "Whiskey Row in Prescott: Arizona's Most Legendary Block." *The Arizona Republic*, February 22, 2018. https://www.azcentral.com/story/travel /arizona/2018/01/08/whiskey-row-prescott-arizona-historic-block/949759001/

Dary, David. 1982. *Cowboy Culture: A Saga of Five Centuries*. New York: Avon Books.

Eliot, Marc. 2011. *Steve McQueen: A Biography*. New York: Crown Archetype.

Evans, Max as told to Robert Nott. 2014. *Goin' Crazy with Sam Peckinpah and All Our Friends*. Albuquerque: University of New Mexico Press.

"400 Contestants: Prescott Rodeo Starts Tomorrow." 1971. *The Arizona Republic*, July 1, 1971, p. 16-B.

Fredriksson, Kristine. 1993. *American Rodeo: From Buffalo Bill to Big Business*. College Station: Texas A&M University Press.

Freeman, Danny. 1988. *World's Oldest Rodeo*. Prescott, AZ: Prescott Frontier Days, Inc.

Fuhrman, John. 1971. "A Million Dollar Boom for Prescott." *The Arizona Republic*, August 8, 1971, p. N-1.

Groves, Melody. 2006. *Ropes, Reins, and Rawhide: All about Rodeo*. Albuquerque: University of New Mexico Press.

Harkins, Bob. 2010. "A Tough Life, but One a Cowboy Can't Resist: Rodeo World Filled with Injury and Hardship, but also with Love of the Sport." MSNBC.com, December 10, 2010.

"History of Rodeo." n.d. Professional Rodeo Cowboys Association. https://www .prorodeo.com/prorodeo/rodeo/history-of-the-prca

Hoffman, Brett. 1990. "Murray Branding His Name among Best." *Fort Worth Star-Telegram,* December 10, 1990, Section 3, p. 7.

Hoffman, Brett. 1998. "Former Champion Bull Rider Paralyzed, not Expected to Walk." *Fort Worth Star-Telegram*, March 17, 1998, Section D, p. 4.

Keating, Michelene. 1972. "A Keating Review: 'Junior Bonner' a Movie, but Mostly in Slow Motion." *Tucson Daily Citizen*, July 29, 1972, p. 6.

LeCompte, Mary Lou. 1982. "Notes, Documents, and Queries: The First American Rodeo Never Happened." *Journal of Sport History*, 9, no. 2 (Summer): 89–96.

Lewis, Tricia. 2020. "History Lives Here." *Prescott Living Magazine*, June 16, 2020. https://prescottlivingmag.com/history-lives-here/

McKinney, Kelsey. 2018. "As Sports Become Safer, Bull Riding Doubles Down on Danger: Inside One of the Most Stubbornly Dangerous Sports in the World." *Gen*, December 13, 2018. https://gen.medium.com/as-sports-become-safer-bull -riding-doubles-down-on-danger-25369587442c

McNamara, Chris. 2010. "Clowns Doing Serious Work." *Chicago Tribune*, February 7, 2010. https://www.chicagotribune.com/news/ct-xpm-2010-02-07-10020 60296-story.html

"Middle Texas." 1869. *Galveston Daily News*, p. 1.

Mootz, William. 1972. "'Junior Bonner': An Appealing Character Study." *The Courier-Journal*, October 12, 1972, p. B26.

Nance, Susan. 2020. *Rodeo: An Animal History.* Norman: University of Oklahoma Press.

Nelson, Murry R., ed. 2009. *Encyclopedia of Sports in America: A History from Foot Races to Extreme Sports. Volume 1: Colonial Years to 1939.* Westport, CT: Greenwood Press.

Nickell, Tom. 1972. "Two Films in One, 'Junior Bonner' Both Awful, Good." *San Antonio Express,* July 10, 1972, p. 12-A.

Nix, David. 1972. "Sensitive Frontier Film Opens at Buena Vista." *The Arizona Daily Star,* July 30, 1972, p. 10.

Nodjimbadem, Katie. 2017. "The Lesser-Known History of African-American Cowboys: One in Four Cowboys Was Black. So Why Aren't They More Present in Popular Culture?" *Smithsonian Magazine,* February 13, 2017. https://www.smithsonian mag.com/history/lesser-known-history-african-american-cowboys-180962144/

Parke, Henry C. 2019. "Cowboy Pens Best Rodeo Movie Ever Made: Jeb Rosebrook's Highly Personal Memoir of the Writing and Producing of the Sam Peckinpah and Steve McQueen Movie Junior Bonner Recounts the Special Relationship between the Historic Arizona City and Its Residents in the Summer of 1971." *True West,* January 16, 2019. https://truewestmagazine.com/cowboy-pens-rodeo-movie/

"Passing Thoughts." 1898. *The Arizona Republican,* February 16, 1898, p. 2.

"Pete Knight, Noted Cowboy, Dies in Action: Vaquero, Well Known in Salinas, Killed by Horse in Hayward." *Salinas Index-Journal,* May 24, 1937, p. 1.

Porter, Willard H. 1990. "Bull Riding Showcases Best of NFR." *The Sunday Oklahoman,* December 23, 1990, Section B, p. 6.

"Prescott Rodeo Riders Split $28,000." 1970. The Arizona Republic, July 7, 1970, p. 10.

ProRodeo Livestock. 2015. Colorado Springs, CO: Professional Rodeo Cowboys Association.

"RCA Suspends Bronc Rider for Cheating." 1963. *Williams News,* November 7, 1963, p. 2.

"Record Crowd Sees Prescott Parade." 1971. *The Arizona Republic,* July 4, 1971, pp. B-1, B-6.

Robertson, Lori. 2012. "Are Rodeos a Form of Culture or Cruelty? Western Rodeos Attract Tens of Millions of Fans from across the US. But Animal Rights Groups Argue That This Part of US Heritage Belongs in the Past." BBC, February 8, 2012. http://www.bbc.com/travel/story/20120207-ethical-traveller-are-rodeos-a -form-of-culture-or-cruelty

Rosebrook, Jeb with Stuart Rosebrook. 2018. *Junior Bonner: The Making of a Classic with Steve McQueen and Sam Peckinpah in the Summer of 1971.* Albany, GA: BearManor Media.

"Scenes at a Rodeo. How Cattle Are Managed in the Far West—Vaccaros, Problamas and Fandangos—Branding Beeves." *The Cincinnati Enquirer,* April 1, 1882, p. 12.

Siskel, Gene. 1972. "'Junior Bonner.'" *Chicago Tribune,* September 18, 1972, Section 2, p. 18.

Smith, Red. 1963. "Views of Sport." *Chattanooga Daily Times,* November 9, 1963, p. 12.

Strassberg, Phil. 1972. "'Junior Bonner' Features Prescott and Stars Suave Steve McQueen." *The Arizona Republic,* July 2, 1972, p. N-5.

United Press International. 1964. "RCA Reinstates, Mayo, Tolbirt." *The Billings Gazette*, June 5, 1964, p. 19.

Untitled Article. 1913. *The Redondo Reflex*, February 21, 1913, p. 4.

Untitled Paragraph. 1888. *Weekly Journal-Miner*, July 4, 1888, p. 1.

Van Steenwyck, Elizabeth. 1977. *Larry Mahan*. New York: Tempo Books.

Waddell, Al G. 1913a. "All to the Fancy. Great Crowd Sees Riders. Twenty-five Thousand People Have Great Day. Noted Cyclone Easily Unseats His Daring Rider. Several Men Injured During the Contests." *The Los Angeles Times*, February 10, 1913, pp. 1–2.

Waddell, Al G. 1913b. "Mucho Combate. Rodeo Riders at Last Clash. Cyclone Is Tamed by Rider from Wyoming. Popular Contestant Handed Blow in Race. Game Girl Stars and Figh [sic] Ends Programme." *The Los Angeles Times*, February 17, 1913, Section III, p. 2

Weddell, David. 1994. *"If They Move ... Kill 'Em!": The Life and Times of Sam Peckinpah*. New York: Grove Press.

"Wednesday's Edition." 1888. *Arizona Weekly Journal-Miner*, May 9, 1888, p. 3.

Westermeier, Clifford P. 1948. *Man, Beast, Dust: The Story of Rodeo*. Denver, CO: World Press.

"West's Daring Thrills Huge Rodeo Throng: 75,000 See First Two Performances." 1925. *Chicago Sunday Tribune*, August 16, 1925, pp. 1, 3.

Chapter 5

A League of Their Own (1992)

Few moviegoers, critics, and baseball fans knew what to expect when *A League of Their Own* opened in theaters in July 1992. While star Tom Hanks (1956–) had earned a Best Actor Academy Award nomination for *Big* (1988), three of his previous four films had flopped at the theaters. And where Geena Davis (1956–) was coming off her Academy Award–nominated performance in the runaway hit *Thelma & Louise* (1991), costar Madonna (1958–) was a controversial rock singer and occasional actress whose music video *Justify My Love* had been banned by network MTV in 1990. Sure, baseball films could often be counted on for strong domestic box office— *The Natural* (1984, $47,951,979); *Bull Durham* (1988, $50,888,729); *Field of Dreams* (1989, $84,431,625); *Major League* (1989, $49,797,148)—but the storyline about a Midwestern women's professional baseball league during World War II seemed to be a gamble.

"When I heard that Tom Hanks and Madonna were going to be in the movie, I was a little bit mortified because I thought that they would just make a travesty of the history of the league," said Merrie A. Fidler, historian for the All-American Girls Professional Baseball League (Merrie A. Fidler, interview with author, February 3, 2020).

Written by Lowell Ganz (1948–) and Babaloo Mandel (1949–), *A League of Their Own* opens in 1988 when Dottie Hinson (Lynn Cartwright 1927–2004) travels to the National Baseball Hall of Fame and Museum in Cooperstown, New York, for the opening of an exhibit about women in baseball. There she remembers her brief time playing professional women's baseball during World War II (1941–45).

Dottie's memories take her back to 1943, when crude baseball scout Ernie Capadino (Jon Lovitz, 1957–) arrives in Willamette, Oregon, seeking to sign

Dottie (now played by Davis), a power-hitting catcher for a women's fast-pitch softball team, to try out for a new women's baseball league. With many major-league baseball players serving in the U.S. military, Walter Harvey (Garry Marshall, 1934–2016), owner of a chocolate company and a major-league team, has asked Ira Lowenstein (David Strathairn, 1949–), Harvey's advertising and promotions executive, to figure out a money-making alternative in case the war shuts down big-league baseball. Lowenstein's idea is to start professional women's baseball league. Dottie, whose husband (Bill Pullman, 1953–) is fighting in Italy, is not interested. But her kid sister, Kit (Lori Petty, 1963–), a pitcher jealous of her sister's success, wants to get away from the dull life of working on a dairy farm. Capadino makes a deal: if Kit can get Dottie to try out, Kit will be allowed to compete for a roster spot too. Dottie reluctantly agrees.

In Chicago, hundreds of women try out for four teams that each will have sixteen players. Dottie and Kit are assigned to the Rockford Peaches, along with Doris Murphy (Rosie O'Donnell, 1962–) and Mae Mordabito (Madonna, 1958–). All four teams require the players to wear skirted uniforms and attend charm and beauty classes. Meanwhile, Harvey hires Jimmy Dugan (Hanks), a former major-league star whose heavy drinking has wrecked his knee and career. Dugan is too drunk to coach, so Dottie handles manager and catcher duties until Dugan finally begins showing an interest in the players—even if he is rude; he urinates in the women's locker room and screams at one of his players for making a mistake. When she bursts into tears, he yells, "There's no crying in baseball."

But attendance is low, the media are apathetic, and Harvey considers closing the league until Lowenstein pleads with Dottie to do something exceptional to get media attention. She makes an amazing catch that a *Life* magazine photographer captures for a cover image, and fans began filling the stands. Life on the team, though, is not always fun and games. Player Betty "Spaghetti" Horn (Tracy Reiner, 1964–) learns that her husband has been killed in action, and the rift between Kit and Dottie widens until Lowenstein arranges for Kit to be traded to the Racine Belles. Kit blames Dottie for that too. After a sober, if still self-serving, Dugan manages the Peaches to the league's World Series against Racine, Dottie's husband, discharged after being wounded in action, returns and the couple plan to go back to Oregon. She doesn't need baseball.

Dottie, however, returns for the deciding seventh game in the World Series that pits her and the Peaches against Kit and the Belles. Trailing 2–1 with two outs in the last inning, Kit ties the score with an extra-base hit and wins the game after colliding at the plate with Dottie, who drops the ball to let Kit enjoy the taste of fame. At the exhibit dedication forty-five years later, Dottie reunites with old teammates, including her sister.

In 1987, Kelly Candaele (1961–) helped produce a documentary for Los Angeles PBS station KCET about the All-American Girls Professional

Baseball League titled *A League of Their Own*. Candaele's mother, Helen Callaghan Candaele St. Aubin (1923–92), had played outfield for the women's league in Minneapolis, Minnesota, and Fort Wayne, Indiana. Actress-turned-director Penny Marshall (1943–2018), an avid baseball fan, saw the documentary and attended the opening of the Women in Baseball exhibit in November 1988. Before becoming a director, Marshall had starred in the hit ABC-TV sitcom *Laverne & Shirley* (1976–83). As a director, she had clout: *Big* (1988) was the first movie directed by a woman to gross more than $100 million domestically, and *Awakenings* (1990) had grossed more than $52 million and was nominated for the Best Picture Academy Award. "I chose to direct *A League of Their Own* because I thought it was a story that needed to be told," Marshall said, "and told with accuracy, inspiration and humor" (Fidler 2006, 280).

Marshall brought the project to 20th Century, where she was directing *Awakenings*, and Jim Belushi (1954–) agreed to play Dugan. But studio chief Joe Roth (1948–) removed Marshall from the baseball project and assigned it to David Anspaugh (1946–), who had earned kudos for the basketball movie *Hoosiers* (1986). "That was my fatal error," Roth said (Dutka 1991). The production faltered, and Roth put *A League of Their Own* in turnaround, meaning that another studio could take on the project and reimburse 20th Century's investment later. When Marshall went to Columbia Pictures in November 1990, the baseball movie came with her. Columbia hired the screenwriters, and cast Debra Winger (1955–) as Dottie Hinson.

Hanks, who reportedly put on 20 to 25 pounds for the role, said the original story had a love interest. "I said, take it out. I like the less-is-more quality," and Marshall agreed, telling Hanks, "we don't want you to be cute because then the audience will wonder why the girls aren't going for you" (Campbell 1992, D-3).

Shortly after Madonna was cast, Winger was replaced—"not voluntarily," her publicist said (Scripps Howard 1991, C9)—and negotiations began to sign Davis to play Dottie. Most actors had been practicing baseball for months, but Davis had only three weeks to prepare before filming began.

Shooting started in July 1991. Chicago's Wrigley Field, home of the Chicago Cubs, became the fictitious Harvey Field. Bosse Field, an early 1900s minor-league ballpark in Evansville, Indiana, was turned into Racine's home field, and the circa-1894 baseball field and grandstands at Huntingburg (Indiana) City Park was rebuilt as the Rockford Peaches' stadium.

The budget, originally around $30 million, grew to between $45 million and $50 million—"the movie cost more to make than the league had cost to operate during its entire 12-year history" (Macy 1995, 106)—a figure that left some studio executives concerned. Driving up the costs, the *New York Times* reported, were period costumes and automobiles; the need for extras for stadium scenes; and because "Marshall, a meticulous director, took a great deal of time in filming and post-production" (Weinraub 1992, C18). Bigger factors were salaries: Hanks, $5 million; Marshall, $3 million; Davis, roughly $2.5 million; and Madonna, $1 million. Columbia also had to pay Winger $2 million.

When the film opened July 1, most reviewers were not kind. Michael Mills of *The Palm Beach Post* said the movie "falls into familiar potholes—easy sentiment and cheap nostalgia—as it skips down the road" (Mills 1992, D1). Wrote the *San Francisco Examiner's* Scott Rosenberg: "The movie is like a series of self-celebratory postcards the characters send between games. Some write, 'Having a great time!'; others say, 'Can't wait to come home and have some kids!' Nobody seems to notice the contradiction" (Rosenberg 1992, D-1). Even reviewers where the movie was shot and set had reservations. "Marshall slings a big gob of sentimentality without a story to hold it together," Jeffrey Westhoff wrote for the *Northwest Herald* of Woodstock, Illinois (Westhoff 1992, 4), while the *Chicago Tribune's* Dave Kehr called Marshall's film "a major disappointment" (Kerr 1992, 1).

Moviegoers paid no attention to reviewers. Receipts for *A League of Their Own's* first weekend hit $13,739,456—Columbia's highest-grossing opener for a movie that was not a sequel. "I honestly don't think [Columbia executives] knew the movie would be so hot this summer," Lovitz said.

By the end of its initial release, *A League of Their Own* had earned more than $107 million in the United States. Worldwide numbers would drive receipts to $132 million. *A League of Their Own* found fans, including Fidler. "When I went to see it, I said, 'Oh thank you, Penny Marshall'," Fidler said, "because I knew the whole country—I didn't predict the whole world but I do think it basically affected the whole world at times—became aware that the All-American Girls Professional Baseball League existed and that it was a significant thing in women's sports history, especially in the United States" (Merrie A. Fidler interview with author, February 3, 2020).

HISTORICAL BACKGROUND

Women had been playing baseball long before World War II. Although baseball's creation is surrounded by myth, the sport surged in the 1840s in New England and New York. After the Civil War (1861–65), the game exploded across the country. It soon became "America's pastime"— just not for women, especially during the Victorian era (1820–1914). Gai Ingham Berlage wrote: "Envisioned as the weaker sex, women were seen as biologically frail and in need of protection. Like porcelain dolls, they were to be treated with special care and were expected to be pure and chaste. Having children was the primary function of married women, and all their energy needed to be conserved for their reproductive role. The "true" woman was expected to devote her life totally to her husband and to motherhood. Her domain was the home. Strenuous activity of any kind was to be avoided. Sports and outdoor activities were male preserves" (Berlage 1994, 1).

Although allowed to attend games as fans—if their husbands or fathers allowed—women weren't supposed to play baseball. Cracks in this philosophy began when doctors began promoting exercise for health. Walking, riding, yachting, and playing cricket, golf, or tennis became acceptable in society for women's activities. So did bicycling. Doctors also discouraged the wearing of constrictive corsets, so some women turned to "bloomers," the loosely fitting, comfortable underwear developed by Amelia Jenks Bloomer (1818–94) in the 1850s. Bloomers became popular for women cyclists—and female baseball players.

Vassar College, which opened in Poughkeepsie, New York, as a women's liberal arts college in 1865 before becoming coeducational in 1869, formed two women's baseball teams in 1866. In 1904, five women participated in a men's baseball game at the University of Pittsburgh. According to the *Harrisburg Telegraph*:

> As there were not enough of the boys to make up the two teams, two of the co-eds students were added. Later three more girls "signed," and all were placed in the field. The news spread and in a short time there was a crowd of cheering students. Each play, or mis-play, in which the gentler sex had a part was applauded long and loud, and pandemonium finally broke loose when one of the stalwart co-eds knocked a two-bagger into Woodland avenue. But the attention of the faculty had been attracted and the result was prohibition. ("Co-eds Mustn't Play Ball on the U. of P. Campus" 1904, 1)

University officials declared that women could not play baseball on campus and instructed the police to "break up all such games" ("Co-eds Mustn't Play Ball on the U. of P. Campus" 1904, 1).

The biggest surge for women's baseball came in the 1890s when a number of Bloomer Girls teams began barnstorming across the country against town teams of men and boys. But not all Bloomer Girls were women. Many teams used "toppers"—wig-wearing males dressed in women's uniforms—as players, usually at the pitcher and catcher positions and elsewhere as needed. Some towns took the ruse in humor; others were outraged. After a Bloomer Girls team defeated the Dewey Blues, 4–0, in Dewey, Oklahoma, in 1906, *The Dewey World* reported: "As ball players they are rank imposters, but as money getters they will do" (Untitled Article 1906, 8).

Years before leading the St. Louis Cardinals to the 1926 World Series championship and being inducted into the Baseball Hall of Fame in 1942, a teenaged Rogers Hornsby (1896–1963) was hired to play as a Bloomer Girl in Dallas, Texas. At age 16, Smoky Joe Wood (1889–1985), who would pitch the Boston Red Sox to the 1912 World Series championship, briefly traveled with a Bloomer Girls team across Kansas in 1906. "Joe has a girlish face,

---

EARLY WOMEN'S BASEBALL STARS

Many women players stood out on baseball fields in the late 1800s and early 1900s.

Elizabeth Stroud, or Stride (1877–1919), played for years under the name Lizzie Arlington and was reportedly paid $100 a week to play for the Philadelphia Reserves in 1898. Later that year, she played briefly in a minor-league game for Reading, Pennsylvania. A woman would not play again in a minor-league game until Sarah Frances "Sonny" Dunlap (1913–90) appeared in a Class D Arkansas–Missouri League game in Fayetteville, Arkansas, in 1936. Although Dunlap did not record a hit, she played the entire game in right field—probably "because league officials had not been alerted by advanced publicity in time to prevent it" (Seymour 1990, 502). Dunlap's Fayetteville Bears defeated the Cassville Blues, 5–1.

Clementina Brida (1881–1944), who played third base as Maud/Maude Nelson/Neilson for various women's teams, later pitched for, coached and owned women's teams. As late as 1927, her performance still impressed reporters.

Ruth Egan (1892–1957) played on the same 1906 Bloomer Girls team with Smoky Joe Wood, who said "she played first base with a catcher's mitt, but she could really catch the ball" (Eberle 2019). By the 1920s, Egan was barnstorming with the Chicago Legioneers and performing stunts like catching a baseball dropped 300 feet from a balloon.

Sources

Eberle, Mark E. 2019. "Who's On First? Kansas City's Female Baseball Stars, 1899–1929." Fort Hays State University, FHSU Scholars Repository, Monographs. https://scholars.fhsu.edu/cgi/viewcontent.cgi?article=1009&context=all_monographs

Seymour, Harold. 1990. *Baseball: The People's Game.* New York: Oxford University Press.

---

and it was easy for him to pass as a girl," *The Hutchinson News* reported ("Manager Andrews" 1907, 7).

By the time the Amateur Softball Association was founded in 1933, the Bloomer Girls baseball teams were fading into history. Softball eventually emerged as a woman's alternative to baseball.

Most accounts have a group of men in Chicago inventing softball in 1887 when they designed a stadium inside a gymnasium so that they could play baseball during winter months. It "was not invented as a game for girls and women so that they would stop playing baseball," historian Debra A. Shattuck wrote (Shattuck 2017, 7). But with the shorter distances and a softer ball, the sport became acceptable for women to play. In the 1927 meeting of the subcommittee on baseball of the National Committee on Women's Athletics of the American Physical Education Association, rules were modified for a form of women's baseball with shorter base paths. That led to more women beginning to play softball, and by the early 1930s softball became accepted as "an appropriate female sport" (Berlage 1994, 97). That remained the case when the United States entered World War II.

After Japanese naval forces attacked Pearl Harbor on December 7, 1941, Major League Baseball (MLB) commissioner Kennesaw Mountain Landis (1866–1944) wrote to President Franklin D. Roosevelt (1882–1945), asking whether professional baseball should be suspended. A fan of the sport, Roosevelt said baseball should continue but that players would not be exempt from military service. Before the war ended, more than five hundred major-league and more than four thousand minor-league players had either been drafted or enlisted in the armed forces. With a terminally ill father, Cleveland Indians pitcher Bob Feller (1918–2010) was exempt from military service but enlisted in the Navy two days after the bombing of Pearl Harbor. "The last thing on my mind right then was playing baseball," he said (*The New York Times* 2010). Feller missed four years of baseball, spending most of his naval career on the U.S.S. *Alabama* in the South Pacific. St. Louis Cardinals outfielder Enos Slaughter (1916–2002) joined the Army Air Corps in 1942. After winning the 1944 National League (NL) batting title for the Cardinals, Stan Musial (1920–2013) was drafted, served in a naval ship repair unit, and missed the 1945 season.

By 1943, the major leagues had lost star players like the New York Yankees' Joe DiMaggio (1914–99), the Detroit Tigers' Hank Greenberg (1911–86), the New York Giants' Johnny Mize (1913–93), the Brooklyn Dodgers' Pete Reiser (1919–81), and the Boston Red Sox's Ted Williams (1918–2002) to the U.S. military. Major-league teams were filling their rosters with players well past their prime and "the kids who should have been learning their profession in Class D baseball but who were now forced to learn it before the fans in big league ballparks" (Turner 1996, 10). Joe Nuxhall (1928–2007) pitched in one game for the Cincinnati Reds in 1944 at age fifteen. Sixteen-year-old Tommy Brown (1927–) played forty-six games that year for the Dodgers. He finished the season with a .146 batting average.

Men were not the only ones joining the war effort. In 1942, Congress established the Women's Army Auxiliary Corps (WAAC) after a heated debate in which one senator said the bill "cast a shadow on the sanctity of the home" (Ziobro 2016). Recruitment for WAACs began in May. Later that year, the war department announced plans to train women as military pilots (Women's Airforce Service Pilots, shortened to WASPs). Almost two thousand women were serving as WASPs by 1945.

Fearing the 1943 baseball season would be ruined or canceled, Philip K. Wrigley (1894–1977), the chewing gum manufacturer and owner of the Chicago Cubs, formed a committee to come up with an alternative to baseball. Wrigley liked the committee's idea of creating a professional women's league to "furnish additional means of healthful recreation to the public, who are all in one way or another under severe pressure from war work" (Macy 1995, vii). Wrigley also had financial reasons for turning to women's athletics. "He had parks in Chicago and Los Angeles that held championship games and he was faced with not having anything in his ballpark after the summer of 1943" (Merrie A. Fidler, interview with author, February 3, 2020).

The sport would be softball. "That was the only talent pool they had," Fidler said. "The philosophy at that time was 'We don't want highly competitive sports for girls and women because of the excesses seen in boys' and men's sports.' And they didn't want to subject girls and women to those things. Also, it wasn't considered feminine for girls and women to play baseball at that time. It was considered a man's sport and it always had been" (Merrie A. Fidler, interview with author, February 3, 2020).

The All-American Girls Softball League was formed as a nonprofit organization. Wrigley wanted the teams to play in major-league stadiums when the home teams were traveling, but when the other NL team owners refused to let women's teams play in their stadiums, Wrigley focused on smaller markets. The inaugural season in 1943 included four teams—the Racine (Illinois) Belles, the South Bend (Indiana) Blue Sox, the Kenosha (Wisconsin) Comets, and the Rockford (Illinois) Peaches. Professional baseball scouts were dispatched to find talent, but the women had to be white. Like major-league baseball at the time, African American players were excluded. In May, roughly 280 women recruits from the United States and Canada tried out for sixty-four roster spots.

What helped parents and spouses agree to let the players leave home and play ball under a male manager was the use of paid female chaperones. Their duties included approving players' social engagements, living quarters, restaurants, as well as enforcing curfews, league rules and room assignments, and being responsible for players' appearance, conduct, and behavior. "In essence, a chaperone acted as an overseer of team personnel, a road secretary, an equipment manager, a trainer, a first aid dispenser, and an assistant manager. Some also assisted in the coaching boxes during games" (Fidler 2006, 174).

The game might have been softball, but except for shorter distances to the fences, between bases and from the pitcher's mound to home plate, big-league baseball rules were used. In the middle of the 1943 season, league officials, wanting to emphasize that the game was baseball, began calling the league the All-American Girls Base Ball League. The name was changed again after the 1943 season to the All-American Girls Professional Ball League, and again in 1945 to the All-American Girls Base Ball League (although more commonly referred to as Baseball) and after the 1950 season to the American Girls Baseball League.

Rockford and South Bend were the only original teams still around after the final season in 1954. The Kenosha Comets lasted through the 1951 season, and the Racine Bells closed after 1950. Other teams came and went in Battle Creek, Michigan (Belles, 1951–52); Chicago (Colleens, 1948–50); Fort Wayne, Indiana (Daisies, 1945–53); Kalamazoo, Michigan (Lassies, 1950–54); Milwaukee, Wisconsin (Chicks, 1944); Minneapolis, Minnesota (Millerettes, 1944); Muskegon, Michigan (Lassies, 1946–50; and Belles,

1953); Peoria, Illinois (Redwings, 1946–51); and Springfield, Illinois (Sallies, 1948–50). The league's peak year was 1948, when ten teams competed and more than 910,000 people attended games.

Some of the press comments were as sexist as the team names. League press agent Eddie McGuire's idea of a "cute" note for newspapers included, "The favorite remark of Eddie Stumpf, manager of the Rockford Peaches, is: 'You have one woman and think you have trouble. Toss a little sympathy my way, brother. I have 15 I had to manage'" (Ward 1943, 19).

It took a while before the women earned respect from fans and the media. "There were women who hated us because they didn't think we should be doing a masculine thing," said Lavonne "Pepper" Paire Davis, who played for Racine and Minneapolis from 1944 to 1946. "Then there were men who just thought it was funny, women playing baseball. But we won them over with our play . . . they could see that we could play" (Smith 1992, F2).

Eleanor Moore Warner, who started her career at age sixteen with the Chicago Colleens in 1950 and played four more seasons with the Fort Wayne Daisies and Grand Rapids Chicks, said the players had to be as tough as men on the field. "If we got a little ache, we might take a little break," she recalled, "but then the coach would come up and say, 'It's your turn to pitch, kid'" (Hrabal 1992, 5).

Wrigley left the league after the 1944 season, and his advertising executive, Arthur Meyerhoff (1895–1986), took over and reorganized the league so that a board of directors with representatives from each franchise governed the league.

In 1948, the league officially became a baseball league. Softballs and underhanded pitching were out. But that meant that the league lacked a talent pool because women were playing softball, not baseball, across America. "When they did recruit an outstanding softball player, they had to give them training time to develop the skills of throwing the longer distances, learning overhanded pitching if they were pitchers and getting used to an overhand pitch instead of an underhanded pitch as batters," Fidler said. "Not only did they have to recruit the good players, then they had to spend time and money to train them before they could put them on the field" (Merrie A. Fidler, interview with author, February 3, 2020).

The league's popularity took a sudden dive in 1949. Attendance fell to 585,813 and continued to drop during the next five years. After the 1950 season, team directors voted to buy the league from Meyerhoff and run the franchises independently. Publicity and promotional budgets were cut, as were budgets for player procurement. Team scouts had to recruit locally. "If any major-league team cut its publicity and player procurement budget today, it wouldn't last long. And that's what happened to the All-American Girls league," Fidler said (Merrie A. Fidler, interview with author, February 3, 2020). A recession also hit the United States in the early 1950s.

Other reasons for the league's demise included the technology boom, which soon put televisions in most American homes; travel technology improved, allowing for new leisure activities, and decreasing the league's fan base. "There was also a shift in the American idea of femininity, which during the previous three decades had seemed to be becoming more liberal. Television and advertising created the 'June Cleever' image [from the 1957–63 TV series *Leave it to Beaver*], and American women began to conform to it" (Heaphy and May 2006, 15–16). Only Fort Wayne, Grand Rapids, Kalamazoo, Rockford and South Bend remained for the 1954 season, which drew 270,000 spectators. The league folded after that season, and although it had given more than 600 women the chance to play professional baseball, it quickly faded from memory.

DEPICTION AND CULTURAL CONTEXT

A League of Their Own is fact-based fiction. The screenwriters turned chewing gum kingpin Philip K. Wrigley into chocolate bar manufacturer Walter Harvey, while the Ira Lowenstein character is easily recognized as Arthur Meyerhoff. Other characters are composites.

Hanks's Jimmy Dugan is a close copy of Jimmie Foxx (1907–67), who played twenty seasons in the major leagues, primarily with the American League's Philadelphia Athletics (1925–35) and Boston Red Sox (1936–42), leading the Athletics to consecutive World Series championships in 1929 and 1930. In Philadelphia's 1931 World Series loss to the St. Louis Cardinals, Foxx hit a home run that went all the way out of Shibe Park in Philadelphia. But knee, feet, and sinus problems plagued Foxx's career. So did a serious drinking problem. In 1952, a year after being inducted into the Baseball Hall of Fame, the forty-four-year-old Foxx was hired to manage the Fort Wayne Daisies, succeeding another Hall of Famer, Max Carey (1890–1976), who had been become the women's league's president. Foxx's stepdaughter was the Daisies' bat girl.

Foxx coached the Daisies to a 67–42 record, good enough for first place in the six-team league, but Fort Wayne lost in the first round of the playoffs to the Rockford Peaches, and Foxx did not return to the Daisies the next year. Said outfielder Wilma Briggs (1930–): "We were all very disappointed that he didn't come back to manage again for the 1953 season" (Millikin 1998, 249).

Hanks's Dugan, however, bore little resemblance to the real Foxx. "If you talked to any players who played under Jimmie Foxx they'll tell you that Tom Hanks wasn't anything like Jimmie Foxx," Fidler said. "They'll tell you Jimmie Foxx was a real gentleman and would never have gone into the girls locker room at any time, let alone to relieve himself. He treated them very well" (Merrie A. Fidler, interview with author, February 3, 2020).

Daisies shortstop Dottie Schroeder (1928–96) said Foxx "did enjoy a drink, but it never affected his performance on the ball field. He was a good manager. He never lost his temper" (Millikin 1998, 247). Said Briggs: "Jim did enjoy his drinks. He occasionally took a swig from a bottle in the bus on road trips, but it never changed his behavior or demeanor. He never lost his temper; he was never violent. He was a kind man, a gentleman to me and all my teammates. He never used bad language. He was very soft spoken" (Millikin 1998, 247).

Davis's character closely resembles Ruth Lessing (1925–2000), who played from 1944 to 1949 with Minneapolis, Fort Wayne, and Grand Rapids. Instead of coming from Oregon, Lessing was a native of San Antonio, Texas, and was nicknamed "Tex." She set the record for most games played at catcher in a season with 125, and made the league's all-star team in 1946, 1947, and 1948. Highly competitive, she once hit an umpire and was fined $100. Fans chipped in and gave her money to pay the fine, which she did, then donated more money to a charity. Lessing left the league when injuries forced her to retire.

While Lessing did not have a sister on the team, sister combinations were not uncommon. "I wouldn't doubt a bit that there were conflicts between sisters and that one of the sisters was better than the other," Fidler said (Merrie A. Fidler, interview with author, February 3, 2020). Indeed, recruited by a Brooklyn Dodgers scout, Margaret and Helen Callaghan of Vancouver, British Columbia, made up the first sister combination when they signed with the Minneapolis Millerettes for the 1944 season. Margaret (1921–2019), about fifteen months Helen's senior, had been working for Boeing Aircraft as part of the war effort before she signed with the league. After leaving the league after the 1951 season, she remained active in sports, playing basketball and softball. In 1993, she was inducted into the British Columbia Softball Hall of Fame.

Her sister—often suggested as an inspiration for Davis's character—was an outfielder (not a catcher) best known for her offense. Helen won the league's batting average in 1945 with a .299 average. "The reporters of the day called her the 'feminine Ted Williams'," her son, Casey Candaele, recalled (Candaele 1992, 9). An injury kept her from playing in 1947, but she played part of the 1948 season, her last, after giving birth to her son. "I would definitely have taken her swing," wrote her son, who played in the major leagues for parts of nine seasons with the Montreal Expos, Houston Astros, and Cleveland Indians. "It's the kind of swing you associate with Ted Williams or Will Clark: smooth and sweeping, arms extended, weight shifting from the back foot to front at just the right moment, supple wrists that snap the head of the bat through the ball" (Candaele 1992, 9).

Both players took advantage of their speed. "Helen used to lead off," Margaret recalled, "and I batted second, and I did an awful lot of bunting. I would wait until Helen stole second, and I would bunt her to third. If she got to third on her own, or some play didn't work, we had a squeeze play, and I did a lot of bunting on the squeeze play, too" (Sargent 2013, 279).

Scenes involving other characters also rang true, such as when Capadino doesn't want to recruit manly looking Marla Hooch (Megan Cavanagh,

1960). "When Wrigley started the league, if there were two players of equal ability and one was more petite and feminine appearing, that's the one he had his scouts recruit," Fidler said (Merrie A. Fidler, interview with author, February 3, 2020).

As depicted in the film, charm and beauty classes were mandatory, and chaperones traveled with the team. The baseball uniforms worn in *A League of Their Own* closely resembled actual uniforms. "They wore shorts under their dresses, and they had sliding pads that the players could put on underneath dresses but they were too cumbersome so the players didn't wear them," Fidler said. "They put up with strawberries and bruises instead" (Merrie A. Fidler, interview with author, February 3, 2020).

The scene in which Horn is told that her husband has been killed in action was also true to history. "Some of the spouses were killed in the war," Fidler said. "One player was notified before the game that her husband had been killed and she went and played the game anyway" (Merrie A. Fidler, interview with author, February 3, 2020).

The depiction of Lowenstein's fight to keep the league going also has historical basis, although that happened in 1944, not 1943, after Wrigley decided to drop his support. By the fall of 1944, the United States and its allies had turned the tide of the war. The Allied invasion of France, beginning June 6, had been successful, and Paris was liberated on August 25. Gains were being made in the Pacific theater, too. Baseball executives no longer thought the war would shut down the sport, but Meyerhoff argued that women's baseball remained financially viable. He bought the league from Wrigley for $10,000. The following year, he changed the league's name to the All-American Girls Base Ball League.

"Wrigley released the league to Meyerhoff for two reasons," Fidler wrote. "First, because Meyerhoff demonstrated a sincere interest in developing the league's potential. Secondly, Wrigley was confident that Meyerhoff would maintain the ideals and professional standards on which the league had been established" (Fidler 2006, 69). Meyerhoff continued to serve as the league's commissioner until being forced out by team owners after the 1950 season.

The biggest misconception created by the film, however, was that the women started out playing baseball. Even the league's first name used *Softball*, not *Baseball*. The ball was 12 inches, base paths were 65 feet, and the pitching distance was 40 feet.

The war had forced the major leagues to change the baseballs being used. "It looked and felt like a real baseball, but it had a granulated cork center instead of the high-grade cork and rubber mixture, and there was no rubber shell or rubber wrapping around that core," Noel Hynd wrote. "Instead, to give it a little pop, there were two hard shells of a rubberlike substance inside the ball, hugging the core. One shell was red and the other black. For the first time, Americans heard the ominous word 'balata,' which was what the two shells were made of" (Hynd 1985). While the circumference and weight of the ball had been increased slightly—one-eighth of an inch and one-eighth of an ounce to between 9 and 9¼ inches and 5 to 5¼ ounces—the pitching distance remained 60½ feet and the bases were still 90 feet apart.

In the women's league, pitchers made underhanded deliveries to the batter. Still, league officials wanted to stress the baseball aspects, so reporters were told to replace the word *softball* with *baseball* in their articles. "During the 1944 season sportswriters said, 'You can't call this baseball because they're using an underhanded pitch,'" Fidler said. "What they didn't bother to look at was that baseball rules don't indicate how the pitch has to be delivered. We're just used to overhand pitching because that's what's most effective at that distance" (Merrie A. Fidler, interview with author, February 3, 2020).

Rules continued to be tweaked. Midway through the 1944 season, the circumference of the ball was reduced to 11½ inches, while the base paths were increased to 68 feet. The pitching distance was lengthened to 42 feet halfway through the 1945 season. In 1946, the ball became 11 inches, with 72-feet base paths and a pitching distance of 43 feet. The pitching distances were changed to allow stealing bases.

Underhanded pitching remained enforced until a limited sidearm pitch was allowed in 1947. "The basic rule was that the delivery had to be below the waist of the pitcher," Fidler said. "That became too difficult for umpires to legislate, so they went to a full overhand pitch in 1948" (Merrie A. Fidler, interview with author, February 3, 2020). By that year, the baseball was 10 3/8 inches and the pitching distance was 50 feet. The latter went up to 55 feet the following year and the ball was reduced to 10 inches. Those regulations remained in effect until 1953, when 1 foot was added to the pitching distance and the base paths were stretched by 3 feet. In 1954, the league's final season, the ball's circumference was 9 inches, the base paths 85 feet, and the pitching distance 60 feet.

Those changes took a toll on players. "I pitched underhand for three years and tried sidearm," said Viola Thompson Griffin (1922–2017), who pitched ninety-eight games in 1944, helping lead the Milwaukee Chicks to the league championship. "I couldn't handle overhand pitching. It was the end of my career" (Fidler 2006, 72). She joined Chicago Bluebirds of the National Girls' Baseball League, a Chicago-based league that was founded in 1944 and played traditional softball. That league also closed after the 1954 season.

Many pitchers joined the National Girls Baseball League "because they couldn't transition to overhand pitching and they weren't skilled at any other pitching," Fidler said (Merrie A. Fidler, interview with author, February 3, 2020). The adjustment also proved hard for Karen Kunkel (1934–2017), a catcher who played one season, 1953, with the Grand Rapids Chicks. Kunkel said:

> I think probably the hardest thing to adjust to was the fact that . . . I went from being the best to just another ball player having to work my way into

the position, plus switching from softball as a catcher to catching baseball. We were playing regulation baseball at the time with [75-foot] base paths and [a 10-inch] ball. That was a real transition as a catcher. I think the only thing that maybe saved someone like myself who came in very quickly from fast-pitch softball and didn't come through the transition of the league was that it was a constant challenge every day. . . . It took absolute dedication and concentration in order to be able to do the job. (Fidler 2006, 73)

The movie's other major change in history involved the women's World Series. The movie pits the Rockford Peaches against the Racine Belles in a seven-game series, with Racine winning in seven games. Racine did indeed capture the series title, but not against Rockford. Although Rockford won the women's World Series in 1945, 1948, 1949, and 1950, the Peaches finished the 1943 regular season with a 48–54 record in last place in the four-team league. Racine, which finished the first half of the season in first place with a 34–20 record before sliding to a 25–23 record in the second half, met the Kenosha Comets (56–52) in the best-of-five series.

The series opened in Kenosha on Friday, September 3, at Lake Front Stadium, where 1,500 seats had been added to increase seating capacity to roughly 3,800 "in anticipation of the record throngs expected" (McKenna 1943b, 10), but only 2,255 watched the Belles win, 6–2. "The Belles fully deserved the victory off their sound playing, timely hitting, and ability to cash in on Kenosha's miscues and mental slips," the *Kenosha Evening News* reported (McKenna 1943d, 3). Racine won the second game, 7–4, the next day before a crowd of 2,140.

The series moved to Racine for Sunday's third game, a 6–3 Belles victory before 3,362 "roaringly happy fans," making the Belles "the first recognized world champions of girls' professional softball" ("Belles Defeat Comets Three in a Row for World Title" 1943, 12).

Tickets for each game cost $1.10— no discount for children—with gate receipts split 60 percent for Racine and 40 percent for Kenosha. The league also planned to award a $1,000 college scholarship to a woman from the city that won the championship.

"The league . . . has been unique in many respects and entertaining always," Kenosha sports editor Eddie McKenna wrote. "Stress was placed on femininity but not at the expense of ability. As the 108–game season progressed the teams showed marked daily improvement due to the efforts of the baseball men managers. Players competing are professionals, all having received anywhere's [sic] from $45 to $85 per week for 15 weeks" (McKenna 1943b, 12).

The league's popularity continued over the next few years. In 1945, Jim O'Brien, a newspaper reporter for the *Racine Journal-Times*, wrote: "Here in Racine, we even saw girls step out on the baseball diamond and play a game that fell somewhere between baseball and softball, and pack 'em in as few sports have in this city" (Macy 1995, 41).

While Davis's character chooses her husband over baseball in *A League of The Own*, Fidler notes that things sometimes happened that way— but not always. "Sometimes when players got married their husbands said, 'You can't play anymore,' but on the other hand there were those husbands who encouraged their wives to continue to play," Fidler said. "And some players said, 'If it's you or baseball, then I'm taking baseball'" (Merrie A. Fidler, interview with author, February 3, 2020).

CONCLUSION

Dismissed by many critics and ignored by Academy Award voters, *A League of Their Own* made a connection with moviegoers. The movie's impact went beyond box-office numbers. *A League of Their Own* debuted in 1993 on CBS-TV. Starring Sam McMurray (1952–) as Jimmy Dugan and Carey Lowell (1961–) as Dottie Hinson, the series lasted only six episodes, but within a year after the movie's release, nonfiction books began to be published, and former players were invited to sign autographs at baseball events. Today, the movie airs frequently on television, and the women's exhibit remains part of the National Baseball Hall of Fame museum.

Said Shirley Burkovich (1933–), who played in the league from 1949 to 1951 and had a speaking part in the movie's Cooperstown scenes: "If it had not been for Penny Marshall, we would still be obscure, unless you lived in one of those league cities at that time" (Sargent 2013, 150).

FURTHER READING

All-American Girls Professional Baseball League. https://www.aagpbl.org

Associated Press. 1991. "Movie Gives Evansville a Big Boost." *Kokomo Tribune*, September 28, 1991, p. 2.

Associated Press. 1992. "Baseball's Helen St. Aubin Dies: Her Story Inspired Film 'A League of Their Own.'" *San Francisco Examiner*, December 10, 1992, p. A-21.

"Belles Defeat Comets Three in a Row for World Title: Crowd of 3,362 Fans Hails Champs After 6-3 Win Sunday." 1943. *The Racine Journal-Times*, September 7, 1943, p. 12.

Bennett, John. n.d. "Jimmie Foxx." Society for American Baseball Research. https://sabr.org/bioproj/person/e34a045d

Berlage, Gai Ingham. 1994. *Women in Baseball: The Forgotten History*. Westport, CT: Praeger.

Britton, Bonnie. 1991. "Moviemaking: Old Diamond, New Setting: Construction Wizard Helps Build a Big-Screen Ballpark in Huntingbird." *The Indianapolis Star*, July 29, 1991, p. D-1, 4.

Campbell, Bob. 1992. "Hanks Relishes the Chance to Really Get Big: Fat-slob Baseball Manager a Change of Pace in 'League.'" *San Francisco Examiner*, July 3, 1992, p. D-3.

Candaele, Kelly. 1992. "Mom Was in a League of Her Own: She Was a Pro in the 40's with a Sweet Swing and Speed to Burn." *The New York Times*, June 7, 1992, Section 8, p. 9.

"Co-eds Mustn't Play Ball on the U. of P. Campus." 1904. *Harrisburg Telegraph*, May 7, 1904, p. 1.

Dutka, Elaine. 1991. "Batter Up: Yes, Sports Fans, It's 'Truth or Dare' in the Bullpen." *Los Angeles Times*, June 9, 1991. https://www.latimes.com/archives/la-xpm-1991 -06-09-ca-593-story.html

Eberle, Mark E. 2019. "Who's on First? Kansas City's Female Baseball Stars, 1899– 1929." *Monographs*, p. 10. https://scholars.fhsu.edu/all_monographs/10

Fidler, Merrie A. 2006. *The Origins and History of the All-American Girls Professional Baseball League.* Jefferson, NC: McFarland & Company, Inc., Publishers.

Gregorich, Barbara. 1993. *Women at Play: The Story of Women in Baseball.* San Diego, CA: A Harvest Original, Harcourt Brace & Company.

Heaphy, Leslie A., and Mel Anthony May, eds. 2006. *Encyclopedia of Woman and Baseball.* Jefferson, NC: McFarland & Company, Inc., Publishers.

Hrabal, Don. 1992. "Woman Recalls 'a League of Her Own.'" *The Times-Press*, July 17, 1992, p. 5.

Hunt, Alan. 1986. "Casey's a Chip Off the Baseball Block." *Lompoc Record*, September 1, 1986, p. B1.

Hynd, Noel. 1985. "The Inside Story about Baseball in 1943 Was Less Bounce to the Ounce." *Sports Illustrated*, May 13, 1985. https://www.si.com/vault/1985 /05/13/622451/the-inside-story-about-baseball-in-1943-was-less-bounce -to-the-ounce

Kerr, Dave. 1992. "Marshall Strikes Out with 'League.'" *Chicago Tribune*, July 1, 1992, Section 5, pp. 1, 3.

Kronke, David. 1992. "Geena Davis Stresses Feminist Sensibility." *Chicago Tribune*, July 16, 1992, Section 5, p. 4.

Lovell, Gene. 1992. "Can Success, Uh, Get Used to Jon Lovitz?" *Chicago Tribune*, June 30, 1992, Section 5, p. 11A.

Macy, Sue. 1995. *A Whole New Ballgame: The Story of the All-American Girls Professional Baseball League.* New York: Puffin Books.

"Manager Andrews: Dr. Jay Has Played Professional Ball Since 1894. Started in as a Pitcher and Has Played the Game All Over America. Some Base Ball Gossip. Joe Wood Was a Pretty 'Bloomer Girl' Last Year. 'Red' Murray the Wise—Dunham the Funniest Player Ever Seen Here." 1907. *The Hutchinson News*, March 26, 1907, p. 7.

McKenna, Eddie. 1943a. "Comets and Racine Launch Championship Series in Lake Front Stadium Friday." *Kenosha Evening News*, September 2, 1943, p. 12.

McKenna, Eddie. 1943b. "Comets, Belles Launch Championship Play Here Tonight: Add 1,500 Seats Raising Accommodations to 3,800 for Two Title Tilts in Lake Stadium: Gates Open at 5:30 with Game Starting at 8; Both Teams Set to Go." *Kenosha Evening News*, September 3, 1943, pp. 10, 12.

McKenna, Eddie. 1943c. "3,800 Seats Ready; Come and Get 'Em Fans; Lee Harney to Hurl." *Kenosha Evening News*, September 4, 1943, p. 3.

McKenna, Eddie. 1943d. "Comets Lose to Belles; Out to Tie Series Tonight: Nesbitt Beats Nicol in Opener; Harney to Hurl against Winter: First Game in Softball

Championship Series is 6-2 Victory for Racine." *Kenosha Evenings News*, September 4, 1943, p. 3.

McKenna, Eddie. 1943e. "Comets Dip in Three Games; Belles Win Crown: Lose 7-4 Saturday; Score is 6-3 Sunday as 3,362 See Series End: Eagles' Club Presents Helen Nichol with Trophy Recognizing Great Record." *Kenosha Evening News,* September 7, 1943, p. 10.

Millikin, Mark R. 1998. *Jimmie Foxx: The Pride of Sudlersville*. Lanham, MD: The Scarecrow Press, Inc.

Mills, Michael. 1992. "Strong Women Turn 'League of Their Own' into Winner." *The Palm Beach Post*, July 1, 1992, pp. D1, D4.

The New York Times. 2010. "Feller Proud to Serve in 'Time of Need.'" *The New York Times*, December 6, 2010. https://www.nytimes.com/2010/12/17/sports /baseball/17reflect.html

New York Times News Service. 1990. "Madonna Video Too Risque for MTV." *The Daily Dispatch*, November 28, 1990, p. B12.

Ritter, Lawrence S. 2010. *The Glory of Their Times: The Story of the Early Days of Baseball Told by the Men Who Played It*. New York: Harper Perennial.

Rosenberg, Scott. 1992. "'League': Swings and Mrs.: Story of Women's Professional Ballteam Sugared with Star-Spangled Banter." *San Francisco Examiner*, July 1, 1992, pp. D-1, D-5.

Rymer, Sachary D. 2013. "The Evolution of the Baseball From the Dead-Ball Era Through Today." *Bleacher Report*, June 18, 2013. https://bleacherreport.com /articles/1676509-the-evolution-of-the-baseball-from-the-dead-ball-era-through -today

Sargent, Jim. 2013. *We Were the All-American Girls: Interviews with Players of the AAGPBL, 1943–1954*. Jefferson, NC: McFarland & Company, Inc., Publishers.

Scripps Howard. 1991. "Debra Winger Cut from Baseball Movie Lineup." *The Pantagraph*, June 21, 1991, p. C9.

Seymour, Harold. 1990. *Baseball: The People's Game*. New York: Oxford University Press.

Shattuck, Debra A. 2017. *Bloomer Girls: Women Baseball Pioneers*. Urbana: University of Illinois Press.

Smith, Mark Chalon. 1992. "Still Having Ball in League of Own: Movie: Ex-players of the Team That Inspired the Film Speak in Anaheim." *Los Angeles Times*, Orange County edition, pp. F1-2.

Turner, Frederick. 1996. *When the Boys Came Back: Baseball and 1946*. New York: Henry Holt and Company.

Untitled Article. 1906. *Conway Springs Star*, July 5, 1906, p. 8.

Ward, Arch. 1943. "In the Wake of the News." *Chicago Daily Tribune*, November 20, 1943, p. 19.

Weinraub, Bernard. 1992. "Budgets Bloat; Studios Worry." *New York Times*, June 25, 1992, pp. C13, C18.

Westhoff, Jeffrey. 1992. "Sentimentality Strikes Out 'League of Their Own." *Northwest Herald*, July 3, 1992, Sidetracks section, p. 4.

"Women Players in Organized Baseball." 1983. *Society of American Baseball Research Journal*. http://research.sabr.org/journals/component/search/Lizzie%2BArlington /%252F?ordering=&searchphrase=all

Wood, Gerald C. 2013. *Smoky Joe Wood: The Biography of a Baseball Legend*. Lincoln: University of Nebraska Press.

Ziobro, Melissa. 2016. "'Skirted Soldiers': The Women's Army Corps and Gender Integration of the U.S. Army during World War II." National Museum of the United States Army, June 21, 2016. https://armyhistory.org/skirted-soldiers-the -womens-army-corps-and-gender-integration-of-the-u-s-army-during-world -war-ii/

Chapter 6

Ali (2001)

The motion-picture industry found early success in boxing movies. "Spectators could see fights without entering the dubious cultural milieu of the ring," film scholar Dan Streible wrote. "Movie shows gave access to a wider general audience of men who could not afford to attend the big bouts sponsored by clubs. They also granted unexpected access to women" (Streible 2008, 7). In the sound era, boxers showed up in Academy Award–winning tearjerkers (1931's *The Champ*), fantasies (1941's *Here Comes Mr. Jordan*), gritty dramas (1947's *Body and Soul*), romantic comedies (1952's *The Quiet Man*), Westerns (1953's *City of Bad Men*), and surprise blockbusters (1976's *Rocky*).

Studios had likewise found success in film biographies of boxing greats: *Gentleman Jim* (1942), about heavyweight champion James "Gentleman Jim" Corbett (1866–1933); *The Joe Louis Story* (1953), about the 1937–49 heavyweight champion whose real name was Joseph Louis Barrow (1914–81); *Somebody Up There Likes Me*, about middleweight champion Rocky Graziano (1919–90), born Thomas Rocco Barbella; *The Great White Hope* (1970), based on the stage play about John Arthur "Jack" Johnson (1878–1946), the first African American heavyweight champion; *Raging Bull* (1980), which won Robert DeNiro (1943–) an Academy Award for his portrayal of middleweight champion Giacobbe "Jake" LaMotta (1922–2017); and *The Hurricane* (1999), for which Denzel Washington was nominated for an Oscar as Rubin "Hurricane" Carter (1937–2014), a middleweight fighter wrongly convicted of murder in 1967.

Years before *Ali* was released, Muhammad Ali (1942–2016), the three-time heavyweight champion who was selected Sportsman of the 20th Century by *Sports Illustrated*, had played himself in a biopic, *The Greatest*

(1977)—while he was still heavyweight champion. David Wilkening of Orlando, Florida's *Sentinel Star* called that movie "talky, episodic, jarringly disjointed, ridiculous in parts" (Wilkening 1977, 1-B). *Sports Illustrated* writer Frank Deford (1938–2017) noted: "A genuine film about this unique man and his times must wait until Ali can no longer indulge himself as star and censor alike" (Hauser 1992, 344).

When *Ali* began filming January 2001, many believed that time had come. *Ali* was directed by Michael Mann (1943–), whose past three films—*The Last of the Mohicans* (1992), *Heat* (1995), and *The Insider* (1999)—had been well received, if not giant moneymakers. *Ali* starred Will Smith (1968–), who found stardom on NBC-TV's sitcom *The Fresh Prince of Bel-Air* (1990–96) and in blockbuster films *Independence Day* (1996) and *Men in Black* (1997). More importantly, Ali, suffering from Parkinson's disease, had lighted the Olympic flame during the opening ceremonies of the 1996 Games in Atlanta, which "reignited the world's adoration for him, resulting in a sweeping brush fire of new-found popularity" and catapulted "a renaissance for The Greatest, one of the planet's most magical, beloved humanitarians" (Saraceno 1996, C12).

Ali starts in 1964 before Cassius Clay's fight against heavyweight champion Sonny Liston (Michael Bentt, 1965–), although the opening flashback includes scenes of Clay's formative years. Clay, a 7–1 underdog, bests the punishing Liston, winning the heavyweight title. Clay is drawn to Nation of Islam, first by Malcom X (Mario Van Peebles, 1957–) and then Elijah Muhammad (Albert Hall, 1937–). Clay converts to the Muslim religion, marries Sonji (Jada Pinkett Smith, 1971–), and strikes up a friendship with sports broadcaster Howard Cosell (Jon Voight, 1938–), who antagonize one another on screen but respect each other privately. Now calling himself by his Muslim name, Muhammad Ali, the young fighter is distraught when Malcom X is assassinated, but wins his rematch against Liston with a first-round knockout. Ali and Sonji soon divorce. With the Vietnam War escalating, Ali speaks out against the war, drawing criticism from other sports figures, journalists, and boxing fans. And after refusing to be drafted into military service, Ali is stripped of his boxing title.

He is found guilty and sentenced to five years in prison and fined $10,000. Although the sentence is appealed, most states won't allow him to fight; he isn't allowed out of the country to box elsewhere, and for more than three years he cannot fight professionally. The Nation of Islam suspends him, too, although Ali says, "I never stopped being a Muslim. I never stopped being a champion." He marries Belinda Boyd (Nona Gaye, 1974–), and, eventually, the Supreme Court overturns Ali's sentence, allowing Ali to return to the ring, where he loses to heavyweight champion Joe Frazier (James Toney, 1968–).

After George Foreman (Charles Shufford, 1973–) upsets Frazier for the boxing title, promoter Don King (Mykelti Williamson, 1957–) sets up a championship fight in Zaire, Africa, between Ali, now thirty-two years old, and the powerful, twenty-four-year-old Foreman. While that bout is delayed when Foreman is injured while training, Ali begins an affair with Veronica Porché (Michael Michele, 1966–).

In the title fight, Ali uses a defensive strategy to tire Foreman, then knocks out Foreman to regain the heavyweight title.

Amy Pascal (1958–), head of film development at Columbia Pictures, offered screenwriters Stephen J. Rivele (1949–) and Christopher Wilkinson (1950–), the Oscar-nominated writers of *Nixon* (1995), a choice of three projects: Jesus Christ, rock legend John Lennon (1940–80), and Ali. Picking Ali, the writers spent four months doing research, including several conversations with Ali, before starting the screenplay.

"The big challenge," Rivele said, "was reducing this enormous life to a manageable size" (Coppola 2002, 18). The original script covered Ali's Olympic gold medal in 1960 to the present day, but Mann decided to focus on 1964–74, and shortly before filming started, Rivele and Wilkinson were taken off the project. Mann and Eric Roth (1945–), who had cowritten *The Insider* (1999), reworked the screenplay.

Since 1995, Smith had been the top choice to play Ali, but said: "It was just too gargantuan a task and the margin of error was entirely too small. I just refused to be that guy that messed up this story. . . . It was only when I met Michael Mann . . . that I could see how it could be done" (Cheshire 2015, 75).

Actually, Smith and Barry Sonnenfeld (1953–) were first lined up for *Ali*, but Sonnenfeld abandoned the project after the box-office disaster *Wild Wild West* (1999).

Spike Lee (1957–), known for his films dealing with Black America and race relations, wanted to direct the movie. "Spike felt that only a black man could do justice to the story of Cassius Clay," a source told New York's *Daily News*, but Smith reportedly had final say on his director. "If [Smith] really wanted Spike, he could have had him," a source told the *Daily News* (Rush and Molloy 2000, 18). "I wish Spike Lee had made it, somebody with a more focused vision," Ali biographer Jonathan Eig said. "Spike Lee would have made it a racial pride thing" (Jonathan Eig, interview with author, September 2, 2020).

Smith trained for more than a year, upping his weight from 195 pounds to 223.

The project almost died in the fall of 2000 when Mann insisted on filming six weeks in Africa, but Initial Entertainment Group paid $65 million for *Ali*'s foreign rights and Mann and Smith deferred their $5 million and $65 million salaries against cost overruns, saving the project.

The costliest film biography (a $107 million budget), *Ali* hit theaters on Christmas Day 2001. Smith earned solid reviews—he and Voight were nominated for Academy Awards for best actor and best supporting actor—but reaction to the movie overall tended to be lukewarm.

"Smith is the right actor for Ali, but this is the wrong movie," *Chicago Sun-Times* critic Roger Ebert wrote. "Smith is sharp, fast, funny, like the Ali of trash-talking fame, but the movie doesn't unleash that side of him, or his character. . . . The film feels like it's under a cloud" (Ebert 2001). "The real frustration here," the *Fort Worth Star-Telegram*'s Christopher Kelly said, "is that I suspect this is exactly the movie that Mann wanted to make: something florid and brash and hyperbolic, but not dramatically or emotionally coherent; something designed to impress the Ali scholars (the fight scenes are so steeped in specific detail that you feel like you are watching newsreels) rather than to satisfy audiences" (Kelly 2001, 7E).

But in Ali's hometown of Louisville, Kentucky, *The Courier-Journal*'s Judith Egerton praised the movie. "'Ali' doesn't match the emotional clout and devastating beauty of 'Raging Bull' or the realistic glory of Ali at his prime in [the 1996 documentary] 'When We Were Kings.' But Mann's movie reminds us of Ali's role in the U.S. and world politics and his transformation from a loudmouth boxer to a man who roared in the face of racism by standing up for his convictions" (Egerton 2001, C1).

Ali earned only $58.2 domestically and another $29.6 million worldwide.

"The spirit of Ali is lacking in *Ali*, doing little to serve as a tribute to the man," Ellen Cheshire wrote. "It engages but does not inspire" (Cheshire 2015, 77).

HISTORICAL BACKGROUND

Professional boxing's beginnings in America can be traced to an 1816 bout in New York between Jacob Hyer (died 1838) and Tom Beasley—"the first authentic ring fight or contest in America in which rules were partially, if not wholly, observed," boxing historian Nat Fleischer said (Holmes 1949, 21). Hyer won the fight, yet he never defended his title. His son, Tom Hyer (1819–64), however, gained notice as a pugilist in the 1840s, knocking out George "County" McChester in the 101st round in 1841 at Caldwell's Landing, New York, and beating Yankee Sullivan (1811–56) in sixteen rounds in Rock Point, Maryland, in 1849.

As a sport, though, boxing has always had its defenders, and many detractors. Citing the sport's brutality and links to gambling, reformers attacked prizefighting, leading to the banning of such contests in many places. In 1867, John Graham Chambers (1843–83), a member of the British Amateur Athletic Club, wrote new boxing rules that John Sholto Douglas (1844–1900), the ninth Marquess of Queensberry, sponsored. These "Marquess of Queensberry" rules required padded gloves instead of bare knuckles, allotted three minutes per round with a one-minute rest period between rounds, prohibited wrestling techniques, and introduced the 10-second count for knockouts, and the lightweight, middleweight, and heavyweight classes to help equalize competitions. Americans, however, were slow to adapt the new rules, and by 1880, thirty states had banned prizefighting.

That didn't eliminate boxing matches, however. Promoters merely moved the matches to clandestine locations or outside local jurisdictions such as on rivers. On July 21, 1880, Patrick "Paddy" Ryan (1851–1900) defeated Englishman Joe Goss (1837–85) in an eighty-seven-round bareknuckle fight in Colliers, a small town on the Ohio–Pennsylvania border, "to ease potential escapes if authorities should intervene" (Gems 2014, 26). After Goss was arrested in Detroit in September and held for West Virginia authorities, *The Brooklyn Daily Eagle* reported:

> It is necessary for the rowdies and ruffians who thrive by beating each other to pieces, or by filching the pocketbooks of the zanies who attend prize fights in good clothes, to learn that the prize ring of to-day is an anachronism. Prize fighting is brutalizing, degrading and unlawful. It must, by consent of the people, be put down. Every man who engages in one must be punished. The punishment of Mr. Joseph Goss, especially if followed by the punishment of "Paddy" Ryan, will have the effect of convincing the "plugs" and bruisers, sneak thieves and ninnies who countenance prize fighting, in opposition to the will of the people, that its day is over. ("Goss Arrested for Prize Fighting" 1880, 2)

After defeating Ryan in a seventy-five-round bareknuckle fight in Mississippi City, Mississippi, John L. Sullivan (1858–1918) began holding exhibitions under Marquess of Queensberry rules, offering $500 to participants who could last four rounds in the ring against him. Slowly, the Queensberry style began gaining favor in America. Sullivan successfully defended his title, fighting with bare knuckles and under the new rules, until September 7, 1892—in the last of a three-day boxing event called the "Carnival of Champions"—when "Gentlemen Jim" Corbett knocked out Sullivan in the twenty-first round in New Orleans for the heavyweight championship.

Boxing still wasn't respectable or even legal in many places. On February 21, 1896, Ruby Robert "Bob" Fitzsimmons (1863–1917) scored a first-round knockout of Irish champion Peter Maher (1869–1940) on a sandbar in the Rio Grande between Langtry, Texas, and Mexico. Texas Rangers, a state law enforcement agency, had been ordered to Langtry to stop the fight. Believing they had no jurisdiction on the sandbar, the Rangers crossed a rickety bridge with the rest of the crowd to watch the bout.

In 1904, boxing debuted in the Olympics, held that year in St. Louis, Missouri, but the United States was the only country that entered the sport. The United States did not send a boxing team to the 1904 Olympics in London, and boxing was excluded from the 1912 Games in Stockholm because the sport was illegal under Swedish law. Americans have dominated Olympic boxing, earning 109 total medals, including forty-eight gold. Women's boxing made its Olympic debut in 2012 in London.

In 1910, with segregation policies and racial oppression escalating in the United States, Jack Johnson knocked out James J. Jeffries (1875–1953) in the fifteenth round in Reno, Nevada, becoming the first African American to hold the heavyweight championship.

Born in Galveston, Texas, Johnson grew up during the Jim Crow era of strict segregation—and lynching of many African Americas—across the country. Interracial marriages were illegal, while white heavyweight boxing champions refused to fight African American challengers. Johnson started boxing professionally in 1897, and by 1903 was considered the African American champion. Jeffries won the heavyweight title in 1899 with an eleventh-round knockout of Fitzsimmons. Jeffries retired in 1905, unde-feated as a professional boxer. Needing money, Fitzsimmons agreed to fight Johnson, who pummeled the then-forty-four-year-old in 1907 with a second-round knockout. The following year in Australia, Johnson battered Canadian Tommy Burns (1881–1955) for fourteen rounds before police stopped the carnage and Johnson was declared the winner.

Johnson's lifestyle outraged many white Americans. He lived flamboy-antly, taunted opponents in and out of the ring, and had interracial relation-ships with women. "Through Johnson, boxing served as a metaphor for the social, racial, and political struggles of the period, which placed him in the vanguard as a catalyst for the New Negro movement that transpired after World War I" (Gems 2014, 84).

White America searched for "The Great White Hope," someone who could beat Johnson and reestablish racial supremacy in not just the boxing world, but in the Jim Crow era, which would not cease until integration of the Armed Forces in 1948, the end of educational segregation in 1954, and passage of the Civil Rights, Voting Rights and Fair Housing acts in the 1960s. After Johnson annihilated five white opponents in 1909, Jeffries came out of retirement—only to be battered by Johnson.

Jeffries gave credit to Johnson, calling him "a truly great fighter" who won "fairly and squarely," while adding: "The color line should be drawn outside the ring. It cannot be dragged inside the ropes. When two men face each other for battle one of them must not be discriminated against because his skin is black. Keep him out of the ring entirely or give him fair play" ("Jeff Dies Hard, But Is Dead Game" 1910, 5).

Noted sportswriter Bat Masterson (1853–1921) summed up the fight:

Whatever else may be said about Johnson, all who saw him perform today must admit that he knows how to fight. He carries a greater variety of punches in his box of tricks than any heavy-weight I ever saw, not excepting Jim Cor-bett. There never was a man of his inches more fit. His heart and lungs showed strength, while his powers of endurance were superb. His timing of blows, whether delivered by Jeffries or himself, was simply marvelous. He demon-strated his ability to box in clever fashion when it was necessary, and gave unmistakable evidence of possessing a damaging blow in either hand, as Jeffries' face mutely testified to when the end came in the fifteenth round. Although a negro holds the heavy-weight championship, Johnson is an American, and that is some consolation to the people of this country. (Masterson 1910, 3)

Johnson held the title until losing Jess Willard (1881–1968), the 6-foot-7 white boxer from Kansas known as the "Pottawatomie Giant," in twenty-six rounds in Havana, Cuba, in 1915. But Johnson's success paved the way for other African American boxers.

Although the 1920s were dominated by William Harrison "Jack" Dempsey (1895–1983), heavyweight champion from 1919–26 and "one of the most unpopular and despised champions that ever climbed into the ring" (Gallico 1945, 11), in the 1930s, African American Joe Louis began making a name for himself in the ring with knockouts of former heavy-weight champions Primo Carnera (1906–67), Max Baer (1909–59), and Max Schmeling (1905–2005)—although Louis lost his first rematch against Schmeling—and Jack Sharkey (1902–94). With the world on the brink of World War II, Louis's first fight against Schmeling, on September 24, 1935, was instrumental. Schmeling was no Nazi, but Germany used him for Nazi propaganda. "In the eyes of most Americans," biographer Chris Mead wrote, "Joe Louis had exploded the myth of white supremacy. In the process he had won a measure of acceptance as America's national representative, something no black had ever enjoyed before. Louis was a revolutionary by coincidence" (Mead 1985, 159).

On June 22, 1937, Louis knocked out James J. Braddock (1905–74) in the eighth round in Chicago to become the first African American heavyweight champion since Johnson.

With racism rampant, Louis's managers made sure the boxer did not antagonize white Americans the way Johnson had. "He was never to have his picture taken with a white woman, never to enter a night club alone, never to gloat in victory, and he was to fight and live cleanly" (Hickok 2002, 284). "White sports writers got to like this image" (Kelleher 1985).

Louis won his third bout against Schmeling, defending his title sixteen times with fifteen knockouts, before he enlisted in the Army in 1942 after the Japanese bombed Pearl Harbor and America entered the global war. "World War II may have robbed Louis of his peak prize-fighting years, but it worked more wonders for his popularity" (Kelleher 1985). During the war, the Army used Louis for publicity and morale purposes.

After the war, Louis defended his title four more times before retiring in 1949. But a 1950 tax bill for more than $1 million in back taxes forced him back into the ring for financial reasons. He lost in a decision to Ezzard Charles (1921–75) on September 27, 1950, won eight more bouts, then was pummeled by eventual heavyweight champion Rocky Marciano, born Rocco Francis Marchegiano (1923–69), in 1951. Louis retired again. After

Marciano retired in 1956 with a 49–0 record, Floyd Patterson (1935–2006), not quite twenty-two years old, defeated Archie Moore (1916–98) to become the youngest heavyweight champion in history and the first African American heavyweight champion since Louis. Patterson lost the title in 1959 to Sweden's Ingemar Johansson (1932–2009), the first European to beat an American for that title since 1933, but Patterson won the rematch with a fifth-round knockout in 1960 to regain the title. Charles L. "Sonny" Liston (ca 1930–70), however, knocked out Patterson in the first round in 1962 in Chicago, and again in 1963, in another first-round knockout, in Las Vegas.

Liston was a different kind of champion. Born in Arkansas, he grew up poor. "The only thing my old man ever gave me," he said, "was a beating" (Tosches 2000, 34). Liston arrived in St. Louis, Missouri, in 1946, and on June 1, 1950, entered the Missouri State Prison in Jefferson City, sentenced to five years after pleading guilty to three charges of first-degree robbery and two charges of larceny. In prison, he learned how to box. Paroled in 1952, Liston joined the Golden Gloves program, winning the Chicago tournament and the Intercity Golden Gloves Championship (pitting Chicago against New York) in 1953. He turned pro that September. He associated with racketeers. After winning the heavyweight title, Liston "may have been the most unpopular man in all America" (Eig 2017, 106). A 1963 biography by A.S. "Doc" Young was titled *Sonny Liston: The Champ Nobody Wanted.* Liston didn't mind. "A boxing match is like a cowboy movie," he said. "There's got to be good guys, and there's got to be bad guys. I'm the bad guy." But there was a difference, since bad guys lose in cowboy movies. Liston said: "I change that" (Tosches 2000, 163).

"Whether boxing business can endure with a man such as Liston as its ruling monarch is a mite uncertain at this time," columnist Arthur Daley wrote after Liston's first triumph over Patterson. "Its future lies in his massive hands for what may be a long time to come. He looked invincible and overpowering" (Daley 1962, 3-C).

But there was a rising star in the boxing world. Like Liston, Cassius Clay, representing Chicago, was an Intercity Golden Gloves champion, winning in 1960 and then winning the gold medal at the 1960 Rome Olympics. That September, he turned pro and by 1964, he had a 19–0 record with fifteen knockouts.

Clay stirred up controversy of a different sort. He was arrogant, flashy, and flippant. "You have to realize that when Cassius talks he's winking at the world," said William Faversham Jr. (1905–78), who formed a syndicate along with wealthy Kentucky businessmen who backed Clay. "He just wants to see what kind of rise he can get from people" (Cope 1968, 140).

Few gave Clay any chance against Liston, but on February 25, 1964, Clay scored a technical knockout when Liston, claiming a shoulder injury, refused to come out of his corner at the beginning of the seventh round. Standing on the second ring rope after being declared the winner, Clay shouted to the

GOLDEN GLOVES

Golden Gloves amateur boxing started in two cities, thanks to two sportswriters.

In 1927, Paul Gallico, sports editor of New York's *Daily News*, staged an amateur boxing tournament open to New York residents. The first Golden Gloves—Gallico came up with the name—drew 1,084 entries and 21,594 spectators to the finals at Madison Square Garden. The following year, *Chicago Tribune* sports editor Arch Ward (1896–1955) organized a similar tournament in Chicago, taking the Golden Gloves name, after Illinois legalized prizefighting in 1926. Proceeds went to charities.

The popularity spread to other cities, and eventually internationally, while an intercity tournament between New York and Chicago became one of amateur boxing's biggest events.

"Thousands of young men battling in seven or eight states for a place on the Chicago team," Ward wrote. "Then the bouts with New York. Later a fight with the bravest from a foreign country. All for fun. This is amateur sport in its element" (Ward 1934, 19).

Champion boxers including Sugar Ray Robinson (1921–89), Joe Louis, Rocky Marciano, and Muhammad Ali got their starts in Golden Gloves.

Sources

Farrell, Bill. 2011. "1927–1934: Paul Gallico Creates a Classic." *Daily News*, November 8, 2011. https://www.nydailynews.com/sports/more-sports/golden-gloves/1927-1934-paul -gallico-creates-classic-article-1.974660

Griggs, Lee. 1955. "*Fame and Heartbreak in the Golden Gloves:* Amateur Boxing's Giant Elimination Draws 25,000 Young Hopefuls a Year, But Only Eight Can Become Champions." *Sports Illustrated*, March 28, 1955. https://vault.si.com/vault/1955/03/28/fame-and -heartbreak-in-the-golden-gloves

Hickok, Ralph. 2002. *The Encyclopedia of North American Sports History, Second Edition.* New York: Facts on File, Inc.

Ward, Arch. 1933. "Talking It Over." *Chicago Daily Tribune,* February 13, 1933, p. 19.

half-filled arena: "Eat your words" (Smith, W. 1964, 3-1). Shortly after the fight, Clay said he had converted to the Muslim religion and would be called Cassius X, but on March 6, Elijah Muhammad (1897–1975), leader of the Nation of Islam, gave Clay the name Muhammad Ali. "I am honored," Ali said (Associated Press 1964c, 10).

On May 25, 1965, in a rematch against Liston in Lewiston, Maine, Ali scored a controversial first-round knockout.

Ali had failed the Army's military intelligence test in 1963, and was classified 1-Y. "I really tried hard—real hard—on that mental test," he said. "It wasn't too hard, I guess, but I never was a good reader, or a good speller, not brainy with a pencil and paper. I got out of Central High with a D-minus, you know" (Boeck 1964, 20). In 1967, however, with more U.S. troops entering Vietnam, Army standards were lowered and Ali was reclassified

1-A. On April 1, 1967, when Ali refused induction, the World Boxing Association stripped him of his title, and he was sentenced to five years imprisonment for draft evasion.

For more than three years, Ali was unable to fight, although he remained out of prison pending appeals. His exile ended when he secured a fight against Jerry Quarry (1945–99) in Atlanta, Georgia, winning easily on October 26, 1970. A district court ordered the New York Athletic Commission to restore Ali's license, and Ali met Joe Frazier at Madison Square Garden on March 8, 1971. Frazier won in a unanimous decision after fifteen rounds. A few months later, the U.S. Supreme Court overturned Ali's conviction, and Ali began his comeback. After being knocked out by Ken Norton in 1973, Ali won the rematch five months later, then beat Frazier in a twelve-round decision in 1974. On October 30, 1974, Ali regained the heavyweight title by knocking out George Foreman. On October 1, 1975, Ali won the famous "Thrilla in Manilla," his third fight against Frazier, with a fourteenth-round knockout. The fighter once despised for his cockiness, hated for his religion, and loathed as a draft dodger suddenly became a hero.

He lost the title to Leon Spinks (1953–2021) in February 1978, regained it that September, retired in 1979, then came back, unsuccessfully, before retiring permanently in 1981, with a 56–4 record. Despite being diagnosed with Parkinson's in 1982, he traveled, often promoting humanitarian causes. At the 1996 Olympics in Atlanta, he was handed the Olympic torch and climbed the stadium steps to light the Olympic flame.

"When he held that Olympic torch in his shaky hands, the people roared . . . and they weren't roaring for the great fighter," recalled Thom Ross, an artist known for his sports subjects. "They were roaring for the great man. He, elevated as he was on that platform was, in all senses, truly great and, yes, he belonged above us all, floating there on a cloud of our cheers" (Thom Ross, interview with author, January 13, 2020).

In 2005, President George W. Bush (1946–) presented Ali with America's highest civilian award, the Presidential Medal of Freedom. Ali died on June 3, 2016. He was seventy-four.

"I was stunned," Ross said. "I could not imagine a world without him in it. I began to consider his role as a boxer and then as a world-famous figurehead, and I came to realize that he just might be the last man who made that transition from historical figure into a mythic one" (Thom Ross, interview with author, January 13, 2020).

DEPICTION AND CULTURAL CONTEXT

Ali's Olympic gold medal in 1960 made him an American sports hero, but by 1964—when the film opens—he was despised by many. "He came out of nowhere to win an Olympic medal in 1960 and then emerged on the

American sports scene as a person to be reckoned with both as a boxer and as a cultural phenomenon," Ross said. "And as the older generation came to hate him for his outlandish behavior—especially for a Black man of those times—the younger generation saw in him a voice of their own in the same manner as they embraced the music of the Beatles" (Ross, interview with author, January 13, 2020).

As a biopic about a boxer, *Ali* does a credible job of staying close to the facts in the matches depicted. "The fights I thought were fairly accurate," Eig said. "That was probably the area where they were the most accurate. The guy who played Liston as great. The guy who played Frazier was really good and really had his fighting style down" (Jonathan Eig, interview with author, September 2, 2020).

Part of that can be attributed to the casting. Bentt, playing Liston, posted an 11–2 record boxing from 1989–94, winning the World Boxing Organization's heavyweight title in 1993. Toney, as Frazier, went 77–19–3 as a middleweight from 1988–2017. Alfred Cole (1964–), as Ernie Terrell, went 35–16–3 from 1989–2011 in the cruiserweight and heavyweight divisions. Shufford, as Foreman, went 20–8–1 as a heavyweight from 1996 to 2008. Robert Sale, who played Jerry Quarry, was an amateur and professional fighter who served as boxing trainer, consultant, and/or technical adviser for several boxing movies, including *Rocky Balboa* (2006) and *Grudge Match* (2013). Rivele and Wilkinson also relied on a boxed set of videocassettes of Ali's greatest fights while working on the screenplay. "We didn't try to choreograph step by step," Rivele said. "We wanted to get the basic beats of the fights down" (Coppola 2002, 18). Mann, on the other hand, "went farther and tried to re-create the actual moves," Rivele said. "And from what I saw, he did a brilliant job" (Coppola 2002, 18).

Ali starts with the 1964 title fight against Liston. Ali, still fighting as Cassius Clay, was cocksure, confident to the point of arrogance, and that alienated many sportswriters. "I was always surprised the writers couldn't get any fun out of it all," recalled *Sports Illustrated* correspondent George Plimpton (1927–2003). "They stared down at their pads, and sometimes they said under their breaths, 'Aw, come off it, Clay.' They rarely looked up at the fighter" (Plimpton 2016, 81–82). During weigh-ins the day of the fight, Ali called Liston a "chump," and kept acting up so much boxing officials fined him $2,500. Few took the challenger seriously.

"The first punch Liston hits him, out he goes," said Billy Cohn (1917–93), a former light-heavyweight champion. "He can't fight now, and he'll never be able to fight. He hasn't the experience. The only experience he'll get is how to get killed in a hurry" (Tosches 2000, 202).

The *New York Times* didn't even send its boxing writer to cover the event in Miami. "It was basically seen as a feature writer's story," recalled *Times* reporter Robert Lipsyte (1938–), who covered the fight. "Liston would destroy Clay very quickly, the *Times* would do its usual antiboxing editorial;

and they they'd send the real boxing writer back to cover what serious fights came along. In fact, when I went down to Miami for the fight, my basic instruction was to find out the distance from the arena to the nearest hospital, so I wouldn't waste deadline time getting there after Clay was knocked out" (Hauser 1992, 69).

Instead, Ali dominated the fight. The movie "made it look like Liston was beating up on him a little bit in the beginning and it took Ali some time," Eig said. "But really, it's clear from the very beginning that Ali is in control of this fight and at the end of the first round he's landing combinations and is really unafraid of being hit. You see his confidence really lifting" (Jonathan Eig, interview with author, September 2, 2020).

As depicted in the film, Ali was temporarily blinded during the fight, and what followed is one of boxing's unsolved mysteries.

Late in the fourth round, Ali began having trouble seeing. After the round, he told trainer Angelo Dundee (1921–2012) "to cut my gloves off before the fifth round, there wasn't any point in my getting knocked out, and I knew Liston would if he hit me." Dundee refused. "He shoved me right out into the ring, hollering, 'You can't quit now. This is the big one, daddy'" (Pope 1964, 1-C).

While Ali sat on his stool, blinking repeated, referee Barney Felix (1906–85) yelled, "'dammit, Clay, get out here!' If he hadn't moved in a second—and I mean one second—I had made up my mind to stop the bout and award the fight to Liston on a [technical knockout]" (United Press International 1964, 38).

Ali accused Liston of trying to blind him "by putting [liniment] on his glove. I couldn't see a thing. But he couldn't hit me" (Associated Press 1964a, 2).

Theories surfaced. Liniment was put on Liston's glove, although Felix said he found no trace of a foreign substance on the gloves. Liniment had been applied to a cut over Liston's facial cuts, so perhaps that had wound up in Ali's eyes. Others suggested that Dundee had ties with organized crime and had blinded Ali by wiping the boxer's face with a towel that had been doused with a blinding agent. Dundee, however, said he tested his towel and sponge by wiping his own eyes, which were unharmed. "My guess is, it was the coagulant that [Liston's] corner used on the cuts," Dundee said. "Probably Cassius got the solution on his gloves, and when he brushed them against his forehead, it left a layer of something that trickled down with the perspiration into his eyes" (Hauser 1992, 75).

Said Eig: "I think there's certainly a chance that they put something on the gloves, but that's an inefficient way of trying to steal a fight. Like put something on the gloves and hope it gets into his eyes and that nobody's going to notice it, nobody's going to smell it? It's possible that's what really happened, but I don't think we're ever going to really know" (Jonathan Eig, interview with author, September 2, 2020).

Ali's vision cleared, and as depicted in the film, Ali was declared the winner when Liston refused to continue the fight in the seventh round. Felix gave the victory to Ali via a technical knockout.

Ali "fought his way out of the horde that swarmed and leaped and shouted in the ring, climbed like a squirrel onto the red velvet ropes and brandished his still-gloved hands aloft," columnist Red Smith reported. "'Eat your words,' he howled to the working press rows. 'Eat your words.' Nobody had a better right" (Smith 1964, 38).

The two boxers were even on points after six rounds, but Ali was the new heavyweight champion, and the controversy was far from over.

Liston said he could not finish the fight because of numbness in his left shoulder, which he injured in the first round, when both fighters kept punching after the bell sounded to end the round (also accurately covered in the movie). Liston said he attempted to block an Ali punch while simultaneously trying to land a punch. Jack Nilon (1920–2002), Liston's manager, said Liston hurt the shoulder while training.

Eight doctors who examined Liston for 3½ hours at St. Francis Hospital after the fight confirmed the injury was severe enough to end the fight, issuing a statement that: "Sonny Liston received an injury to the long head of the biceps tendon of his left shoulder with the result that there is a separation and tear of the muscle fibers with some hemorrhaging into the inside belly of the [biceps]. This condition could be sufficient to incapacitate him and prevent him from defending himself" (Hand 1964, 10-A).

While *Ali* suggests that something might have been put on Liston's gloves, the film glosses over the post-fight controversy.

Cal Gardner, Miami Beach Boxing Commission vice chairman, announced that Liston's purse would be withheld pending a ruling from surgeons that Liston's injury was legitimate. Reports broke that before the championship fight, International Continental Promoters, Inc., of which Liston was part-owner, had contracted with Ali's management group for the rights to Ali's next fight, paying Ali $50,000 for the commitment—"a staggering amount to pay for the future rights to a single bout by a fighter who was seen as facing almost certain defeat" against Liston (Tosches 2000, 204–205).

Ali screamed at reporters, "you hypocrites can't say it was a fix" (Peterson 1964, 15). But in Washington, D.C., Ohio Representative Michael A. Fieghan (1905–92) asked Congress to investigate professional boxing. "Congress has a duty to turn the spotlight of open inquiry upon it and to effect such legislation as is necessary to prevent fraud and racketeering," Feighan said. "The Liston-Clay affair has brought the long suffering crisis in professional boxing to a head" (Associated Press 1964b, 9-A).

The only thing of consequence to come out of all of this was the May 25, 1965, rematch in Lewiston, Maine—a fight even more controversial than the first fight. *Ali* accurately depicts the stunning first-round knockout of Liston, but again skips the aftermath of what *Sports Illustrated*'s Richard

O'Brien called "perhaps the most confounding and controversial in ring history" (O'Brien 2015).

The fight, originally scheduled for November 16, 1964, at Boston Garden, had been postponed after Ali's emergency hernia surgery three days before the day of the bout. After the hullabaloo surrounding the first fight, state boxing commissions were hesitant to license the rematch. After the fight was delayed because of Ali's surgery, the date was first moved to May 25, 1965, in Boston. But Suffolk County District Attorney Garrett H. Byrne (1897–1989), concerned with Liston's promoters' suspected ties to organized crime, sought an injunction to block the fight. That ended May 6 when organizers withdrew the fight from Boston. Needing a new site quickly, the promoters found Maine Governor John H. Reed (1921–2012) agreeable, and Lewiston (population forty-one thousand) became the smallest city to hold a championship boxing match since Shelby, Montana (population three thousand) held Dempsey's fight against Tommy Gibbons (1891–1960) on July 4, 1923. Liston–Ali II drew only 2,434 spectators to the 5,800-seat St. Dominic's Arena, a youth center, possibly because Malcolm X (1925–65) was assassinated on February 21, and Ali received death threats because he had fallen out with Malcolm X and embraced Elijah Muhammad. Liston also reportedly received death threats, including rumors that the Nation of Islam would kill him if he didn't throw the fight. On the day of the fight, "The arena itself, and the surrounding area, was crawling with troopers and local gendarmes," New York's *Daily News* reported. "Also on hand were two New York detectives assigned to keep an eye peeled for followers of the late Malcolm X who supposedly are out to get Clay. But the way it turned out, Liston was the only one who made a menacing gesture in the direction of Muhammad Ali" (Ward 1965b, 92).

At 10 p.m., the fight began. In less than two minutes, Ali had knocked out Liston and successfully defended his title. Lipsyte wrote for the *New York Times*: "Clay connected immediately with a right to Liston's head. Liston seemed to shake off the blows, as the crowd, for once, cheered for him. For what seemed longer than the official 48 seconds, Clay danced around Liston, counter-clockwise, jabbing him lightly, once more connecting with a solid right. Then he fired the short right and missed a left hook as Liston sagged to his knees. Liston collapsed slowly, like a falling building, piece by piece, rolling onto his back, then flat on his stomach, his face pressed against the canvas. Clay danced around him, waving at him, taunting him" (Lipsyte 1965, 1, 54).

Ali shows the knockout punch, but skips the uproar that followed.

Spectators in the ringside seats, priced at $100 each, called out: "Fake! Fake! Fake!" (Cady 1965, 55). Others called "fix" or "foul." The *Daily News* said Liston had been knocked out by "A righthand punch, thrown with phantom force and landing with the thud of a creampuff" (Ward 1965a, 92).

Once again, calls came for a Congressional investigation of boxing in Washington, D.C. Illinois Representative Robert Michel (1923–2017) complained that people had paid $12 million to watch closed-circuit television broadcasts of Liston's two first-round knockouts of Patterson and his first-round loss to Ali, all of which totaled "less than nine minutes" (Herald Wire Services 1965, 4-D). Several members of the New York Yankees baseball team paid to watch the fight in a theater. First baseman Joe Pepitone (1940–) went to the lobby to buy popcorn. "He came back with ten or twelve sacks, and everyone was leaving," teammate Mickey Mantle (1931–95) said. "Joe just threw the popcorn up in the air and asked, 'What the hell happened?'" (Hauser 1992, 126). News organizations worldwide questioned the fight's legitimacy.

"What unfolded that night," Richard O'Brien wrote for *Sports Illustrated*, "has been analyzed as closely as the Zapruder film [of the 1963 assassination of President John F. Kennedy]: Ali's flashing right hand (did it really land?); Liston's awkward swoon and rolling on the canvas before rising to resume fighting, only to have the referee, former heavyweight champ Jersey Joe Walcott, stop the proceedings and declare Ali the winner by KO; Ali's own reaction, seemingly one of outrage; cries of 'Fix!' from fans and the press" (O'Brien 2015).

"Where did that right hand come from?" Liston asked after the knockout. "I only 'partly' saw it" (Associated Press 1965, 12).

"That punch is so fast you can't see it!" Ali told reporters. "But if you were hit with it, all of you'd be down. . . . It's a twisting right-hand punch that's hard to see. But you can't use it unless the other man is coming at you. It's like a head-on collision" (Cady 1965, 55).

Slow-motion replays reveal that Ali landed a right counter punch. But was it a knockout blow?

"Ali was saying to his brother, 'I don't think I hit him. I don't really think I knocked him out,' and in Ali's corner, they're going, 'Oh, no, no, no, really, you knocked him out'," Eig said. "'That was a good punch.' And a few minutes later Ali's describing the anchor punch and how he'd been planning it all along" (Jonathan Eig, interview with author, September 2, 2020).

The FBI investigated, but found no evidence of a fix. Liston's wife said she thought Liston threw the fight, but if he was paid to lose, she never saw any of the money.

"That did not look like a knockout punch to me," Eig said, "and I think there's a very good chance that Liston just decided to roll over and play dead on that one" (Jonathan Eig, interview with author, September 2, 2020).

The movie minimizes Ali's relationship with Frazier, his biggest and best rival. Ali did spout poetry about Frazier, as early as 1968, and he did use his poem that starts "Ali comes out to meet Frazier/But Frazier starts to retreat/ If Frazier goes back any further/He'll wind up in a ringside seat," as depicted in the movie. But a version of that poem was first used before Ali's 1964 fight against Liston.

While *Ali* stays close to the facts regarding the fights shown, the movie falters in the depictions of Ali's wives—Sonji Roi (1946–2005), Belinda Boyd (1950–), and Veronica Porché (1955–). Ali married his last wife, Lonnie Williams, in 1986, and they remained married until Ali's death.

Sonji "doesn't appear until after the Liston fight, whereas she was a big bone of contention before the Liston fight," said Ferdie Pacheco (1927–2017), Ali's doctor. "Belinda shows up in Africa to have a her-or-me confrontation over Veronica. That happened in the Philippines in the Frazier-Ali third fight, two years later" (Pacheco 2001, 2).

"The movie was a really serious blind spot when it comes to the women," Eig said. "None of the characters are developed at all. Sonji is probably the best developed of all. Those years when he's exiled from boxing, Belinda is really important character. It's sort of like they've lost their superpowers. Ali can't box anymore, and they become a normal married couple in a way. She has to support the family. And then he starts cheating on her during those years. None of that comes through" (Jonathan Eig, interview with author, September 2, 2020).

But the biggest stretch is the relationship between Ali and sportscaster Howard Cosell (1918–95). Certainly, the movie got part of the relationship right, how they relied on each other and played off one another, and "how they were twins—cartoonish and clownish on the exterior, but underneath it, two pioneers who knew more than the rest of us and had the courage and chutzpah to set us straight" (Ostler 2001). But "Cosell wasn't even wearing a hairpiece in the early days of Ali's career" (Jonathan Eig, interview with author, September 2, 2020), and Ali and Cosell "didn't have intimate moments where they talked about their problems and their wives," Lipsyte said. "It was a very respectful business relationship" (Cruz 2002).

Nor did Cosell telephone Ali to let him know the Supreme Court had overturned his draft-evasion conviction as shown in *Ali*. A fan heard the news on his transistor radio and got Ali's attention while he was driving in Chicago to tell him. Another problem with that scene is that it is placed while Ali preps for his fight against Frazier. Ali fought Frazier for the first time at Madison Square Garden on March 8, 1971, more than a month before the Supreme Court heard arguments on April 19, 1971. The court's ruling was not announced until June 28, 1971, more than three months after the first Frazier-Ali fight and more than 2½ years before their first rematch.

The movie ends with Ali's knockout of Foreman—called by Cosell. But Cosell left Zaire after the championship bout against Foreman was postponed. Bob Sheridan (1944–), who broadcast more than 725 championship bouts, called the "Rumble in the Jungle."

"I don't know why Cosell got such incredible treatment as Ali's adviser, almost like his rabbi," Eig said. "He's giving him all this great advice on what he really needs. That bothered me a little bit. It almost made out that Ali needed the white man to offer him this political and spiritual counseling.

That was strange to me" (Jonathan Eig, interview with author, September 2, 2020).

What might hurt *Ali* the most as a sports biopic is its omissions. As the *Chicago Tribune*'s Mark Caro pointed out:

> Mann has made an awfully narrow epic. What he has left out includes: a sense of Ali's childhood beyond a glimpse of him moving to the back of a segregated bus; why he became a boxer; how his popularity soared to globe-conquering heights; his specific religious/spiritual connection to Islam; the 'phantom punch' controversy surrounding his second defeat of Liston; his fierce, bitter rivalry with Joe Frazier, including their on-air scuffle before their second fight and any mention of 'The Thrilla in Manilla' (which followed the Foreman bout); and any reference to his physical decline, the Atlanta Olympics or just about anything that has happened over the past 27 years.
>
> That's a lot to omit. (Caro 2001, 1)

CONCLUSION

Film historian C. Courtney Joyner explained cinema's success with boxing movies:

> There are moments from boxing movies that have stayed with us: [James] Cagney going blind during the last rounds in *City for Conquest*, Kirk Douglas's defeat in *Champion*, or Robert Ryan's victory in *The Set-Up*. The blood dripping from the ropes in *Raging Bull*, and the eternal hope of Sly [Stallone] in *Rocky*.
>
> There are great scenes in other sports movies too, but they seem to fall into the "do you remember" category. Remember Redford swatting the homer in *The Natural* or Burt Reynolds picking up the game ball in *The Longest Yard*? Of course. But the images—the feelings—from the ring don't need reminders. Once seen, they're with us forever. (C. Courtney Joyner, interview with author, August 27, 2020)

Ali lacks those moments. While the film has its admirers—*American History* magazine's *100 Greatest Sports Movies* special edition (2010) ranked *Ali* No. 65—and the history is solid, the focus is lacking. It tries to tell too much, yet doesn't tell enough. Eig suggested than an eight- to ten-part miniseries would be the best way to tell Ali's story. Even Mann wasn't happy with the 2001 release. He reedited *Ali* for television, and a third time for a 2017 Blu-ray release. "I wasn't satisfied with how I felt at the end of the film—which is to say, the story that was being told wasn't complete," Mann told *Vanity Fair*. "It needed to be reorganized, or re-authored, in a way" (Fear 2017).

"I still don't know what to make of the movie," Eig said. "It's interesting, it's beautiful, and it's a mess" (Jonathan Eig, interview with author, September 2, 2020).

FURTHER READING

Ali, Muhammad with Richard Durham. 1979. *The Greatest: Muhammad Ali: My Own Story*. New York: Ballantine.

Associated Press. 1964a. "I'll Fight Any Man Alive, Thunders Clay." *Fort Worth Star-Telegram*, February 26, 1964, Section 3, p. 2.

Associated Press. 1964b. "Fumigation of Professional Boxing Sought." *Messenger and Inquirer*, February 27, 1964, p. 9-A.

Associated Press. 1964c. "Muhammad Ali New Name for Cassius Clay." *Indiana Evening Gazette*, March 6, 1964, p. 10.

Associated Press. 1965. "Dressing Rooms: Liston Barely Saw Punch." *Spokane Daily Chronicle*, May 26, 1965, p. 12.

Boeck, Larry. 1964. "Clown No More: A Quiet Champ Comes Home: But He Warms to Familiar Surroundings." *The Courier-Journal*, March 8, 1964, pp. 1, 20.

Cady, Steve. 1965. "Big Punch a 'Twisting Right,' Victory Says: It's So Fast It Can't Be Seen, Exuberant Winner Explains." *The New York Times*, May 26, 1965, p. 55.

Caro, Mark. 2001. "'Ali' Doesn't Go the Distance: While Will Smith Is Magnetic, the Movie Can't Compare to the Real Man and Legend." *Chicago Tribune*, December 25, 2001, Tempo, pp. 1, 15.

Carruth, Gorton, and Eugene Ehrlich. 1988. *Facts & Dates of American Sports: From Colonial Days to the Present*. New York: Perennial Library.

Cheshire, Ellen. 2015. *Bio-Pics: A Life in Pictures*. New York: Wallflower Press.

Cope, Myron. 1968. *Broken Cigars*. Englewood Cliffs, NJ: Prentice-Hall, Inc.

Coppola, Don. 2002. "Bringing Historical Characters to Life: An Interview with Stephen J. Rivele." *Cinéaste* 27, no. 2 (Spring): 16–19.

Cruz, Clarissa. 2002. "How Closely Does 'Ali' Stick to the Truth? This Season's Biographical Films Take Varying Degrees of Cinematic License." *Entertainment Weekly*, January 8, 2002. https://ew.com/article/2002/01/08/how-closely-does-ali-stick-truth/

Daley, Arthur. 1962. "It Was Almost Too Fast." *St. Petersburg Times*, September 26, 1962, p. 3-C.

Ebert, Roger. 2001. "Ali." https://www.rogerebert.com/reviews/ali-2001

Egerton, Judith. 2001. "Will Smith Impresses as Muhammad Ali." *The Courier-Journal*, December 25, 2001, p. 1C.

Eig, Jonathan. 2017. *Ali: A Life*. New York: Houghton Mifflin Harcourt.

Fear, David. 2017. "Michael Mann on Political New 'Ali' Cut: 'He Was a Symbol of Resistance:' Filmmaker Talks about Revising His 2001 Biopic on the Boxing Legend into a Political Thriller and What Ali Means in the Trump Era." *Rolling Stone*, January 26, 2017. https://www.rollingstone.com/movies/movie-features/michael-mann-on-political-new-ali-cut-he-was-a-symbol-of-resistance-124275/

Gallico, Paul. 1945. *Farewell to Sport*. New York: Pocket Books, Inc.

Gems, Gerald R. 2014. *Boxing: A Concise History of the Sweet Science*. Lanham, MD: Rowman & Littlefield.

Goldstein, Patrick. 2001. "Keeping 'Ali' Grounded in Reality." *Chicago Tribune*, December 28, 2001. https://www.chicagotribune.com/news/ct-xpm-2001-12-28-0112280003-story.html

"Goss Arrested For Prize Fighting." 1880. *The Brooklyn Daily Eagle*, September 15, 1880, p. 2.

Grindon, Leger. 2011. *Knockout: The Boxer and Boxing in American Cinema*. Jackson, MS: University Press of Mississippi.

Hand, Jack. 1964. "MBBC Is Satisfied Liston Suffered 'Honest' Injury." *Messenger and Inquirer*, February 27, 1964, p. 10-A.

Hauser, Thomas. 1992. *Muhammad Ali: His Life and Times*. New York: Touchstone.

Herald Wire Services. 1965. "As Maine Goes, So Goes World." *The Miami Herald*, May 27, 1965, p. 4-D.

Hickok, Ralph. 2002. *The Encyclopedia of North American Sports History, Second Edition*. New York: Facts on File, Inc.

Holmes, Tommy. 1949. "A Sports History of Brooklyn." *Brooklyn Eagle*, July 17, 1949, p. 21.

"Jeff Dies Hard, But Is Dead Game." 1910. *The Buffalo Commercial*, July 5, 1910, p. 5.

Kelleher, Terry. 1985. "'Champion' Mostly Captures the Times of Joe Louis." *South Florida Sun-Sentinel*, September 4, 2020. https://www.sun-sentinel.com/news/fl-xpm-1985-11-24-8502230078-story.html

Kelly, Christopher. 2001. "Down for the Count: Heavyweight Performances Can't Save 'Ali.'" *Fort Worth Star-Telegram*, December 25, 2001, pp. 1E, 7E.

Kram, Mark. 2001. *Ghosts of Manila: The Fateful Blood Feud between Muhammad Ali and Joe Frazier*. New York: HarperCollins.

Leogrande, Ernest. 1977. "Ali Stars as Ali." *Daily News*, May 21, 1977: 17C.

Lipsyte, Robert. 1965. "Clay Knocks Out Liston in One Minute; Bout, Like First, Ends in Controversy." *The New York Times*, May 26, 1965, pp. 1, 54.

Masterson, Bat. 1910. "Masterson Gives Credit to Johnson: Fistic Writer Declares That Negro Champion Is Greatest Fighter of the Age and That White Supremacy in Ring Is Gone. Says Jeffries Never Had Slightest Chance to Win. Defeated Man in His Palmiest Days Would Have Found Black Man His Equal—Like Sullivan at New Orleans." *The Inter Ocean*, July 5, 1910, p. 3.

Mead, Chris. 1985. *Champion Joe Louis: Black Hero in White America*. Mineola, NY: Dover Publications, Inc.

"Muhammad Ali vs. Sonny Liston (2nd Meeting)." n.d. https://boxrec.com/media/index.php/Muhammad_Ali_vs._Sonny_Liston_(2nd_meeting)

Nelson, Murry R., ed. 2009a. *Encyclopedia of Sports in America: A History from Foot Races to Extreme Sports. Volume 1: Colonial Years to 1939*. Westport, CT: Greenwood Press.

Nelson, Murry R., ed. 2009b. *Encyclopedia of Sports in America: A History from Foot Races to Extreme Sports. Volume 2: 1940 to Present*. Westport, CT: Greenwood Press.

O'Brien, Richard. 2015. "Remembering One of Boxing's Most Controversial Fights: Ali-Liston II: Remembering Muhammad Ali vs. Sonny Liston II on the 50th Anniversary of the Controversial Boxing Fight." *Sports Illustrated*, May 21, 2015. https://www.si.com/boxing/2015/05/21/ali-liston-ii-neil-leifer-50-years-later

Ostler, Scott. 2001. "Stronger Than Fiction/Sticking to the Truth in 'Ali' Pays Off for Filmmaker and Fans Alike.'" *San Francisco Chronicle*, January 29, 2012. https://www.sfgate.com/sports/ostler/article/Stronger-than-fiction-Sticking-to-the-truth-in-2819279.php

Pacheco, Ferdie. 2001. "Fight Doctor: 'Ali' Packs Very Little Punch." *The Tampa Tribune*, December 30, 2001, Sports, p. 2.

Peterson, Leo H. 1964. "Clay Stages Shocking TKO to Grab Heavyweight Crown: Loudmouth Clay's Boasting Stands Up in Title Upset; Suspicions Voiced Over Win." *Evening Herald*, February 26, 1964, p. 15.

Plimpton, George. 2016. *Shadow Box: An Amateur in the Ring*. New York: Little, Brown and Company.

Pope, Edwin. 1964. "Cassius Wanted to Surrender: 'Couldn't See.'" *The Miami Herald*, February 27, 1964, p. 1-C.

Romano, Frederick B. 2017. *Boxing on Radio and Television: A Blow by Blow History from 1924 to 1964*. New York: Carrel Books.

Rush, George, and Joanna Molloy. 2000. "It's Kid Gloves for Slighted Spike." *Daily News*, March 8, 2000, p. 18.

Saraceno, Jon. 1996. "The Renaissance of Muhammad Ali: Olympics Set His Life Afire Anew." *The Sacramento Bee*, October 13, 1996, p. C12.

Smith, Red. 1964. "Menu for Day Turns Out to Be Crow." *The Philadelphia Inquirer*, February 26, 1964, p. 38.

Smith, Wilfrid. 1964. "Clay Champ! TKO's Liston: Sonny Fails to Answer Bell in 7th." *Chicago Tribune*, February 26, 1964, section 3, p. 1.

Streible, Dan. 2008. *Fight Pictures: A History of Boxing and Early Cinema*. Berkeley: University of California Press.

Tosches, Nick. 2000. *The Devil and Sonny Liston*. Boston: Little, Brown and Company.

United Press International. 1964. "Referee Almost Gave Liston Win in Fifth." *The Boston Globe*, February 27, 1964, p. 38.

United Press International. 1965. "Fight Is Shifted: Title Bout Reset in Maine." *Kingsport News*, May 8, 1965, p. 13.

Ward, Gene. 1965a. "Creampuff right KO's Liston in 1st: Clay Punch Ends 1-Minute Bout." *Daily News*, May 26, 1965, pp. 92, 96.

Ward, Gene. 1965b. "Cocky Clay 206; Sonny Scales 215: Champ Playful at Guarded Weigh-In." *Daily News*, May 26, 1965.

Weiss, David Ansel. 2005. "Boxing Impresario Nonpareil: Judge Roy Bean's Fighting Matches Could Drive One to Drink." *True West*, August 1, 2005. https://truewestmagazine.com/boxing-impresario-nonpareil/

Wilkening, David. 1977. "'The Greatest' Ali's Movie Isn't." *Sentinel Star*, May 21, 1977, p. 1-B.

Woulfe, Jimmy. 2010. "'Rumble in the Jungle' Commentator to Speak at Ali Event." *Irish Examiner*, August 31, 2010. https://www.irishexaminer.com/news/arid-20129388.html

Chapter 7

Seabiscuit (2003)

Released nationally on July 25, 2003, *Seabiscuit* was among the year's most anticipated movies. Two years earlier, Laura Hillenbrand's *Seabiscuit: An American Legend,* published by Random House, skyrocketed to critical and commercial success. Topping the *New York Times*'s bestseller list for forty-two weeks, the nonfiction account of a successful 1930s racehorse sold more than three million copies; was finalist for the National Book Critics Circle Award; and wound up on the *Los Angeles Times, New York Times, St. Louis Post-Dispatch, Washington Post,* and *Time* magazine's best-book-of-the-year lists. *USA Today* named it Sports Book of the Year.

Hillenbrand's book started out as a 1998 magazine article for *American Heritage* that won the Eclipse Award, sponsored by the *Daily Racing Form*, National Turf Writers Association, and National Thoroughbred Racing Association, for magazine writing. In 1999, Hillenbrand sold book and movie rights in one week.

The racehorse doesn't show up until more than 40 minutes into the film. Before that viewers follow the troubled lives of Charles Howard (Jeff Bridges, 1949–), Tom Smith (Chris Cooper, 1951–), and Johnny "Red" Pollard (Tobey Maguire, 1975–). In the early 1900s, bicycle-shop owner Howard realizes that automobiles are the future, and soon becomes one of California's wealthiest entrepreneurs—telling one customer, "I wouldn't spend more than $5 on the best horse in America." A taciturn horseman and wrangler, Smith sees the end of wide-open ranges rapidly drawing to a close, but he's always trying to save horses about to be killed. "You don't throw a whole life away just because he's banged up a little," he says. Young Pollard grows up in a well-to-do family where reading and discussing books are favorite pastimes.

But the stock market collapses in 1929, sending the United States and the world into the Great Depression (1929–39). After his young son is killed in an automobile accident, Howard becomes melancholy, and his wife leaves him; Smith finds himself living the life of a hobo on the rails; and Pollard's parents lose their home, eventually abandoning Pollard at a horse track because the boy's riding ability gives him a future. Within years, Pollard is drifting, boxing, and riding for money, eventually losing sight in his right eye after being pummeled in a boxing match.

In Mexico for a quick divorce, Howard meets Marcela Zabala (Elizabeth Banks, 1974–), whom he later marries. After deciding to go into horse racing, Howard meets Smith, who talks Howard into buying a small but temperamental stallion, barely fifteen hands, named Seabiscuit. Pollard gets the job as jockey because Smith sees similarities between the feisty horse and easy-to-rile jockey.

The bonding of owner-trainer-rider-stallion works well, and Seabiscuit's success, despite being trivialized by journalists, captures the attention of many struggling Americans. Howard begins lobbying for a match race against War Admiral, winner of the 1937 Triple Crown (Kentucky Derby, Preakness Stakes, Belmont Stakes). Eventually, War Admiral owner Samuel Riddle (Eddie Jones, 1934–2019) agrees, and the "Match Race of the Century" is set for November 1, 1938, at Pimlico Race Course in Baltimore. Pollard, however, breaks his leg badly while riding another horse, and recommends his friend George Woolf (Gary Stevens, 1963–) as his replacement. Seabiscuit wins the race handily, only to rupture a leg ligament in another race. Neither Pollard nor Seabiscuit is expected to compete again, but Pollard starts working with the horse, and at the Santa Anita Handicap, the race that had denied Seabiscuit victory for years, Pollard rides Seabiscuit to an easy win.

"You know, everybody thinks we found this broken-down horse and fixed him," Pollard's narration begins as Seabiscuit approaches the finish line. "But we didn't. He fixed us. Every one of us. And I guess in a way, we kinda fixed each other, too."

The wife–husband producing team of Kathleen Kennedy (1953–) and Frank Marshall (1946–) hired Gary Ross (1956–) to write and direct *Seabiscuit*. Ross seemed the perfect fit for the project. On his thirteenth birthday, Ross's parents took him to Santa Anita, and in later years Ross frequently attended horse races as a bettor. He was even part-owner of Atswhatimtalknbout, a fourth-place finisher in the 2003 Kentucky Derby.

One of the first actors cast was Maguire, who had worked with Ross on the fantasy *Pleasantville* (1998), ridden horses in the Civil War drama *Ride with the Devil* (1999), and was best known for his starring role in the mega-hit *Spider-Man* (2002). "There was an incredible toughness and sensitivity to Red that few people could capture," Ross said, "and Tobey is uniquely capable of doing that" ("Maguire to portray fabled horse jockey" 2002, 4C). The thin Maguire still had to lose more than 20 pounds to play Pollard, who, at 115 pounds, was fairly heavy for a jockey.

Cooper, a well-known character actor who won a supporting actor Academy Award for *Adaptation* (2002), landed the part of Smith. "One big choice I made was in the voice," Cooper said. "I found a voice that is much more highly pitched than mine and I tried to put a quality to it, a softness to it, that I hope the viewer would translate as a part of his sensitivity to the animals that he was working with" (Breznican 2003, E5). Cooper even dyed his sandy hair "old man yellow" (Dutka 2003, 6E).

Bridges came from a family of actors that included his father Lloyd Bridges (1913–98) and brother Beau Bridges (1941–). Acting steadily since 1970, Bridges had been Oscar-nominated for best supporting actor for *The Last Picture Show* (1971) and *Thunderbolt and Lightfoot* (1974). Stevens, a veteran jockey who had won three Kentucky Derbies and whose mounts had earned more than $200 million, was given his first acting job as Woolf. "They were basically taking a favorite for the Kentucky Derby and putting an apprentice jockey on him," Stevens joked (Long 2003, S-8). David McCulloch (1933–), a two-time Pulitzer Prize-winning biographer and narrator of many documentary films, was hired to narrate.

Meanwhile, wranglers searched nationwide for more than forty horses—ten for Seabiscuit, four as War Admiral, and the rest to fill in other racehorses. "We started with the physical description," said veteran movie horse wrangler Rusty Hendrickson (1953–). "Seabiscuit, we decided, [stood] about 15-1 [hands]. He was a red bay. The next qualification was, he had to be a sound horse with no aches or pains or frailties. This is a strenuous schedule and we wanted him to be as problem-free as possible" (Welkos 2003, E6).

More than four thousand extras were hired for the recreation of the match race against War Admiral, where, on a 36-degree November morning, Keeneland Race Course in Lexington, Kentucky, subbed for Pimlico. Other locations for the movie included Santa Anita Park & Racetrack in Arcadia, California, and Saratoga Race Track in Saratoga Springs, New York.

Budgeted at an estimated $80 million (some sources go as high as $98 million), the joint production of Universal Pictures, DreamWorks Pictures, and Spyglass Entertainment waited to see, as the *Los Angeles Times* reported, if "a tale of thoroughbred racing can ignite contemporary passions the way it did in the '30s, when superstar horses like Seabiscuit rivaled today's celebrity athletes in the popular imagination" (Welkos 2003, E6).

After previews in Kentucky, the movie opened nationally to, for the most part, favorable reviews—just not many raves.

The Philadelphia Inquirer's Carrie Rickey called *Seabiscuit* "corny but effective" (Rickey 2003, W4), while Hap Erstein of *The Palm Beach Post* said: "Ross wants to make a thinking person's picture, rather than the easier goal of an emotionally engrossing movie. In that, he may have succeeded too well, for the results are frequently intelligent and never less than interesting but also oddly muted and fairly pokey" (Erstein 2003, 8).

The Christian Science Monitor's David Sterritt wrote: "Feel-good movies have an excellent track record, and I won't be surprised if this one pulls in profits worthy of Seabiscuit himself. 'Seabiscuit' may bring a tear to your eye and a lump to your throat, but don't expect to be cheering at the finish line" (Sterritt 2003). Michael Sragow, film critic for Baltimore's *The Sun*, however, gave the movie a four-star rating, predicting that it "will move large audiences to applause and tears while deepening their feelings for the mysteries of character, the majesty of athletics and the thrill of our democratic culture at its best, when figures from nowhere become true popular champions" (Sragow 2003, 1E).

Seabiscuit's U.S. opening weekend brought in almost $21 million, and the movie went on to earn $120,227,854 domestically and another $28 million worldwide. "The real Seabiscuit may have been a long shot at times," *The Orlando Sentinel*'s Jay Boyar wrote, "but the heart-warming horse film was always figured as a favorite in the Oscar race." The movie garnered seven Academy Award nominations, including best picture, but the fantasy epic *The Lord of the Rings: The Return of the King* won all eleven categories in which it was nominated. *Seabiscuit* earned no Oscars—but few would call the movie unsuccessful.

In *Sports Cinema 100 Movies*, Randy Williams ranked *Seabiscuit* No. 23, writing: "Ross's masterful orchestration of all the elements makes this the most successful sports movie in establishing a twentieth-century period piece setting since *The Natural* [a 1984 baseball movie set in the 1930s]" (Williams 2006, 290).

HISTORICAL BACKGROUND

An ancient sport, horse racing broke into various forms that made their way to America: Hurdles and steeplechases, both developed in Great Britain, required the horse and the rider to leap over obstacles. Harness racing had a trotting horse pulling a driver in a sulky. In 1859, a fourteen-year-old horse named Flora Temple was timed in at 2 minutes, 19¾ seconds in Kalamazoo, Michigan, becoming the first trotter to run the mile in under 2 minutes, 20 seconds. In Colonial Virginia, thoroughbreds were bred with native mares, creating the line of quarter horses that were known for running fast over short distances of a quarter-mile. Quarter-horse racing soon developed, as did endurance racing, especially in Western states and territories, where horses were raced over long distances. In 1908, the *Denver Post* sponsored a 600-mile race from Evanston, Wyoming, to Denver, an event that inspired the 1975 movie *Bite the Bullet*. By far, however, thoroughbred racing remained the most popular form of horse racing in America.

Once considered a sport for the upper classes, thoroughbred racing began to attract not only the American wealthy, but also middle class and poor fans by the mid-1800s. On May 10, 1842, thousands attended Union Course in Long Island, New York, where Fashion defeated Boston in a four-mile,

$20,000 match race. In 1854, President Millard Filmore (1800–74) traveled to New Orleans and watched Lexington defeat Lecomte in a match race reportedly before twenty thousand spectators.

Horse racing's real rise came after the Civil War. In 1867, the filly Ruthless won the first Belmont Stakes thoroughbred race, then held at Jerome Park in Westchester County, New York. Baltimore's Pimlico Race Course was opened on October 26, 1870, when a colt named Preakness won the track's inaugural race, Bowie's Dinner Party Stakes; the winner's name was adopted for Pimlico's premier race. In 1875, Aristides won the first running of the Kentucky Derby at Louisville's Churchill Downs before a crowd of ten thousand. In the years after jockey Johnny Loftus (1895–1976) rode Sir Barton to victory in all three races in 1919, the Derby, Belmont, and Preakness became known as thoroughbred racing's Triple Crown.

Some 314 race tracks could be found in the United States by 1890. Racing also began to organize. The American Jockey Club was founded in 1894.

At first, admission fees paid by spectators determined the prize money for winners—the bigger the crowd, the better the purse—which often did not make owning a horse a financially rewarding business. By 1910, however, that began to change as major tracks began implementing entry fees be paid by horse owners. The windfall was short-lived in many states, however, when reform movements led to the abolition of horse racing because of its ties to gambling. Laws passed in New York in 1910 effectively eliminated horse racing in the state for two years. Ratification of the Eighteenth Amendment, which prohibited manufacturing, transporting, and selling alcoholic beverages, in 1919 also hurt the sport. Attendance at racetracks that year hit a twenty-year low.

It took a fast stallion to reignite interest in the sport.

On March 29, 1917, a mare named Mahubah gave birth to a chestnut thoroughbred. Sired by Fair Play, the colt named Man o' War was bought for $5,000 as a yearling by Samuel D. Riddle (1861–1951)—and only at the urging of Riddle's trainer.

On June 6, 1919, Man o' War, a 3-to-5 favorite, won his first race easily at Belmont Park. "He went to the post nicely enough," *The Evening World* of New York reported, "but when he got there he kicked and fussed so much that it was feared he would leave his race there. When the break finally came he got away flying and was never caught" (Treanor 1919, 6). Man o' War won his next six races before losing—ironically to a horse named Upset—by a half-length at the Sanford Memorial Stakes in Saratoga. In 1920, the three-year-old won the Preakness and Belmont, but missed out on a possible Triple Crown because Riddle did not believe in running three-year-olds at the Derby's 1¼-mile distance. After beating Canadian champion Sir Barton, the 1919 Triple Crown winner, in an $80,000 match race in Windsor, Ontario, on October 12, 1920, Man o' War was retired. A sportswriter wrote of that decision: "If a cold stream of water had suddenly been

---

BETTING ON HORSES

Paraphrasing a line from the classic film *Casablanca* (1942), *Chicago Sun-Times* movie critic Roger Ebert (1942–2013) pointed out that "If 'Seabiscuit' has a weakness, it's the movie's curious indifference to betting. Horses race and bettors bet, and the relationship between the two is as old as time, except in this movie, where the Seabiscuit team seems to be shocked! Shocked! to learn that there is gambling at the track" (Ebert 2003, 8W).

One reason for the boom of horse racing during the Great Depression was the legalization of pari-mutuel betting in which the money wagered is placed into a pool, a percentage deducted, and the remaining distributed to the winners. Needing to boost tax revenues and employment, many states began to look at legalizing gambling. First came bingo, followed by horse racing and pari-mutuel betting. By 1935, twenty-seven states allowed pari-mutuel betting and "the money handled in legalized wagering has risen to about $500,000,000 annually" (Nilsson 2011).

Many of those flocking to watch Seabiscuit run weren't just rooting for an underdog. They were hoping to win big. But while Seabiscuit was a fan favorite, the bettors at the famous match race of 1938 favored War Admiral.

Sources

Ebert, Roger. 2003. "'Seabiscuit' Will Make Your Heart Race." *The Gazette*, July 24, 2003, p. 8W.

Nilsson, Jeff. 2011. "Depression America Goes to the Horses: With the Economy in Shambles, Businesses Folding, and Unemployment Rising, Many Americans Were Pinning Their Hopes on Thoroughbreds." *The Saturday Evening Post*, April 30, 2011. https://www.saturdayeveningpost.com/2018/04/advantage-risk-takers/

---

turned upon race-goers . . . they could not have felt more uncomfortable and wretched" (Vreeland 1920, 2). Man o' War won twenty of twenty-one races and remains "Still the yardstick many use to measure great racehorses" (Von Borries 1999, 127).

In an era during which sports figures like New York Yankees slugger George Herman "Babe" Ruth (1895–1948) and boxer William Harrison "Jack" Dempsey (1895–1983) became major celebrities, so did Man o' War. "The register in Man o' War's stable tells the story of his fame and his greatness," the *Chicago Tribune* reported in 1937. "From practically every country on the face of the globe his visitors have come. They represent every walk of life. As accurate an estimate as can be made sets his yearly number of callers at 50,000" (Lane 1937, 4). Between 1922 and 1947, an estimated one million to one and half million people visited the horse at Faraway Farm near Lexington, Kentucky.

The retired champion sired many colts, including one, born in 1934, named War Admiral. Another Man o' War offspring, Hard Tack, born in 1926, sired a colt named Seabiscuit that was born in 1933.

Man o' War might have stimulated interest, but the stock market crash that began on "Black Thursday," October 24, 1929, and worsened five days later on "Black Tuesday," sent the world reeling. The panic left millions of Americans in financial ruin, but not only the rich suffered. Four million Americans were out of work by 1930, a number that rose to six million a year later. By 1933, roughly fifteen million had lost their jobs, and almost half of U.S. banks had failed. Making matters worse, droughts turned the plains from Nebraska to Texas into a "Dust Bowl," killing crops and live-stock, as well as men, women, and children. Meanwhile, the Kentucky Derby, considered America's crown jewel of thoroughbred racing, saw its purse fall from $50,000 to $37,000.

Forced to increase revenues, some state governments looked at horse rac-ing. In 1933, California legalized betting on horse racing, and a $3 million track called Santa Anita Park opened in Arcadia near Los Angeles. The track was the brainchild of dentist and businessman Charles "Doc" Strub (1884–1958), whom the crash had left $1 million in debt. Strub lined up investors, and Santa Anita opened on Christmas Day 1934. "Strub spent the money well. He built a track like none other on earth, a cathedral to the Thorough-bred so resplendent that writer David Alexander described his first sight of it as one of the most stirring visual experiences of his life" (Hillenbrand 2001, 16). The Santa Anita Derby, a winner-take-all stakes race for three-year-olds—first run at $1\frac{1}{16}$ miles (now contested at $1\frac{1}{8}$ miles)—debuted in 1935 and became a popular annual event. The track's other big event, the Santa Anita Handicap, was also first run in 1935. "The Big 'Cap," as that race was known, was open to horses three years old or older, and offered a minimum purse of $100,000. "But the fondest ambition of the California sportsmen was to develop a horse capable of winning the great event against the fastest Thoroughbreds the East could produce. They expected the task to take many years, for it had required more than a century to establish the royal Thoroughbred families in the East, and the wealthy owners there would not give up a colt that showed promise of becoming a champion" (Moody 2003, 64).

On May 23, 1933, Seabiscuit was foaled at Claiborne Farm near Lex-ington, Kentucky. Despite his sound pedigree, Seabiscuit was stubby-legged, thick-bodied, and when he galloped, his left foreleg jabbed out oddly. His first trainer, James E. Fitzsimmons (1874–1966), called him "Dead lazy" (Hillenbrand 2001, 39). As a two-year-old, Seabiscuit raced thirty-five times, roughly three times the usual number. He didn't win until his eighteenth race.

On June 29, 1936, Tom Smith (1878–1957) watched Seabiscuit win a minor claiming race at Suffolk Downs in Massachusetts. Known as "Silent Tom," Smith worked as a wrangler on Western cattle drives and had been a drifting horsebreaker, trainer, veterinarian, and blacksmith until hired by Charles S. Howard (1877–1950), who made his fortune distributing Buick automobiles in eight Western states during the early 1900s. Now interested in horse racing, Howard hired Smith as trainer. After Smith and Howard watched Seabiscuit win a race at Saratoga in July 1936, Howard bought Seabiscuit for $7,500 ($8,000 by some accounts). When Johnny "Red" Pollard (1909–81), who began riding horses at age fifteen, walked into a barn in at Fair Grounds Racecourse in Detroit in August 1936, Smith thought the jockey might be able to handle the stormy Seabiscuit.

The Howard–Smith–Pollard–Seabiscuit partnership worked. The colt won its third and fourth starts before setting a track record at the Scarsdale Handicap in New York. In 1937, Seabiscuit lost to a fast-charging, and favored, Rosemont in a photo finish at the Santa Anita Handicap. Ever the salesman, Howard began promoting his horse. "Seabiscuit had that relationship with people that some ball players and fighters and other sports figures had . . . ," Francis E. Stan wrote for Washington, D.C.'s *The Evening Star*, "a common ground that has made, makes, and always will make, their victories heart-warming and popular" (Stan 1938, A-14).

With many thoroughbred owners and trainers of the eastern United States dismissing Seabiscuit as an inferior horse that beat also-rans in weak competition, Howard began a marketing campaign. Howard and his second wife, Marcela Zabala Howard (1903–87), didn't go into horse racing to make money. "To them racing was a sport, a friendly rivalry between California and the big eastern owners for the honor of winning the richest prize in racing— the Santa Anita Handicap" (Moody 2003, 84).

The two best horses of 1937 were Seabiscuit and War Admiral. On August 21, William P. Kyne (1887–1957), general manager of Bay Meadows Racetrack in San Mateo, California, offered to hold a winner-take-all $40,000 match race in October, pitting the four-year-old Seabiscuit against three-year-old War Admiral over a distance of 1⅛ miles. Almost immediately, Howard agreed to the race. "War Admiral won't meet Seabiscuit at Bay Meadows any more than I will," the *Los Angeles Times*'s Bob Ray reported. "If the champion 3-year-old and the king of the handicap ranks do get together, it'll probably be in the 'hundred' at Santa Anita next winter" (Ray 1937, 14). Riddle, Seabiscuit's owner who had also owned Man o' War, eventually rejected the Bay Meadows offer, and the horses didn't meet at Santa Anita, either, leaving Howard to comment:

> I've always wanted a shot at War Admiral. We were all ready to race at Pimlico last November, when Al Vanderbilt guaranteed us a fine purse for a match race. But Mr. Riddle didn't see fit to send his horse against us. Then I figured we would have to wait until the Santa Anita handicap. I couldn't see how any man who thought he had the best horse in the country could refuse to run him for a purse of $100,000.
>
> But War Admiral isn't here. He is going to run in Florida for half the money that is offered here. That's his business. But I can't help but feel that if a horse is the greatest horse—and I have heard that War Admiral is—he should go for the biggest money in the biggest race. (McLemore 1938, 14)

But Seabiscuit, ridden by George Woolf (1910–46) because Pollard had been injured, didn't win the 1938 Santa Anita Handicap, either. For the second consecutive year, Seabiscuit lost in photo finish, this time falling to Stagehand, a three-year-old that two weeks earlier won the Santa Anita Derby. On the same day Seabiscuit lost, War Admiral, a 3-to-10 favorite, won the Widener Challenge Cup in Hialeah, Florida, boosting his earnings to $231,525.

Talks continued of a Seabiscuit–War Admiral matchup, and on October 1, a Pimlico official announced that Howard and Riddle had agreed to terms for a match race. The race was held on November 1 before a crowd of forty thousand. Ridden by Woolf, Seabiscuit led from start to finish. "The only question of doubt regarding that mad, headlong dash was the winning margin," *Brooklyn Eagle* correspondent W.C. Vreeland wrote. "Was it four lengths or was it three?" (Vreeland 1938, 21).

"He's the best horse in the world," Woolf said. "He proved that today," while War Admiral jockey Charles "Charley" Kurtsinger (1906–46) said, "I have no excuses. What else can I say? I just couldn't make it" (Associated Press 1938d, 13).

Seabiscuit's 1938 victory over War Admiral was heard over the radio by an estimated forty million listeners. When President Franklin D. Roosevelt (1882–1945) arrived late for a news conference, he explained that he had been listening to Seabiscuit's victory.

"I would like to have Seabiscuit defeat War Admiral again," Howard said in December, "and I am keen to have him beat Stagehand if he can" (United Press 1938b, 22).

But Seabiscuit was injured on February 14 in a prep race for the Santa Anita Handicap. The *San Francisco Examiner* ran a Page 1 story under the headline:

'BISCUIT HURT;
MAY NEVER BE
IN RACE AGAIN
(Special to the Examiner 1939, 1)

Seabiscuit, still being ridden by Woolf, had ruptured a left front tendon. "[W]e hope to keep Seabiscuit in training," Howard said, "but we won't know until tomorrow just how serious the injury may be" (Special to the Examiner 1939, 34).

The injury, however, was quite serious: a ruptured suspensory ligament. Many people thought that Seabiscuit would never race again, just as many thought Pollard, after breaking his leg badly, would never race horses again. But both recovered. With Pollard back in the saddle, Seabiscuit won the 1940 Santa Anita Handicap, one length ahead of his stablemate, Kayak II, boosting Seabiscuit's career earnings to $437,730, the most in horse-racing history at that time. In May, Howard officially retired Seabiscuit, announcing a stud fee of $2,500—second only to Man o' War's $5,000 fee. Seabiscuit finished his career with thirty-three wins in eighty-nine races.

Seabiscuit, less than a week from his fourteenth birthday, died on May 17, 1947, of "Acute heart failure," veterinarian John W. Britton said. "It takes a lot of thoroughbreds of this age" (Sullivan 1947, 20).

The loss, Howard said as he walked away from the horse's grave, was "Like losing one of the family" (Sullivan 1947, 20).

DEPICTION AND CULTURAL CONTEXT

After *Seabiscuit*'s release, jockeys praised the film's treatment of their profession. "They showed at one point Tobey trying to make weight, and they showed him regurgitating," said jockey Richard Migliore (1964–). "And another point where he wasn't eating very much at a dinner with the trainer and owners because he was weight-conscious" (Ross 2003, 56). The scenes depicting Pollard struggling to find work touched jockey Mike Luzzi (1969–). "[E]very one of us has our stories of how we started riding and the tough times we went through," he said. "You muck stalls, you live in a tack room. I basically started from the ground up and I think nine out of 10 jockeys did" (Ross 2003, 56). And jockeys, especially at smaller tracks, could get physical with each other. "It doesn't happen much now because there are cameras everywhere," former jockey Diane Zippi said. "But it did happen, more on the bush tracks. You had to fight to ride. But they didn't wear chin straps and goggles back then" (Jones 2003, D-2).

Yet *Seabiscuit* is far from a documentary.

Ross's script slightly follows the known histories of Tom Smith and Charles Howard, with some liberties, including giving the Howards only one son in the movie. Actually, they had three other sons, Charles Stewart Howard (1902–55), Lindsay Coleman "Lin" Howard (1904–71), and Robert Stewart Howard (1916–62). While his parents were away, Frank "Frankie" R. Howard (1911–26) was killed in a truck accident on his way fishing, but he wasn't alone, and no other vehicle was involved. Two friends were with him when he swerved to miss a rock in the road. Frankie lost control, and the truck crashed into a canyon. His friends survived, but Frankie was dead. Charles Howard grieved for months, but paid for construction of the Frank R. Howard Memorial Hospital, which opened in 1928, and Charles Howard served on the board of directors until his death.

Frankie's death took a toll on the Howard marriage, and the couple divorced in 1931. In 1932, Fannie Mae Smith Howard (1879–1942) married attorney Edmond E. Herrscher (ca 1890s–1983), the same year Howard married Marcela Zabala (1903–87). There was no quickie divorce for the Howards, and Howard didn't meet Marcela in Tijuana, though Howard frequently attended Mexican horse tracks during Prohibition, and Tom Smith spent 1935 at a horse track in Mexico. Howard met Marcela in 1929 when Howard's son Lin invited him to the rodeo in Salinas, California. Marcela was the older sister of Lin's wife, and Lin might have influenced his father's interest in horse racing; an outstanding polo player, Lin partnered with singer Bing Crosby (1903–77) in horse-breeding and stable operations. Like Howard, Marcela loved horses, and after tracks opened in Santa Anita in 1934 and Bay Meadows a year later, the Howards decided to get into horse racing. Howard met Smith through a mutual friend who owned several racehorses.

Pollard's biography is more heavily fictionalized. While he was an avid reader in a large family, it was not the Great Depression that left Pollard fending for himself. A flash flood in Edmonton, Alberta, destroyed the business owned by Pollard's father and left him bankrupt. Young Pollard started boxing and began delivering groceries on horseback. Before long, he was trying to trade manual labor for jockeying at a nearby horse track. He wanted to race full time, and his parents compromised; a family friend became Pollard's guardian, and in 1925 the guardian and teenager arrived in Butte, Montana. The guardian left Pollard on his own, but about a year later, a former jockey turned traveling trainer saw Pollard and signed him. Pollard began riding summers in western Canada, spring and fall in California, and winters in Tijuana. In 1927, Pollard met jockey George Monroe Woolf (1910–46). The Canadian-born Woolf had been racing horses since he was in his teens. He dressed flamboyantly in Western attire: cowboy hat, tailored shirts, and fancy boots. Pollard and Woolf, who struggled to control diabetes and keep his riding weight, struck up a friendship, often picking on each other. On a live NBC radio broadcast while hospitalized with his broken leg, Pollard gave Woolf instructions to ride Seabiscuit: "Why, Georgie boy, get on the horse—face to the front—put one leg on each side of him, get someone to lead you into the gate, and then f— it up like you usually do" (Hillenbrand 2001, 222).

When Pollard wasn't riding horses, he still tried prizefighting, and the movie implies that Pollard lost the vision in his right eye during a fight. The blindness came early in his riding career, when a rock flew up while he was working a horse and struck Pollard in the forehead. Both Hillenbrand's book and Ross's screenplay blame Seabiscuit's loss in his first running in the Santa Anita Handicap on Pollard's blindness. In the movie, Pollard confesses that he can't see out of his right eye. That's not in Hillenbrand's book, because, in all likelihood, Pollard never told Smith or Howard. "Had he let on that he was blind in one eye," Hillenbrand notes, "his career would have been over" (Hillenbrand 2001, 125).

Whether vision played a part in the loss can only be speculated. But the movie's version of the race is fairly accurate.

"At the 70-yard pole, Seabiscuit looked a winner," the *San Francisco Examiner* reported (Kemp 1937, 1). After passing early leader Special

Agent, Pollard kept Seabiscuit on the inside. Jockey Harry Richards, however, drove Rosemont to Seabiscuit's withers.

"I got off a little slow," Pollard said, "and when I hit the eighth pole I didn't think anything was close to me until Richards yelled at me. It was a clean race and Rosemont beat me squarely" (Kemp 1937, 2).

Pollard thought Seabiscuit might have fared better on the outside, but he couldn't move his horse over without fouling Rosemont.

The *San Francisco Examiner* described the finish: "The real race developed when the turn into the home stretch was reached with Pollard finally giving Seabiscuit his head and he went into the lead. It was a vicious riding duel at the eight pole home between Rosemont and Seabiscuit and furnished the record crowd [estimated at 50,000] with a thrill it will long talk about" (Kemp 1937, 2).

Minutes passed before Rosemont was declared the winner in a photo finish. "I knew we had lost before they took the picture," Pollard said. "They caught us in the last jump" (Potts 1937, 2).

"The best horse won," Richards said, "but it was too close for comfort" (Potts 1937, 2).

In the film, after Seabiscuit's narrow loss in the Santa Anita Handicap, Howard begins his relentless campaign for a match race against War Admiral, who is said to stand just under 18 hands, towering over diminutive Seabiscuit. War Admiral was nowhere near that tall, which Beverly Smith wrote for *The Globe and Mail*, "would make him just about the most giant-sized thoroughbred that ever lived" (Smith 2003). Horses are measured from the ground to the highest point of their withers, the ridge between the shoulder blades at the base of the neck; one hand equals four inches. An average racehorse stands 15.3 hands. While the largest thoroughbred, Holy Roller, stood 18.1 hands, and Phar Lap was 17.1, and Man o' War 16.2½, most sources put War Admiral at 15.3 hands, not much taller than Seabiscuit. Horse-racing journalist Steve Haskin complained that "there was no reason to describe War Admiral as being nearly 18 hands, with the average moviegoer not knowing what that means and the racing fan laughing over such an absurdity" (Haskin 2003).

The elitism between Eastern horsemen and those, like Howard, from the West Coast, however, was accurate. "It really was a territorial thing," said horse trainer and racing historian John Shirreffs. "Anything west of the Rockies in those days in racing was not really taken seriously. That helped make this a big national event" (Loverro 2013). But there were several potential matchups before the famous race at Pimlico. Seabiscuit was scratched from some races—twice due to the muddy track, once because of leg issues—and War Admiral was scratched once.

In the film, Pollard badly breaks his leg in a riding accident shortly before the match race against War Admiral, and Woolf is brought in as his replacement for the key race. This is another leap from the historical record. Pollard wasn't injured once, but twice. On February 19, 1938, in a warm-up for the Santa Anita Handicap, Howard scratched Seabiscuit from running in the $5,000-added San Carlos Handicap because of muddy conditions, and Pollard chose to ride Fair Knightess, another Howard horse. Around the far turn, the horse, caught in close quarters, stumbled and threw Pollard hard to the turf. Mandingham, ridden by Maurice Peters, fell over Fair Knightess. Peters sprained an ankle, but Pollard sustained a shattered collarbone and fractured ribs. Pollard was not expected to race for at least four months, denying him a chance at the Santa Anita Handicap. "Seabiscuit'll run," Howard said, "even if I have to ride him myself" (Henry 1938, 9).

A handful of jockeys were considered for the next warm-up race, the San Antonio Handicap at Santa Anita, before Sonny Workman (1909–66) was chosen. When Seabiscuit finished second in that race, Woolf, backed by Pollard, was hired as jockey for the $100,000 race. Seabiscuit lost the 1938 Santa Anita Handicap in another thriller—a race the movie omits—but Woolf said he had been fouled at the start of the race when Count Atlas, ridden by jockey Johnny Adams (1914–95), bumped Seabiscuit so hard, the horse almost fell to the ground. When race stewards reviewed film, they saw that Woolf had repeatedly struck Adams with his whip. Woolf was suspended for the rest of the Santa Anita meet, and the stewards recommended that the California Racing Board add fifteen days to the suspension. Howard stuck by Woolf, saying, "I don't blame Woolf for not standing idly by and allowing another rider to ruin his chances in a $100,000 race" (Otis 1938, 11). Jockey Noel Richardson rode Seabiscuit to his next victory, March 28 at the Agua Caliente Handicap, before Woolf returned to the saddle at Bay Meadows in April.

Meanwhile, Pollard recovered from his injuries and by April, when a match race was being set up between Seabiscuit and War Admiral—this one for Belmont Park on Memorial Day (then known as Decoration Day)—he had recovered from his injuries and was riding again. Howard withdrew Seabiscuit from that race, citing the horse's leg troubles, but still hoped to run him on June 29 at the $50,000 Massachusetts Handicap at Suffolk Downs in yet another possible Seabiscuit–War Admiral pairing. But on June 23, after working out Seabiscuit in Boston, Pollard volunteered to exercise a friend's two-year-old horse. Something spooked the horse, which bolted out of control, ran through the rail and toward the barns, where it fell and slid sideways into the barn and lay in a heap. Pollard's leg was badly broken.

"It's the most dangerous sport in the world," Ross said. "If you don't win, you don't get paid, and you don't eat. And yet there is this amazing camaraderie. It's like golf. Except you can't get killed playing golf" (Horn 2003, E4).

Again, Woolf was brought in to ride Seabiscuit. But the record crowd of sixty-six thousand was disappointed on race day when Seabiscuit was scratched because of a swollen tendon and War Admiral finished out of the money for the first time in his career.

Those two horses finally faced one another on November 1 in the Pimlico Special. Riddle wanted a walkup start because War Admiral had troubles with starting gates. Races had been started by dropping flags, ropes, ribbons, or wooden barriers. In the late 1800s, the "Gray Gate," named after inventor Reuben G. Gray of Australia, strung six strands of rope on a frame that stretched across the track. When released, the "gate" flew up 12 feet, allowing horses to start. Electronic starting gates, invented by Clay Puett (1899–1998), made their debut in Canada in 1939 and were soon being installed on many American tracks.

Seabiscuit got much of the match race correct, though it eliminated the first two false starts—common in walkup starts. The turnout for the match race was huge. Pimlico had a capacity of sixteen thousand, but some thirty thousand crammed into the stands and another ten thousand stood in the infield. Announcer Clem McCarthy (1882–1962) couldn't make it upstairs and had to call the race from the winner's circle.

Howard and Riddle agreed to a bell start, as depicted in the film. The bell intended to start the race wasn't there on race day, and Smith provided his own as a replacement. What no one outside of the Howard crew knew was that Smith had been training Seabiscuit to break fast by using an alarm clock and a whip.

In match races, the horse that starts fast usually wins, and 1 minute, 57 seconds after the bell rang, Seabiscuit had won. "Seabiscuit," Orlo Robertson wrote for Baltimore's *The Evening Sun*, "the hard-hitting little equine warrior from the West, stands unchallenged today as the king of the American turf" (Robertson 1938, 26). For all the sizable purses that had been bandied about in attempts to land the horse-racing duel, Howard and Riddle agreed to race for $15,000.

As depicted in the film, Woolf did pull up Seabiscuit during a prep race for the 1939 Santa Anita Handicap, and the ruptured suspensory ligament was serious enough to end a racehorse's career. But by the end of the year, Howard, Smith and Pollard were thinking about racing Seabiscuit again.

On February 9, 1940, Pollard rode Seabiscuit to a third-place finish in the La Jolla Handicap. "Seabiscuit didn't win his comeback race . . ." United Press reported, "but he proved his soundness and recovery since a sprained ligament knocked him out of training a year ago" (United Press 1940a, 8). But in the next race, an eighth-place finish at the San Carlos Handicap at Santa Anita on February 17 left the *San Francisco Examiner* proclaiming "Seabiscuit is definitely through as a first line contender for the '100 grander' . . ." (Special to The Examiner 1940, 3). Seabiscuit, however, came back to win the San Antonio Handicap on February 24 in "a sizzling performance that will go down in the dramatic annals of the turf as one of the greatest of all time," the *Los Angeles Times* reported. "It was a comeback that will live forever" (Lowry 1940a, 17).

Seabiscuit omits those three tune-ups for the Santa Anita Handicap for both horse and rider, although the film correctly captures the atmosphere of Seabiscuit's last race. "At nine o'clock in the morning all roads leading to Arcadia were packed with people. The vast parking area of the plant began filling in the early hours. Long lines formed outside the gates awaiting the opening. At eleven no seat in the grandstand or clubhouse was left, and the human stream was pouring out through the tunnel onto the lawns of the infield, eddying around the blazing beds of flowers.

"And still they came . . ." (Beckwith 2003, 13).

Yet Ross stretched the truth greatly in the film version of the 1940 Santa Anita Handicap. Woolf was riding another horse in that race, Heelfly—which finished sixth, not dead last. In the movie, Seabiscuit falls far behind—a good fifteen to twenty lengths by many estimates—early in the race before powering to victory. That makes a good movie comeback, but Seabiscuit never trailed by much. According to the *Los Angeles Times*' Handicap Form Chart: "SEABISCUIT, close to the pace from the start, was urged forward and out of trouble when it seemed as if he might be caught in close quarters nearing the far turn, then came on to catch WHICHEE entering the final furlong and going in his best form to the finish won handily" (Handicap Form Chart 1940, 13). Seabiscuit's track record 2 minutes, 1 1/5 seconds was the second-fastest 1 1/4-mile time of all time.

What the film and Hillenbrand's book leave out, however, is a rumored deal Howard put in place before the race. Howard also owned second-place finisher Kayak II, the 1939 Santa Anita Handicap winner that was ridden by Leon "Buddy" Haas (1915–82). Rules of that period had horses owned by the same party coupled in the betting line, meaning bettors backing either Seabiscuit or Kayak II could cash their tickets on either horse. Rules also allowed an owner with more than one horse in the field to declare his intention to win with a particular horse. That meant if Howard declared his intention to win with Seabiscuit, then Haas would be obligated not to try to win if no other horse was challenging. Decades later, Haas's sister said, "My brother said many times that C.S. Howard had instructed him to let Seabiscuit win" (Christine 2003, D8). The Handicap Form Chart noted that Kayak II "might have been closer to the winner had he been vigorously ridden in the last sixteenth" (Handicap Form Chart 1940, 13). Hillenbrand told the *Los Angeles Times* that she left out the rumored deal. "I didn't want to take the focus off of Seabiscuit's accomplishment for the sake of belaboring a minor issue" (Christine 2002, D8).

The movie ends with Pollard riding to victory. Any epilogue of what happened afterward would not fit in a feel-good movie.

After falling off a horse during a race at Santa Anita, Woolf never regained consciousness, dying at age thirty-six on January 4, 1946. "Horses are in my blood," he once told a friend. "I'll be with 'em till I die" (Wade 1946, 36).

Smith eventually joined Maine Chance Farm in Lexington, Kentucky, but in 1945, a steward caught a groom using a decongestant spray on one of Smith's horses. Smith might have not known what the groom was doing, and the spray was not performance enhancing, but Smith was suspended for a year. After his reinstatement, he trained Kentucky Derby winner Jet Pilot in 1947. Smith died in 1957, but wasn't inducted the Horse Racing Hall of Fame until 2001.

Pollard also retired after the 1940 Santa Anita Handicap, became a trainer, then resumed racing until 1955, and afterward worked odd jobs at tracks until he wound up in a nursing home where he died in 1981. According to his daughter, "he had just worn out his body" (Hillenbrand 1998).

Howard died of a heart attack at age seventy-three in 1950, leaving behind an estate valued at more than $1.7 million. His will included his hope that his trustees would "continue the operation of the racing stables . . . even though it may be necessary to continue such operation on a smaller scale" (Associated Press 1950, 1). While several horses were kept in training, 109 horses were auctioned off at Santa Anita in November 1950. "It will be a long time," one journalist wrote, "before another such combination as Howard and Seabiscuit appears on the racing scene" (Underwood 1950, 8).

CONCLUSION

Seabiscuit wasn't Hollywood's first crack at the famous stallion. In 1949, Warner Bros. released *The Story of Seabiscuit*, a Technicolor film with former child star Shirley Temple (1928–2014) and Barry Fitzgerald (1888–1961). That movie's problems included a highly fictionalized script. When the horse playing Seabiscuit kept losing to the horse playing War Admiral, filmmakers had to resort to one of the movie's highlights: actual footage from Seabiscuit's races. "Never a great film," a reviewer opined in *Leonard Maltin's 2012 Movie Guide*, "this is now rendered meaningless (if not downright ludicrous) by Laura Hillenbrand's book and the 2003 adaptation, SEABISCUIT" (Maltin 2011, 1327).

Seabiscuit also took liberties with some facts, but overall stayed true to Hillenbrand's story and Ross's vision. "It wouldn't be the biggest-selling book in America if it was just about horse racing," Ross said (Williams 2006, 290).

"Across the board," Williams wrote, "horse racing movies have produced very few winners. Of the genre's 200-plus films, most have ended up in the also-ran category."

"A sports and social history, *Seabiscuit* joins a precious few (including *National Velvet, Phar Lap, A Day at the Races,* and *The Black Stallion*) in the winners circle" (Williams 2006, 292).

FURTHER READING

Associated Press. 1931. "Divorcee Gets Half Fortune." *The Spokesman-Review*, May 9, 1931, p. 5.

Associated Press. 1937. "Howard Agrees to Proposed Race." *Los Angeles Times*, August 24, 1937, Part II, p. 11.

Associated Press. 1938a. "New Jockey Will Ride Seabiscuit." *Fort Worth Star-Telegram*, February 21, 1938, p. 13.

Associated Press. 1938b. "Biscuit and War Admiral Are Matched." *Casper Star-Tribune*, October 2, 1938, p. 8.

Associated Press. 1938c. "Woolf Says 'Biscuit Best: 'He's the Best Horse in the World,' Avers Winning Jockey." *Los Angeles Times*, November 2, 1938, Section II, p. 13.

Associated Press. 1938d. "Roosevelt Gets Kick Out of Match Race." *Los Angeles Times*, November 2, 1938, Section II, p. 13.

Associated Press. 1950. "Howard Relatives to Get Huge Estate." *Los Angeles Times*, June 18, 1950, p. 1.

Beck, Marily. 2002. "Kim Cattrall Planning Her 2nd Sex Book." *Kenosha News*, June 13, 2002, p. D3.

Beckwith, B. K. 2003. *Seabiscuit: The Saga of a Great Champion*. Yardley, PA: Westholme Publishing.

Bernard, Maurice. 1938. "Seabiscuit's Jockey Is Suspended: George Woolf Set Down for Hitting Adams: In Big Race: Stewards Act after Seeing Movies." *San Francisco Examiner*, March 10, 1938, p. 22.

Beyer, Andrew. 2003. "A Thin Line between Fact and Fiction." *The Washington Post*, July 25, 2003. https://www.washingtonpost.com/archive/sports/2003/07/25/a-thin-line-between-fact-and-fiction/8ed0d092-c555-4a47-a4dd-d9e47602199a/

Boyar, Jay. 2004. "No Surprise: 'Lord of Rings' Rules Oscars with 11 Nominations." *Messenger Inquirer*, January 28, 2004, p. 4.

Breznican, Anthony. 2003. "Chris Cooper Gives 'Seabiscuit' His Silent Passion." *The Desert Sun*, July 27, 2003, p. E5.

Buckley, James, Jr., and John Walters. 2010. *Sports in America: 1920–1939, Second Edition*. New York: Chelsea House.

Carruth, Gorton, and Eugene Ehrlich. 1988. *Facts & Dates of American Sports: From Colonial Days to the Present*. New York: Perennial Library.

Christine, Bill. 2002. "Ending Is Seen as a Real Stretch: Ever since Legendary Seabiscuit Won the 1940 Santa Anita Handicap, There Have Been Suspicions That Result Was Decided by Owner, not the Horse." *Los Angeles Times*, November 20, 2002, pp. D1, D8.

Christine, Bill. 2003. "Getting Lost in a Legend: Kayak II Is Ignored in 'Seabiscuit' Movie, But Two Jockeys' Relatives Say the Horse Might Have Been Held Back from Winning the 1940 Big 'Cap." *Los Angeles Times*, December 24, 2003, pp. D-1, D8.

Dutka, Elaine. 2003. "Chris Cooper (Who?) Blooms in an Unconventional Role: 'Adaptation' Brings Critical Acclaim to an Actor Who Has Yearned for a Chance to Do Something Different." *The Des Moines Register*, February 4, 2003, p. 6E.

Erstein, Hap. 2003. "A Winner in Accuracy, but Thrills Get Nosed Out." *The Palm Peach Post*, Section TCIF, p. 8.

"Former Wife of Chas. S. Howard Dies." 1942. *Oakland Tribune*, October 10, 1942, p. 13.

Frey, Jennifer. "Author's Struggle Evident in Book Theme." *The Honolulu Advertiser*, March 18, 2001, p. F3.

Gwynne, Tom. 1939. "Racing." *Santa Ana Register*, 1939, p. 6.

"Handicap form Chart." 1940. *Los Angeles Times*, March 3, 1940, Part II, p. 13.

Haskin, Steve. 2003. "Historical Liberties Aside, Seabiscuit Is 'Excellent Piece of Movie-Making'." *BloodHorse*, July 21, 2003. https://www.bloodhorse.com /horse-racing/articles/180863/historical-liberties-aside-seabiscuit-is-excellent -piece-of-movie-making

Henry, Bill. 1938. "Seabiscuit Definitely in $100,000 Race." *Los Angeles Times*, February 20, 1938, Part II, pp. 9, 11.

Hillenbrand, Laura. 1998. "Four Good Legs Between Us: When the Lives of a Failed Prizefighter, an Aging Horsebreaker, and a Bicycle-Repairman-Turned-Overnight-Millionaire Converged Around a Battered Little Horse Named Seabiscuit, the Result Captivated the Nation and Transcended Their Sport." *American Heritage*, July-August 1998. https://www.americanheritage.com/four-good-legs-between-us#1

Hillenbrand, Laura. 2001. *Seabiscuit: An American Legend*. New York: Random House.

Hillinger, Charles. 1988. "King of the Turf: Inventor's Electrical Gate Revolutionized Horse Racing." *Los Angeles Times*, August 26, 1988, Part IV, pp. 2–3.

History.com editors. No Date. "Great Depression History: The Great Depression Was the Worst Economic Downturn in the History of the Industrialized World, Lasting from the Stock Market Crash of 1929 to 1939." History.com. https:// www.history.com/topics/great-depression/great-depression-history

Horn, Jeff. 2003. "One-track Mind: Before Directing 'Seabiscuit,' Gary Ross Had a Love for the Races." *Los Angeles Times*, July 23, 2003, pp. E1, E4.

"Howard Horses Go on Block in Big Auction." 1950. *Valley Times*, November 25, 1950, p. 9.

Isaacs, Stan. 2004. "Truth an Also-Ran in 'Seabiscuit' Film." *Newsday*, January 31, 2004. https://www.newsday.com/sports/truth-an-also-ran-in-seabiscuit-film-1.715799

Jackson, Christine. 2018. "After the Finish: Eighty Years Ago, Two Horses at Pimlico Gripped the Nation, but for Many It Was Far More Than a Race." *Baltimore Magazine*, November 2018. https://www.baltimoremagazine.com/2018/10/30 /eighty-years-ago-seabiscuit-war-admiral-gripped-nation-pimlico-race-course

Jones, Diana Nelson. 2003. "Movie Took Jockey on Trot Down Memory Lane." *Pittsburgh Post-Gazette*, July 31, 2003, p. D-2.

Kemp, Abe. 1937. "Seabiscuit Gets Second Place in Thrilling Finish: Indian Broom Third: Photo Needed to Determine Winner; 50,000 Fans Watch Classic." *San Francisco Examiner*, February 28, 1937, Section SE, pp. 1–2.

Keyser, Tom. 2003. "A Race for the Ages." *The Baltimore Sun*, July 22, 2003. https:// www.baltimoresun.com/news/bs-xpm-2003-07-22-0307220081-story.html

"Keyser Wins Eclipse for Newspapers." *The Courier-Journal*, December 29, 1998, p. D3.

Kocher, Greg. 2009. "Kentucky Derby Offers History Lesson from Great Depression." *The Lexington Herald-Leader*, April 28, 2009. https://www.mcclatchydc .com/news/nation-world/national/article24536059.html

Lane, Frenchy. 1937. "Man O' War Is 20, and Is Butler Harbut Proud! 850,000 Visit Big Red in Sixteen Years." *Chicago Tribune*, April 4, 1937, Part 2, p. 4.

Long, Gary. 2003. "Stevens Loves Being in Front of Camera." *The Record*, May 2, 2003, p. S-8.

Loverro, Thom. 2013. "Seabiscuit vs War Admiral: The Horse Race that Stopped the Nation: 75 Years ago a Match Race at Baltimore's Pimlico Race Course Took US Minds Off the Depression and Impending War." *The Guardian*, November 1, 2013. https://www.theguardian.com/sport/2013/nov/01/seabiscuit-war-admiral -horse-race-1938-pimlico

Lowry, Paul. 1938. "Pompoon Wins; Two Riders Injured in Spill: Pollard and Peters Hurt as Horses Fall: Mandingham and Fair Knightess in Mishap as Favorite Romps Home in San Carlos." *Los Angeles Times*, February 20, 1938, Part II, pp. 9, 11.

Lowry, Paul. 1940a. "Seabiscuit, Kayak II Run One-Two in San Antonio Handicap: Howard Aces Come Back: Whichee Also Shows Form in Capturing Six-Furlong Handicap." *Los Angeles Times*, February 25, 1940, Section I, pp. 17, 21.

Lowry, Paul. 1940b. "Seabiscuit and Kayak II Run One-Two in Handicap: Howard Great Campaigner Eclipses Sun Beau's Money-Winning Record." *Los Angeles Times*, March 3, 1940, Part II, pp. 13–14.

"Maguire to Portray Fabled Horse Jockey." 2002. *Springfield News-Leader*, August 7, 2002, p. 4C.

Maltin, Leonard, ed. 2011. *Leonard Maltin's 2012 Movie Guide*. New York: Plume.

McGraw, Eliza R. L. 2020. "6 Things You May Not Have Known about Man o' War: In the 100 Years Since the Original 'Big Red' Was Foaled, He Became One of the Most Famous Horses in History. But There Are Still a Few Things to Be Learned about Him." *Equus*, May 6, 2020. https://equusmagazine.com/horse -world/man-o-war-facts

McLemore, Henry. 1938. "Owner of Seabiscuit Believes He's Fastest Horse on U.S. Tracks: Regrets Fact War Admiral Isn't Entered in Santa Anita Handicap." *The Dayton Herald*, January 26, 1938, p. 14.

Moody, Ralph. 2003. *Come on Seabiscuit!* Lincoln: University of Nebraska Press.

"Mrs. Fannie May Howard, Divorced, Will Wed Her Attorney." 1931. *Oakland Tribune*, August 4, 1931, p. 6.

Nelson, Murry R., ed. 2009a. *Encyclopedia of Sports in America: A History from Foot Races to Extreme Sports. Volume 1: Colonial Years to 1939*. Westport, CT: Greenwood Press.

Nelson, Murry R., ed. 2009b. *Encyclopedia of Sports in America: A History from Foot Races to Extreme Sports. Volume 2: 1940 to Present*. Westport, CT: Greenwood Press.

Ockerman, Foster, Jr. 2019. *Hidden History of Horse Racing in Kentucky*. Charleston, SC: The History Press.

"Offers $40,000 for 'Biscuit, War Admiral." 1937. *San Francisco Examiner*, August 22, 1937, Section SF, p. 1.

Otis, Oscar. 1938. "Seabiscuit Withdrawn: Handicap Star Out of Tomorrow's Feature Turf Race." *Los Angeles Times*, March 11, 1938, p. 11.

Pate, Nancy. "Book Buzz: Reel Deal." *Orlando Sentinel*, April 8, 2001, p. F8.

Potts, Bill. 1937. "Best Horse Won—Richards Agrees." *San Francisco Examiner*, February 28, 1937, Section SE, p. 2.

"Racing in the Depression." n.d. *American Experience*. https://www.pbs.org/wgbh /americanexperience/features/seabiscuit-racing-depression/

Ray, Bob. 1937. "The Sports X-Ray." *Los Angeles Times*, August 25, 1937, p. 14.

Rice, Grantland. 1938. "War Admiral Runs Fourth to Menow in Massachusetts Handicap: Ace First Time Out of Money: 66,000 See Star Trail Busy K and War Minstrel at Suffolk: Seabiscuit Is Scratched Because of Swollen Tendon Just Before Race." *The Sun*, June 30, 1938, p. 13.

Rickey, Carrie. 2003. "Spirited 'Seabiscuit' Beats the Odds." *The Philadelphia Inquirer*, July 25, 2003, pp. W4, W12.

Robertson, Orlo. 1938. "Smith Vindicated: Seabiscuit's Owner, also Gains Satisfaction of Knowing Son of Hard Tack Is Best Race Horse in Country." *The Evening Sun*, November 2, 1938, p. 26.

Rolfe, Costa. 2014. "Holy Roller - Australia's Biggest Racehorse." *Sporting News*, March 7, 2014. https://www.sportingnews.com/au/other-sports/news/holy-roller -australias-biggest-racehorse/8pk4viepggxf1l799j9ijo43f

Ross, Sherry. 2003. "'Seabiscuit' a Winner: Blockbuster Scores with Spa Jockeys." *New York Daily News*, July 27, 2003, p. 56.

Schaefer, Jack. 1963. *The Great Endurance Horse Race*. Santa Fe, NM: Stagecoach Press.

Scott, Walter. 2001. "Walter Scott's Personality Parade." *Parade Magazine*, September 16, 2001, p. 2.

Smith, Beverly. 2003. "Hollywood's Shaggy-Horse Story from the Past." *The Globe and Mail*, July 26, 2003. https://www.theglobeandmail.com/arts/hollywoods -shaggy-horse-story-from-the-past/article25287949/

Special to the Examiner. 1939. "'Biscuit Hurt; May Never Be in Race Again: Howard Champion Horse 'Pops' Knee, Loses Gruelling [sic] Run in Contest at Santa Anita: Under Whip: Beaten by McCarthy's Today; Start of American Monarch in $100,000 Handicap Doubtful." *San Francisco Examiner*, February 15, 1939, pp. 1, 31, 34.

Special to the Examiner. 1940. "Biscuit, Kayak Blow Up; Specify Wins! Anita 'Cap Favorites Finish Out of Money: Jockey Pollard Reports Champion 'Didn't Have It When Called Upon.'" *San Francisco Examiner*, February 18, 1940, Section S, pp. 2, 6.

Sragow, Michael. 2003. "A Great Ride: 'Seabiscuit' Is a Winning Tale of a Fantastic Race Horse, Extraordinary Men—And America Itself." *The Sun*, July 23, 2003, pp. 1E, 5E.

Stan, Francis E. 1938. "Win, Lose or Draw: Seabiscuit, Best in Land, Came Up Hard Way. Howard Horse's Victory Made the Better Story." *The Evening Star*, November 2, 1938, p. A-14.

Sterritt, David. 2003. "'Seabiscuit' Swerves Off Track: Racehorse Movie Has Heart, but Falls Short of Winners' Circle." *The Christian Science Monitor*, July 25, 2003. https://www.csmonitor.com/2003/0725/p15s02-almo.html

Sullivan, Prescott. 1947. "Seabiscuit Dies: One of the Turf's All-Time Greats, Howard Horse Won $437,730." *San Francisco Examiner*, May 19, 1947, p. 20.

Thompson, Eva. 2014. "American Horse Racing Through the Years." *Sports Then and Now*, August 18, 2014. http://sportsthenandnow.com/2014/08/18/american -horse-racing-through-the-years/

Treanor, Vincent. 1919. "Field of Eleven in the Suburban at Belmont To-Day: Open Cotest Is Promised, and Winner of Annual Feature Is Hard to Select." *The Evening World*, June 7, 1919, p. 6.

Underwood, Carl. 1950. "The Second Guess." *Lodi News-Sentinel*, June 8, 1950, p. 8.

United Press. 1938a. "War Admiral Hialeah Victor: Man O' War's Son First in $50,000 Widener Cup Race in Florida." *Oakland Tribune*, March 6, 1938, pp. A-7, A-9.

United Press. 1938b. "Weights Will Determine Where Seabiscuit Runs." *Binghamton Press*, December 7, 1938, p. 22.

United Press. 1940a. "Seabiscuit Is Impressive in La Jolla Event." *The Newark Advocate*, February 10, 1940, p. 8.

United Press. 1940b. "Seabiscuit Retired to Stud." *Tulare Daily Advance Register*, May 8, 1940, p. 7.

Von Borries, Philip. 1999. *Racelines: Observations on Horse Racing's Glorious History.* Chicago: Masters Press.

Vreeland, W. C. 1920. "Is Mr. Riddle Afraid to Race Man o' War Next Year." *Brooklyn Daily Eagle*, October 18, 1920, p. 2.

Vreeland, W. C. 1938. "Seabiscuit Master in Speed and Stamina." *Brooklyn Daily Eagle*, November 2, 1938, p. 21.

Wade, Horace. 1946. "'I'll Be Riding 'Til I Die' Proved Prophetic for Woolf." *Pasadena Independent*, January 6, 1946, p. 36.

Wagoner, Ronald. 1938. "Victory in Santa Anita 'Cap Glorifies Sande: Photo Picks Winner; $1,635,071 Handled in Record Betting Day." *Oakland Tribune*, March 6, 1938, pp. A-7, A-8.

Welkos, Robert W. 2003. "Going to Great Lengths: There May Have Been Only One Seabiscuit, but It Takes a Full Stable to Re-create His Race with War Admiral." *Los Angeles Times*, January 19, 2003, p. E6.

Williams, Randy. 2006. *Sports Cinema 100 Movies: The Best of Hollywood's Athletic Heroes, Losers, Myths, and Misfits.* Pompton Plains, NJ: Limelight Editions.

Chapter 8

Miracle (2004)

The U.S. men's hockey victory over the Soviet Union during the 1980 Winter Olympics—dubbed the "Miracle on Ice"—remains one of the biggest events in American sports history. The final call—"Do you believe in miracles? Yes!" by ABC-TV broadcaster Al Michaels (1944–)–became a catchphrase. ABC-TV rushed a movie, *Miracle on Ice*, that aired in 1981; cable-television network HBO produced a documentary in 2001, *Do You Believe in Miracles? The Story of the 1980 U.S. Hockey Team*; and several books were published about the game. Hockey in America, however, had never been as popular as baseball, boxing, football, or basketball, and Hollywood rarely produced hockey movies. Yet the biggest challenge for Walt Disney Pictures, director Gavin O'Connor (1963–) and first-time screenwriter Eric Guggenheim (1973–) and reportedly an uncredited Mike Rich (1959–) was how to bring audiences into theaters when the ending was known to practically every moviegoer in the country.

Miracle opens in 1979, when University of Minnesota hockey coach Herb Brooks (Kurt Russell, 1951–) interviews for and lands the job as coach of the U.S. Olympic men's team. At the team tryouts in Colorado Springs, Colorado, Brooks surprises his assistant coach, Craig Patrick (Noah Emmerich, 1965–), and Olympic committee officials when he selects his preliminary twenty-six-player squad on the first day, a process that typically takes at least a week. "I'm not looking for the best players," Brooks says, "I'm looking for the right ones."

Brooks relentlessly works and antagonizes his players. "Well, maybe if they hate him," team physician Doc Nagobads (Kenneth Welsh, 1942–) tells Patrick, "they won't have time to hate each other." After tying the Norwegian National Team in an exhibition game, Brooks works his players on the ice for hours, even after the rink's lights are turned off. "When you pull on that jersey, you represent yourself and your teammates," he bellows. "And the name on the front is a hell of a lot more important than the one on the back."

Other players are cut to reach the roster maximum of twenty, and in a final Olympic tune-up, the team is crushed, 10–3, by the Soviet Union, the powerhouse expected to win the Olympic gold medal. Jack O'Callahan (Michael Mantenuto, 1981–2017) injures his knee, but Brooks keeps him on the team even though it's uncertain if he will be able to get into a game, and Brooks challenges goaltender Jim Craig (Eddie Cahill, 1978–) to play to his potential.

In the Olympics, the Americans survive a tie against Sweden in the opening game, then rally from behind to fight their way into a rematch against the Soviets in the medal round. The young American players fight back and hold on to a stunning 4–3 victory before going on to come from behind once more to beat Finland for the gold medal.

But it is the game against the Soviet Union that will be talked about, as Brooks remembers. "It was a lot more than a hockey game, not only for those who watched it, but for those who played it."

Once known for its animated and children/family-oriented features, Walt Disney Pictures had branched out with a string of successes in sports movies, including *Remember the Titans*, (football, $115.65 million domestic box office) in 2000, and *The Rookie* (baseball, $75.6 million) in 2002.

Russell, who appeared in a number of Disney family films in the late 1960s and early 1970s, had become known for his roles in a wide range of films, including the futuristic *Escape from New York* (1981), the drama *Silkwood* (1983), and the Western *Tombstone* (1993). A high school baseball standout, Russell knew a thing or two about hockey; his teenage son Wyatt (1986–) was a goaltender for a Pacific International Junior Hockey League team in Richmond, British Columbia.

But like the debut screenwriter, the rest of the cast and crew were practically unknowns. Even O'Connor had only recently gained notice for directing the independently produced *Tumbleweeds* (2001).

With principal photography set in British Columbia, an estimated seventeen hundred showed up at a casting call in Vancouver in February 2003. That number was cut to four hundred fifty, who began trying out on the ice. "If you hadn't played junior [league] hockey, they didn't even look at you," said Darren Webb, a junior and semipro hockey player from British Columbia who became one of sixty-five extras cast as hockey players (Corbett 2003, A13).

"The thing is you can't fake hockey," said Rob Miller of ReelSports Solutions Inc., which was hired to handle the hockey scenes after choreographing sports scenes in *Jerry Maguire* (1996), *Any Given Sunday* (1999), and *The Rookie*. "It takes such unique skills to play the game at a high level that you can't fake it. You see it right away" (Mason 2003, E6).

But O'Connor realized he needed more than hockey-playing extras. "Do I get hockey players and teach them how to act or do I get actors and teach them how to play hockey?" he said. "Once I asked myself that it was very clear which way to go" (Mason 2004, G1).

Patrick O'Brien Demsey (1978–), cast as Mike Eruzione, had played hockey at Fitchburg (Massachusetts) State College. Mantenuto, who had played at the University of Maine, might have landed his role as the hot-headed O'Callahan after fighting with another player in the on-ice tryouts. "I went up to Gavin to apologize," Mantenuto said, "but he was very happy. He was pumped" (Globe Staff, and Wires 2017, B14). Alaska-born Nathan West (1978–), who played Rob McClanahan, had been a goaltender in the Ontario Hockey League. Billy Schneider (1981–) played his dad, William "Buzz" Schneider (1954–), who scored five goals in seven games for the 1980 Olympic champions.

On August 13, 2003, shortly after principal shooting ended, Brooks was killed in an auto accident when his minivan rolled over on Interstate 35 in Forrest Lake, Minnesota, while driving home from a fund-raising golf event. He was sixty-six. "He was 100 percent at home with hockey players," Russell said. "One of the last conversations Herb and I had, he talked about coming to watch Wyatt play. He never made it" (Strickler 2004b, E11).

Released by Disney's Buena Vista subsidiary, *Miracle* opened on February 6, 2004.

"Hockey movies have often been a disappointment to hockey fans," Canadian journalist Neil Corbett wrote, citing *Slap Shot* (1977), "the uncontested king of the small mountain of hockey films"; *Youngblood* (1986), "surely the least authentic sports film ever produced"; *The Mighty Ducks* (1992), a Disney family film; and *Mystery, Alaska* (1999), a comedy set in a small Alaska town. But Webb said: "People are going to be surprised how authentic this will be" (Corbett 2003, A13).

In hockey country, *Miracle* scored solid reviews. "Like all great sports movies, 'Miracle' is about more than hockey," Jeff Strickler wrote for the *Star Tribune* in Minneapolis, giving the film a four-star rating, its highest. "You don't need to be a sports fan to appreciate the enormity of the challenge the team faced and the depth of its dedication to overcoming it. This is a movie about winners and what it takes to be one" (Strickler 2004a, E1). "I don't know that I've ever felt more involved in fictional competition than I was throughout this movie," Jack Mathews wrote for New York's *Daily News*, "and I can't tell a hockey puck from a cow pie" (Mathews 2004, 57). And Ron Weiskind of the *Pittsburgh Post-Gazette* said, "For all the zeal Russell invests in the movie, 'Miracle' succeeds largely because of its restraint" (Weiskind 2004, W-23).

But outside of hockey country, reviews were decidedly more mixed. "No matter how much (or little) you know about ice hockey," Bob Ross wrote for *The Tampa Tribune*, "this fact-based story speaks eloquently about the virtues of determination and teamwork" (Ross 2004, 10). Jason Cohen of the *Austin American-Statesmen*, however, said the movie "never quite transcends its formula" and "spends much of its 115 minutes proving there was no miracle at all. The United States triumphed at Lake Placid because a hockey lifer realized that the best way to beat the Russians was to embrace their way of life—that is to say, communism" (Cohen 2004, E3-E4). And Anita Katz of San Francisco's *The Examiner* called it "an impressively choreographed but depressingly formulaic film" (Katz 2004, 13).

Miracle grossed a better-than-respectable $64,378,093 domestically, and Michael Sragow, film critic for *The Sun* in Baltimore, named it one of the best films of year, citing Russell's performance and his powerful speech to the players before their Olympic victory against the Soviets:

> Great moments are born from great opportunity. That's what you have here, tonight, boys. That's what you've earned here tonight. One game. If we played them 10 times, they might win nine, but not this game. Not tonight. Tonight, we skate. Tonight, we stay with them, and we shut them down, because we can! Tonight, *we* are the greatest hockey team in the world. You were born to be hockey players, every one of you. And you were meant to be here tonight. … This is your time. Their time is done, it's over. I'm sick and tired of hearing about what a great hockey team the Soviets have. Screw 'em. This is your time. Now go out there and take it! (Sragow 2004, C1)

HISTORICAL BACKGROUND

Stick-and-ball games had been played in prehistoric Europe, ancient Egypt, and by Native Americans, including the Mi'kmaq, a First Nations group that played a blend of lacrosse and hockey in Canada. Field hockey was played on lawns, but in colder climates, ice hockey took root on frozen ponds. By the 1820s, British soldiers were ice-skating on frozen Canadian ponds, using hooked sticks to push around whiskey-barrel corks called bungs.

Those early games were played on ice-covered ponds and lakes, but in 1875, James G.A. Creighton (1850–1930), an engineer from Halifax, Nova Scotia, moved the game indoors. On March 3, Creighton organized a hockey game at the Victoria Skating Rink in Montreal, Quebec, his home since 1872. Instead of a ball, Creighton used a wooden disc to protect the players and the forty spectators; by the following year, the disc in hockey was being called a puck. Because of the rink's size (80 feet wide and 204 feet long), Creighton limited the number of players on ice to nine per team.

> The tight space also meant that rules would have to be imposed to avoid anarchy. Creighton resorted to the rules he had learned in Halifax, ones that regulated a game quite different to the modern eye: the puck was not allowed

to leave the ice, there was no forward passing ahead of the puck carrier, and goalies could not fall or kneel to make saves. The sixty-minute match would have an intermission in the middle, partly for the players to recover, as no substitutions would be allowed during the game. Everyone played the full hour, unless removed due to injury or penalty—and, in either case, players were not replaced. (McKinley 2006, 7–9)

Two years later, Creighton had published rules for his "Montreal Game." In 1877, Montreal's McGill University founded a hockey club. The game spread across the globe. In 1885, Oxford University in England formed a hockey club, and John Hopkins University staged an "ice polo" game against Yale University in 1893. The Amateur Hockey League was formed by New York City–area teams in November 1896, and the New York Athletic Club won the league's first championship for the 1896–97 season. Although that league folded during World War I (1914–18), in 1913 Minnesota and Michigan teams had organized the American Amateur Hockey Association. The first professional team in the United States was formed in Houghton, Michigan, in 1903, although its players were largely Canadians. The National Hockey League (NHL) was founded in 1917, but a U.S. team would not join until the Boston Bruins came aboard in 1924. The New York Americans and Pittsburgh Pirates entered the league the following year, followed by the New York Rangers, Chicago Blackhawks, and Detroit Cougars when the NHL expanded to ten teams in 1926. As a cold-weather sport that required ice, hockey's popularity remained strongest in the northern regions of the United States, but the NHL eventually took the sport south. Los Angeles and Oakland, California, were awarded franchises in 1966, part of a six-team expansion beginning with the 1967–68 season, although Oakland's California Golden Seals were never successful competitively or commercially, moving to Cleveland, Ohio, in 1976 before merging with the Minnesota North Stars for the 1978–79 season. The Atlanta Flames joined the league for the 1972–73 season before moving to Calgary, Alberta, in 1980. "This is the Southern United States," a season-ticket holder told *The Atlanta Constitution* in 1980, shortly before the team was sold to Nelson Skalbania (1938–), a real estate entrepreneur from Vancouver, British Columbia, for a reported $16 million U.S., "and I really think hockey's not gonna get it here" (Newman 1980, 1D).

As in professional big-league baseball, basketball, and football, the National Hockey League was challenged briefly by rival leagues. The Western Canada Hockey League started with four teams in 1921, expanded to six teams for the 1924–25 season, and changed its name to the Western Hockey League for its last season, 1925–26. A bigger challenge came in 1971 with the founding of the World Hockey Association (WHA). "Not only did the WHA place franchises in existing NHL markets such as Chicago, Los Angeles, New York, Philadelphia, and Boston, it also ignored NHL contracts, emboldened by an antitrust investigation of the NHL by the U.S. Department of Justice and a slew of lawsuits, and actively pursued NHL star players" (Nelson 2009b, 412). Gordie Howe (1928–2016), the star known as "Mr. Hockey" who had played twenty-five seasons with the Detroit Red Wings before retiring after the 1970–71 season, signed with the WHA's Houston Aeros and played six seasons in the league, guiding Houston to the 1974 and 1975 league championships. After fifteen seasons with the Chicago Black Hawks, Bobby Hull (1939–) signed with the WHA's Winnipeg franchise, helping the Jets win three titles. The WHA's biggest coup came when Skalbania, then owner of the Indianapolis Racers, signed seventeen-year-old Wayne Gretzky (1961–), considered hockey's biggest talent since Bobby Orr (1948–), to a seven-year, $1.75 million contract. Gretzky went on to play twenty-one professional seasons, setting sixty-one NHL records and powering the NHL's Edmonton Oilers to four Stanley Cup championships. After his retirement in 1999, the Hockey Hall of Fame waived its three-year waiting period for only the tenth time and inducted him into the hall only seven months after his retirement. But the WHA lacked stability, and by the end of the 1978–79 season, only six teams remained. That summer, the WHA and NHL worked out a deal. Four WHA franchises, the Edmonton Oilers, Hartford Whalers, Quebec Nordiques, and Winnipeg Jets, would join the NHL, and the Cincinnati Stingers and Birmingham Bulls would both be paid $1.5 million and disband.

Although planned for the 1916 Olympic Games, hockey's first Olympic appearance had to wait when the Games were canceled because of World War I (1914–18). Instead, the sport debuted at the Summer Olympics in Antwerp, Belgium, in 1920, with Canada winning the gold medal and the United States taking the silver; women's hockey debuted at the Games in 1998 in Nagano, Japan.

Medals were determined on a points system; the playoff format would not begin until 1992. In 1924, at the first Winter Olympics, Canada again defeated the United States for the gold medal. Canadian hockey dominated the next five Olympics—none was played in 1940 and 1944 because of World War II—winning the gold medal every year except in 1936, when Canada lost to Great Britain in the championship game. But in 1956, the Soviet Union powered its way to Olympic gold in Cortina d'Ampezzo, Italy. The United States, overpowered 4–0 by the Soviets, took the silver, and Canada finished with the bronze. "Russia," said U.S. coach John Mariucci (1916–87), "was out of this world" (Gordon 1956, 1). Asked how Russia would fare against a top American collegiate team filled with Canadian players, Mariucci laughed. "It wouldn't be a game," he said. "Russia would kick the heck out of them. They'd do the same to any amateur team I've seen. After all, I think this American team of ours is pretty good, and look what they did to us" (Gordon 1956, 1).

The Soviets became a new power in Olympic hockey, but the following year, the Winter Games were being held in Squaw Valley, California. One of the players trying out for that team was Brooks, a forward from the University of Minnesota whose high school team in St. Paul, Minnesota, had won the 1955 state championship. The Soviet Union and Canada were considered favorites for Olympic gold.

"Not many people gave us much of a chance," said Bill Cleary Sr. (1934–), one of five players returning from the Americans' 1956 team. "I remember all the press, I think they were picking us to finish 12th, and then there were only nine teams in the finals—that's what they thought of us" (Bates 2018).

But the U.S. team beat Czechoslovakia and Australia to advance to the medal round, then defeated Sweden and Germany before upsetting Canada, 2–1. Two nights later, the U.S. team overcame a 2–1 deficit to shock the Soviet Union, 3–2. The next morning, the United States faced Czechoslovakia in a rematch. Trailing 4–3 after two periods, the Americans scored six goals to pull off a 9–4 victory.

Brooks, however, received no gold medal. A few days before the Olympic team had to be finalized, coach Jack Riley (1920–2016) decided he needed Cleary and John Mayasich (1933–), who had powered the 1956 Olympic gold-medal run by combining for fourteen goals and eleven assists. Cleary accepted, but only if his brother Bob (1936–2015) also made the team. Riley agreed, but only seventeen players could be on the roster, so Brooks was cut. After learning what had happened, Brooks's teammates almost walked out. Said Dick Meredith (1932–):

> The boys held a meeting and decided that we'd all quit if Riley decided to bring up Bill and Bob Cleary and let Herb Brooks go. We all realized that Bill would help us. But we didn't think it was fair for Bill to insist that his brother come along in the deal.
>
> Finally it was Weldon Olson [1932–] who pointed out that if we quit we would all be barred by the Amateur Hockey association. He also said this would be a black mark on the Americans. So we went along with the deal and both the Clearys joined the team and Brooks was cut. (Hartman 1960, 13)

The move worked. The Cleary brothers totaled eleven goals and nine assists, and Mayasich had two goals and three assists. Back home in St. Paul on February 28, Brooks watched the game final game on television with his father. After the rout, his father said, "Well, I guess the coach cut the right guy" (Coffey 2005, 4).

The Soviet Union dominated Olympic hockey for the next four Games 1964 through 1976, winning gold medals in those Games, outscoring opponents 175–44, and posting a 27–1–1 record. During the same period, the United States managed only one hockey medal, a silver in 1972. Brooks played on the 1964 and 1968 teams, scoring one goal and two assists as the U.S. team went 3–5, including a 5–1 loss to the Soviets, for a fifth-place finish in 1964, and getting two assists in the United States' 2–4–1, sixth-place finish in 1968 that saw the Americans fall, 10–2, to the Soviet Union. In the

THE 1950 'MIRACLE ON GRASS'

What the Olympics are to many sports, the World Cup is to soccer. Thirty years before the "Miracle on Ice," a ragtag United States team upset England, 1–0, in Belo Horiizonte, Brazil, in the world-championship tournament.

Started in 1930 by international soccer's governing body, the World Cup had been played every four years except for 1942 and 1946 because of World War II.

London bookmakers made England a 3–1 favorite to win the 1950 World Cup. The United States, which hadn't qualified for the World Cup since 1934, was the 500–1 underdog. But Joe Gaetjens (1924–64), a Haitian attending Columbia University, scored a first-half goal, and goaltender Frank Borghi (1925–2015), one of six players from St. Louis, saved a penalty kick late in the game to preserve U.S. victory. How big was the upset? "Americans [in London] said it compared to a major-league all-star team being beaten in London by nine part-time English baseball players" (Associated Press 1950a, 3B), while a Page 1 article in London's *Daily Express* proclaimed: "This is the biggest soccer upset of all time" (Associated Press 1950b, 13).

Another St. Louis player, Harry Keough (1927–2012), said the Americans "were almost sorry" to beat England. "We felt it was going to be a terrible blow to them," Keough said, "and we knew we were not yet strong enough to win the championship" (Post-Dispatch Archives 2020). Neither England nor the Americans made it out of the first round of play, finishing with 1–2 records. Uruguay went on to win the tournament; Brazil finished second.

The game was recreated in the 2005 movie *The Game of Their Lives* (retitled *The Miracle Match* for video), directed by David Anspaugh (1946-) and based on Geoffrey Douglas's book.

Sources

Associated Press. 1950a. "London Writers Weep." *St. Louis Post-Dispatch,* June 30, 1950, p. 3B.
Associated Press. 1950b. "Boston Tea Party Was Minor Upset." *Spokane Daily Chronicle,* June 30, 1950, p. 13.
Douglas, Geoffrey. 2005. *The Game of Their Lives: The Untold Story of the World Cup's Biggest Loss.* New York: First Perennial Currents.
Post-Dispatch Archives. 2020. "70 Years Go a Bunch of St. Louis Kids Helped to Pull Off Soccer's 'Miracle on Grass.'" *St. Louis Post-Dispatch,* June 29, 2020. https://www.stlto day.com/sports/soccer/70-years-ago-a-bunch-of-st-louis-kids-helped-to-pull-off-soccers -miracle/article_37c6929d-881e-5e92-8556-1a06e3cc4320.html
"U.S. Upsets England in Soccer: Gaetjens Scores the Only Goal." *St. Louis Post-Dispatch,* June 30, 1950, p. 3B.

1972 Games, the Soviets beat the silver-medalist U.S. team, 7–2; in 1976, the Americans fell 6–2 to the Soviets and placed fifth.

Before the Olympics began in Lake Placid in 1980, the Soviet Union and Czechoslovakia were expected to compete for the gold medal. Many thought the United States might have a chance at the bronze if it could handle Sweden and Finland. But after the Soviet Union invaded Afghanistan in late

December 1979, President Jimmy Carter (1924–) threatened to boycott the Moscow Games scheduled for that summer (the official boycott announcement came after the Winter Olympics, and Canada, West Germany, Japan, and more than sixty other countries refused to participate in Moscow that summer). The Soviets, however, refused to boycott the Winter Games, and no Soviets were banned from participation, but the Soviet Union retaliated by leading a boycott of the 1984 Olympics in Los Angeles. "An athlete has to realize he or she is very insignificant in the overall world situation," Brooks said. "I don't think you can separate politics and athletics, [but] hockey players here don't determine government policy and I'm sure they don't there, either" (Vincent 1980, 1D).

The Americans' first hockey game for the 1980 Games, against Sweden, was played the day before the opening ceremonies. With the arena only half full, the U.S. team trailed 2–1 with less than just a minute remaining in the game. A loss would knock the Americans out of medal contention. With 41 seconds left, Brooks removed goaltender Craig for an extra offensive player. But Sweden's goaltender Pelle Lindbergh had been tough all night. Dan Stoneking, sports editor of *The Minneapolis Star*, wrote that Lindbergh "at times looked as if he could stop inflation" (Stoneking 1980, 20B). But Bill Baker (1956–) made a 55-foot shot—"It was a little bit of a Hail Mary shot," Baker said (Stoneking 1980, 20B)—that gave the United States a 2–2 tie that felt like a victory.

The Americans went on a run after that opening round, trailing but rallying to beat Czechoslovakia, 7–3; Norway, 5–1; Romania, 7–2; and West Germany, 4–2, before meeting the undefeated, untied Soviet Union on February 22.

Again, the United States fell behind early, came back to tie the score, fell behind again before Mark Johnson (1957–) tied the score in the third period. Team captain Mike Eruzione (1954–) then gave the United States a 4–3 lead, and some 10 minutes later, Michaels was yelling into his microphone, "Do you believe in miracles? Yes!"

"I must have said at least 100 Hail Marys in the last 10 minutes," Eruzione's mother said (Wendel 2009, 41).

Two days later, the Americans rallied again, defeating Finland, 4–2, to claim the country's first hockey gold in twenty years.

"When the buzzer sounded, I didn't know what to do," Craig said. "Then, it struck me. We had just won the Olympic gold medal. I kept repeating that in my mind. We're gold medalists! We're gold medalists!" (Bodley 1980, 13).

"This is a group of young people who have startled the athletic world here," Brooks said. "I'm not just talking about the hockey world. I'm talking about the entire athletic world. It just goes to show what a group can do when it makes up its mind. To me, it brings to the front the beliefs in our country—that you do not have to prove our way of life through a state-supported athletic body" (Bodley 1980, 13).

1980's "miracle" marked the United States' last gold medal in men's hockey to date; the Americans placed second to Canada in the 2002 Games—with Brooks coaching the U.S. team—and again in the 2010 Games. The Soviet Union won gold in 1984 and 1988, but inner turmoil and unrest led to the dissolution of the Union of Soviet Socialist Republics at the end of 1991. A team from the newly formed Commonwealth of Independent States of former Soviet nations won gold in 1992, and Russian Olympians took gold in 2018. The world was changing, and so were the Olympics. In 1986, the International Olympic Committee began allowing professional athletes to compete in the Games, and in 1998, the NHL allowed its players to play in the Olympics. In 1998, the average salary of a U.S. men's hockey player was $3 million.

"There's no progress without change," said Brooks, who coached the French men's hockey team in the 1998 Games. "The Olympics are still real special to me. Olympians were always my heroes. . . .

"I watched the flag go up in the Olympic village the other day. Those things that are part of the tradition are very emotional and moving.

"That has not changed. A lot of the symbols are still there, but they have dollar signs in front of them" (Gugger 1998, C10).

DEPICTION AND CULTURAL CONTEXT

One goal of the Olympics is to promote world unity and peace, but wars had canceled the Olympics in 1916 (Berlin), 1940 (Tokyo), and 1944 (London), and politics came into play. The 1956 Games (Melbourne) were boycotted by Egypt, Iraq, and Lebanon over Israel's role in the Suez Canal seizure, and by Holland, Spain, and Switzerland over the Soviet Union's invasion of Hungary. A number of African nations boycotted the 1976 Games (Montreal) in protest of New Zealand's rugby tour of then-segregated South Africa. Tragedy struck the 1972 Games (Munich) when Palestinian terrorists kidnapped several Israeli athletes. During a rescue attempt, eleven athletes, five terrorists, and a policeman were killed.

In December 1979, Soviet troops invaded Afghanistan, airlifting three divisions into Kabul, capital of the Central-South Asia country. The Soviets said they were upholding the 1979 Soviet–Afghan Friendship Treaty. The U.S. State Department called it "blatant military interference" (Shlachter 1979, 1-A). President Carter threatened to boycott the Summer Olympics in Moscow, but the Soviets never really considered a boycott of the Lake Placid Games. Before long, Soviets, with some one hundred thousand troops in the country, had control major Afghan cities, but Mujahideen rebels, supported by several other countries, including the United States, struck back. For nine years the war raged, leaving an estimated one million civilians, ninety thousand Mujahideen fighters, eighteen thousand Afghan troops, and fourteen thousand five hundred Soviet soldiers dead. After the Soviets withdrew, the Taliban took control of Afghanistan.

That made the 1980 U.S.–U.S.S.R. Olympic hockey matchup more than just a game. "It was a game of our ideals against the Russian way of life," said Gary Smith, trainer for the 1980 U.S. hockey team (Gary Smith, interview with author, September 4, 2020).

Yet when *Miracle* was released, the United States and the U.S.S.R. might not have been allies, but their relationship was far from possible nuclear annihilation during the Cuban Missile Crisis (1962). Years before reports of Russian interference in U.S. presidential elections or bounties offered for dead American soldiers, the United States and Russia were cooperating on anti-terrorism measures. Osama bin Laden (1957–2011), who helped found the terrorist group al-Qaeda and planned the September 11, 2001, terrorist attacks on U.S. soil that claimed more than three thousand American lives, remained at large. So did Saddam Hussein (1937–2006), leader of Iraq, which the United States had invaded in 2003. Under President Vladimir Putin (1952–), Russia had shared intelligence and contributed logistical support to the American-led effort to drive the Taliban out of power in Afghanistan. U.S. president George W. Bush (1946–) reportedly sought to improve ties with Russia, but was voted down by other members of his administration, including Secretary of Defense Donald H. Rumsfeld (1932–), who "saw Russia as a second-rate power; not worth a hill of beans" (Kuchins 2016).

The Russians might have been America's biggest threat in 1980, but not in early 2004. That was one challenge for *Miracle*. Another was that sports movies usually shied away from politics.

"To have a sports film with an international, political crisis happening with the Cold War—I remember that there was a real fear we'd be in a war with Russia, a nuclear war—it was incredibly tense," said Mark Ciardi (1961–), one of *Miracle*'s producers. "Leading up to that game it played to a bigger stage" (Harris 2020).

The not-quite U.S.–Russia alliance proved short-lived. Months after *Miracle* was released, Russian commandos attacked a school in Beslan, where armed Chechen rebels had talked twelve hundred adults and children hostage and demanded Russian withdrawal and independence for Chechnya. More than three hundred thirty people were killed, half of them children. Putin suggested that the United States supported the Chechen terrorists. Later that year, during an election protest in Ukraine, Putin said the United States was interfering in Russian elections.

Miracle stayed fairly close to history, but as *New York Times* critic Elvis Mitchell wrote: *Miracle* "faces a hurdle that most fact-based films don't have to contemplate: the actual story the picture is based on was so corny and rousing that it hit all the notes many filmmakers would have too much shame to embrace" (Mitchell 2004).

The biggest stretch comes when Brooks makes his selections after the first day of tryouts in Colorado Springs, failing to seek input from the committee or assistant coach Craig Patrick (1946–). The cut to twenty-six players didn't come until August 1, 1979, after the hockey championship game at the National Sports Festival in Colorado Springs, Colorado, and took, *Minneapolis Tribune* sports columnist Dan Stoneking wrote, "an evaluating, re-evaluating and re-re-evaluating process" that started when the festival began on July 26. Even Brooks said, "I wish there were spots for 36, or even, 46. Some of the decisions were very, very close. There were jobs up for grabs right through the last period of tonight's championship game" (Stoneking 1979, 8B). Brooks received input from several college coaches, including Harvard's Bill Cleary, who had cost Brooks a place on the 1960 Olympic roster; New Hampshire's Charlie Holt (1922–2000); Wisconsin's Bob Johnson (1931–91); Boston University's Jack Parker (1945–); and Colorado College's Jeff Sauer (1943–2017).

The festival, started in 1978 by U.S. Olympic Committee chairman Robert Kane (1911–92), drew two thousand three hundred prospects in thirty-one sports.

"It's no fun standing up here in front of you this evening," Brooks told players and media before announcing his team. "I am not trying to pacify any of you or make this over dramatic. But I have been sitting right where you are sitting, feeling what you are feeling. I was the last guy cut before the team played in Squaw Valley in 1960. The coach must have made the right decision because the team won the gold medal" (Stoneking 1979, 8B).

The decision wasn't without controversy.

"I think this team has confused the selection committee a bit," said Bill Selmen (1939–), who coached the festival's gold-medal-winning team. "Some of the guys should have played themselves right on the team during tonight's game. Some players come to a tryout session like this one with a reputation. Others leave with a reputation" (Stoneking 1979, 8B). But Boston University's Parker countered: "Brooks should be given a lot of credit or the team that was selected. In the past, it was usually Western or [Western Collegiate Hockey Association] players who were picked. But from the point of view of the Eastern people he was extremely fair. I don't think anyone could have done a better, more rational job" (Wendel 2009, 9).

In a letter to his Olympians four months after winning the gold, Brooks explained that "I did not want the U.S. Hockey Community to say that regionalism and/or favoritism entered into my final decision" (Coffey 2005, 263).

"The common denominator of all the guys . . . was that they were really competitive, very hungry, very focused and mentally tough—to go along with whatever talent they had," Brooks said (Chin and Granat 2010).

Before the festival, Brooks told one of his assistant coaches, Warren Strelow (1934–2007), that a panel of coaches would pick the players for the U.S. team but that Strelow, goalies coach for the University of Minnesota from 1974–83, would pick the goaltenders. When Strelow asked, "What if I pick someone you don't like," Brooks answered: "I don't care who you pick, you just better be right" (Coffey 2005, 177). When Brooks coached the U.S. Olympic hockey team in 2002, Strelow again served as his goalies coach.

Strelow isn't included in *Miracle,* and Patrick and Dr. George Nagobads (1921–) are given little to do. Trainer Smith and physician Nagobads are combined into one character, Doc Nagobads. "I was the one in the middle of the skating punishment in Finland when the rink people turned off the lights and wanted us to leave," Smith said (Gary Smith, interview with author, September 23, 2020).

The movie depicts Brooks as a dictator. "Russell got Herbie to a T," Smith said. "He knocked it out of the park on how Herbie acted, how he stood" (Gary Smith, interview with author, September 4, 2020).

After the team is announced, Boston University's Jack O'Callahan (1957–) and Minnesota's Rob McClanahan (1958–), get into a fight at practice over a grudge from a college game. In the movie, O'Callahan claims that a cheap shot by McClanahan cost his team a chance at winning the college hockey championship in 1976. Minnesota defeated BU, 4–2, in the semifinals that year, but McClanahan was still playing high school hockey.

"What was real was the animosity between the guys from Boston and the guys from Minnesota," McClanahan said. "You only have two hours to tell the story, so they created that scene to show that we really didn't like each other" (Shipley 2020a).

Joked O'Callahan "Robby was much too smart to start a fight with an Irish guy from Charlestown" (Pallasch 2007).

For the most part, *Miracle* sticks to the key facts afterward.

Brooks, who had graduated with a degree in psychology from the University of Minnesota, gave his Olympic team a three hundred-question psychology test. Goaltender Jim Craig (1957–) was one of the few players who refused to take it. "Brooks could've taken his refusal as insubordination or as a sign that Craig had some latent vulnerability he didn't want exposed. Instead he took it as evidence of Craig's take-on-the-world mentality, which the coach had liked so much in the 1979 world championships" (Coffey 2005, 185). Brooks also needed smart players flexible enough to learn a new style of play. "He described his rigorous off-ice conditioning program, featuring anaerobic, flexibility and other exercises that he'd picked up from swimming and track coaches," E.M. Swift wrote for *Sports Illustrated.* "That was all quite revolutionary to hockey, and he knew he was putting his players through a lot" (Swift 2004).

Brooks said: "There are two schools of thought on the Olympics. One is to forget about trying to beat the Russians, Czechs and Swedes and concentrate on winning the games that are possible in the 12-team competition. The second is to go after the whole thing, try to innovate and surprise them. That second one is where I'm at. I'm idealistic as well as realistic. I want to try to beat the Russians, but we won't cut our throats if we do" (Gilbert 1979, 14)

The challenge for Brooks and his players was to learn this system in a matter of months. The North American style of hockey at that time was "dump-and-run" (Wendel 2009, 11), in which the player's objective was to get the puck into the defending team's zone and hope for a shot at the goal—not much speed, and not often exciting—and that worked often in the NHL. But the NHL plays on rinks 85 feet wide; internationally, including at the Olympics, hockey is played on rinks 100 feet wide. With more open space, players needed to be agile and creative. So Brooks came up with a game that blended American hockey—specifically forechecking (applying defensive pressure in the offensive zone to create a turnover)—and the European's open-ice game. He worked his players relentlessly hard because he knew that to win against Europe's top teams, especially the Soviet Union, his players had to be in top physical shape.

"Gentlemen," Brooks tells his players in *Miracle*, "you don't have enough talent to win on talent alone." That was one of what Brooks's players called "The Best of Brooksisms," slogans and catchwords he would bellow during practices or in locker rooms. Some of the players even began compiling a notebook of his comments, such as "Passes come from the heart and not from the stick" and "Don't dump the puck in. That went out with short pants" (Wendel 2009, 12).

When the U.S. team played halfheartedly to a 3–3 tie against Norway during a European tour, Brooks had the team leave the locker room and return to the ice—as depicted in the film—where he proceeded to work the players for 45 minutes.

Ever the psychologist, Brooks played mind games with his players, praising them, then antagonizing them. "He blew up on Rob McClanahan after the first period against Sweden," Smith recalled. "I had sent [McClanahan] in to get ice on a bruised thigh and Herbie called him soft and that he would never make it to the NHL. They went at it, and I thought Herbie had lost it, but he was using it to get the team motivated. They all kind of rallied around their teammate" (Gary Smith, interview with author, September 23, 2020).

In the movie, Craig and Nagobads suggest that Brooks is playing the bad-guy role hoping that if the players hate his guts, they will bond as a team. Which wasn't that far from the truth. Brooks, McLanahan said, "was not my friend, he was my coach. I was afraid of him. I think anyone from Minnesota would tell you that—and it was a different era, where he was the dictator. We called him 'Ayatollah Khomeini'" (Shipley 2020b). Sayyid Ruhollah Musavi Khomeini (1902–89) was the leader of Iran when Iranian college students gained control of the U.S. embassy in Tehran on November 4, 1979, and held them hostage for four hundred and forty-four days.

The scene in the film when players, exchanging gag gifts at a Christmas party, present Brooks with a whip actually happened.

The Americans' last game before Olympic play came at New York City's Madison Square Garden when they met the Soviet team. "I said to Herbie, 'We don't have a chance against these guys,' and he said, 'No s—'," Smith said. The Soviets, as expected, crushed the U.S. team, 10–3. But what the movie doesn't suggest is that, in this game, Brooks might have been playing mind games with the Russians. Before the game, Brooks told his players to have fun—something he never uttered before any game, and when Strelow suggested that Craig split goaltending duties with backup Steve Janaszak (1957–), Brooks agreed. Both coaches thought that the plan would keep Craig from being demoralized in a potential drubbing while the Russians wouldn't get to learn Craig's strengths and weaknesses. "I think [Brooks] was OK with the beating because then the Russians might be overconfident," Smith said, "that we presented no challenge to them" (Gary Smith, interview with author, September 23, 2020).

Soviet coach Viktor Tikhonov (1930–2014) wasn't fooled. "I think that we showed what we can do and they didn't," he said after the February 9 exhibition game. "We have a feeling that they have a lot of reserve. I anticipate it was the tactics of the coach. I think if they had been playing a little more cold minded (less physical), they would be playing better" (Morganti 1980, 1D).

Coaches, however, understand the difficulty in convincing young players that the team they just annihilated is not that bad. Years later, Tikhonov said, "No matter what we tried we could not get that 10–3 game out of the players' minds. The players told me it would be no problem. It turned out to be a very big problem" (Coffey 2005, 28).

The Soviets were relative newcomers to the world of international sports. Having shunned sports, including the Olympics, since coming to power in 1917, the country began rethinking that after seeing more than an estimated twenty-six million deaths, including from disease and famine, during World War II. Only after the war did the Russians begin playing hockey, organizing its first league in 1946. Before that, the closest amateur hockey game in Russia had been a sport called bandy, "essentially field hockey on ice" (Coffey 2005, 31). Yet in the world hockey championship tournament of 1954, the Soviet Union defeated Canada, 7–2, in the final game to complete an undefeated run and win its first world title. Their first Olympic championship came two years later—and this in a country where players often wore bicycle helmets on ice, and practiced and played in snowstorms. But unlike U.S. players, the Russians were a national team, practicing and playing together on club and national teams. They did not just come together every four years in the Winter Olympics.

"The Russians came and went as a group, never showered at rink, had bad equipment, and did not look happy," Smith said (Gary Smith, interview with author, September 4, 2020).

Entering the 1980 Games, Soviet teams had won twenty-four world championships, posting 176–23–10 record while scoring 1,492 goals and allowing only 394. Shortly before the game against the United States in Lake Placid, a U.S. newspaper reporter wrote: "They are the quietest the least-known group of athletes in these mountains. They are the Russians. As a hockey team, they are heavily favored to win a fifth straight Olympic Games gold medal. They are unemotional, thoroughly programmed on the ice. They don't hug each other and celebrate after goals. They just head back to center ice for the faceoff. Fans consistently root for the opposition here. But the Russians remain unmoved. . . . These guys don't lose" (Gannett News Service 1980, 7B).

Filmmakers went to great lengths to recreate the U.S.–Soviet game as accurately as possible, even bringing in Michaels to announce the game as he did on ABC-TV (tape-delayed for prime-time viewing) in 1980. While Michaels did voice-overs for most of his play-by-play call for the film, when he was asked to recreate "Do you believe in miracles?", he said, "Over my dead body" (Harris 2020), and so the final call came from the tape made in 1980.

Michaels was a veteran broadcaster, but he had called only one hockey game during his career—the 1972 gold-medal game between the Soviet Union and Czechoslovakia in Sapporo, Japan. As a boy, Michaels had attended some pro hockey games with his father, and other ABC broadcasters weren't lobbying for the U.S.–U.S.S.R. game. "I was pretty happy about it," he said, "because among other things, when you're doing a Winter Olympic sport, you want to be inside" (Frederick 2020).

Bill Ranford (1966–), who had retired after fifteen seasons and was coaching the Los Angeles Kings goalies, doubled for Cahill as U.S. goaltender Craig. "We were really focused on trying to make it as real as possible," Ranford said. "We let the hockey make the events, versus the other way around" (Harris 2020).

Brooks's pregame speech was pieced together from memories. According to O'Callahan, O'Connor asked him to write down what he remembered, but what appeared on screen wasn't exactly what O'Callahan recalled. "I don't know if Herbie said, 'Great moments are made from great opportunities'," O'Callahan said, "or if those are my words that sorta have taken a life of their own" (Littlefield 2015). One of the earliest versions of the speech came in Tim Wendel's book *Going for the Gold*, first published in 1980. In Wendel's account, Brooks read from a crumpled yellow paper: "You were born to be a player. You were meant for this moment. You were meant to be here. So let's have poise and possession of ourselves at this time" (Wendel 2009, 34).

The game, however, is accurate. After Vladimir Krutov (1960–2012) put the Soviets up in the first period, the teams exchanged goals, the last coming from Johnson with one second to play. That sent the Americans into the locker room tied 2–2—a huge confidence builder. "That's quite a turnabout," O'Callahan said, "and things like that just don't happen naturally.

It's almost like the parting of the Red Sea" (Wendel 2009, 35). When the players returned to the ice for the second period, Russian goaltender Vladislav Tretiak (1952–) had been benched.

The Soviets scored on a goal by Alexander Maltsev (1949–) early in the second period, but goals by Johnson and Eruzione midway into the final period had the Americans on top, 4–3. But Finland had led by one in the third period in its Olympic game against the U.S.S.R. only to allow three goals in under two minutes and lose 4–2. Canada held a 4–3 lead in the third period before Aleksandr Golikov (1952–) scored three goals, including two in 12 seconds, sending Canada to a 6–4 loss. But this game was different. "We were panicking," Soviet defenseman Sergeo Starikov (1958–) said. "We were stiff" (Coffey 2005, 239). Brooks kept yelling at his team to "Play your game," and Michaels started thinking that the Americans might have a chance. The Russians did not pull goaltender Vladimir Myshkin (1955–) for an offensive advantage. They had never even practiced it. Moments later, American players, coaches, and fans were celebrating. Inside the losing locker room, Tikhonov told his biggest stars, "This is your loss" (Coffey 2005, 243).

Miracle, however, underplays the final game, a 4–2 U.S. victory over Finland. The U.S. victory on February 22 did not assure the Americans of a gold medal. Round-robin tournaments are based on points—two points for a win; one for a tie. Entering the final game, the United States had to win to secure the gold. A loss, coupled with a Soviet victory against Sweden, would have put the U.S. and U.S.S.R. in a tie, which the Soviets would have broken because of its overall advantage in goal differential. In fact, the Americans would have not even medaled in the Games had Finland won by two goals and Sweden and the Soviets tied. Before the game against Finland, Brooks kept his speech short and to the point: "If you lose this game, you'll take it to your bleeping grave" (Coffey 2005, 254).

"For some, it was a hockey victory," Eruzione said of the "Miracle on Ice." "For some it was a political meaning, something as a country, for a shot in the arm. I guess we brought a lot of pride back to a country that was looking for something, and it happened to be us" (Elliott 2020, D2).

CONCLUSION

Like Brooks, *Miracle* knew what buttons to push to get good results. Without being overly preachy, the movie kept relatively faithful to the facts, and its hockey scenes were authentically put together. Ray Didinger and Glen Macnow rank it seventeenth in *The Ultimate Book of Sports Movies*. In *Sports Cinema 100 Movies,* Randy Williams places it thirty-sixth. Both might be a little high, but *Miracle* did something many underdog films failed to do. It inspired a new generation of fans.

"We watched it all the time on the road as a team, just to get inspiration," said Alex Iafallo (1993–), a forward for the Los Angeles Kings who grew up in Buffalo, New York, while Noah Hanifin (1997–), a Calgary Flames defenseman from Boston, said: "A lot of American kids now grew up watching that movie and got interest in the game from it. My buddies back home all have it memorized. It's a legendary movie" (Harris 2020).

Said Smith: "The movie is now used to motivate teams in every sport before big games that involve David versus Goliath" (Gary Smith, interview with author, September 4, 2020).

But Brooks, Smith said, probably wouldn't have liked it.

"Herbie wanted things done his way," Smith said. "He had to control everything and did not like people telling him what to do" (Gary Smith, interview with author, September 4, 2020).

FURTHER READING

Allenspach, Kevin. 2003. "'Miracle' Coach Killed in Rollover: Gold Medal Winner Pushed SCSU Hockey to Division I." *St. Cloud Times*, August 12, 2003, pp. 1A, 5A.

Associated Press. 1999. "'The Great One' Ready to Enter Hall of Fame." *The Sentinel*, November 21, 1999, p. C5.

Associated Press. 2002. "Young Goalie Makes Switch from Hollywood to Hockey." *Billings Gazette*, September 27, 2002, p. 1B.

Bates, Greg. 2018. "The 1960 U.S. Olympic Men's Hockey Team Was the First 'Miracle on Ice': Twenty Years before the 1980 'Miracle on Ice' U.S. Men's Olympic Hockey Team, the First 'Miracle on Ice' Took Place at the 1960 Winter Olympic Games." *Sports Collectors Digest*, January 16, 2018. https://sportscollectorsdigest.com/news/olympic-hockey-gold-medal

Bodley, Hal. 1980. "The Miracle Really Did Happen." *Poughkeepsie Journal*, February 25, 1980, p. 13.

Canadian Press. 1978. "Top Junior Goes to Work for Skalbania." *The Province*, June 13, 1978, p. 17.

Carruth, Gorton, and Eugene Ehrlich. 1988. *Facts & Dates of American Sports: From Colonial Days to the Present.* New York: Perennial Library.

Chin, Carlton J., and Jay P. Granat. 2010. "How Miraculous Was the Miracle?" *The New York Times*, February 22, 2010. https://vancouver2010.blogs.nytimes.com/2010/02/22/how-miraculous-was-the-miracle/?searchResultPosition=1

Coffey, Wayne. 2005. *The Boys of Winter: The Untold Story of a Coach, a Dream, and the 1980 U.S. Olympic Hockey Team.* New York: Broadway Books.

Cohen, Jason. 2004. "It's Hard to Believe in This 'Miracle': Familiar Ending Leaves Audiences Little to Root for in Flat Rendition of 1980 Olympic Hockey." *Austin American-Statesman*, February 6, 2004, pp. E3–E4.

Corbett, Neil. 2003. "Making Miracles: Shinny Standout Hits the Big Screen." *The Abbotsford News*, March 22, 2003, p. A13.

D'Agati, Philip A. 2013. *The Cold War and the 1984 Olympic Games: A Soviet-American Surrogate War.* New York: Palgrave Macmillan

Elliott, Helene. 2020. "Do Eruzione, Michaels Believe in Nostalgia? Yes!" *Los Angeles Times*, February 14, 2020 p. D2.

Feldman, Jason. 2017. "'Miracle on Ice' Doctor Has Fond Memories of Brooks, 'U.'" *Post Bulletin*, September 29, 2017. https://www.postbulletin.com/sports /sports/localsports/miracle-on-ice-doctor-has-fond-memories-of-brooks-u/arti cle_00a4868c-874e-517f-9af0-7c1233198f08.html

Fosty, Darril, and George Fosty. 2014. *Tribes: An International Hockey History.* New York: The Stryker-Indigo Publishing Company, Inc.

Frederick, Jace. 2020. "Al Michaels Got the Miracle on Ice assignment Because of His Hockey Experience. One Game." *Pioneer Press*, February 16, 2020. https:// www.twincities.com/2020/02/16/al-michaels-got-the-miracle-on-ice-assignment -because-of-his-hockey-experience-one-game/

Gannett News Service. 1980. "Russian Hockey Team Remains an Enigma." *The Journal News*, February 20, 1980, p. 7B.

Gilbert, John. 1979. "Hockey Team/Coach Herb Brooks." *Minneapolis Tribune*, March 25, 1979, Picture section, p. 14.

Globe Staff, and Wires. 2017. "Michael Mantenuto, Holliston Man Who Starred in 'Miracle.'" *Boston Sunday Globe*, April 30, 2017, p. B14.

Gordon, Dick. 1956. "Mariucci by Phone: 'We Rose to Heights; Russia Too Good.'" *Minneapolis Sunday Tribune*, February 5, 1956, Sports, p. 1.

Gugger, John. 1998. "Hockey's Miracle Man: Brooks Back in Spotlight as Coach for French Team." *Oshkosh Northwestern*, February 8, 1998, p. C10.

Hardy, Stephen, and Andrew C. Holman. 2018. *Hockey: A Global History.* Urbana: University of Illinois Press.

Harris, Jack. 2020. "'Miracle' Revived the Memory and Glory of the 1980 U.S. Hockey Team's Triumph." *Los Angeles Times*, February 21, 2020. https://www .latimes.com/sports/olympics/story/2020-02-21/miracle-on-ice-film-1980-herb -brooks-al-michaels-kurt-russell

Hartman, Sid. 1960. "Teammates Credit John Mayasich for U.S. Olympic Title." *Green Bay Press-Gazette*, March 4, 1960, p. 13.

History.com Editors. n.d. "1875, March 3: First Indoor Game of Ice Hockey." *History*. https://history.com/this-day-in-history/first-indoor-game-of-ice-hockey

"James George Aylwyn Creighton: Hockey Pioneer." Society for International Hockey Research. https://sihrhockey.org/_creightoon.cfm

Katz, Anita. 2004. "Hockey Shtick: 'Miracle' Is not a Gold-medal Winner." *The Examiner*, February 6, 2004, p. 13.

Kuchins, Andrew C. 2016. "That Brief U.S.-Russia Strategic Partnership 15 Years Ago? New Interviews Reveal Why It Derailed." *The Washington Post*, September 23, 2016. https://www.washingtonpost.com/news/monkey-cage/wp/2016/09/23 /that-brief-u-s-russia-strategic-partnership-15-years-ago-new-interviews-reveal -why-it-derailed/

Littlefield, Bill. 2015. "Hollywood Scores a 'Miracle' with Lockerroom Speech." WBUR-FM, June 6, 2015. https://www.wbur.org/onlyagame/2015/06/06/us-mir acle-olympics-herb-brooks

Mason, Gary. 2003. "It's a Miracle When Hockey and Hollywood Score: This Try at a Movie Based on Our National Sport May Get It Right." *The Vancouver Sun*, February 6, 2003, pp. E1, E6.

Mason, Gary. 2004. "It Was a Miracle Turning Jocks into Actors." *The Vancouver Sun*, February 6, 2004, p. G1.

Mathews, Jack. 2004. "You Will Believe in 'Miracle.'" *Daily News*, February 6, 2004, p. 47.

McKinley, Michael. 2006. *Hockey: A People's History.* Toronto: McClelland & Stewart Ltd.

McNamara, Lynne. 2003. "Kurt Russell to Shoot Hockey Film Here: Contrary to Rumours, His Goalie Son, Wyatt, 16, Will Not Join Him in This Movie, But He Has Played with Him in Another." *The Vancouver Sun*, January 25, 2003, p. D-22.

Miller, Ed. 2020. "The WHA—A Look Back at the Upstart Hockey League." *The Hockey Writers*, July 6, 2020. https://thehockeywriters.com/the-wha-a-look -back-40-years-later

Mitchell, Elvis. 2004. "Film Review; a Hollywood Ending from Real Life." *The New York Times*, February 6, 2004. https://www.nytimes.com/2004/02/06/movies/film -review-a-hollywood-ending-from-real-life.html?searchResultPosition=1

Morganti, Al. 1980. "Flunked: Americans Fail Test against Soviet Hockey Team." *The Philadelphia Inquirer*, February 10, 1980, pp. 1-D, 6-D.

Nelson, John. 1980. "Speedskaters Hold America's Olympic Hopes." *Pottsville Republican*, January 26, 1980, p. 8.

Nelson, Murry R., ed. 2009a. *Encyclopedia of Sports in America: A History from Foot Races to Extreme Sports. Volume 1: Colonial Years to 1939.* Westport, CT: Greenwood Press.

Nelson, Murry R., ed. 2009b. *Encyclopedia of Sports in America: A History from Foot Races to Extreme Sports. Volume 1: 1940 to Present.* Westport, CT: Green-wood Press.

Newman, Warren. 1980. "Many Fans Frustrated, Feel Franchise Is on Way Out." *The Atlanta Constitution*, March 11, 1980, p. 1-D.

"The 1980 Moscow Olympics Boycott." 2017. Wilson Center, February 27, 2017. https://wilsoncenter.org/blog-post/the-1980-moscow-olympics-boycott

O'Neill, Bill, and Ryan Black. 2017. *The Great Book oof Ice Hockey: Interesting Facts and Sports Stories.* No City: LAK Publishing.

Pallasch, Abdon M. 2007. "Miracle: An Interview with Jack O'Callahan." *Irish America*, August/September 2007. https://irishamerica.com/2007/08/10662/

Reid, Heather L., and Michael W. Austin, eds. 2012. *The Olympics and Philosophy.* Lexington: University Press of Kentucky.

Reusse, Patrick. 2007. "Strelow, Pioneering Goalie Coach, Dies." *Star Tribune*, April 12, 2007, p. C3.

Rosenthal, Bert. 1979. "National Sports Festival Slated to Begin Tonight." *Winona Daily News*, July 26, 1979, p. 3B.

Ross, Bob. 2004. "'Miracle' of Lake Placid Evokes Warm Olympic Spirit." *The Tampa Tribune*, February 6, 2004, Friday Extra, p. 10.

Sherman, John. 2019. "Gary Smith, the Veteran Trainer for Olympians, Collegians and High School Athletes." *Sun Current,* September 9, 2019. https://www.home townsource.com/sun_current/community/bloomington/gary-smith-the-veteran -trainer-for-olympians-collegians-and-high-school-athletes/article_cae2b328 -c9ee-11e9-b4d9-dfc944611898.html

Shipley, John. 2020a. "A Brooks Tale: 'Miracle' Movie Melded Myth, Magic." *Pioneer Press*, February 16, 2020. https://www.twincities.com/2020/02/16/a-brooks-tale-miracle-movie-melded-myth-magic/

Shipley, John. 2020b. "St. Paul Native Rob McClanahan Takes Coach Cues from 'Miracle' Mentor." *Pioneer Press*, February 17, 2020. https://www.twincities.com/2020/02/17/st-paul-native-rob-mcclanahan-takes-coach-cues-from-miracle-mentor/

Shlachter, Barry H. 1979. "Soviet Troops Land in Afghanistan." *The Philadelphia Inquirer*, December 27, 1979, pp. 1-A, 6-A.

Smith, Al. 1980. "Flames' Farewell not Without Tears." *The Atlanta Constitution,* May 24, 1980, pp. 1-C, 5-C.

Sragow, Michael. 2004. "Michael Scragow's 10 Best Films of 2004." *The Sun*, December 31, 2004, pp. 1C, 4C.

Stoneking, Dan. 1979. "Brooks Gulps, Cuts Olympic Team." *Minneapolis Tribune*, August 2, 1979, p. 8B.

Stoneking, Dan. 1980. "Baker Keeps U.S. Cooking." *The Minneapolis Star*, February 13, 1980, pp. 20B, 14B.

Strickler, Jeff. 2004a. "Do We Believe in 'Miracle'? Yessssss!" *Star Tribune*, February 6, 2004, pp. E1, E11.

Strickler, Jeff. 2004b. "Russell, Brooks Found Common Ice." *Star Tribune*, February 6, 2004, p. E11.

Swift, E. M. 2004. "Miracle, the Sequel a New Film, With a Spoot-On Portrayal of Herb Brooks by Kurt Russell, Takes the Author Back to 1980 and Brings to a New Generation the Thrill of the U.S. Hockey Team's Olympic Triumph." *Sports Illustrated*, February 9, 2004. https://vault.si.com/vault/2004/02/09/miracle-the-sequel-a-new-film-with-a-spot-on-portrayal-of-herb-brooks-by-kurt-russell-takes-the-author-back-to-1980-and-brings-to-a-new-generation-the-thrill-of-the-us-hockey-teams-olympic-triumph

Taylor, Alan. 2014. "The Soviet War in Afghanistan, 1979–1989." *The Atlantic*, August 4, 2014. https://www.theatlantic.com/photo/2014/08/the-soviet-war-in-afghanistan-1979-1989/100786/

Vincent, Charles. 1980. "Dollar Detente: Soviets Help Keep Placid Out of the Red." *Detroit Free Press*, February 13, 1980, p. 1D.

Wendel, Tim. 2009. *Going for the Gold: How the U.S. Olympic Hockey Team Won at Lake Placid*. Meneola, NY: Dover Publications, Inc.

Weiskind, Ron. 2004. "'Miracle' Shoots—And Scores." *Pittsburgh Post-Gazette*, February 6, 2004, pp. W-24, W-25.

Chapter 9

Battle of the Sexes (2017)

By 2017, tennis had found its way into plots of many popular movies—director Alfred Hitchcock's thriller *Strangers on a Train* (1951) and the comedy-drama *The Royal Tenenbaums* (2001) come to mind—but finding a good, accurate movie about the sport was a different matter altogether.

Kerri Craddock, programming director for the 2017 Toronto International Film Festival said "there really hasn't been a quintessential tennis movie the way there have been for other sports, like baseball, football, or hockey" (Clarke 2017).

Tennis coach Nick Bollettieri (1931–) was harsher. "If I'm totally honest," he said, "there are none" (Clarke 2017).

Bollettieri, who coached tennis champions such as Andre Agassi (1970–), Boris Becker (1967–), Monica Seles (1973–), and sisters Venus (1980–) and Serena Williams (1981–), and his tennis academy were the subjects of a documentary, *Love Means Zero,* that debuted in 2017 at the 42nd Toronto International Film Festival. Two feature films about tennis—*Borg vs McEnroe*, a Swedish–Danish–Finnish production depicting the 1980 rivalry between Björn Borg (1956–) and John McEnroe (1959–); and *Battle of the Sexes*, chronicling the 1973 tennis match between women's star Billie Jean King (1943–) and former men's standout Bobby Riggs (1918–95)—were also on the 2017 Toronto lineup.

Battle of the Sexes, directed by the married team of Jonathan Dayton (1957–) and Valerie Faris (1958–), premiered in U.S. theaters on September 24.

The movie opens after King (Emma Stone, 1988–) has become the first women's athlete to reach $100,000 in earnings after winning the U.S. Open women's singles championship. But when King and women's tennis promoter Gladys Heldman (Sarah Silverman, 1970–) learn that promoter Jack Kramer (Bill Pullman,

1953–) has organized a tournament that will pay the men's champion $12,000 but the women's winner only $1,500, they threaten a boycott. The men don't take the women seriously, so King and Heldman decide to form a women-only tour despite Kramer's threat that the United States Lawn Tennis Association (USLTA), the governing body of U.S. tennis, will ban any women playing in a competitive association from playing in the USLTA events—which include some of the world's most prestigious tennis tournaments.

Undeterred, King and Heldman push forward and create the Women's Tennis Association. King and eight other professionals sign contracts with the association for $1 each. Virginia Slims, a cigarette brand, signs on as a sponsor, agreeing to pay $7,000 for every tournament. That leads Australian star Margaret Court (Jessica McNamee, 1986–) to join the circuit. During the tour, King begins an affair with hairdresser Marilyn Barnett (Andrea Riseborough, 1981–).

Meanwhile, former tennis champion and hustler Riggs (Steve Carell, 1962–) struggles with his addiction to gambling and his love for the spotlight, which jeopardizes his relationship with his wife, Priscilla (Elisabeth Shue, 1963–), and his oldest son, Larry (Lewis Pullman, 1993–). King's marriage to Larry King (Austin Stowell, 1984–) also suffers.

Kicked out of his house after winning a Rolls Royce on a tennis bet, Riggs, an unrepentant sexist, comes up with the idea to challenge the top women's player to a match. He first seeks King, but when she declines, he goes after Court, who beats King in a Virginia Slims final in Los Angeles to inherit the No. 1 ranking. King pleads with Court not to accept Riggs's challenge. "He wants to make himself look great and women look stupid," she says, but Court won't back down, and loses in straight sets in the match televised nationally.

King bounces back from a slump, and when Riggs offers $100,000 to any woman who can beat him, King accepts. Riggs, fifty-five years old, doesn't train much, but King does, and on September 20, 1973, the twenty-nine-year-old King beats Riggs, 6–4, 6–3, 6–3, at the Houston Astrodome and before ninety million viewers on ABC-TV—the highest rated TV broadcast since the Apollo 11 moon landing in 1969.

"Times change," Ted Tinling (Alan Cumming, 1965–), the women's tour's fashion designer, tells King, speaking of her sexual orientation as well as the women's liberation movement. "You should know—you changed them."

Producer Christian Colson (1968–) came up with the idea for *Battle of the Sexes* during the 2012 London Olympics, and pitched the project to director Danny Boyle (1956–). They took the concept to Fox Searchlight, which backed the project for $24 million. Boyle and Colson then approached British screenwriter Simon Beaufoy (1966–), an Oscar winner for his adapted screenplay for *Slumdog Millionaire* (2008), which Boyle codirected and Colson produced. Beaufoy went to King's apartment in New York City and said he wanted to tell the story about the 1973 tennis match. "She looked me in the eyes and said: 'I've seen every single one of your films, and I like them—you're the right person to do this,'" Beaufoy said (Sutherland 2017). Although King helped Beaufoy with script details, she visited the set just once.

Boyle, however, abandoned the project in 2015, electing to make *T2 Trainspotting*, a sequel to his 1996 hit *Trainspotting*. Instead of shelving the project, in April 2015, Fox Searchlight announced the shooting was ready to begin that fall, with Stone and Carell to star and Dayton and Faris to direct.

The directors were drawn to the project because "It is a sports movie and a love story that is about finding one's true self and the quest for social change," Dayton said. "It touches on so many levels of human emotions. Sadness, happiness, disappointments, setbacks, thrills and joys—so our goal was to empathize with all of the characters and to experience the complexity of the situation" (Behan 2017).

Scheduling conflicts almost caused Stone to back out—Brie Larson (1989–) was sought as a replacement—before Stone, who won a best actress Oscar for *La La Land* (2016), managed to rearrange her schedule to get the part.

Principal photography began in Los Angeles in April 2016.

"An actor can train to box, run or throw a football or baseball. But it's very difficult to train in tennis," said *Love Means Zero* director Jason Kohn (1984–). "It's also difficult to capture the beauty and elements of the game" (Clarke 2017).

Playing tennis as an out-of-shape fifty-five-year-old wasn't that hard for Carell, an avid tennis player, but the lithe Stone, who had never played tennis, had to put on 15 pounds of muscle with physical training—in addition to working with a dialect coach to pick up King's speech patterns. King gave Stone a couple of lessons, and Stone began intensive training with Vince Spadea (1974–), a former professional player ranked in the Top 20. Spadea also doubled for Carell to recreate Riggs's backhands and forehands. Kaitlyn Christian (1992–), who had played tennis for the University of Southern California, doubled for Stone and also portrayed Kerry Melville (1947–), one of the Women's Tennis Association players, in the film. "I could focus on the details," Stone said, "how [King] bounced her ball or the beginning of her serve or her backhand and could really try to perfect moments rather than become the No. 1 role player" (Pantic 2017).

Filming around Los Angeles took thirty-five days, with Los Angeles Sports Arena—demolished that September—subbing for the Astrodome.

The film premiered at Colorado's Telluride Film Festival on September 2, 2017, then showed at Toronto before a national release. Reviews were generally favorable.

"These actors aren't doing impersonations," critic Richard Roeper wrote for Universal Press Syndicate. "They're creating full-fledged, complex characters—each flawed, each making mistakes that hurt others, but both quite sympathetic and endlessly fascinating" (Roeper 2017, C5). But *The Chicago Tribune's* Michael Phillips wrote: "The movie's determined not to demonize any of its major players. But there are tricky obstacles in 'Battle of the Sexes.' The climactic match wasn't much in terms of suspense . . ., and to the degree this is a sports movie, it's not a very exciting one" (Phillips 2017, D6).

"Like real life, the movie loses some steam when the big match rolls around," the *Tampa Bay Times'* Steve Persall wrote. "Nothing on the court could match what led King and Riggs there and the same goes for Dayton and Faris' movie. Up to that point, *Battle of the Sexes* had me smiling wider more often than usual, winning at least one love" (Persall 2017, 12W). The *Los Angeles Times'* Kenneth Turan, on the other hand, wrote: "'Battle' is most involving when it deals not with sports or society but the personal struggles both players, especially King, were going through in the runup to the match" (Turan 2017, E1).

Hollywood buzzed that Carell and Stone might be nominated for Academy Awards. But the movie tanked at the box office, earning just more than $12.6 million domestically, and received no Oscar nominations; Carell and Stone were nominated for Golden Globe awards.

Detroit News film critic Adam Graham, however, said *Battle of the Sexes* should have been better received, calling it "Unfairly ignored by audiences" and "also ignored by the Academy" despite being "an engaging look back at an odd pop culture moment and a smart riff on gender issues that are dominating the headlines today" (Graham 2018).

HISTORICAL BACKGROUND

Tennis was an offspring of a twelfth-century French game called *paume* (palm), which led to handball and, with the introduction of the racket, tennis. Originally popular in France, tennis spread to England, Australia, and eventually the United States, but the sport did not surge until the 1870s after the founding of the All England Croquet Club in London's Wimbledon district.

Mary Outerbridge (1852–86) was vacationing in Bermuda when she saw British army officers play the game—called *sphairistiké* (Greek for *playing at ball*). Fascinated by the sport, she returned home to New York with equipment, including a net and rackets, but it took help from her brother, A. Emilius Outerbridge (1845–1921), a shipping executive, to get the equipment cleared by customs officials.

In the spring of 1874, the Outerbridges laid out a court on the Staten Island Cricket and Baseball Club lawns. The court was designed like an hourglass, with the net 24 feet wide and both bases 30 feet wide. The rectangular tennis court came into use at Wimbledon in 1877.

In Newport, Rhode Island, Henry "Harry" Stevens (1859–85) returned from England, where he had been studying, and also brought tennis equipment. He set up a court on the lawn at his mother's mansion on Bellevue Avenue. Stevens was briefly engaged to author Edith Wharton (1862–1937), who in an August 1876 letter described the sport as "difficult, tiresome, & destructive to pretty dresses & to the complexion, but nevertheless delightful" (Mead 2009).

Appleton's Journal, a then-weekly journal of literature, science, and art based in New York City, noted the rise of lawn-tennis in 1875:

> We spare the reader a description of lawn-tennis, as it is destined to be played on the lawn of English country houses during this and probably many future summers; we fear he would understand as little of "nets," and "right and left hand hazard," and "service courts," and "volleyed service" and "hand in," and "hand out," as we ourselves. Certain it is, however, that lawn-tennis requires the use of balls, and the exercise of many muscles; and whatever game requires balls compels respect. . . . A zealous admirer of the new pastime says of it that "it is graceful and pleasant to watch; it gives great opportunity for skill and judgment; it is played in the open and under the fresh sky, and upon the bright-green turf; and it obliges the player, even malgre lui, to get through a great amount of very hard exercise." If so, let us have "lawn-tennis" playing, as well as "coaching," over here as soon as may be. The summer hotel proprietors might probably take the hint, have a tennis ground marked off in front of the mammoth plazzas [sic], and even provide a professor of tennis for the ignorant; thus getting up a fashionable sensation which would be provocative of brisk blood and the building up of languid bodies. (*Appleton's Journal* 1875, 1)

It did not take long for tennis to catch on across the rest of America. Tennis soon spread to Boston, Philadelphia, and as far west as Chicago, New Orleans, and San Francisco.

In September 1880, the Staten Island club held a lawn-tennis tournament, organized by the Outerbridges and open to all comers. "Long nets, looking like seines, were stretched between posts at different points in the field," the *New York Times* reported. "The boundary fences had received fresh coats of whitewash, and camp-stools for spectators were placed in rows on either side of the several tennis courts" ("The Lawn-Tennis Tournament" 1880, 3). Some Boston players withdrew because the balls being used in New York weren't the same weight or size as those found in Boston. Wimbledon champion O.E. Woodhouse (1855–87) defeated Canadian J.F. Helmuth to earn the title "Champion of America." But organizers realized that the growing sport needed unified organization, and a convention was announced for May 21, 1881, at New York City's Fifth Avenue Hotel.

Thirty-six delegates from nineteen clubs (and having proxy to vote for sixteen other clubs) attended the meeting in which they agreed to adopt for one year the All England Club rules, formed a committee to organize tournaments, and elected Robert S. Oliver president of the newly formed U.S. National Lawn Tennis Association (*National* was deleted from the organization's name in 1920; *Lawn* was cut in 1975). Representatives also agreed to stage an official championship tournament, which was scheduled in August at the Newport Casino, which opened on July 26, 1880, in Newport, Rhode Island. Richard Sears (1861–1943) defeated William E. Glyn (1859–1939) for the United States National Championship's singles championship, and Clarence Clark (1859–1937) and Frederick Winslow Taylor (1856–1915) claimed the doubles title. Newport continued holding what became the U.S. Open Championship until 1915, when the tournament was moved to Forest Hills, New York.

Once a pastime for the wealthy, tennis soon surged. In 1890, Bostonian Henry A. Ditson (1856–91), who, with partner George Wright (1847–1937), founded the sporting goods business Wright & Ditson in 1871, set out west to learn "just how far tennis had advanced in places where the game is supposed to be new" and learned that "The future of the game never looked brighter . . ." Ditson told a reporter:

> At Denver, I visited the Denver Athletic Club, which, by the way, has a building six stories high, and found everything flourishing. On the top of this building I was very much surprised to find a tennis court, from which the Rocky Mountains could easily be seen. It was a sight well worth witnessing, to see the men playing at such a distance from the ground.
>
> At Colorado Springs I found every one playing tennis. There was a lot of fine courts and plenty of enthusiasm, and at Salt Lake City found tennis booming. At Ogden the same interest was shown in the game.
>
> San Francisco, the objective point of the trip, was next reached, and I went immediately to see the California Lawn Tennis Club. It has a spacious club house, and the courts are situated conveniently for the members who are engaged in business in town. The house is well arranged, having not only lockers and bathrooms, but a well-furnished reading room. A broad sheltered veranda runs around the house, from which spectators can view the games.
>
> The club's courts are made of bituminous rock, and consequently are very lively. ("Tennis in the Air" 1890, 13)

Part of the surge could be attributed to women. Tennis was a sport that welcomed women, although social norms of the time required them to wear corsets and long skirts (men, at that time, wore blazers and trousers). "This game . . . combines a most perfect exercise for all the muscles, with a singular charm for girls as well as boys, for men and women" (St. Nicholas 1879, 1).

Women's tennis first appeared at Wimbledon in 1884, and three years later, the Cricket Club in Philadelphia played host to the first U.S. Women's National Singles Championship. Seventeen-year-old Ellen Hansell (1869–1937) defeated Laura Knight in the championship match, 6–1, 6–0. The first women's French Tennis Championship also was contested in 1887.

Men's tennis debuted at the 1896 Olympics in Athens, Greece, and women's tennis was added in 1900. But a dispute between the International Olympic Committee and the International Tennis Federation led to the removal of the sport from the official Games in 1928. Although tennis was staged as a demonstration sport during the 1968 and 1984 Games, it would not officially return to the Olympic program until 1988 in Seoul, South Korea.

In 1899, four Harvard University tennis players came up with an idea to stage an international tournament pitting amateur teams from the United States against amateur teams from Great Britain. Harvard player Dwight F. Davis (1879–1945) designed the format for the biennial International Lawn Tennis Challenge Trophy, renamed the Davis Cup. France and Belgium were added to the tournament in 1904, and in 1912 the International Lawn Tennis Federation took over supervision. By 1921, thirteen nations competed. By 2020, when COVID-19 forced postponement of the finals to 2021, one hundred thirty-three nations were competing.

"Lawn tennis is no longer a rich man's game," Davis wrote in 1921. "It is every man's game. Lawn tennis not only has become nationalized—it has become internationalized. . . . Golf, cricket, polo, baseball and football have their devotees in a few countries at most. Interest in lawn tennis is becoming universal and its enthusiasts can now boast that lawn tennis is THE WORLD'S SPORT" (Davis 1921, 12).

As the sport grew worldwide, the International Tennis Federation was formed in 1913 to standardize rules. The United States joined the federation in 1923.

Bobby Riggs burst onto the tennis scene in the late 1930s. The son of a Los Angeles minister (one of six children), Riggs came out of the Southern California Tennis Association and Los Angeles Tennis Club, but Perry T. Jones (1890–1970), who helped establish both organizations, did not think Riggs, at 5-foot-7½, had much of a future in tennis.

Jones and others declared that Riggs "was too short," "didn't hit the ball hard enough," lacked a powerful serve, and "will never have the reach to play a good net game," Riggs recalled in his autobiography (Riggs with McGann 1974, 18). But at age twenty, Riggs was good enough to help the U.S. team win the Davis Cup in 1938. In 1939, he lost in the French Championships finals but won three titles at Wimbledon: singles, doubles with Elwood Cooke (1913–2004), and mixed doubles with Alice Marble (1913–90). He also won the U.S. Championships singles title to become the top-ranked amateur.

After winning the U.S. Championships again in 1941, he signed a $25,000 contract to play professional tennis. "I was an honest tennis player at last," Riggs recalled (Riggs with McGann 1974, 58). World War II (1941–45) interrupted, and Riggs joined the Navy, helping the 14th Naval District Navy Yard Tennis Team win the league title in 1945. After the war, he returned to professional tennis, retiring in 1959. "The records say that Riggs won three singles majors," British tennis correspondent Simon Briggs wrote, "small beer by Roger Federer's standards [Federer (1981–) has 103 singles championships, including a record 30 Grand Slam titles]. But it's worth remembering that he turned professional in 1941, aged twenty-three. Even then, he lost what should have been his peak years to the Second World War" (Briggs 2017).

In March 1947, the men's-only World Professional Tennis League was formed, opening with a $10,000 tournament in Philadelphia. Among the professional players was Riggs, but the league disbanded nine months later because, league commissioner Tony Owen said, "there are not enough top-notch pros to give the public the brand of competition it deserves" (Gipe 1978, 144). "What [Owen] didn't say was that the main attraction of the new league, Bobby Riggs, often failed to play in scheduled tournaments when a better offer for a personal tour came along" (Gipe 1978, 144).

Postwar America brought about better paying jobs and more leisure time, allowing sports like tennis and golf to move beyond the wealthy and country clubs.

First denied membership in the U.S. Tennis Association because of her race, African American Althea Gibson (1927–2003) played in the all-Black American Tennis Association. After winning ten consecutive ATA events, she was allowed to play in USTA events beginning in 1950 and was allowed to compete at Wimbledon in 1951. In 1952 Gibson teamed with Angela Buxton to win the doubles championship at Wimbledon, the first African American and Jewish players to win titles at the historic venue. Gibson went on to win Wimbledon's singles and doubles championships in 1957 and 1958, and the Associated Press named her Female Athlete of the Year in both years.

Wimbledon and tennis's other three Grand Slam events (the Australian, French, and U.S. championships) might have been prestigious but they did not help tennis players financially as the events were open only to amateurs. Professional men's tennis players competed in other tournaments for money, but women's players didn't have anywhere near as many options. In 1968, the Grand Slam events began awarding prize money. That year, Billie Jean King (1943–) won the women's title at Wimbledon for a prize of £750—£1,250 less than men's champion Rod Laver (1938–) received. In 1970, King's Italian Open championship won her $600, but men's singles winner Ilie Nastase (1946–) won $3,500. "Everyone thinks women should be thrilled when we get crumbs," King said, "and I want women to have the cake, the icing and the cherry on top too" (Barajas 2016).

Born Billie Jean Moffitt in Long Beach, California, King lost in the first round of the 1959 U.S. Championships at age fifteen, played in her first Wimbledon two years later, and by the mid-1960s was one of women's tennis best players. By the 1970s, she was speaking up for women's rights. That fight, she said years later, began when she was twelve years old. "I was daydreaming about my little tiny universe of tennis, and I thought to myself:

'Everybody's wearing white shoes, white socks, white clothes, playing with white balls, everybody who plays is white. Where is everybody else?'" she said. "That was the moment I decided to fight for equality and freedom and equal rights and opportunities for everyone. Everyone. Not just girls. Everyone" (Nicholson 2017).

Things were beginning to change in the 1970s. The National Organization for Women was founded in 1966. Title IX, which prohibited discrimination based on sex in education programs or activities (including athletics) receiving federal assistance, became law in 1972. That same year, Congress passed the Equal Rights Amendment guaranteeing American citizens legal equality and prohibiting discrimination on the basis of sex and sent it to the states for ratification. Congress set the deadline for 1979, then extended it to 1982, but by that time only thirty-five states had passed the amendment—three states shy of the needed thirty-eight for ratification. The amendment was declared dead.

In 1970, King led a boycott of the Pacific Southwest tennis tournament because of a disparity between men's and women's prize money. She eventually served as the Women's International Tennis Association president, lobbying for equal treatment.

Joining this fight, but on the opposite side, was Riggs, the self-proclaimed "hero of all middle-aged men smarting under the taunts of the Women's Libbers, the leader of Bobby's Battalions, and the undisputed number-one male chauvinist in the world" (Riggs with McGann 1974, 1). Riggs, then fifty-five, challenged Margaret Court, Australia's No. 1 player, to a $10,000 winner-take-all match, beating her, 6–2, 6–1, on May 13, 1973, "a cruel Mother's Day gift for Margaret" (Daley 1973, E4).

Then Riggs met King at the Houston Astrodome on September 20, 1973, in a winner-take-all $100,000 match. This time, Riggs was humbled in a 6–4, 6–3, 6–3 loss.

"I tossed my wood racket into the air and Bobby jumped over the net to congratulate me," King recalled. "Even though we had a rivalry on the court, we truly did like each other. Now proven athletic peers, as well as friends, we walked off the court arm in arm" (King with Brennan 2008, 32).

King continued to dominate much of women's tennis. She retired shortly after winning her last tournament in 1983 at age thirty-nine having won 168 open-era tennis championships. In 1987, she was inducted into the International Tennis Hall of Fame.

After the Battle of the Sexes loss, Riggs hit the talk-show and lecture circuit and even appeared in TV shows. In an episode of the ABC sitcom *The Odd Couple* that first aired on November 16, 1973, he and King played Ping-Pong. Riggs died of prostate cancer in 1995. Before his death, King called him to say good-bye. After the call, he told his daughter, "She's a real good gal. I got a lot of respect for her. She's the best female tennis player there was" (LeCompte 2003, 426).

DEPICTION AND CULTURAL CONTEXT

Battle of the Sexes does a good job in the historical accuracy department. Most events depicted actually happened, but the filmmakers fiddled with the chronology and tightened the narrative for storytelling purposes. For instance, the movie opens after King has been congratulated by President Richard Nixon (1913–94) on becoming the first female athlete to earn $100,000 in history and then King has a run-in with tournament organizer Jack Kramer (1921–2009) over the prize differential between women and men.

King had reached the landmark in October 1971, when Nixon called her on October 4. It took the president three tries; the first two calls got King's voice recording. When King answered, Nixon began the conversation: "Billie Jean, I want to congratulate you. I'm glad to see a fellow Californian has won more than $100,000." Some chitchat followed, then Nixon praised King for promoting physical fitness. After a pause, King asked, "Are you through?" (Associated Press 1971, 12).

A month later, King had earned another $15,000. King pointed out, however, that the reason she could make that much money was because of Virginia Slims, which sponsored the women's tennis tour. She said:

> Normally, I break my back to earn $30,000 a year. Now I break my back and am able to earn more than three times as much.
>
> If someone told me 10 years ago I was going to win $100,000, I would have laughed and told them they were crazy.
>
> But I think it's great I was able to accomplish what I set as my goal last January. I just hope my success might motivate some youngsters to take up the sport.
>
> What a lot of people don't realize is that Rod Laver will probably make more than $300,000 this year. (Hower 1971, B1)

The reason King earned that much money was because of the rift with Kramer, which came first.

Before the 1947 U.S. Championships, Kramer, the defending champion of that tournament and that year's Wimbledon winner, decided to turn professional because "I needed the money" (Dwyer 2009, A17).

After winning the 1947 U.S. Championships, Kramer's pro tour drew more than fifteen thousand spectators to New York City's Madison Square Garden during a blizzard. "Soon the success of the pro tours, Kramer's the most prominent, put pressure on tennis federations, whose tournaments were no longer offering fans all the best players," *Los Angeles Times* sports columnist Bill Dwyer wrote. "That pressure eventually led to the establishment of Open tennis in 1968, featuring prize money for all players" (Dwyer 2009, A17).

After a bad back forced his retirement in 1954, Kramer continued promoting the sport, helping found the Association of Tennis Professionals in 1972 and serving as the organization's first executive director. Kramer developed a long relationship with the Pacific Southwest tennis tournament—he won the singles championship there in 1943, 1946, and 1947—which began at the L.A. Tennis Club in 1927—and served as tournament director and tournament chairman.

In 1970, the Southwest Pacific Open announced that the winning purse for the men's singles would be $12,500 (the movie makes the purse $12,000). The women's champion would win $1,500.

King, who was recovering from knee surgery and wasn't playing in the tournament, called the inequality "ridiculous," while Rosemary Casals (1948–), the third-ranked women's singles player in 1970, argued: "We use the same amount of energy as the men. We work and practice just as hard. There should not be so much discrimination in the money" (Grimsley 1970, B11).

The tournament's prize money totaled $65,000, with $51,500 going to the men, another $6,500 going into the international Grand Prix pool (to be divided by the men), and $7,500 to the women. Kramer, running the tournament that year for the dying Perry Jones, agreed that the women were being treated "shabbily," but argued: "But you have to analyze who's coming: First of all, Margaret Court, who won Forest Hills [site of the U.S. Open], is fishing in Florida with her husband. Billie Jean King is out with

---

OTHER MAN VERSUS WOMAN MATCHUPS

Tennis isn't the only sport to stage a "Battle of the Sexes." Three years before Billie Jean King defeated Bobbie Riggs, professional golfer Doug Sanders (1933–2020) met women's professional Carol Mann (1941–2018) on a windy September 1, 1970, at Grossinger (New York) Golf Club. Play was close until Mann carded an 8 on the par-4 No. 9 hole.

"I feel that I let the women down," said Mann, whose ten-year earnings of twenty-nine victories totaled $200,000—compared to Sanders's $550,000 earnings in seventeen victories in fourteen years. "I don't think women should compete against men," Sanders said. "A woman should have feminine characteristics and stay at home and raise the kids" (Associated Press 1970, 45).

In 1999 in Seattle, however, thirty-six-year-old Margaret MacGregor (1963–) beat thirty-three-year-old Loi Chow (1965–) in what was believed to be the first woman-versus-man boxing match in America. "I hit her with a couple good shots," said Chow, who earned his third consecutive loss in his third, and last, career fight. MacGregor improved to 4–0, cheered on by the crowd's yells of "Kill him, Margaret," and "He's a bum" (Cook 1999, B5). All three judges scored the four-round bout in favor of MacGregor, who finished her career with a 5–1 record.

Sources

Associated Press. 1970. "Woman vs. Man Golf Test Hurts Cause of Liberation." *The Courier-News*, September 2, 1970, p. 45.

Cook, Rebecca. 1999. "Fans Give First Man-vs.-Woman Bout Generally Favorable Reviews." *The York Dispatch*, October 11, 1999, p. B5.

a knee operation. Virginia Wade is home in England. What's left is hardly center-court Stuff" (Murray 1970, 1).

Women's players weren't just protesting the lack of pay at the Los Angeles tournament. Another tournament was considering moving its women's finals to the middle of the week in an attempt to increase attendance during weekdays. "Phooey on that," King said. "I'm just as big a ham as any of the men and I like to play in front of the big crowds, too" (Martin 1970, C-5).

The women sought out Gladys Heldman (1922–2003) to intervene with Kramer on their behalf. Heldman discovered tennis when she was twenty-three, playing in the U.S. National Championships four times and at Wimbledon once. In 1953, she founded *World Tennis* magazine and became its "publisher, editor, proof reader, paste-up man, janitor, head of the circulation and promotions departments, etc." (Saylor 1979, 2D). After twenty years, she sold the magazine to CBS Publications for $2 million.

When Heldman told Kramer that the women were considering a boycott of the tournament, Kramer replied: "Fine with me. I'll take the $1,500 and throw it in the men's singles." Heldman reported back to the women that "Kramer's an a—" (Roberts 2005, 1976).

Boycotting the Pacific Southwest event wouldn't accomplish anything, but Heldman had connections. She reached out to Joseph Cullman III (1912–2004), a tennis fan and CEO of tobacco conglomerate Philip Morris Company. Cullman agreed to have Virginia Slims, a cigarette brand aimed at female smokers, to sponsor a women's tennis tournament in Houston with $7,500 in prize money even though Virginia Slims' advertising slogan— "You've come a long way, baby"—prompted criticism from women's movement leaders: "Is this what we've come a long way for? To have our own cigarette?" (Buck 1970, 3).

Here's another instance of where *Battle of the Sexes* switches the timeline of events. In the movie, nine women's players sign a token $1 professional contract to play in the newly founded Women's Tennis Association (WTA). Later, Virginia Slims agrees to sponsor a 12-month tour for women with a purse of $7,000 for each event. But in reality, Virginia Slims came before the WTA. King and eight other players—eventually known as the Original Nine—signed a personal-service contract for $1 each with *World Tennis* and would play in the Virginia Slims tournament in Houston, which was offering a $5,000 purse. Heldman later named two cats Virginia and Slim.

At first, the U.S. Lawn Tennis Association refused to sanction the event unless Philip Morris eliminated the prize money. The company agreed, electing to pay the players expenses instead. King wasn't pleased, saying:

"We thought we'd like to play above board rather than get expenses under the table. We're all pros so why should we become amateurs for a week? Why should we go backward?

"We're trying to make this game honest. I've received as much as $4,500–5,000 under the table for playing in one tournament, even if I lost in the first round. Why can't we just get paid like the other pros?" (United Press International 1970a, 5B).

Signing the contracts made the nine women "contract pros," technically making the Virginia Slims event a professional event and removing the tournament from the U.S. Lawn Tennis Association's control. But Kramer and the U.S. Lawn Tennis Association retaliated, kicking the nine players out of the USLTA.

"We knew this would happen," King said. "This is no surprise and it is fine with us" (United Press International 1970c, 11).

Casals won the Houston tournament, "but the real winner was the cause of women's tennis, which received more media coverage that week than it had the entire previous year" (Ware 2011, 32).

Battle of the Sexes doesn't give King's counterparts much to do, but the eight other players were standouts in 1970. Casals was King's partner as they won Wimbledon's doubles championship that year. The last of the nine to sign, Julie Heldman (1945–), Gladys Heldman's daughter, was ranked fifth in the world. Nancy Richey (1942–) was ranked No. 1 player in the United States when she signed the contract. World-ranked Jane "Peaches" Bartkowicz (1949–), Kristy Pigeon (1950–), Melville and fellow Australian Judy Tegart Dalton (1937–), and Valerie Jean Ziegenfuss (1949–) helped give the new group "about eight of the top 10 [women's tennis players] in the world," King said (United Press International 1970a, 5B).

"We felt we had no choice," Richey said. "What was there to lose? The money wasn't there" (Roberts 2005, 78).

The Virginia Slims Series began in 1971, with nineteen tournaments and with purses totaling $309,100.

Other women's tennis stars—including Court, Chris Evert (1954–), Evonne Goolagong (1951–), and Virginia Wade (1945–)—remained in the USLTA. "[T]hey had the support of the USLTA and the entrée of being the good guys," Casals said. "We were the bad guys" (Roberts 2005, 79). After two months, the USLTA reversed course and ended its ban against the rebelling tennis stars and began a competing tour, but the next years would reveal that there wasn't enough interest to support two competing women's tennis tours. In 1972, Heldman formed the Women's International World's Tennis Foundation to "work with, but not under, other national organizations such as" the USLTA (Associated Press 1972, 8). That year, King won the U.S. Open and was chosen *Sports Illustrated*'s Sportswoman of the Year. The Women's International Tennis Federation attracted some holdouts, including Court. "If we can make it go over on a large scale the way I think we can," Court said, "women's tennis will come through in the end" (Recchi 1972, 1D).

By 1973—the year the U.S. Open became the first major tournament to award equal prize money to the men and women—the women's tennis rift had been mended. That year at Wimbledon, King met at the Hotel

Gloucester with the professional women players and formed a players union called the Women's Tennis Association.

By that time, Bobby Riggs was putting out challenges that he could beat anyone his age. A newspaper reporter wrote: "He doesn't play tennis for just nickels and quarters. He plays for the kind of money that buys stocks or pays off the mortgage. It's tennis, cash-and-carry style. Riggs fast-talks spectators or opponents into putting up the cash—$100 . . . $500 . . . $3,000— and Riggs usually carries it away. He's good at other things, too. Since Jack Kramer served and volleyed him into retirement from the pro tour decades ago, Riggs has amassed a fortune (one estimate: $500,000) hustling wagers on not just tennis, but golf, poker, craps, backgammon and dominoes" (Prugh 1972, B8).

Battle of the Sexes gets Riggs down right as a compulsive gambler who doesn't think he's an addict. "In his mind, gambling addicts were compulsive losers: people bent on self-destruction," biographer Tom LeCompte wrote. "Gambling addicts were people who wouldn't rest until they had gambled away everything—their paycheck, the mortgage, money for a spouse's birthday present . . . Sure, he might entertain himself by playing baccarat or betting on football, but his big play was games in which he felt he had the edge, the advantage, whether from athletic skill, competitive toughness, inside information, or chicanery" (LeCompte 2003, 266).

By the early 1970s, Riggs was dominating the men's senior tennis circuit. But seeing King winning $100,000 a year and women's players getting national attention irritated him. He thought men's senior tennis was better than women's tennis. He didn't like playing for small purses while women, in his estimation, were making money and winning glory. Mostly, though, Riggs admitted: "I didn't like being kept out of the spotlight" (Riggs with McGann 1974, 2). That's how Riggs got the idea to challenge a top women's player to a winner-take-all match.

His first choice, as depicted in the film, was King, but they barely knew one another. Riggs began "bugging me to play him, but I didn't even give that a serious thought," King recalled. "Women's tennis was starting to take off; the last thing we needed was a sideshow" (King with Deford 1982, 24). *Sports Illustrated* reported Riggs's challenge, and other outlets picked up the story, but King declined the offer, which at the time was only $5,000. Riggs went after his second choice, Court. A sponsor added $5,000, Riggs recalled, bringing the purse to $10,000—not $35,000 as in the movie. When CBS decided to televise the event, the network offered Court $10,000 and Riggs $7,500 just to appear. After Riggs easily won the match, Kramer said: "I guess it proves that the top ladies are about equal to a 15-year-old boy or a 55-year-old man, or maybe not as good" (LeCompte 2003, 311).

King didn't see the match on TV, either, as depicted in the movie. She learned of Court's loss on an airplane while returning from a tournament in Japan, and didn't view the match, she said, until the night before her own

"Battle of the Sexes" against Riggs. But when Court lost, King recalled, "I immediately knew what I had to do: I had no choice—I had to play Bobby, and I had to beat him" (King with Brennan 2008, 25).

The film certainly captures the carnival atmosphere of the King–Riggs match. Riggs, who was on a 415-vitamins-a-day routine, was paid $50,000 to wear a Sugar Daddy jacket. King did present Riggs with a small pig before play began and came into the stadium in a "Cleopatra" litter. Both the pig and the litter were the ideas of promoter Jerry Perenchio (1930–2017). "He said to me, 'I know you're a feminist. So you probably won't get on this Egyptian litter, will you?'" King said. "I said, 'Yes, I love it. 'Let's go.' He was shocked. I got on it, and we walked out" (Alexander 2017).

"On Bobby's side, it was a huge promotion, and on Billie Jean's side, it had huge meaning," King's husband, Larry, said. "The marriage of the two made for great theater. They have all this reality TV nowadays, but that was reality TV" (Roberts 2005, 131).

The film's accurate enough, also, depicting Riggs's lackadaisical approach to the King match—he had trained hard for the Court match—while King pushed herself to be physically ready for her meeting with Riggs. "He really underestimated me, and I was prepared," King said. "That was the difference" (Cone 1990, 2C). Riggs's son, believing that his father would be humiliated by King, did not stay on the court to watch the match—also accurately depicted.

King, however, did not burst into tears alone in the locker room after her victory. "They kept me so busy after that, but that's how I was feeling, such relief," King said (Alexander 2017).

Battle of the Sexes also adjusts the timeline of King's affair with hairdresser Marilyn Barnett (1948–). Instead of meeting at the beginning of the women's tour, King met Barnett in 1972, and Barnett did cut King's hair before the Riggs match, but in Los Angeles before they left for Houston. Nor did they reunite before the match, as depicted in the movie. In fact, during the final set, when Riggs went to the sidelines to fight off hand cramps, King's own legs were cramping. Barnett "rubbed down Billie's calves to keep the muscles warm while everyone waited to see if Bobby could continue" (Roberts 2005, 129).

The film also leaves out the fact that King's homosexuality became public because Barnett filed a palimony suit against King in 1981, two years after King ended their relationship. At first King denied the affair, but on May 1 at a news conference in Los Angeles, she said: "I did have an affair with Marilyn, but it was over quite some time ago. I'm very disturbed and shocked that Marilyn would do this in such a selfish way" (United Press International 1982, A2). The suit was eventually dismissed. In 1987, Billie Jean and Larry King, a former college tennis standout who served as the Women's Tennis Association's attorney, divorced.

Riggs's relationship with his wife worked out better—eventually. The film shows Priscilla returning to Riggs after his loss, and notes that they renewed their wedding vows. They divorced in 1971, but remarried on Valentine's Day 1991. "What can I say?" Riggs said. "We truly love each other. We just had an intermission for 20 years . . ." (Roberts 2005, 411).

They remained married until Priscilla's death in 1995.

CONCLUSION

Battle of the Sexes is inaccurate mainly in its timeline, but King called the movie roughly 99 percent right, saying, "They certainly captured the essence" (Alexander 2017).

Though it wasn't a hit, *Battle of the Sexes* succeeds as a sports film because, as the Toronto International Film Festival's Craddock said: "With any sports film, what makes it good is looking beyond the sport itself. It comes down to the storytelling and the character" (Clarke 2017).

Maybe it isn't needed, but the movie's epilogue did not note that equality between men and women in tennis, and elsewhere, had not improved. While the Equal Rights Amendment was declared dead in 1982, advocacy groups have fought for passage of the amendment. Nevada ratified it in 2017, and since the release of *Battle of the Sexes*, Illinois (2018) and Virginia (2020) have approved, enough for ratification, but Congress has yet to act.

And around the time of the film's release, McEnroe said that Serena Williams would be ranked only seven hundred in the men's seeds.

"It's terrifying . . . ." King said. "Not really as much has changed as one would hope. All those debates about gender rights and equal pay have all bubbled up to the surface again and there's a huge groundswell among women to go back on the battle lines again."

"What is great is the debate about sexuality has moved on, that's in a different place now thank goodness" (Sutherland 2017).

Added Beaufoy: "The film is becoming more and more horrifyingly relevant as time goes on" (McClintock 2018).

FURTHER READING

Alexander, Bryan. 2017. "'Battle of the Sexes': How Accurate is the Movie about the Infamous Match." *USA Today*, September 21, 2017. https://www.usatoday.com/story/life/movies/2017/09/21/battle-sexes-how-accurate-movie-infamous-tennis-match/681093001/

Appleton's Journal. 1875. "An Old Game." *Lancaster Intelligencer,* June 25, 1875, p. 1.

Associated Press. 1971. "Billie Jean King Keeps President Nixon Waiting." *The Greenville News*, October 5, 1971, p. 12.

Associated Press. 1972. "Billy Jean in Tennis Tour Plan." *The Evening Sun*, October 3, 1972, p. 8.

Baltzell, E. Digby. 1995. *Sporting Gentlemen: Men's Tennis from the Age of Honor to the Cult of the Superstar*. New York: Free Press.

Barajas, Joshua. 2016. "Equal Pay for Equal Play. What the Sport of Tennis Got Right." *PBS News Hour*, April 12, 2016. https://www.pbs.org/newshour/econ omy/equal-pay-for-equal-play-what-the-sport-of-tennis-got-right

Behan, Beau. 2017. "Inside the Making of 'Battle of the Sexes' with Directors Valerie Faris and Jonathan Dayton." *Patch*, September 27, 2017. https://patch.com/california /hollywood/inside-making-battle-sexes-directors-valerie-faris-jonathan-dayton

Briggs, Simon. 2017. "Bobby Riggs—The Bizarre Career of a Great Tennis Show-man." *The Telegraph*, November 8, 2017. http://68416521.weebly.com/women x27s-tennis-in-the-60s.html

Buck, Jerry. 1970. "'TV.'" *The Childress Index*, April 8, 1970, p. 3.

Carruth, Gorton, and Eugene Ehrlich. 1988. *Facts & Dates of American Sports: From Colonial Days to the Present*. New York: Perennial Library.

Clarey, Christopher. 2020. "Attach an Asterisk to This U.S. Open? Tennis History Mocks That Idea: The Field Is Considerably Diminished Because of Complica-tions Related to the Pandemic, But Our Columnist Can Tell You about Many Other Grand Slam Draws That Lacked the Best Players of the Day." *The New York Times*, September 9, 2020. https://www.nytimes.com/2020/08/31/sports /tennis/-us-open-serena-djokovic.html

Clarke, John. 2017. "Tennis Movies Are Usually Terrible—But These Three Might Break the Curse: The Trio of Tennis-focused Movies at the Toronto Film Festi-val This Year—*Battle of the Sexes, Borg/McEnroe,* and *Love Means Zero*—Are Ready to Shatter the Sport's on-Screen Losing Streak." *Vanity Fair*, September 7, 2017. https://www.vanityfair.com/hollywood/2017/09/battle-of-the-sexes-borg -mcenroe-love-means-zero-tennis-movies-toronto

Cone, Tracie. 1990. "The Hustle of His Life: Bobby Riggs Always Bets on Himself. Now He's Matched Up Against Cancer." *The Miami Herald*, 1990, pp. 1C–2C.

Daley, Arthur. 1973. "How It All Began: Bad Boy of Tennis Pulls Classic Con Job." *The Sacramento Bee*, May 16, 1973, p. E4.

Davis, Dwight F. 1921. "Tennis Is World Sport, Says Donor of Davis Cup." *The Brainerd Daily Dispatch,* September 1, 1921, p. 12.

Dockterman, Eliana. 2017. "The True Story Behind the *Battle of the Sexes* Movie." *Time*, September 22, 2017. https://time.com/4952004/battle-of-the-sexes-movie -true-story/

Dwyer, Bill. 2009. "Jack Kramer, 1921–2009: Champ Ushered in Era of Pro Tennis." *Los Angeles Times*, September 14, p. A17.

Evry, Max. 2016. "First Battle of the Sexes Photo as Filming Begins." *Coming Soon*, April 13, 2016. https://www.comingsoon.net/movies/news/676181-first-battle -of-the-sexes-photo-as-filming-begins#/slide/1

Fleming, Mike, Jr. 2015. "Game, Set Match? Searchlight Serves Up 'Battle of the Sexes;' Dayton & Faris Direct Emma Stone as Billie Jean King, Steve Carell as Bobby Riggs." *Deadline*, April 20, 2015. https://deadline.com/2015/04/battle -of-the-sexes-emma-stone-billie-jean-king-steve-carell-bobby-riggs-fox-search light-1201412970/

Gillmeister, Heiner. 1998. *Tennis: A Cultural History*. London: Leicester University Press.

Gipe, George. 1978. *The Great American Sports Book*. Garden City, NY: Doubleday & Company, Inc.

Goodykoontz, Bill. 2017. "Serving Her a Game: Emma Stone Talks Preparation for Role in 'Battle of the Sexes." *The Arizona Republic*, September 24, 2017, pp. 1D, 8D.

Graham, Adam. 2018. "Academy Ignored: 10 Movies the Oscars Overlooked: From 'Wind River' to 'Wonder Woman,' Here Are 10 Movies That Should Have Been in the Oscar Conversation." *The Detroit News*, January 26, 2018. https:// www.detroitnews.com/story/opinion/columnists/adam-graham/2018/01/26 /academy-ignored-movies-oscars-overlooked/109819524/

Grimsley, Will. 1970. "Pro Tennis Dispute: Liberationists Plan to Pass Up Tournament Over Pay Disparity." *The Post-Crescent*, September 8, 1970, p. B11.

Hower, George. 1971. "Billie Jean King Earns $100,000." *Naples Daily News*, December 19, 1971, p. B1.

King, Billie Jean with Christine Brennan. 2008. *Pressure Is a Privilege: Lessons I've Learned from Life and the Battle of the Sexes*. New York: TimeLife Media, Inc.

King, Billie Jean with Frank Deford. 1982. *Billie Jean*. New York: The Viking Press.

Kroll, Justin. 2015. "Emma Stone Set to Star as Billie Jean King in Fox Searchlight's 'Battle of the Sexes.'" *Variety*, November 18, 2015. https://variety.com/2015/film /news/battle-sexes-emma-stone-billie-jean-king-1201644084/

Law, Tara. 2020. "Virginia Just Became the 38th State to Pass the Equal Rights Amendment. Here's What to Know About the History of the ERA." *Time*, January 15, 2020. https://time.com/5657997/equal-rights-amendment-history/

"The Lawn-Tennis Tournament. First Day of the Meeting at Camp Washington, Staten Island." *The New York Times*, September 2, 1880, p. 3.

LeCompte, Tom. 2003. *The Last Sure Thing: The Life & Times of Bobby Riggs*. Easthampton, MA: Skunkworks Publishing.

Lindsey, Robert. 1981. "Billie Jean King Is Sued for Assets Over Alleged Lesbian Relationship." *The New York Times*, April 30, 1981, p. A18.

Martin, Bob. 1970. "Billie Jean Pleads for Equal Money." *Independent*, August 25, 1970, p. C-5.

McClintock, Pamela. 2018. "Making of 'Battle of the Sexes': How Emma Stone Mastered the Signature Move of a Tennis Legend." *The Hollywood Reporter*, January 9, 2018. https://www.hollywoodreporter.com/features/making-battle -sexes-how-emma-stone-mastered-signature-move-a-tennis-legend-1071797

Mead, Rebecca. 2009. "The Age of Innocence: Early Letters from Edith Wharton." *The New Yorker*, June 29, 2009. https://www.newyorker.com/magazine/2009/06/29 /the-age-of-innocence-rebecca-mead

Meyers, Naila-Jean. 2013. "The Open's Breakthrough of 1973." *The New York Times*, August 24, 2013. https://www.nytimes.com/2013/08/26/sports/tennis/the -opens-breakthrough-of-1973.html

Murphy, Melissa. 2020. "King, Original 9 Mark 50 Years of Women's Pro Tennis Tour." *Journal Review*, September 6, 2020. https://www.journalreview.com/sto ries/king-original-9-mark-50-years-of-womens-pro-tennis-tour,130290

Murray, Jim. 1970. "The Girls Are Upset." *Los Angeles Times*, September 24, 1970, Part III, p. 1.

Nelson, Murry R., ed. 2009a. *Encyclopedia of Sports in America: A History from Foot Races to Extreme Sports. Volume 1: Colonial Years to 1939*. Westport, CT: Greenwood Press.

Nelson, Murry R., ed. 2009b. *Encyclopedia of Sports in America: A History from Foot Races to Extreme Sports. Volume 2: 1940 to Present.* Westport, CT: Greenwood Press.

Nicholson, Rebecca. 2017. "Billie Jean King: 'Be Ahead of Your Time—That's What You Have to Do." *The Guardian,* November 12, 2017. https://www.theguardian.com/world/2017/nov/12/billie-jean-king-tennis-equality-battle-of-the-sexes

Overman, Steven J., and Kelly Boyer Sagert. 2012. *Icons of Women's Sport: From Tomboys to Title IX and Beyond: Volume One.* Santa Barbara, CA: Greenwood.

Padnani, Amisha. 2018. "Mary Ewing Outerbridge: Established What May Have Been America's First Tennis Court in the 1870s." *The New York Times,* March 8, 2018. https://www.nytimes.com/interactive/2018/obituaries/overlooked-mary-ewing-outerbridge.html

Pantic, Nina. 2017. "How Battle of the Sexes Made Tennis Look Real." *Baseline,* September 26, 2017. http://baseline.tennis.com/article/69549/how-battle-sexes-made-tennis-look-real

Persall, Steve. 2017. "Ace Off the Court: Battle of the Sexes Serves a Fine Time Capsule Comedy That's Easy to Cheer for." *Tampa Bay Times,* September 28, 2017, p. 12W.

Phillips, Michael. 2017. "A Crowd-Pleasing Recreation: Movie a Study in Gender Wars, Love Matches." *Hartford Courant,* September 29, 2017, pp. D1, D6.

Prugh, Jeff. 1972. "Net Profit: At 54, Bobby Riggs Challenges Tennis 'Racketeers' and Usually Pockets Their Cash." *The Courier-Journal,* June 21, 1972, p. B8.

Recchi, Ray. 1972. "Qualifying Rounds Scheduled in Boca Tennis." *Fort Lauderdale News,* October 7, 1972, p. 1D.

Riggs, Bobby with George McGann. 1974. *Bobby Riggs: Court Hustler.* New York: Signet.

Roberts, Selena. 2005. *A Necessary Spectacle: Billie Jean King, Bobby Riggs, and the Tennis Match That Leveled the Game.* New York: Crown Publishers.

Roeper, Richard. 2017. "Stone, Carell Bring 'Battle' to Life." *Albany Democrat-Herald,* October 5, 2017, p. C5.

Saylor, Jack. 1979. "Ex-netter's Next Smash Probably a Suspense Novel." *Detroit Free-Press,* October 30, 1979, p. 2D.

St. Nicholas. 1879. "Origin of Lawn Tennis." *Abbeville Press & Banner,* August 14, 1879, p. 1.

Sutherland, Gill. 2017. "Interview: The Battle of the Sexes Scriptwriter Simon Beaufoy." *Stratford-upon-Avon Herald,* October 10, 2017. https://www.hollywoodreporter.com/features/making-battle-sexes-how-emma-stone-mastered-signature-move-a-tennis-legend-1071797

"Tennis in the Air. Played on the Top of a High Building in Denver. The Game Booming to the Shores of the Pacific. H.A. Ditson Talks of His Recent Trip to the West." *The Boston Sunday Globe,* December 28, 1890, p. 13.

Tignor, Steve. 2015. "1970: The Women's Tour Begins." *Tennis Magazine,* February 26, 2015. https://www.tennis.com/pro-game/2015/02/1970-womens-tour-begins/54184/

Turan, Kenneth. 2017. "Good Match: Stone and Carell Serve Up Surprises in Strong 'Battle of the Sexes.'" *Los Angeles Times,* September 22, 2017, p. E1, E12.

United Press International. 1970a. "Uslta Move Sparks Gals' Tennis Revolt." *The Monitor,* September 24, 1970, p. 5B.

United Press International. 1970b. "Honolulu Listed: Gals Plan Own Tennis Tour." *The Honolulu Advertiser,* September 25, 1970, p. F-4.

United Press International. 1970c. "9 Players Expelled." *Waxahachie Daily Light,* September 27, 1970, p. 11.

United Press International. 1982. "Billie Jean King Admits Lesbian Affair with Ex-secretary Suing for Support." *The San Francisco Examiner*, May 2, 1981, p. A2.

Ware, Susan. 2011. *Game, Set, Match: Billie Jean King and the Revolution in Women's Sports*. Chapel Hill: The University of North Carolina Press.

Webb, Christopher. 2009. "Jack Kramer; Tennis Champ Helped Develop Sport in US." *The Boston Globe*, September 14, 2009, p. B10.

Wilson, Elizabeth. 2014. *Love Game: A History of Tennis, from Victorian Pastime to Global Phenomenon*. Chicago: The University of Chicago Press.

Chapter 10

Ford v Ferrari (2019)

Of all sports, perhaps the hardest to turn into a dramatic film that is a commercial and critical success and depicts its subject accurately is motorsports. "So many of them have been horrible," said Steven Cole Smith, longtime motorsports writer and former editor of *Car and Driver* magazine (Steven Cole Smith, interview with author, January 31, 2020).

Steve McQueen (1930–89) couldn't make *Le Mans* (1971) a hit, and Burt Reynolds (1936–2018) later pegged his career downfall on *Stroker Ace* (1983). *Days of Thunder* (1990) and *Talladega Nights: The Ballad of Ricky Bobby* (2006) were box-office hits, but reviews tended to use words like *unsatisfying* and *inane*.

"Scroll back to a time long before *Rush* [2013] or even *Le Mans*, and racing flicks could be divided into two groups: big-budget melodramas where the central protagonist was a ruthless so-and-so in search of redemption (or a good woman), or B-movies where camp dialogue and stock footage were no substitute for an actual plot," motorsports writer Richard Heseltine wrote (Heseltine 2016). While Hollywood has found success with car chases since *Runaway Match* (1903), movies about motorsports have been a tougher sell. *Grand Prix* (1966) won three Academy Awards and is known for its racing footage, but "It is hard to stay awake while the auto racers . . . are muddling through their personal problems" (Hunt 1987, C13). When *Heart Like a Wheel* (1983), a biopic of drag racer Shirley Muldonney (1940–), was first released, "To say that nobody came is an understatement" (Harmetz 1983, C21). 20th Century Fox rereleased the movie in the fall of 1983, with a new marketing campaign, and the movie found an audience and many stellar reviews, even if it didn't make a lot of money. *The Last American Hero*, based on an *Esquire* article by celebrated author Tom Wolfe

(1930–2018) about whiskey runner-turned-NASCAR star Junior Johnson (1931–2019) is admired by many, but it hardly documents Johnson's actual career.

"Motorsports is a massive sport, if you add all the motorsports together, which is unlike anything else," Smith said. "If you're covering baseball, it's baseball. If you're covering football or soccer, it's football or soccer. If you cover motorsports, you've got drag racing, and dirt-track racing, you've got stock-car racing, IndyCar, you've got Formula One. And there are not many people who are fans of all of those, so if you narrow it down to where it's just IndyCar or just Formula One or just NASCAR, you're talking about a fairly limited audience" (Steven Cole Smith, interview with author, January 31, 2020).

Those were the obstacles director James Mangold (1963–) and Chernin Entertainment/Turnpike Films faced when the $97 million production *Ford v Ferrari* premiered nationally in November 2019.

It's 1959 when American driver Carroll Shelby (Matt Damon, 1970–) drives an Aston Martin to victory in the 24 Hours of Le Mans, the world's oldest and most prestigious automobile endurance race. Shelby's career as a driver ends shortly afterward because of a heart condition, and the film flashes forward to the 1960s, where Shelby is building sportscars and running an auto-racing team with Ken Miles (Christian Bale, 1974–), a cantankerous Brit, driving for him. Shelby's business and Miles's day job, running a garage, are struggling. The Internal Revenue Service even seizes Miles's garage.

Ford Motor Company is also in dire straits. With Ford's sales and prestige dropping, Henry Ford II (Tracy Letts, 1965–) demands that if a "man comes to my office with an idea–that man gets to keep his job." Lee Iacocca (Jon Bernthal, 1976–) brings an idea that Ford's racing program spread from regional NASCAR to Le Mans. Italy-based Ferrari has dominated Le Mans, winning four of the past five races, but Iacocca points out that Ferrari is for sale, so Ford sends Iacocca to negotiate a merger. Instead of agreeing, Enzo Ferrari (Remo Girone, 1948–) declines the offer, insults Henry Ford II, and prefers to merge with Fiat. When Ford hears of Ferrari's insult, he agrees to enter Le Mans no matter the cost.

That brings Iacocca to Shelby, who agrees to join the Ford team. But Ford's corporate ways clash with Shelby's methods and Miles's personality. Ford executive Leo Beebe (Josh Lucas, 1971–) wants another driver because "Ken Miles is not a Ford man. Put a Ford-type driver in a Ford car. That's the Ford way."

Miles is passed over as a driver for Ford's three Le Mans cars, and the Fords fail to finish, but Ford sticks with Shelby, telling him, "Go to war."

Beebe is then put in charge of Ford racing, and Shelby has to take Ford for a spin in a race car to show him what it takes to drive fast. Ford breaks down crying, but agrees that if Miles can win the Le Mans tune-up race, the 24 Hours of Daytona, then Miles can drive at Le Mans. Miles does, and despite setbacks at Le Mans, he is cruising to victory when Beebe orders all three Ford drivers to cross the finish line at the same time—for a photo op. Shelby doesn't order Miles to slow down, but Miles does, thinking he will win anyway.

Le Mans rules give the victory to one of Miles's teammates because that car started farther back in the field so it covered more ground than Miles. Shelby is furious, but Miles takes it in stride. "We're gonna get the b— next year," he says.

But shortly afterward, while testing a race car in California, Miles is killed in a wreck.

Ford v Ferrari began in 2009 when Bantam Books published *Go Like Hell . . . Ford, Ferrari and Their Battle for Speed and Glory at Le Mans* by A.J. Baime (1971–). Jason Keller (1968–), an Indianapolis native familiar with motorsports, wrote the first draft of the screenplay, and Michael Mann (1943–) was originally pegged as director, but by 2013, director Joseph Kosinski (1974–) was attached to the project and was trying to cast Cruise as Shelby and Brad Pitt (1963–) as Miles. "I wouldn't say we got close to production, but I got to the point where I had Tom Cruise and Brad Pitt at a table read, reading the script together," Kosinski said. "But we couldn't get the budget to the number it had to be at, and it was the right number" (Lattanzio 2020). The project was shelved until Mangold expressed interest in 2017 and made the pitch to 20th Century Fox, which had released Mangold's Oscar-winning *Walk the Line* (2005), a biopic of country music legend Johnny Cash (1932–2003). Mangold's last film, *Logan* (2017), had grossed $619 million worldwide, so Fox green-lighted the project but told Mangold that the budget could not exceed $100 million. Mangold brought in brothers Jez (1969–) and John-Henry Butterworth (1976–) to work on the script, moving the focus to Shelby and Miles.

Bale, whom Mangold directed in *3:10 to Yuma* (2007), signed on, and Damon had "been wanting to work with both Jim and Christian, so it seemed too good to be true" (McClintock 2019).

To make the racing scenes authentic—and without computer-generated special effects—Mangold hired Robert Nagle as stunt coordinator. Shooting at Le Mans wasn't possible (the track today doesn't resemble the 1966 version), so a bridge at Road Atlanta became Le Mans's Dunlop bridge; and a road course in Savannah, Georgia, subbed for other corners. The start–finish line was recreated at an airport in the Los Angeles area, and the 3.7-mile Mulsanne straight was filmed along a five-mile stretch of country road near Statesboro, Georgia, where, Nagle said, "We were able to run the picture cars there at 180 mph" (Ceppos 2019).

Ford v Ferrari opened predominantly to rave reviews.

"A barnburner of a motion picture than mainlines heart-in-mouth excitement and tug-at-the-heart emotion, 'Ford v Ferrari' is made the way

Hollywood used to make them," wrote the *Los Angeles Times'* Kenneth Turan, "a glorious throwback that combines a smart modern sensibility with the best of traditional storytelling" (Turan 2019, E1). "I don't know bupkes about cars and you may not either," *The Boston Globe's* Ty Burr wrote, "but I do know this: 'Ford v Ferrari' feels custom-built for maximum audience pleasure" (Burr 2019, G6).

Praising it as "an infectious and engrossing story," Mark Kennedy of The Associated Press also noted that "you don't need to be a motorhead to enjoy Matt Damon and Christian Bale as a pair of rebels risking it all for purity and glory" (Kennedy 2019, G20).

Nominated for four Academy Awards, including Best Picture, *Ford v Ferrari* won for film editing and sound editing. It took in more than $117.6 million domestically at the box office and added more than $107.8 million internationally for a $225,508,210 total gross.

"I'm glad it got made," Smith said, "because I think it's bringing a lot of eyes to sports-car racing" (Steven Cole Smith, interview with author, January 31, 2020).

HISTORICAL BACKGROUND

Auto racing officially began in France in 1894, with a "Reliability Trial" competition from Paris to Rouen. The following year motor races were staged in France, Italy, and metropolitan Chicago.

Americans soon became fascinated with the speed these automobiles could reach.

Michigan native Henry Ford (1863–1947) began experimenting with engines in the 1880s and by the 1890s was building automobiles. He founded the Detroit Automobile Company in 1899, but was forced to close it less than two years later. Undeterred, Ford tweaked his designs and built a new automobile with 26 horsepower by the fall of 1901. Ford named the car Sweepstakes. He turned to another Detroit resident, Tom Cooper (1874–1906), a bicycle-racing champion and member of the Detroit Athletic Club cycling team who had been lured into racing motorized vehicles. Cooper tutored Ford about racing, and on October 10, 1901, Ford entered Sweepstakes in a match race in Grosse Pointe, Michigan, near Detroit.

Before racetracks built specifically for automobiles were first constructed in Australia and England, horse tracks were repurposed for cars, including Grosse Pointe, Michigan.

"A mettlesome pacer, with sleek coat, high head, extended nostrils, stood uneasily in a stall at the Grosse Pointe race track yesterday," a *Detroit Free Press* reporter wrote. "As he pawed the floor and jerked at his halter, it was easy to see that something was wrong with his equine majesty. For the first time in his career the horse was getting no attention, though a crowd stood about, and he resented it as earnestly as a horse ever resented anything" ("Alex Winton's Fast Mile" 1901, 1).

The event, a series of races featuring steam, electric and gasoline-powered vehicles, drew a crowd estimated from seven thousand five hundred to ten thousand. Officials weren't prepared for anywhere near that number.

Between the third and fourth races, Alexander Winton (1860–1932), owner of Cleveland-based Winton Carriage Car Company, set a world record by covering a mile in 1 minute, 12 2/5 seconds in his car—although at that time France's Henri Fournier (1871–1919) was breaking the record in New York with a 1:06 4/5 mile.

A leaky cylinder forced Pittsburgh millionaire William N. Murray to withdraw his car from the major race, leaving only Winton and Ford in the field. *The Detroit Free Press* described the race:

> For the first seven miles Mr. Winton led and gradually increased his lead to nearly a half mile. Mr. Ford had not had experience in driving his machine and did not dare keep her on the pole as Mr. Winton did. E.S. Huff, Fords mechanician, hung far out in his effort to ballast the car, but she swung wide at every turn, and Mr. Ford had to shut off the power. Suddenly the Winton machine began to slow down.
>
> Then a thin wreath of blue smoke appeared at the rear of the machine and it gradually increased to a cloud. Mr. Shanks, who was riding, poured oil on it, but it did no good, and Mr. Ford swept by them as though they were standing still. Down the stretch he came like a demon and the crowd yelled itself hoarse. In the next three miles Ford increased his lead to fully three-quarters of a mile and won amid great cheering, his time being 13:23 4-5 for ten miles. Mr. Winton made the best times in 1:14-25. Several of Mr. Ford's backers, among them whom are W. H. Murphy, Mark Hopkins, Clarence A. Black, A. E. F. White and L. W. Bowen, were present and they were heartily congratulated upon the success of the new motor car which has been named Sweepstakes. Before the car left the grounds they received two offers, one from a New York man and another from a Chicagoan, who wished to purchase the racer. Several brasses in Mr. Winton's machine became heated, which caused his break down. ("Alex Winton's Fast Mile" 1901, 2)

The victory was enough for investors to back Ford's Henry Ford Company, which became Ford Motor Company in 1903.

"That was my first race," Ford recalled in his autobiography, "and it brought advertising of the only kind that people cared to read. The public thought nothing of a car unless it made speed—unless it beat other racing cars" (Ford 2017, 31).

In 1902, Cooper wrote another cycling champion, Barney Oldfield (1878–1946), "The Bicycle Champion of Ohio" who was turning to racing motorcycles, to come to Detroit to help Cooper and Ford build race cars. "Cooper was supposed to be Ford's driver, but in fact no one was anxious to handle the cars. They were nothing but engine and frame, steered by handle bars, with exposed crankshafts that sprayed oil over the driver. Oldfield was enchanted by them" (Snow 1977).

Ford's latest car was named 999, after a locomotive for the New York Central Railroad, which he let Oldfield drive. The former cyclist cover the Grosse Pointe mile in just more than a minute, and Ford let him drive in a race against Winton, who would be driving his car known as the Bullet. "Well," Oldfield reportedly said, "this damn chariot may kill me, but they will say afterward that I was goin' like hell when she took me over the bank" (Snow 1977).

Oldfield drove the 999 to victory over the Bullet, and the following spring became the first driver to take a gas-powered vehicle faster than 60 mph. A month later, he clocked a mile in 55 seconds. On January 12, 1904, he broke the world record by driving a Ford 91.37 miles per hour in what the *Detroit Tribune* called "the wildest ride in the history of automobiling" (Lewis 1976, 25). In 1910, driving the German-made 200-horse-power Blitzen Benz on the sands of Daytona Beach, Florida, Oldfield set a world record with a speed of 131.7 miles per hour.

"I have realized my life's ambition," Oldfield said. "I have traveled faster than any other person in the whole world. I have shot along the rock-line sand of Daytona Beach at a greater speed than any of the wise men believed was possible without encountering disaster" ("Fast as a Bullet" 1910, 7).

Even before his retirement from racing in 1918, Oldfield was appearing in motion pictures, beginning in 1913 with *Barney Oldfield's Race for a Life*, a short directed by Mack Sennett (1880–1960) that had Oldfield racing his car against a locomotive to save the proverbial heroine tied to a railroad track.

In 1904, William K. Vanderbilt (1849–1920) began the 300-mile Vanderbilt Cup, held on Long Island, New York, at a 28-mile road course, a series that continued until World War I (1914–18). In the coastal town of Savannah, Georgia, what is considered the first American Grand Prix race in the United States, sponsored by the Automobile Club of America, began in 1908, drawing an estimated crowd of two hundred thousand, and continued through 1911.

Another onetime bicycle racer, Carl Graham Fisher (1874–1939), thought up the idea to build a race course specifically for automobiles where manufacturers could test new models for safety and performance. The track could also double as a racecourse. Fisher and partners bought 328 acres of farmland near Indianapolis and built a 2.5-mile rectangular track that costs more than $350,000. After a series of motorcycle races in early August, the Indianapolis Motor Speedway—dubbed the "Brooklands of America" after the fabled, high-banked English speedway—scheduled its first car races for August 19–21, 1909. Anticipation for racing records ran high, but on the day of the inaugural, 250-mile event, *The Indianapolis News reported*: "In reality the track is now in poor condition for racing" and that Fisher "made a statement to the effect that he wished it were possible to postpone the race meeting" ("Speedway Opening Today Big Event" 1909, 10).

The first day brought a crowd of sixteen thousand, and Oldfield set a world record by covering a mile in 43.1 seconds. But the event turned tragic when the Knox Company's No. 3 car, driven by twenty-six-year-old William Borque with twenty-two-year-old mechanic Harry Holcomb, skidded, slammed into a ditch at an estimated speed of 75 miles per hour and flipped into the fence, tossing the driver and mechanic to their deaths. "This will probably end our racing," a Knox representative said. "We will probably enter no more cars in automobile racing. It is simply suicide, that's all it is" ("Death Demands Toll in Record Speedway Races" 1909, 1).

Another driver and another mechanic suffered minor injuries in separate incidents. On August 21, a car driven lost a tire and slammed through a fence, killing the mechanic and two spectators and injuring another spectator; the driver was not hurt.

Most accounts for the three-day event put the deaths at two drivers, two mechanics, and two spectators.

The problems were attributed to the track's surface: crushed rock and tar. When the track reopened in December, the surface had been replaced with 3.2 million paving bricks secured in sand with mortar, which gave the speedway a new nickname—"The Brickyard." Attendance dropped dramatically, leading the owners to switch from multiple events to one long race. On May 30, 1911, Ray Haroun (1879–1968) won the first Indianapolis 500, averaging 74.59 miles per hour and winning $14,250 in prize money.

Money ruled early races in America. It took capital to develop and build race cars and travel to, usually, larger cities for competition. "The vast majority of Americans never saw an auto race," Don Radbruch wrote. "World War I changed all this. When Johnny came marching home he'd seen a chunk of the world. Maybe Johnny was restless and wanted excitement. Maybe he was inspired by Henry's wonderful Model T which could so easily be converted to a race car. Johnny and his Model T went racing at the local fairgrounds, and a new era began" (Radbruch 2004, 5).

Dirt-track racing, often on short, quarter-mile ovals and sometimes even smaller, became popular, and led to the creation of "midget" cars, usually open-cockpit, open-wheel miniature versions of larger open-wheel race cars like those driven at Indianapolis Motor Speedway.

The Great Depression shuttered many tracks, and gasoline shortages during World War II stopped most racing altogether, but after the war, auto racing rebounded as various forms took root—sprint cars, stock cars, Indy cars, Formula One cars, dragsters—across the country.

The National Association for Stock Car Auto Racing became largely popular in the South, with fabled tracks in Darlington, South Carolina (Darlington Raceway, 1950); Daytona Beach, Florida (Daytona International

THE RACE THAT MADE NASCAR

Seeking to broaden NASCAR's popularity, founder Bill France Sr. (1909–92) worked on national television coverage in the 1970s. In 1979, CBS televised start-to-finish the Daytona 500, "one of the high points of NASCAR, put NASCAR on a nationwide map," said Richard Petty (1937–), who won two hundred races in his NASCAR career, including the 1979 Daytona 500 (Long 2019).

But Petty's victory wasn't what most of the fifteen million TV viewers were talking about after the race—or what race fans discuss more than forty years later.

On the last lap, Cale Yarborough attempted to pass Donnie Allison (1939–) for the lead with both cars traveling more than 200 miles per hour. Allison made what he called a blocking maneuver. "Cale had made up his mind he would pass me low and I made up my mind he would pass me high," Allison said. "He went off the track when he tried to pass low. He spun and hit me" (Gossett 1979, 1D).

Yarborough countered, "you don't cut left on a man who's up beside you on the backstretch going that fast" (Pearce 1999, 2). The two cars wrecked—the second accident involving Yarborough, Allison, and Allison's racing brother, Bobby (1937–) that day. This one allowed Petty to win NASCAR's biggest race. Then spectators, press, and TV viewers watched as Yarborough got into a fight with the Allison brothers after Bobby stopped to help his brother.

Television ratings soared, and NASCAR's popularity moved from mostly regional to national.

Said Yarborough: "All I ended up with was a wrecked car and fifth place. France and NASCAR got a lot more out of that afternoon than I ever did" (Pearce 1999, 3).

Sources

Gossett, Peggy. 1979. "Petty Captures Sixth 500: Yarborough, Allison Brothers Fighting Mad." *The Palm Beach Post,* February 19, 1979, pp. 1D, 6D.

Long, Gary. 1979. "Petty Inherits Wild 500 Victory: Frontrunners Fight After Last-Lap Crash." *The Miami Herald,* February 18, 1979, pp. 1D, 2D.

Long, Mark. 2019. "Perfect Storm: The 500 and Fight That Changed NASCAR Forever." *Daily Herald,* February 17, 2019. https://www.dailyherald.com/sports/20190216/perfect-storm -the-500-and-fight-that-changed-nascar-forever

Pearce, Al. 1999. "Feb. 18, 1979, Daytona International Speedway: A Race, a Fight, a TV Winner." *Daily Press, Racing* section, February 10, 1999, pp. 2–3.

Speedway, 1959); Bristol, Tennessee (Bristol Motor Speedway, 1961); and Talladega, Alabama (Talladega Superspeedway, 1969). Sara Christian (1918–80) became the first female driver in a NASCAR event when she started at Charlotte (North Carolina) Motor Speedway on June 19, 1949 in NASCAR's first official race. Janet Guthrie (1938–), the first woman to qualify for the Indianapolis 500 and the Daytona 500, finished sixth at Bristol in 1977, the highest finish for a woman driver in NASCAR's top series in the modern era; Danica Patrick (1982–) tied that in 2014 in a race at Atlanta. Wendell Scott (1921–90) became the first, and, at this date, only African American to win race in NASCAR's top series, then called the Grand National, when he was declared the winner—after much argument—in Jacksonville, Florida, in 1963. Shirley Muldowney, the first woman to be licensed in the National Hot Rod Association's top-fuel drag-racing category, won three championships between 1977 and 1982 and was inducted into the International Motorsports Hall of Fame.

NASCAR and the Indianapolis 500 dominated American motorsports, but an event in France still topped the auto-racing world. "LeMans is to all of Europe what Daytona and Indianapolis are to this country," said Cale Yarborough (1939–), a NASCAR driver who raced at Le Mans in 1981 (Higgins 1981, 12B).

Actually, the 24 Hours of Le Mans was widely considered the world's most prestigious motorsports event. It started in 1923 as an endurance race pitting passenger cars, not specially built race cars, on a muddy, 17.26-kilometer track (roughly 10.7 miles) that was later shortened to roughly 13.6 kilometers, or 8.45 miles. Twenty-four hours later, André Lagache (1885–1938) and René Léonard (1889–1965) drove a Chenard & Walcker to victory. Of the thirty-three cars that started, only three did not finish. Strikes canceled Le Mans in 1936, and no races happened from 1940 to 1948 due to World War II and postwar rebuilding, but the 24 Hours of Le Mans returned in 1949 when Luigi Chinetti (1901–94), an Italian who emigrated to the United States during World War II, teamed with British driver Peter Mitchell-Thomson (1913–63) to win in a Ferrari 166 MM. In 1958, Phil Hill (1927–2008) became the first American-born driver to win at Le Mans, when he partnered with Belgian Olivier Gendebien (1924–68) to drive a Ferrari 250 TR58 to win; the team would also drive to Le Mans victories in 1961 and 1962. In 1959, Texas-born Carroll Shelby (1923–2012) won at Le Mans in an Aston Martin DBR1, driving with England-born Roy Salvadori (1922–2012) for an England-based team.

"The 24 Hours of Le Mans was (and still is) a sports car race," A.J. Baime wrote. "But in the 1950s and 1960s, it was more than that. It was the most magnificent marketing tool the sports car industry had ever known. Renowned manufacturers built street-legal machines that would prove on the racetrack that their cars were the best in the world" (Baime 2010, 11–12).

In the early 1960s, Henry Ford II (1917–87), Ford Motor Company's CEO, decided to develop a sports car to race at Le Mans, partly fueled by a rivalry with Italian Enzo Ferrari (1898–1988), whose cars dominated Le Mans in the early 1960s. When Fords failed to finish in the 1964 and 1965 races, Ford turned to Shelby, then designing sports cars in Los Angeles, to take charge. Shelby hired his friend, test driver and engineer Ken Miles (1918–66), and they came up with the GT40 to run at Le Mans in 1966. Fords placed 1-2-3 when Miles, who was leading much of the race, slowed down to allow his teammates to cross the finish line together. Teammates Bruce McLaren (1937–70) and Chris Amon (1943–2016), both New

Zealand natives, were declared the winners in one of the race's most controversial finishes. Miles was killed while testing a car later that year. The following year, Shelby's team of American drivers Dan Gurney (1931–2018) and A.J. Foyt (1935–) won for Ford again. While Ford cars won Le Mans in 1969 and 1970 for an England-based team, a U.S. team would not win the race again until 2005 when ADT Champion Racing's Audi R8, driven by non-American drivers, won.

"In the 1970s, the grandeur of the 24-hour classic began to fade," Baime wrote. "The race is still held every June, and still draws hundreds of thousands of spectators. But the glory days are past. Many fans believe that the Ford-Ferrari rivalry represents automobile racing's true Golden Age" (Baime 2010, 354).

John Sturbin, a reporter at RacinToday.com who helped with the Associated Press's coverage of Le Mans as a freelancer in 1989, agrees. "Fifty-four years later, Ford's 1-2-3 Le Mans sweep in 1966 stands as the seminal moment in international competition by an American auto manufacturer," he said. "A program admittedly begun to salve Henry Ford II's ego, and as a marketing tool to attract the attention and wallets of Baby Boomers, had whipped Ferrari on its sacred turf" (John Sturbin, interview with author, August 22, 2020).

DEPICTION AND CULTURAL CONTEXT

In 1981, while filming secondary footage of the Southern 500 at Darlington Raceway, producer Walter Wood (1921–2010) said that, unlike so many motorsports movies, his goal was to capture accurately the *esprit de corps* of NASCAR, "the color of the crowd, the cars and the drivers, and what goes on in the infield area" (Boggs 1981, 3A). The film was *Stroker Ace* (1983), which the *New York Times's* Vincent Canby called "the must-miss movie of the summer" (Canby 1983) and the *San Francisco Examiner's* Allan Ulrich said "makes 'Smoky and the Bandit' look like 'Citizen Kane'" (Ulrich 1983, E12).

Filmmakers might have had good intentions when they set out to make movies about auto racing, but they rarely succeeded. But while *Ford v Ferrari* might not have been completely accurate, it succeeded as an accurate depiction of what all goes into a successful racing team. "Every movie takes liberties with the truth, and I thought all the liberties were well within the parameter of drama," said Smith, a TV critic at the *Dallas Times Herald* before reporting on motorsports.

One of the liberties was in its depiction of Miles.

"Ken's son, who was there for the fatal crash and the other stuff, asked some of his dad's contemporaries, 'Was my dad really that big of an a—?'" Smith said, "and the answer was 'no.' He was prickly but he was genuinely a generous guy" (Steven Cole Smith, interview with author, January 31, 2020).

A veteran of the 1944 D-Day campaign with the British army, Miles—who didn't get his first car until he was twenty years old—started racing after World War II. Settling with his wife in Hollywood, he became well known in Southern California's racing scene of the 1950s and served as president of the California Sports Car Club in 1957. The "transplanted Britisher" became "generally acknowledged to be the greatest smallbore sports car driver in America" (Alexander 1960, 11). In the 200-mile Riverside (California) Grand Prix race in 1960, Miles finished second to Shelby. But while Miles was a fantastic mechanic, engineer, and driver, he wasn't much of a businessman. In 1963, the Internal Revenue Service padlocked the doors of his Hollywood garage—accurately depicted in the movie—and that's why Miles joined Shelby American.

While *Ford v Ferrari* shows the ups-and-downs home life of Miles, it ignores Shelby's. "The elision of Shelby's private life is a sleight of hand that obscures, above all, the complexity of life—it suggests a sheer unwillingness to contend with facts that don't easily fit into a sentimental schema," Richard Brody wrote for the *New Yorker*. "The real Shelby was married seven times, and two or three of those marriages overlapped with the eight-year span covered in 'Ford v Ferrari,' and extramarital affairs appear to have been involved, too. To place details of Shelby's complicated life in the movie would be to offer a hero whose characteristics stand in contrast to the sanitized image of Hollywood heroes (even flawed ones) in family-oriented movies" (Brody 2019).

That said, Damon "did a pretty good job as Shelby," Smith said, however the film "didn't quite show what kind of a flimflam man Shelby was. He was a lot more outgoing, not nearly as countrified. If you wrote something bad about Carroll, it actually hurt his feelings. He was such a legend, he couldn't imagine anybody would be critical of him. And it was hard to be because he was such a charming guy" (Steven Cole Smith, interview with author, January 31, 2020).

After serving as a flight instructor during World War II, Shelby went into the trucking business, then worked in oil fields, and next began raising chickens. None worked out. In 1948 and 1949, Shelby and his wife attended the Indianapolis 500 and although Shelby had attended dirt-track races in Texas, he "had no connection whatever with Gasoline Alley or any of the builders, entrants, or drivers of that time" (Shelby 2020, 29). In 1952, however, a friend asked Shelby to drive a home-built race car in a drag race at the Grand Prairie (Texas) Naval Air Station. Shelby won easily and found a new career, racing friends' cars in Texas and Oklahoma. In 1955, a wealthy colleague took Shelby with him to Italy where the friend planned to buy fifteen Ferraris. Shelby was introduced to Enzo Ferrari, who, after hearing of Shelby's success, offered him a job as a racer. When Shelby turned down the offer, Ferrari felt insulted. In 1957, Shelby began driving for the Aston Martin team and made the cover of *Sports Illustrated* as the Sports Car Driver of the Year. He won Le Mans in 1959, but the following year, his racing career ended after he was diagnosed with angina pectoralis. With an ex-wife and three kids to support, Shelby decided that if he couldn't race cars, he could build them. In 1962, he went to Ford Motor Company and pitched an idea to executive Lee Iacocca (1924–2019) to put powerful Ford engines in lightweight English coupes. Iacocca backed the idea, Shelby founded Shelby American, and the Shelby Cobra was about to be born.

The film's loosest interpretation of an actual person is likely that of Ford executive Leo Beebe (1917–2001)—"depicted as the kind of self-important p— found in any corporation" (John Sturbin, interview with author, August 22, 2020). Movies need a villain, and Beebe was given that role. But while Beebe was involved in the controversial decision that cost Miles a victory at Le Mans in 1966, Shelby never had to lock Beebe in an office in order to take Henry Ford II on a wild ride in a race car in order to convince the CEO that Miles needed to drive at Le Mans. In the film, after stopping the car, Shelby says if Miles doesn't win at the race in Daytona, Ford can take over Shelby American. "There is no record of any such ultimatum in print," Sturbin said (John Sturbin, interview with author, August 22, 2020).

A Michigan native, Beebe held a number of positions in his twenty-eight years with Ford Motor Company. In the 1950s, Ford loaned Beebe to the U.S. government help supervise the resettlement of refugees fleeing the Hungarian revolution, a job he repeated in the 1960s with Cuban refugees in Florida.

In 1964, John Wyer (1909–89), who joined Ford in 1963 after guiding Shelby to his 1959 Le Mans win and becoming general manager of Aston Martin Lagonda Ltd., was running Ford's sports program. Ford Advanced Vehicles built three Ford Mark 1s, but all three cars failed to finish in the 1964 Le Mans. Nor did a Ford finish the next month in the 12 Hours of Reims in France. In the final race of the series, Ford driver Phil Hill finished twenty-sixth. Roger Penske (1937–), driving a Chevrolet Corvette Grand Sport, won that race. A Chevy embarrassing Fords was too much for Beebe to take.

"I don't know anything about racing," Beebe told Wyer. "But there is one thing that has become increasingly apparent to me in the past few months. You don't either" (Baime 2010, 186). Beebe turned Ford's racing program over to Shelby. Later, Wyer and John Willment (1925–97) formed JW Automotive, which acquired Ford's racing program and led Ford back to Le Mans victories, for an English team, in 1968 and 1969.

Ford v Ferrari skips Ford's 1964 failures. The filmmakers also has Beebe clashing with Miles at the unveiling of the Ford Mustang in California—a bit of fiction since the 1964 Mustang was launched on April 17, 1964, at the New York World's Fair. The incident sets the fictional tone of the Beebe–Miles relationship, ending when Beebe has Miles removed from the team for the 1965 Le Mans team. In the film, Miles works on a car in an airport hangar while listening to the Le Mans race on a radio. That's not accurate, either. "Look it up and you'll find that Miles was paired with McLaren in one of six Fords—theirs was one of two Mark IIs—to record DNFs [Did Not Finish]," Sturbin said. "In fact, because of gearbox and head-gasket failures, not one of the Ford fleet lasted until Sunday morning" (John Sturbin, interview with author, August 22, 2020).

Miles called the 1965 Le Mans "the greatest defeat ever suffered by a team in the history of motor racing" (Lerner 2015, 6).

What the movie does get right is what brought Ford to Le Mans.

Iacocca started working at Ford in 1946 as a student engineer. A mild recession in the United States in the 1950s caused Ford sales slipped, and Iacocca, assistant sales manager for Ford's Philadelphia district, came up with a marketing idea that he called *56 for '56* . . . for a 20 percent downpayment, a buyer could pay $56 a month for three years on a 1956 Ford. The financing plan went national, increasing Ford sales by seventy-five thousand. In 1960, Henry Ford II called Iacocca into his office—"it was like being summoned to see God," Iacocca recalled (Iacocca 1984, 46)—and put him in charge of the Ford Division.

Henry Ford II wasn't all that interested in racing. After World War II, Congress had pressured major American automobile companies to stop promoting auto racing. In 1957, Ford, General Motors and Chrysler—the "Big Three"—agreed to the Automobile Manufacturers Association's Safety Resolution, which stated that the companies would not promote "the specific engine size, torque, horsepower, or ability to accelerate or perform, in any contest that suggest speed" (Baime 2010, 39). Chevrolet, part of General Motors, cheated, funding racing under the guise of a marine engine program. When Chevies won races, sales increased, proving truth to the adage *Win on Sunday, Sell on Monday.* Iacocca talked Henry Ford II into returning to racing, and Ford withdrew from the Safety Resolution on June 11, 1962.

Ford was going racin'.

At the Daytona 500 on February 25, 1963, Tiny Lund (1929–75) drove a Ford to victory. The next four drivers—Fred Lorenzen (1934–), Ned Jarrett (1932–), Nelson Stacy (1921–86), and Don Gurney (1931–2018)—also drove Fords for a 1-2-3-4-5 finish. By March, Ford was running newspaper ads that touted, "1st 2nd 3rd 4th 5th! In the test that tears 'em apart . . . the Daytona '500' . . . Ford durability conquered the field" (Advertisement 1963, 11).

Meanwhile, Iacocca, overseeing the launch of the Ford Mustang, learned that Ferrari was for sale and brought that to Henry Ford II's attention. Ford agreed. Accountants and engineers were sent to Italy, attorneys came up with contracts, and a $10 million offer was made that would have one company, Ford–Ferrari, designing and selling factory cars, and another company, Ferrari–Ford, overseeing the racing component. The reasoning? "At Le Mans, Ferrari was invincible. Buying Ferrari meant buying Le Mans"

(Baime 2010, 108). For twenty-two days in April–May 1963, Ford and Ferrari entered negotiations.

In the film, Iacocca goes to Italy to close the deal. In reality, Iacocca sent his No. 2 man, Don Frey (1923–2010), whom Ferrari drove around in his cars. "He drove like a mad man," Frey recalled. "He loved to get me in the car and try to scare me" (Baime 2010, 107).

When Ferrari read the offer, he wasn't happy. A clause "required Ferrari to submit to Ford, 'for quick approval,' any racing team budget over 450 million lire. That equaled $257,000 at the time, the amount of Ferrari's race budget for the 1963 season" (Ciferri 1998). Worse, though, was that Frey told Ferrari that if Ferrari wanted to enter cars at, say, Indianapolis, and Ford rejected the proposal, Ferrari could not race at Indianapolis.

Ferrari exploded: "My rights, my integrity, my very being as a manufacturer, as an entrepreneur, cannot work under the enormous machine, the suffocating bureaucracy of the Ford Motor Company" (Baime 2010, 109).

Frey returned to Dearborn, Michigan, with no deal.

Although Iacocca is put in Italy, *Ford v Ferrari* gets the essence of the meeting right, but there is no record that Ferrari personally insulted Henry Ford II. Ford, in fact, had never really been interested in merging with Ferrari—that had been Iacocca's idea—but Ford took Ferrari's rejection as an insult. Ford's "temper flared when he realized that Ferrari had essentially given him the finger," historian Preston Lerner wrote. "'You go to Le Mans,' he told Frey after an awkward interrogation in a private dining room, 'and beat his a—'" (Lerner 2015, 15).

The movie also adjusts the historical timeline by having Ferrari merge with Fiat immediately after the Ford deal fell through. Fiat and Ferrari announced a joint merger in 1969, years after Ford had won at Le Mans.

Though the fact that Ford had eight cars—not just three—in the 1966 Le Mans is left out, the film gets most of the controversy right about Ford's 1-2-3 finish at Le Mans in 1966, a decision that cost Miles his chance at winning.

"The most commonly accepted explanation is that Beebe and the cadre of Ford yes-men came up with the staged finish idea about two hours before the checkered flag, as the Fords were running 1-2-3 and the Ferraris were long gone," Sturbin said. "Shelby is reported to have reluctantly agreed" (John Sturbin, interview with author, August 22, 2020).

Lerner said the Automobile Club de l'Ouest, the organization that sanctioned the Le Mans race, at first OK'd the idea to allow the Fords to finish in a dead heat, thinking that Miles, having led the race, would be declared the winner. Yet after officials studied the rules, a representative was sent to the Ford team with news that a tie was not possible. "Instead of calling it a dead heat," Sturbin said, "the ACO would award the win to the car covering the greatest distance" (John Sturbin, interview with author, August 22, 2020).

Ford's No. 2 car, driven by McLaren and Amon, having started roughly 20 feet farther back than Ford's No. 1 car, driven by Miles and New Zealand's

Denny Hulme (1936–92), had traveled farther, thus recording a faster over-all speed—even though the McLaren/Amon car had once trailed the Miles/Hulme car by four laps.

The movie continues to make Beebe the villain, suggesting that he knew Miles would not win the race. Beebe, who was promoted to head of market-ing for Lincoln–Mercury after the Le Mans triumph, took responsibility for the decision for the 1-2-3 finish. "The decision regarding the outcome of that race was mine as the manager of the Ford racing effort at Le Mans," he said, but he denied having any dislike of Miles, saying: "I was always fond of Ken Miles and I had great respect for him in that race. Miles was devilish, not only for himself but for others" (Lerner 2015, 158).

Had Miles won, he would have become the first driver to win endurance races at 12-hour Sebring, 24-hour Daytona and Le Mans in the same year. Miles "did exactly what he was told, and at the end, he slowed down on the back chute and all over the place to let McLaren unlap himself," crew chief Charles Agapiou (1942–) said. "He followed his orders and then he got f—. That's what happened" (Considine 2019).

"To all of us enthusiasts, Ken Miles will always be that race's winner," said Bruce Meyer, founding chairman of the Peterson Automotive Museum in Los Angeles, "but for the record books, he wasn't" (Fretts 2019).

Ford's victory had been costly. The company declined to confirm or deny the figures, but published reports said the trip to Le Mans had cost $400,000 and that Ford had spent $9 million in its three-year-old racing program. (For perspective, Ford reportedly spent $75 million developing the Mustang.)

It was "a hollow victory," Canadian motorsports writer Bill Mantle wrote. "When Miles and McLaren came down the pit straight side by side to take the checkered flag, three years of intense planning effort, scientific know how and close to 9 million collars in expenditures seemed a high price to pay for such a victory" (Mantle 1966, 29).

Ford, however, wasn't in motorsports for glory. "At Ford, racing was essentially a marketing tool," Lerner wrote. "This was a fundamental con-trast to Ferrari, where racing was a function of Enzo's thirst for victory, and Porsche, where the motorsports program was driven by the engineer-ing department. Despite all the lip service paid to the notion that racing improves the breed, there was no realistic expectation that any of the lessons learned on the Le Mans prototypes would be applied to street cars" (Lerner 2015, 215–216).

The film's depiction of the perils and intensity of auto racing is accurate. The sport has always been dangerous. In 1906, Tom Carpenter, who taught Henry Ford I how to drive race cars, died of a broken neck in a wreck while racing, illegally, after midnight in New York near West 75th Street and Eighth Avenue in 1906. IndyCar drivers Eddie Sachs (1927–64) and Gordon Smiley (1946–82); drag racers Lee Shepherd (1944–85) and Scott Kalitta (1982–2008); and NASCAR drivers Edward Glenn "Fireball" Roberts

(1929–64); Adam Petty (1980–2000), Richard Petty's grandson; and seven-time Winston Cup champion Dale Earnhardt (1951–2001) are just a few of the noted drivers to die in qualifying, practice, or race accidents. Riverside International Raceway, a road course that opened in 1957, saw ten racing fatalities while it was in operation until 1989. In the first event held at the road course in September 1957, driver John Lawrence was killed when his MG sports car flipped at Turn 6. NASCAR champion Joe Weatherly (1922–64), who refused to wear a seat belt for fear of being trapped inside a burning car, was killed when his head went outside the window and struck a retaining wall.

Miles was killed at Riverside while testing a Ford two months after Le Mans, but *Ford v Ferrari* makes a *faux pas* by having engineer Phil Remington (1921–2013), played by Ray McKinnon (1957–) tell Shelby, "Sometimes, they don't get out of the car."

With Ford increasing its motorsports budget to $10 million for the 1967 season, Miles expected to return to Le Mans. At Riverside International Raceway on August 17, 1966, Miles was testing a prototype called the J Car when it veered sharply, went airborne, crashed down a steep embankment, and burst into flames. Miles was thrown 15 feet, his seatbelt ripped from its mount, and died instantly.

Miles's teenage son, Peter—depicted as a younger boy in the film—raced from the parking lot to the crash site, where he saw the burning wreckage of a car and asked where his father was. A crewman pointed at the dead body.

"We have nobody to take his place," Shelby said of Miles. "Nobody. He was our baseline, our guiding point. He was the backbone of our program. There will never be another Ken Miles" (Baime 2010, 349).

The cause of the accident was never determined, and Shelby never forgave himself for the 1966 Le Mans finish. "That was my f—up," Shelby said. "I take full responsibility for it, and I'm very sorry . . . " (Lerner 2015, 159).

CONCLUSION

Like *Moneyball* (2011), the Oscar-nominated movie about the Oakland A's unorthodox method of fielding a major-league baseball team in the early 2000s, *Ford v Ferrari* succeeded for revealing another side to what it takes to build a successful sports franchise.

But the screenwriters "exercised poetic license with their script," Sturbin said. "Perhaps only diehard Shelby and/or Ford Racing fans noticed, and those embellishments certainly added to the movie's entertainment value" (John Sturbin, interview with author, August 22, 2020). Motorsports writer Steven Cole Smith added: "I thought all the liberties were well within the parameter of drama" (Steven Cole Smith, interview with author, January 31, 2020).

Ford v Ferrari's legacy in the racing-movie canon will be determined over the upcoming years. "Hollywood is nothing if not influenced by the very, very recent past," Smith said. "I don't know about movies, but we're likely to see some scripts as people try to revive *Ford v Ferrari*" (Steven Cole Smith, interview with author, January 31, 2020).

The movie, entertaining, critically acclaimed and slightly accurate, accomplished one thing, though. It returned Ken Miles to the general public's consciousness, and that was something his friend, Carroll Shelby, who died before the film began production, always wanted.

"I got to do something for him," Shelby said. "I don't want him to be forgotten. I don't want him to be forgotten" (Baime 2010, 358).

FURTHER READING

Advertisement. 1909. *Fort Wayne Daily News*, August 18, 1909, p. 10.

Advertisement. 1963. *Enquirer and News*, March 8, 1963, p. 11.

Alexander, Jim. 1960. "Top Drivers at Vaca." *Valley Times*, April 27, 1960, p. 11.

"Alex Winton's Fast Mile: Cleveland Expert Made the Distance in 1:12 2-5 at Grosse Pointe. Detroit Free Press Cup Won by Edgar Apperson, of Buffalo, in a 10 Mile Event. About 8,000 People Attended the First Big Auto Race Meet of the West." *The Detroit Free Press*, October 11, 1901, pp. 1–2.

Associated Press. 1957. "Ken Miles Elected Sports Car President." *The Desert Sun*, February 7, 1957, p. 9.

Associated Press. 1966. "1-2-3 LeMans Finish Dethrones Ferrari." *The News-Palladium*, June 20, 1966, p. 14.

Associated Press. 1981. "Ickx Returns to Win Le Mans." *Messenger-Inquirer*, June 15, 1981, p. 3B.

Bailey, Tanya A. 2014. *The First American Grand Prix: The Savannah Auto Races, 1908–1911*. Jefferson, NC: McFarland & Company, Inc., Publishers.

Baime, A. J. 2010. *Go Like Hell: Ford, Ferrari and Their Battle for Speed and Glory at Le Mans*. London: Bantam Books.

Boggs, Johnny. 1981. "For Movie, 'Stand on It': Crew Tries to Capture Color." *Florence Morning News*, September 7, 1981, p. 3-A.

Brody, Richard. 2019. "The Airbrushed Racing History of 'Ford V Ferrari.'" *The New Yorker*, November 19, 2019. https://www.newyorker.com/culture/the-front-row/the-airbrushed-racing-history-of-ford-v-ferrari

Brudenell, Mike. 2016. "Detroit Cyclist Taught Henry Ford How to Race: Tom Cooper Coached Automotive Pioneer to Victory 115 Years Ago That Helped Launch Ford Motor Co." *Detroit Free Press*, October 10, 2016. https://www.freep.com/story/sports/motor/2016/10/10/motor-sports-history-henry-ford-motor-company/91880258/

Burr, Ty. 2019. "In 'Ford v Ferrari,' a Lot More Than Just Vroom-Vroom." *The Boston Globe*, November 15, 2017, p. G6.

Canby, Vincent. 1983. "'Stroker Ace' at Wheel." *The New York Times*, July 1, 1983. https://www.nytimes.com/1983/07/01/movies/stroker-ace-at-wheel.html?

Carter, David M., and Darren Rovell. 2003. *On the Ball: What You Can Learn about Business from America's Sports Leaders*. Upper Saddle River, NJ: Prentice Hall Financial Times.

Ceppos, Rich. 2019. "Ford v Ferrari: How They Shot All Those Cool Racing Scenes the Man Who Made It Happen Takes Us Behind the Scenes—Literally." *Car and Driver*, November 8, 2019. https://www.caranddriver.com/features/a29738370/ford-ferrari-movie-race-scenes/

Ciferri, Luca. 1998. "Story Reveals Why Enzo Ferrari Said No to Ford." *Automotive News*, August 31, 1998. https://www.autonews.com/article/19980831/ANA/808310794/story-reveals-why-enzo-ferrari-said-no-to-ford

Considine, Tim. 2019. "Foul Play in Ford's 1966 Le Mans 24 Hour Photo Finish? 'Yanks at Le Mans' Extract." *MotorSport*, June 25, 2019. https://www.motorsportmagazine.com/articles/sports-cars/le-mans/foul-play-fords-1966-le-mans-24-hour-photo-finish-yanks-le-mans-extract

Cotton, Mike. 1989. "Obituary: John Wyer." *MotorSport*, May 1989. https://www.motorsportmagazine.com/archive/article/may-1989/6/john-wyer

"Death Demands Toll in Record Speedway Races: Two Men Killed in Crash on Speedway: William Bourque and His Mechanician, Harry Holcomb, Hurled to Death Through Fence: Fatality in Long Event: Auto Racers Meet Accident When 250-Mile Contest Is More Than Half Finished." *The Indianapolis Star*, August 20, 1909, pp. 1, 12.

De La Garza, Alejandro. 2019. "The True Story Behind the Movie *Ford v Ferrari*." *Time*, November 15, 2019. https://time.com/5730536/ford-v-ferrari-true-story/

Donovan, Brian. 2008. *Hard Driving: The Wendell Scott Story: The American Odyssey of NASCAR's First Black Driver*. Hanover, NH: Steerforth Press.

Dougall, Angus. 2013. *The Greatest Racing Driver: The Life and Times of Great Drivers, with a Logical Analysis Revealing the Greatest*. Bloomington, IN: Balboa Press.

Eastman, Chuck. 1957. "Fatality Mars Track Opening in Riverside." *Valley Times*, September 23, 1957, p. 11.

"Fast as a Bullet: Oldfield's Horrific Speed in His 200-H. P. Benz. Rate of 132 Miles an Hour: Man Who Made Speed That Is Appalling to Think of Will Race at the Illinois State Fair Every Day." *The Joliet Daily News*, September 23, 1910, p. 7.

"Favors British Track: Autoist Likes Brooklands: Finds England's Motor Race Course Superior in Some Points, but Inferior in Others, to Local Speedway." *The Indianapolis Star*, August 15, 1909, Auto Section, p. 6.

Ford, Henry. 2017. *My Life and Work*. Los Angeles: Enhanced Media Publishing.

Fretts, Bruce. 2019. "In 'Ford v Ferrari,' a Race with Plenty of Real-Life Characters: The Matt Damon-Christian Bale Movie Is Based on the Still-Controversial 24 Hours of Le Mans Run in France in 1966." *The New York Times*, November 15, 2019. https://www.nytimes.com/2019/11/15/movies/ford-v-ferrari-facts.html

Gilboy, James. 2018. "The 10 Most Lethal Racetracks in America." *The Drive*, March 29, 2018. https://www.thedrive.com/accelerator/19210/the-10-most-lethal-racetracks-in-america

Gorzelany, Jim. 2012. "The Oscars' Favorite Car Movies." Forbes, February 24, 2012. https://www.forbes.com/sites/jimgorzelany/2012/02/24/the-oscars-favorite-car-movies/#5548474179d7

Hannerstein, B. J., compiler. 2013. "Jamie Dornan to play Grey in 'Fifty Shades' Movie." *Detroit Free Press*, October 25, 2013, p. 3C.

Harmetz, Aljean. 1983. "Fox Will Re-release Abandoned Film That Flopped." *The New York Times*, October 5, 1983, p. C12.

Heseltine, Richard. 2016. "50 Years on—Frankenheimer's Grand Prix." *MotorSport*, August 2016. https://www.motorsportmagazine.com/archive/article/august -2016/70/50-years-frankenheimer-s-grand-prix

Hickok, Ralph. 2002. *The Encyclopedia of North American Sports History, Second Edition*. New York: Facts on File, Inc.

Higgins, Tom. 1981. "Yarborough Says Au Revoir NASCAR, Bonjour LeMans." *The Charlotte Observer*, June 7, 1981, p. 12B.

Hunt, Dennis. 1987. "'Star Trek IV' Video Due to Dock in September." *The Gazette*, July 24, 1987, p. C13.

Iacocca, Lee with William Novak. 1984. *Iacocca: An Autobiography*. Toronto: Bantam Books.

Kaufman, Amy. 2019. "5 Films We're Excited to See after CinemaCon." *The Miami Herald*, April 20, 2019, p. 6C.

Kennedy, Mark. 2019. "Buckle Up: 'Ford v Ferrari' Is a Fast but Pleasant Ride: Matt Damon and Christian Bale Play a Pair of Rebels Who Risk It All in a 1966 Showdown on a French Racetrack." *St. Louis Post-Dispatch*, November 15, 2019, p. G20.

Lattanzio, Ryan. 2020. "Why the Unmade Version of 'Ford v Ferrari' with Pitt and Cruise Never Happened: 'Top Gun: Maverick' Director Joseph Kosinski Was Originally Set to Direct the Project That Became Oscar Winner 'Ford v Ferrari,' Titled 'Go Like Hell.'" *IndieWire*, July 25, 2020. https://www.indiewire .com/2020/07/ford-v-ferrari-tom-cruise-brad-pitt-go-like-hell-1234576232/

Lauring, Art. 1955. "McAfee Wins Desert Race in Ferrari." *Los Angeles Times*, March 28, 1955, Part IV, p. 4.

Lerner, Preston. 2015. *Ford GT: How Ford Silenced the Critics, Humbled Ferrari and Conquered Le Mans*. Minneapolis, MN: Motorbooks.

Lewis, David L. 1976. *The Public Image of Henry Ford: An American Folk Hero and His Company*. Detroit: Wayne State University Press.

Mantle, Bill. 1966. "Racing Rallying." *The Ottawa Journal*, August 31, 1966, p. 29.

McClintock, Pamela. 2019. "Making of 'Ford v Ferrari': Christian Bale, Matt Damon, Silly Fights and Real-Life Racing Effects: From Crash Diets to Crashed Cars (and a Disappearing Studio), the Movie's Decade-Long Journey to the Screen Was a Bumpy One: 'Obviously, Movies Like This Are Scary to Studios.'" *The Hollywood Reporter*, November 15, 2019. https://www.hollywoodreporter .com/features/making-ford-v-ferrari-christian-bale-matt-damon-silly-fights-real -life-racing-effects-1254131

Muldowney, Shirley with Bill Stephens. 2013. *Tales from a Top Fuel Dragster: A Collection of the Greatest Drag Racing Stories Ever Told*. New York: Sports Publishing.

Nelson, Murry R., ed. 2009a. *Encyclopedia of Sports in America: A History from Foot Races to Extreme Sports. Volume 1: Colonial Years to 1939*. Westport, CT: Greenwood Press.

Nelson, Murry R., ed. 2009b. *Encyclopedia of Sports in America: A History from Foot Races to Extreme Sports. Volume 2: 1940 to Present*. Westport, CT: Greenwood Press.

New York Times News Service. 1969. "Fiat, Ferrari Auto Builders Will Merge." *The Sacramento Bee*, June 23, 1969, p. B5.

Olney, Ross R. 2012. *The Exciting History of Auto Racing*. Morrisville, NC: Lulu.

Payne, Henry. 2019. "The Real Story Behind 'Ford v Ferrari.'" *The Detroit News*, November 14, 2019. https://www.detroitnews.com/story/opinion/columnists/henry -payne/2019/11/14/real-story-behind-ford-v-ferrari/2567859001/

Pezdirtz, Rick. 1963. "Lund Almost Didn't Make It." *The Miami News*, February 25, 1963, pp. 1C, 4C.

Phelan, Matthew. 2019. "What's Fact and What's Fiction in Ford v. Ferrari: The New Racing Movie Plays Fast and Loose with the Facts, but Some of Its Most Unbelievable Details Are Straight from the Record Books." *Slate*, November 18, 2019. https://slate.com/culture/2019/11/ford-v-ferrari-fact-vs-fiction-le-mans-ken -miles.html

Radbruch, Don. 2004. *Dirt Track Racing, 1914–1941: A Pictorial History*. Jefferson, NC: McFarland & Company, Inc., Publishers.

Shelby, Carroll. 2020. *The Carroll Shelby Story*. Los Angeles: Graymalkin Media.

Snow, Richard F. 1977. "Barney Oldfield: A scrappy and Reckless Farm Boy from Ohio Became America's Most Legendary Race Car Driver, and His Widely Publicized Victories in Henry Ford's Racing Cars Helped the Aspiring Entrepreneur Launch Ford Motor Company." *American Heritage*, February 1977.

"Speedway Opening Today Big Event: Eyes of Automobile Enthusiasts of Two Hemispheres on Indianapolis: Records Expected to Fall: New Track Not Yet Perfect, but Believed to be Faster Than Any Other American Course to Date." *The Indianapolis News,* August 19, 1909, p. 10.

Starer, Taylor. n.d. "Women in NASCAR," NASCAR.com. https://www.nascar.com /gallery/women-in-nascar/#photo-2

Szymanski, Stefan, and Silke-Maria Weineck. 2020. *City of Champions: A History of Triumph and Defeat in Detroit*. New York: The New Press.

Tannert, Chuck. 2019. "Ford vs. Ferrari: The Real Story Behind The Most Bitter Rivalry in Auto Racing." *Forbes*, November 14, 2019. https://www.forbes.com/wheels/news /ford-vs-ferrari-the-real-story-behind-the-most-bitter-rivalry-in-auto-racing/

Thomas, Bob. 1966. "Ken Miles Killed in Riverside Crash." *Los Angeles Times*, August 18, 1966, Part III, pp. 1, 4.

Thompson, Gary. 2019. "Philly Friends of Leo Beebe Say 'Ford v Ferrari' Gets the Ford Exec Wrong." *The Philadelphia Inquirer,* November 14, 2019. https:// www.inquirer.com/news/leo-beebe-ford-ferrari-k-tron-ron-jaworski-20191114 .html

"Three More Lives Toll of Auto Speed Mania: National Car, Driven by Charles Merz, of Indianapolis, Dashes Through Fence into Group of Spectators. Two Onlookers and Mechanic Killed and Several Others Hurt. Driver Miraculously Escapes Death, Saving Himself from Being Burned Alive—Total Fatalities Now Seven." *The Muncie Sunday Star*, August 22, 1909, pp. 1, 3.

"'Tom' Cooper Killed in Park Auto Race: Noted Cyclist and Driver Breaks His Neck in Collision. Two Others May Die: Broker Barlow and Helen Hall Badly Crushed—Machines Came Together at Curve." *The New York Times*, November 20, 1906, p. 1.

Turan, Kenneth. 2019. "All Cylinders: Strong Acting, Fast Cars. 'Ford v Ferrari' Is a Finely Tuned Film." *Los Angeles Times*, November 15, 2019, p. E1.

Turmell, Kitte. 1960. "Teen Etiquette: After You Get That Driving License." *Daily Press*, June 19, 1960, p. 10B.

Ulrich, Allan. 1983. "Burt's Going Around in the Wrong Circles." *San Francisco Examiner*, July 1, 1983, pp. E1, E12.

United Press International. 1960. "Shelby Captures Prix: Argentine Driver Killed." *Progress-Bulletin*, April 4, 1960, Section 2, p. 4.

Willis, P. P. 1909. "Records Broken in First Auto Events: Sixteen Thousand People Witness Opening Races at Indianapolis Motor Track. Oldfield Sets a New Mark. Makes Mile From Flying Start in: 43-1—Chevrolet Lowers Record for Ten Miles." *The Indianapolis Star*, August 20, 1909, pp. 1, 4.

"Wonderful Automobile Records." 1901. *The Lima Times-Democrat*, October 11, 1901, p. 1.

Bibliography

Ali, Muhammad with Richard Durham. 1979. *The Greatest: Muhammad Ali: My Own Story*. New York: Ballantine.

Ambrose, Stephen E. 1999. *Duty, Honor, Country: A History of West Point*. Baltimore, MD: The Johns Hopkins University Press.

Baime, A. J. 2010. *Go Like Hell: Ford, Ferrari and Their Battle for Speed and Glory at Le Mans*. London: Bantam Books.

Beckwith, B. K. 2003. *Seabiscuit: The Saga of a Great Champion*. Yardley, PA: Westholme Publishing.

Belsky, Gary, and Neil Fine. 2016. *On the Origins of Sports*. New York: Artisan.

Berlage, Gai Ingham. 1994. *Women in Baseball: The Forgotten History*. Westport, CT: Praeger.

Bernstein, Joel H. 2007. *Wild Ride: The History and Lore of Rodeo*. Salt Lake City, UT: Gibbs Smith, Publisher.

Bonderoff, Jason. 1982. *Alan Alda: An Unauthorized Biography*. New York: Signet.

Bowen, Edward L. 2007. *War Admiral: Man O' War's Greatest Son*. Lexington, KY: Eclipse Press.

Breslin, Jimmy. 2011. *Branch Rickey*. New York: Viking.

Carruth, Gorton, and Eugene Ehrlich. 1988. *Facts & Dates of American Sports: From Colonial Days to the Present*. New York: Perennial Library.

Cheshire, Ellen. 2015. *Bio-Pics: A Life in Pictures*. New York: Wallflower Press.

Coffey, Wayne. 2005. *The Boys of Winter: The Untold Story of a Coach, a Dream, and the 1980 U.S. Olympic Hockey Team*. New York: Broadway Books.

Cohen, Stanley. 2001. *The Game They Played*. New York: Carroll & Graff Publishers, Inc.

Didinger, Ray, and Glen Macnow. 2009. *The Ultimate Book of Sports Movies*. Philadelphia: Running Press.

Douglas, Geoffrey. 2005. *The Game of Their Lives: The Untold Story of the World Cup's Biggest Loss*. New York: First Perennial Currents.

Eig, Jonathan. 2007. *Opening Day: The Story of Jackie Robinson's First Season*. New York: Simon & Schuster.

Eig, Jonathan. 2017. *Ali: A Life*. New York: Houghton Mifflin Harcourt.

Eliot, Marc. 2011. *Steve McQueen: A Biography*. New York: Crown Archetype.

Fidler, Merrie A. 2006. *The Origins and History of the All-American Girls Professional Baseball League*. Jefferson, NC: McFarland & Company, Inc., Publishers.

Ford, Henry. 2017. *My Life and Work*. Los Angeles: Enhanced Media Publishing.

Fosty, Darril, and George Fosty. 2014. *Tribes: An International Hockey History*. New York: The Stryker-Indigo Publishing Company, Inc.

Fredriksson, Kristine. 1985. *American Rodeo: From Buffalo Bill to Big Business*. College Station, TX: Texas A&M University Press.

Frommer, Harvey. 1982. *Rickey & Robinson: The Men Who Broke Baseball's Color Barrier*. New York: Macmillan Publishing Co., Inc.

Gallico, Paul. 1945. *Farewell to Sport*. New York: Pocket Books, Inc.

Gems, Gerald R. 2014. *Boxing: A Concise History of the Sweet Science*. Lanham, MD: Rowman & Littlefield.

Gipe, George. 1978. *The Great American Sports Book*. Garden City, NY: Doubleday & Company, Inc.

Golenbock, Peter. 1986. *Bums: An Oral History of the Brooklyn Dodgers*. New York: Pocket Books.

Goodman, Matthew. 2019. *The City Game: Triumph, Scandal, and a Legendary Basketball Team*. New York: Ballantine Books.

Gregorich, Barbara. 1993. *Women at Play: The Story of Women in Baseball*. San Diego, CA: A Harvest Original, Harcourt Brace & Company.

Groves, Melody. 2006. *Ropes, Reins, and Rawhide: All about Rodeo*. Albuquerque: University of New Mexico Press.

Hardy, Stephen, and Andrew C. Holman. 2018. *Hockey: A Global History*. Urbana: University of Illinois Press.

Hauser, Thomas. 1992. *Muhammad Ali: His Life and Times*. New York: Touchstone.

Heaphy, Leslie A., and Mel Anthony May, eds. 2006. *Encyclopedia of Woman and Baseball*. Jefferson, NC: McFarland & Company, Inc., Publishers.

Hickok, Ralph. 2002. *The Encyclopedia of North American Sports History, Second Edition*. New York: Facts on File, Inc.

Hillenbrand, Laura. 2001. *Seabiscuit: An American Legend*. New York: Random House.

Holtzman, Jerome, recorder and ed. 1974. *No Cheering in the Press Box: Recollections— Personal & Professional—By Eighteen Veteran American Sportswriters*. New York: Holt, Rinehart and Winston.

Horrigan, Joe. 2019. *NFL Century: The One-Hundred-Year Rise of America's Greatest Sports League*. New York: Crown.

Kahn, Roger. 1973. *The Boys of Summer*. New York: Signet.

Karras, Alex with Herb Gluck. 1978. *Even Big Guys Cry*. New York: Signet.

King, Billie Jean with Christine Brennan. 2008. *Pressure Is a Privilege: Lessons I've Learned from Life and the Battle of the Sexes*. New York: TimeLife Media, Inc.

King, Billie Jean with Frank Deford. 1982. *Billie Jean*. New York: The Viking Press.

Lang, Brandon with Stanley Cohen. 2009. *Beating the Odds: The Rise, Fall, and Resurrection of a Sports Handicapper*. New York: Skyhorse Publishing, Inc.

LeCompte, Tom. 2003. *The Last Sure Thing: The Life & Times of Bobby Riggs.* Easthampton, MA: Skunkworks Publishing.

Lerner, Preston. 2015. *Ford GT: How Ford Silenced the Critics, Humbled Ferrari and Conquered Le Mans.* Minneapolis, MN: Motorbooks.

Macy, Sue. 1995. *A Whole New Ballgame: The Story of the All-American Girls Professional Baseball League.* New York: Puffin Books.

Mann, Arthur. 1951. *The Jackie Robinson Story.* New York: Grosset & Dunlap.

Margolies, Jacob. 1993. *The Negro Leagues: The Story of Black Baseball.* New York: Franklin Watts.

Mead, Chris. 1985. *Champion Joe Louis: Black Hero in White America.* Mineola, NY: Dover Publications, Inc.

Moody, Ralph. 2003. *Come on Seabiscuit!* Lincoln: University of Nebraska Press.

Naismith, James. 1996. *Basketball: Its Origin and Development.* Lincoln: University of Nebraska Press.

Nance, Susan. 2020. *Rodeo: An Animal History.* Norman: University of Oklahoma Press.

Nelson, Murry R., ed. 2009a. *Encyclopedia of Sports in America: A History from Foot Races to Extreme Sports. Volume 1: Colonial Years to 1939.* Westport, CT: Greenwood Press.

Nelson, Murry R., ed. 2009b. *Encyclopedia of Sports in America: A History from Foot Races to Extreme Sports. Volume 2: 1940 to Present.* Westport, CT: Greenwood Press.

Overman, Steven J., and Kelly Boyer Sagert. 2012. *Icons of Women's Sport: From Tomboys to Title IX and Beyond: Volume One.* Santa Barbara, CA: Greenwood.

Paige, Leroy (Satchel) as told to David Lipman. 1962. *Maybe I'll Pitch Forever.* Garden City, NY: Doubleday & Company, Inc.

Plimpton, George. 1961. *Out of My League.* New York: Harper & Row, Publishers.

Plimpton, George. 1966. *Paper Lion.* New York: Harper & Row, Publishers.

Plimpton, George. 2016. *Shadow Box: An Amateur in the Ring.* New York: Little, Brown and Company.

Rampersad, Arnold. 1997. *Jackie Robinson: A Biography.* New York: Alfred A. Knopf, Inc.

Riggs, Bobby with George McGann. 1974. *Bobby Riggs: Court Hustler.* New York: Signet.

Ritter, Lawrence S. 2010. *The Glory of Their Times: The Story of the Early Days of Baseball Told by the Men Who Played It.* New York: Harper Perennial.

Roberts, Selena. 2005. *A Necessary Spectacle: Billie Jean King, Bobby Riggs, and the Tennis Match That Leveled the Game.* New York: Crown Publishers.

Robinson, Jackie as told to Alfred Duckett. 1972. *I Never Had It Made: An Autobiography.* New York: G.P. Putnam's Sons.

Robinson, Jackie as told to Wendell Smith. 1948. *Jackie Robinson: My Own Story.* New York: Greenberg.

Rosebrook, Jeb with Stuart Rosebrook. 2018. *Junior Bonner: The Making of a Classic with Steve McQueen and Sam Peckinpah in the Summer of 1971.* Albany, GA: BearManor Media.

Rosen, Charley. 1999. *Scandals of '51: How the Gamblers Almost Killed College Basketball.* New York: Seven Stories Press.

Rosen, Charley. 2001. *The Wizard of Odds: How Jack Molinas Almost Destroyed the Game of Basketball*. New York: Seven Stories Press.

Seymour, Harold. 1990. *Baseball: The People's Game*. New York: Oxford University Press.

Shattuck, Debra A. 2017. *Bloomer Girls: Women Baseball Pioneers*. Urbana: University of Illinois Press.

Shelby, Carroll. 2020. *The Carroll Shelby Story*. Los Angeles: Graymalkin Media.

Sperber, Murray. 1998. *Onward to Victory: The Crises That Shaped College Sports*. New York: Henry Holt and Company.

Strait, Raymond. 1983. *Alan Alda: A Biography*. New York: St. Martin's Press.

Streible, Dan. 2008. *Fight Pictures: A History of Boxing and Early Cinema*. Berkeley: University of California Press.

Tamte, Roger R. 2018. *Walter Camp and the Creation of American Football*. Urbana: University of Illinois Press.

Tosches, Nick. 2000. *The Devil and Sonny Liston*. Boston: Little, Brown and Company.

Ware, Susan. 2011. *Game, Set, Match: Billie Jean King and the Revolution in Women's Sports*. Chapel Hill: The University of North Carolina Press.

Weddell, David. 1994. *"If They Move … Kill 'Em!": The Life and Times of Sam Peckinpah*. New York: Grove Press.

Wendel, Tim. 2009. *Going for the Gold: How the U.S. Olympic Hockey Team Won at Lake Placid*. Meneola, NY: Dover Publications, Inc.

Westermeier, Clifford P. 1948. *Man, Beast, Dust: The Story of Rodeo*. Denver, CO: World Press.

Williams, Randy. 2006. *Sports Cinema 100 Movies: The Best of Hollywood's Athletic Heroes, Losers, Myths, and Misfits*. Pompton Plains, NJ: Limelight Editions.

Wilner, Barry, and Ken Rappoport. 2014. *Crazyball: Sports Scandals, Superstitions, and Slick Plays*. Lanham, MD: Taylor Trade Publishing.

Wilson, Elizabeth. 2014. *Love Game: A History of Tennis, from Victorian Pastime to Global Phenomenon*. Chicago: The University of Chicago Press.

Index

About the Author

JOHNNY D. BOGGS, winner of a record nine Spur Awards from Western Writers of America, has been praised by *Booklist* magazine as "among the best western writers at work today." His novels include *Return to Red River, Camp Ford*, and *Hard Winter*. He is also a film historian, author of *Jesse James and the Movies* and *Billy the Kid on Film, 1911–2012*, and is working on a book about U.S. newspaper movies.

Boggs also won a Western Heritage Wrangler Award from the National Cowboy and Western Heritage Museum in Oklahoma City for *Spark on the Prairie: The Trial of the Kiowa Chiefs* and an Arkansiana Juvenile Award from the Arkansas Library Association for *Poison Spring*. He was honored as a 2011 Distinguished Alumnus from the University of South Carolina School of Journalism and Mass Communication.

A native of South Carolina, Boggs worked almost fifteen years in Texas as a sports journalist at the *Dallas Times Herald* and *Fort Worth Star-Telegram* before moving to New Mexico in 1998 to concentrate full time on his novels, nonfiction books, and freelance magazine articles.

When not writing, Boggs has acted onstage in local theater and is a volunteer umpire, manager, and league official with Little League baseball. He lives with his wife, son, two dogs, and extensive DVD collection in Santa Fe, New Mexico. His website is www.johnnydboggs.com.